Contemporary Higher Education

International Issues for the Twenty-First Century

Series Editor

Philip G. Altbach
Boston College

A GARLAND SERIES

Contents of the Series

College Student Development and Academic Life

Psychological, Intellectual, Social, and Moral Issues

Edited with an introduction by

Karen Arnold and Ilda Carreiro King
Boston College

GARLAND PUBLISHING, INC.
A MEMBER OF THE TAYLOR & FRANCIS GROUP
New York & London
1997

Library of Congress Cataloging-in-Publication Data

College student development and academic life : psychological,
    intellectual, social, and moral issues / edited with an introduction by
    Karen Arnold and Ilda Carreiro-King.
        p.   cm. — (Contemporary higher education ; 4)
    Includes bibliographical references.
    ISBN 0-8153-2663-7 (alk. paper)
    1. College students—United States—Psychology. 2. Developmental
psychology—United States. 3. College student development
programs—United States. 4. Student affairs services—United States.
I. Arnold, Karen D. II. Carreiro-King, Ilda. III. Series.
LA229.C62 1997
378.1'98—dc21   97-26201
                                                             CIP

Printed on acid-free, 250-year-life paper
Manufactured in the United States of America

Contents

Volume Introduction

by Karen Arnold and Ilda Carreiro King

Reflections on Student Development

Voices inside and outside the academy are calling for a rededication to student learning and personal development as the core of higher education (American College Personnel Association, 1994; Wingspread Group on Higher Education, 1993). Over the past decade, increased attention to general education and to the preparation of graduates for enlightened citizenship in a global community has accompanied mounting concern about student behavior, campus civility, and institutional accountability for the outcomes of a college education (Astin, 1995; Boyer, 1990). Prominent among contemporary problems and crises on individual campuses are student retention, minority recruitment, academic remediation, campus violence, alcohol abuse, and incidents of hate speech, violence, and protest related to race, gender, and sexuality. Effective responses to such issues require an understanding of the developmental tasks of undergraduate students and the social processes of learning.

Public criticisms of higher education also feature student concern for maximizing individual potential. Students desire an education with greater apparent usefulness and personal meaning. Against the backdrop of high tuition, scarce grant aid and a tight professional labor market, consumers of higher education are demanding that faculty devote more time to undergraduate teaching, advising, and mentoring. Legislators, parents, and the general public further demand that post-secondary institutions be accountable for demonstrating positive student outcomes as a result of college attendance. In a technological world with an ever-increasing knowledge base, those outcomes have shifted from accumulation of facts to a focus on developing habits of mind in which graduates engage in lifelong learning, seek understanding, and adapt skills to changing situations. As Grant Wiggins (1993) has noted, "The aim of education is thoughtful action, not knowledge. A capacity for autonomous learning and a thirst for unending education are more important than accurate recall or simplistic application of the particular knowledge taught" (p. 34).

Fostering student development is a central task of higher education when learning is broadly construed in terms of potential for lifelong growth and effective citizenship. For the past quarter century, theoretical conceptions of the characteristics of young adults and their development during the undergraduate years have guided the study of college students. The purpose of this anthology is to draw together theories of late-adolescent and adult development that constitute the essential knowledge base about college students. In addition to presenting classic and contemporary theories that pertain directly to students and have been widely influential in student affairs administration, this volume attempts to extend the student development literature by incorporating relevant readings from the leading edge of developmental and social psychology that have not previously been connected to higher education and college students.

What is student development and why is it important for higher education? In general, development refers to the process of human growth and change. Development can also refer to the characteristics of the outcomes of the unfolding change process (King, 1994; Miller and Winston, 1991; Vygotsky, 1978). Student development theory is the application of principles of human growth and change to the context of higher education (Garland and Grace, 1993). Student development theories provide maps or guides by which to understand the ways individuals and groups experience higher education and the factors that interact with their satisfaction, achievement, and persistence (Stage, 1989). With the lens of theory, postsecondary professionals can observe, understand, and influence patterns of student change, capabilities, behavior, and preoccupations. Just as important, developmental theory provides systematic ways of making sense of individual differences among college students and their responses to educational environments.

In answering the question "why bother with theory?" Kneflekamp, Widick, and Parker (1978) outlined four issues that developmental theory addresses. Each is central to teaching and administration concerned with promoting student learning and positive personal growth. First, educators need to understand the changes that occur in college students and how those changes manifest themselves. Second, we need to comprehend how development occurs and what internal and external processes cause growth. Third, we must understand how factors in college environments facilitate or inhibit growth. Fourth and finally, we must have a clear picture of our goals for students, to know "toward what ends development in college should be directed" (Kneflekamp et al., 1978).

Formal theories of student development have been the basis for the American student-affairs profession only since the 1960s. However, the acceptance of human development as the theoretical basis for the student-affairs profession was enabled by a constellation of factors within both the student-affairs profession and the field of psychology during the early part of the 20th century. With the first deans of men and women, the student-affairs profession was formed to carry out the American higher education mission of character building and parental oversight of students that was being abandoned by an increasingly scholarly and professionalized professoriate (Fenske, 1990). As the first deans of students took office, Freudian concepts of human psychology were taking hold; the profession matured between World War I and the Depression under the influence of the vocational guidance and personnel movement (Garland and Grace, 1993; Strange, 1994). Taking up William Rainy Harper's call for "the scientific study of the student," (Herr and Cramer, 1979) and codifying a statement of professional philosophy, early student personnel professionals made education of the "whole person" the foundation of the influential 1937 "Student Personnel Point of View" (American Council of Education, 1937).

Psychological theories of adult development and specific models of college student growth emerged in the 1960s during the same period in which colleges relinquished their role "in loco parentis" (Moore, 1990). No longer focused on controlling student behavior, higher education professionals attempted to promote student growth through understanding patterns of individual change and specifying the conditions necessary to promote development. In addition to the influence of this fundamental shift in the relationship between the college and the student, student development theories stemmed from the cognitive revolution of the 1960s, which refuted behaviorist learning theory. Behaviorists came to view learning as associated with relatively small accumulations of skills and knowledge, whereas development referred to global or radical psychological changes resulting in increased capacity to learn (Canfield and Ceci, 1992). Early theoretical work in development focused on childhood. In particular, the Piagetian model of development which propelled this revolution defined the apex of intellectual development as early adolescent, formal operative thought, emphasizing solutions to well-structured problems based on logical analyses. This prompted theorists such as Perry (1970) to develop models of postformal thought that captured the intellectual demands of adulthood and higher education involving "real life" problems that require a capacity to accept contradiction, uncertainty, and the relative and changing nature of knowledge. The emergence of the first student development theories in the 1960s provided student affairs with an intellectual framework with which to foster the intellectual, social, ethical, and vocational growth of students as complementary to the academic goals of the professoriate.

The first generation of college student development models relied heavily on psychological-stage theories, empirically based on limited populations but positing universal sequences of human development. However, evidence that developmental changes in adulthood relate strongly to individual experience (Flavell, 1970) led to the formulation of theories accounting for individual differences such as those based in gender, race, and class. Therefore, contemporary views of college students draw from sociological as well as psychological perspectives and from diverse undergraduate populations.

Currently, theorists place intensified focus on the social context of development. Featuring the reciprocal influence of the individual and the environment (Scarr, 1992), recent theories incorporate the complex effects of historical era, culture, and immediate environment along with personal characteristics (Moen, Elder, and Luscher, 1995). Such an expanded definition of context embedding the person/environment interaction adds significant complexity to the understanding of human development. These sociohistoric theories, while well known within the disciplines of developmental and social psychology, have not yet been incorporated explicitly into the student development literature.

Despite the differences between theories, there are several hallmarks of developmental change that characterize the body of theory as a whole. Theories of college student development outline patterns of qualitative cyclical change in late adolescence and adulthood (Strange, 1994). The movement toward more adequate adaptation to change and a more mature perspective occurs through an iterative process of becoming aware of differential components within issues and perspectives followed by integrating this new awareness into a complete, stable understanding (King, 1994). The direction of growth is toward greater complexity, broader and more differentiated frames of reference, more authentic interpersonal relations, greater ethical and aesthetic awareness, and more adequate coping with ideas, life tasks, and external demands. Development theories depict a movement from an externally bound identity to an internal sense of self, and from conformist to self-evaluated standards of belief and behavior (Loevinger, 1976). As individuals develop, they move from dependence through autonomy to mature interdependence (Chickering and Reisser, 1993).

Each theory acknowledges environmental influences on development. The study of college students has frequently conceptualized these influences in terms of challenge and support (Roark, 1989; Sanford, 1962). Related to the concepts of cognitive dissonance (Festinger, 1957) and zone of proximal development (Vygotsky, 1968), challenge and support refers to the environmental conditions under which individuals are likely to change. Challenges from the environment that require responses are likely to result in positive growth when they are neither incomprehensible nor unduly threatening (Diener and Dweck, 1978; Dweck, 1986). Without external challenge, no change occurs, but support is necessary during the differentiation period of leaving behind comfortable old ways of understanding and behaving. Student-affairs functions, such as residence life programs, counseling, and student activities, have traditionally provided much of that support.

Although psychologically based theories form the intellectual cornerstone of their profession, student-affairs administrators have not generally shared the developmental perspective with other college personnel. Faculty, academic and financial administrators, and scholars of the organization and administration of higher education generally remain unaware of student development theory and research. Beginning in the late 19th century, the American professoriate became increasingly focused on scholarship, disciplinary specialization, and a narrowly defined concern with student intellectual development and formal academic study (Vesey, 1965). Administrators and scholars outside of student affairs concerned themselves with management issues and the study of higher education institutions as organizations. It is vital that these groups familiarize themselves with the student development literature in order to respond effectively to the many institutional issues implicating students.

Developmental theory illuminates a question at the center of the work of all postsecondary professionals: how can college environments be structured to influence student growth and change toward valued individual and societal goals? It is developmental theory that provides a rationale for framing student goals and designing optimal learning environments (Brown and Barr, 1990; Kneflekamp, et al., 1978; Stage, 1991). Student development theory also explains the interrelationship of student intellectual and personal growth, a necessary conceptual link in connecting student affairs and academic affairs around a common goal of student learning (American College Personnel Association, 1994; Chickering and Reisser, 1993). Finally, current formulations of developmental theory also provide the tools with which to better analyze the wider context of development, encompassing the college campus, society, and historical era.

Taken together, this body of theory suggests that college environments will produce positive growth when appropriate challenges and supports are provided that take into account students' levels of maturity within a particular social context. This anthology provides the conceptual guide for the realization of that goal. We have chosen theories based on two criteria. First, we have included the most widely cited, useful, and influential theoretical models of Western college student development. Second, the collection includes contemporary critiques of traditional stage theories and monocultural perspectives as well as emerging conceptions of development in sociohistoric context.

Classic Integrative Theories of Development

The volume begins with two integrative theories of student development. Arthur Chickering's 1969 book, *Education and Identity*, outlined the first comprehensive theory of college student development. This classic text for student-affairs administrators was updated and revised in 1993 (Chickering and Reisser, 1993). The Chickering model of vectors of development has been highly influential because of its realistic, practical application to higher education contexts. The seven vectors of development represent psychosocial tasks of late adolescence and adulthood that characterize the college experience. Such vectors as developing competence, establishing genuine relationships, and crystallizing purpose occur simultaneously in a loose chronological and hierarchical fashion, rather than in strict stages. Innumerable educational interventions have used the model as a guide to identifying, measuring, and fostering developmental change in students. A widely used assessment instrument, the Student Development Task Inventory (SDTI), provides empirical measurement of the vectors (Prince, Miller, and Winston, 1974).

Unlike Chickering's model, the ego development theory of Jane Loevinger (1976) was not specifically composed for the college student population. The value of the theory for higher education faculty and administrators lies in its rigorous conception of the interrelation between facets of development. The ego, according to Loevinger, is a master trait that encompasses impulse control, character development, interpersonal style, conscious preoccupations, and cognitive style. Her theory outlines nine stages through which these integrated factors change qualitatively to form increasingly mature structures of beliefs, values, and reasoning. The article represented in this anthology is the only piece written by someone other than the theorist. Rita Weathersby's work both outlines Loevinger's theory and provides an empirical and conceptual link to college student development. The lens of ego development theory reveals patterned variations in college student motivations and reactions to the college experience.

Cognitive and Ethical Development: Construction of Meaning

The primary mission of higher education is the fostering of intellectual development. In a recent study, more than three-fourths of all professors cited students' intellectual development as their institution's highest goal (Mooney, 1991). Cognitive theories are particularly important, therefore, as guides to optimal teaching and learning processes.

Cognitions are psychological structures, or patterns of making meaning of the self and the world resulting from experience (Kohlberg and Mayer, 1972). Changes in how students think—the underlying structures of using evidence to form solutions to problems—are assumed more enduring than the accumulation of facts within a content area. Cognitive theorists created models for conceptualizing these qualitative shifts in thinking and learning by studying students' ways of knowing and reasoning. Differences in how students construct and interpret their experiences offer important guides for structuring the education process (Strange, 1994). From a cognitive developmental perspective, educational experiences that stimulate development are those that arouse interest and challenge in the immediate experience of the student. The five pieces chosen for this section exemplify the evolving knowledge base of cognitive theories that have informed student development in Western cultures.

Our first selection in this cluster is the classic work of William Perry. Based on longitudinal interviews with male Harvard undergraduates, Perry derived a series of cognitive and ethical positions. Students progress from an unquestioning, dualistic framework of thinking in which sources of knowledge or authorities are viewed in polar terms such as "right or wrong," through various positions in which multiple views and diversity of opinions are considered legitimate, to a contextual and relativistic view of knowledge and authority. Students who reach this last stage have made an active commitment to their responsibilities in a pluralistic world, establishing their identities in the process. Perry's studies of intellectual and ethical development document the important interrelationships between cognitive processes and the ways in which values and belief systems are acquired. His work also indicates expected sequences of changes in students' reasoning that hold implications for instruction and other educational interventions.

The work of Nancy Rule Goldberger, Blythe McVicker Clinchy, Mary Field Belenky, and Jill Mattuck Tarule, based on interviews with women, represents both an extension and modification of the Perry scheme of developmental epistemology. Dissatisfied that Perry had not captured females' experience, these researchers examined women's ways of constructing meaning and making judgments about truth and knowledge. Their research on epistemology focused exclusively on women's experiences and on attributes more commonly associated with women, such as interdependence, intimacy, nurturance, and contextual thought. Using a similar qualitative approach to Perry's, they formulated a model of five perspectives based on the metaphor of voice that ranges from silence to an integration of voices. In recommending pedagogy that facilitates development, the researchers propose theoretically based educational practices of potential benefit to both sexes. (See also, Belenky, Clinchy, Goldberger, and Tarule, 1986).

Marcia Baxter Magolda offers a different perspective on the question of gender differences in intellectual development. She claims that while there is little evidence for gender-based structural differences in reasoning, gender-related patterns do exist within epistemological structures. This article describes students' assumptions about the nature, certainty, and limits of knowledge through four ways of knowing. The author follows students' epistemic development through college in order to clarify students' perceptions of specific academic experiences. Urging that postsecondary education start with students' knowledge rather than teachers' knowledge, Baxter Magolda details how to translate student ideas into new forms of pedagogy. She further challenges educators to question traditional assumptions of objectivist pedagogy and consider replacing them with "relational pedagogy guided by listening, valuing, and engaging with students' epistemologies" (Baxter Magolda, 1992, p. 286).

Karen Kitchener and Patricia King formulate a well-articulated seven-stage model of reflective judgment. This model brings together theories of intellectual development with educational philosophers' descriptions of "good thinking." Based on the work of Dewey (1933), who identified reflective thinking as a goal of education, Kitchener and King define a reflective thinker as someone who understands that judgments are made in problem solving using criteria such as evaluation of evidence, consideration of expert opinion, adequacy of argument, and implications of the proposed solution. This piece describes the model as well as the dialectical relationship between learning and development. The authors then go on to describe learning objectives, tasks, and assignments that can be used to create transformative learning experiences to both challenge and support students. Unlike many developmental theories, the Kitchener and King model rests on a comprehensive empirical base of several dozen studies, conducted over a 15-year period, that have tested their claims (Brabeck, 1994). Their recent book outlines both the reflective judgment theory and studies, making it a useful reference for student affairs staff as well as researchers (King and Kitchener, 1994).

James Fowler proposes a cognitive stage model for spiritual development related to Kohlberg's (1973) theory of moral development and Selman's (1976) theory of social perspective taking. The theory is cognitive because it examines the ways in which individuals make meaning and reason in the moral and spiritual domain. Unlike Kohlberg, who separated faith from moral reasoning by positing a rational core requiring detachment, Fowler sees cognition as socially mediated. Attempts to construct meaning rely upon our trust in "significant others who are companions or mediators in our acts of meaning construction" (Fowler, 1980, p.135). Faith is by necessity a relational matter. Faith stages are broader constructs that move toward multidimensional approaches to life, truth, and commitments. As Perry (1981) commented, "It is in the affirmation of Commitments that the themes of epistemology, intellectual development, ethics, and identity merge" (p. 97). Theories of moral and spiritual development, such as Kohlberg's and Fowler's, are important reminders that advances in moral understanding and action rely on intellectual complexity and interpersonal engagement.

Robert Kegan's model of adult development concerns cognitive complexity and the making of meaning beyond Piaget's late adolescent formal operations. The subject-object relations theory first proposed in the influential *The Evolving Self* (Kegan, 1982) describes how, at each stage of development, previously embedded ways of constructing the self, relationships, values, and beliefs become themselves the objects of reflection. *In Over Our Heads: The Mental Demands of Modern Life* (Kegan, 1994) is the most recent and comprehensive exposition of this important theory. In this book, Kegan makes a persuasive case that our cultural "curriculum" requires metasystems thinking for adult work, relationships, and learning.

Identity Development

Erik Erikson's (1968) lifespan theory of development portrays the main dilemma of adolescence as the interactive conflict between identity achievement and identity diffusion. Although a complex term, identity can be generally understood as the sense of self that remains stable despite environmental change and individual growth (McKinney, 1994). Answering the question "Who am I?" is the central task of Erikson's identity stage. Traditional-age college students—those in their late teens and early 20s— fall into the life stage in which identity issues are paramount. Self-definition becomes particularly urgent at this juncture because of societal expectations and institutions that require individuals to define themselves apart from their families and externally derived childhood self-images.

Erikson's theory remains influential but is only tangentially applicable to contemporary college students. Too broad to specify hallmarks of early adulthood development, the theory also suffers from the assumption that male patterns of individuation apply to women and across cultures. An important body of theory emerged in the 1980s that examines identity as the interaction between personal and perceived social images of self. In particular, these theories recognize that being a member of a minority or less-valued social group strongly affects the formation of identity.

The minority-identity development theory of Donald Atkinson, George Morten, and Derald Wing Sue begins the section on group-specific patterns of identity development. These authors postulate a sequence of identity development for members of ethnic minority groups that takes into account "their shared experience of oppression" (Atkinson, Morten, and Sue, 1983, p. 39). In order to develop a healthy sense of self within a society in which their group is denigrated, members of minority groups must confront views of the self, their group, other minority groups, and the majority. Identity development follows a trajectory in which low levels of development are characterized by lack of consciousness of difference and group identity. As negative encounters force the acknowledgment of racism and other forms of oppression, this theory claims, individuals begin to identify with their group in opposition to the dominant culture. At the highest levels of development, people view their minority status as a positive facet of self that is neither all-encompassing nor oppositional to other groups and cultures. The minority-identity development theory illuminates the debilitating effects of numerical underrepresentation and racism on the development of college students who are members of societal and campus minority groups. The theory also suggests necessary conditions for achievement and persistence by students of color.

Janet Helms provides a model of white racial identity that relates to the development of college students who are members of the dominant group in multi-cultural societies. Helms, like Atkinson, Morten, and Sue, recognizes that individuals form their sense of self within a social context where groups are differentially valued and privileged. Members of minority groups have little choice about confronting the realities of oppression, but progress in ending racism depends upon on the perceptions and behavior of members of the majority. Forms of racism, Helms claims, become part of the identity of majority individuals and are harmful because they preclude the achievement of a positive racial sense of self. The theory of white racial identity is a six-stage model in which white individuals first recognize and then actively confront internalized and societal racism, finally defining a positive, nonracist white identity. Helms' model holds important practical implications for colleges and universities. The model provides a theoretical rationale for involving majority students in racial awareness and other anti-racism efforts. It also demonstrates that significant interactions with members of minority groups are necessary for majority students to develop a positive racial identity.

The homosexual development theory of Vivienne Cass provides another model that demonstrates how the social construction of groups interacts with individual identity development. In this case, identifying oneself as gay, lesbian, or bisexual occurs within a social matrix in which heterosexuality is the presumed norm, homosexuality is negatively perceived, and active hostility and homophobia are directed at gay and lesbian individuals. Developing a positive, integrated homosexual identity in this larger environment involves cognitive, behavioral, and affective dimensions. Of particular importance at various stages of development is the need to disclose one's sexuality to others and the need to affiliate with a community in which homosexuality is valued and accepted. Like minority identity development in general, homosexual development moves through a broad pattern of differentiating oneself from the majority, taking pride in one's minority identity, and seeing oneself as a multifaceted person who can interact with individuals both within and outside of one's own group. This theory also points to the ways in which current college environments can inhibit development of certain students to the detriment of their success, persistence, and satisfaction with the undergraduate experience.

In the context of colleges and universities, identity theories offer guides to the campus experiences and responses of students according to their membership in minority or majority groups. These models can be particularly relevant to colleges around the world committed to increasing the cultural and socioeconomic diversity of their student populations. Among the most important practical aspects of this set of theories are the role of the college environment in identity development, the need to integrate students fully into college academic and social systems (Tinto, 1993), the importance of majority as well as minority understanding of oneself in cultural and historic context, and the need for access to culturally specific groups, activities, and knowledge.

The Social, Historical, and Cultural Context of Development

Student development theory has historically been concerned with the context of development as it seeks to apply itself to the particular environments provided by colleges. Lecture halls, seminars, laboratories, studios, residence halls, sports programs, and student organizations are some of the environments intended to influence student development through their content and interpersonal interactions. With an increasingly diverse student body, it is important to enhance our understanding of the ways in which context and college environments provide the conditions for the development of certain individuals and groups of undergraduates. Some of the most promising theoretical models for this goal have not yet been adopted in the college student literature.

The goals of student development are typically grounded in the needs of society. Historically, student development theories have been based on a Western perspective of independence and autonomy. Models of college student development, therefore, have focused on individual development, such as the fostering of complex, creative and ethical thought and a bounded self. This is only one of many ways of socially constructing reality. What has become equally clear is that the college graduate of the twenty-first century will be participating in a global community dependent upon its human resources and awareness of interdependence. Hence, student development theory should also look to models that view development and learning as socially, culturally, and historically situated.

The final cluster of readings, while not all strictly developmental, helps the reader to appreciate the complexity of contexts in which development occurs and the reciprocal, interactive effects of individuals, their environments, and the larger social, cultural, and historic contexts. These contexts range from face-to-face settings to the cultural values and beliefs in which they are embedded.

Alexander Astin's theory of student involvement views student development as a function of student interactions with college environments. Student involvement refers to the amount of physical and psychological energy that the student devotes to academic and student life experiences. Development occurs as a result of involvement. Focusing on student actions, it is possible to determine the level of student involvement with various aspects of the campus and with the college experience as a whole. For example, time spent studying, time spent on campus, participation in student organizations, and relationships with other students and faculty can be measured along a continuum of involvement. College environments can also be assessed in terms of their ability to elicit student involvement. According to the theory, the greater the student's involvement in college, the greater will be the amount of student learning and personal development. Astin uses his theory to make the case that traditional indications of institutional effectiveness, such as faculty disciplinary expertise and campus resources, are poor measures of student learning outcomes. Involvement theory offers faculty, administrators, counselors, and student-affairs workers a practical principle for designing and evaluating effective learning environments.

In contrast to Astin's behavioral approach, Hazel Rose Markus and Shinobu Kitayama focus on the underlying phenomenology of a culture's construal of self, of others, and of the interdependence of the two in order to understand culturally based differences in self-perceptions and styles of behavior. While not yet connected to the student development literature, their comparison of the interdependent self of the East with the independent self of the West lends insight into the nature of two contrasting bases of individual experience that in turn influence cognition, emotion, and motivation differently for each. The authors argue that the view one holds of the self is critical in understanding individual behavior.

One of the most influential theories that accounts for personal development in sociological context is Urie Bronfenbrenner's theory of the ecology of human development. This model requires that behavior and development be examined as a joint function of the characteristics of the person and environment. The developmental environment is modeled as a system of nested, interdependent, dynamic structures ranging from proximal (face-to-face) to broader social contexts, such as social class or cultural beliefs. Both biological and psychological attributes of the person are studied. This model helps in analyzing the many and complex factors that contribute to particular people acting in specific environments. It has transformed the way social, developmental, and behavioral scientists think about and study human beings in their environments (Moen, et al., 1995) and holds great promise for understanding the complexity of social dilemmas facing campuses of the twenty-first century.

Conclusion

As Patricia King (1994) states in her critique of the adequacy of the knowledge base of student development theory, models of student development need to go beyond a Eurocentric perspective of focusing on individuals to include attention to the development of community-oriented goals of interdependence and altruism. Facing the challenge of living in a world of shrinking natural resources, we must maximize our human resources by focusing on the development of human potential in order to prepare our students to live effectively in a society of global and international social and economic interdependence. Incorporating the new generation of human development models into student development theory and practice holds great promise for this core goal of higher education worldwide.

References

American College Personnel Association (1994) *The Student Learning Imperative*. Washington, D.C.: American College Personnel Association.

American Council of Education (1937) *Student Personnel Point of View*. In G.L. Saddlemire and A.L. Rentz, eds., *Student Affairs: A Profession's Heritage* (pp. 122–40) Alexandria, Va.: American College Personnel Association.

Astin, A.W. 1995. The Cause of Citizenship. *Chronicle of Higher Education*. October 6, B1–2.

Atkinson, D.R., Morten, G., and Sue, D.W. 1983. *Counseling American Minorities: A Cross-cultural Perspective*, 2d. ed. Dubuque, Iowa: Brown.

Baxter Magolda, M.B. 1992. Students' Epistemologies and Academic Experiences: Implications for Pedagogy. *Review of Higher Education* 15(3): 265–87.

Belenky, M.F., Clinchy, B.M., Goldberger, N.R., and Tarule, J.M. 1986. *Women's Ways of Knowing: The Development of Self, Voice, and Mind*. New York: Basic Books.

Boyer, E. 1990. *Campus Life: In Search of Community*. Princeton, N.J.: Carnegie Foundation for the Advancement of Teaching.

Brabeck, M. 1994. A Review of Developing Reflective Judgment. *Journal of Adult Development* 1(4): 261–63.

Brown, R.D., and Barr, M. 1990. Student Development: Yesterday, Today, and Tomorrow. In L.V. Moore, ed. *Evolving Theoretical Perspectives on Students* New Directions for Student Services, no. 51. San Francisco: Jossey-Bass.

Canfield, R.L., and Ceci, S.J. 1992. Integrating Learning into a Theory of Intellectual Development. In R.J. Sternberg and C. Berg, eds. *Intellectual Development*. New York: Cambridge University Press.

Chickering, A., and Reisser, L. 1993. *Education and Identity*. 2d ed. San Francisco: Jossey-Bass.

Dannefer, D. 1984. Adult Development and Social Theory: A Paradigmatic Reappraisal. *American Sociological Review* 49: 100–16.

Dewey, J. 1933. *How We think*. Lexington, Mass.: Heath.

Diener, C., and Dweck, C. 1978. An Analysis of Learned Helplessness: Continuous Changes in Performance, Strategy, and Achievement Cognitions Following Failure. *Journal of Personality and Social Psychology* 36: 451–62.

Dweck, C. 1986. Motivational Processes Affecting Learning. *American Psychologist* 41: 1040–48.

Erikson, E. 1968. *Identity: Youth and Crisis*. New York: W.W. Norton.

Fenske, R.H. 1990. Historical Foundations of Student Services. In U.A. Delworth and G.R. Hanson, eds. *Student Services: A Handbook for the Profession*. San Francisco: Jossey-Bass.

Festinger, L. 1957. *A Theory of Cognitive Dissonance*. New York: Row, Peterson.

Flavell, J.H. 1970. Cognitive Changes in Adulthood. In L.R. Goulet and P.B. Baltes, eds. *Life Span Developmental Psychology: Theory and Research*. New York: Academic Press.

Fowler, J. 1980. Moral Stages and the Development of Faith. In L. Kohlberg and B. Munsey, eds. *Moral Development, Moral Education*. Birmingham, Ala.: Religious Education Press.

Garland, P.H., and Grace, T.W. 1993. *New Perspectives for Student Affairs Professionals: Evolving Realities, Responsibilities and Roles*. ASHE-ERIC Higher Education Report no. 7. Washington, D.C.: The George Washington University, School of Education and Human Development.

Herr, E.L., and Cramer, S.H. 1979. *Career Guidance Through the Life Span*. Boston: Little, Brown.

Kegan, R. 1982. *The Evolving Self: Problem and Process in Human Development*. Cambridge: Harvard University Press.

Kegan, R. 1994. *In Over Our Heads: The Mental Demands of Modern Life*. Cambridge: Harvard University Press.

King, P. 1994. Theories of College Student Development: Sequences and Consequences." *Journal of College Student Development* 35: 413–21.

King, P., and Kitchener, K.S. 1994. *Developing Reflective Judgment: Understanding and Promoting Intellectual Growth and Critical Thinking in Adolescents and Adults*. San Francisco: Jossey-Bass.

Kneflekamp, L., Widick, C., and Parker, C.A. 1978. Applying New Developmental Findings. *New Directions for Student Services* no. 4. San Francisco: Jossey-Bass.

Kohlberg, L. 1973. Continuities in Childhood and Adult Moral Development Revisited. In P.B. Baltes and K.W. Schaie, eds. *Life-Span Developmental Psychology: Personality and Socialization*. New York: Academic Press.

Kohlberg, L., and Mayer, R. 1972. Development as the Aim of Education. *Harvard Educational Review* 42(4): 449–96.

Loevinger, J. 1976. *Ego Development: Conceptions and Theories*. San Francisco: Jossey-Bass.

McKinney, J.P. 1994. Identity Formation. In R.J. Corsini, ed. *Encyclopedia of Psychology*. 2d ed. New York: John Wiley and Sons.

Miller, T.K., and Winston, R.B., Jr. 1991. *Administration and Leadership in Student Affairs: Actualizing Student Development in Higher Education*. 2d ed. Munci, Ind.: Accelerated Development.

Moen, P., Elder, G., and Luscher, K., eds. 1995. *Examining Lives in Context: Perspectives on the Ecology of Human Development*. Washington, D.C.: American Psychological Association.

Mooney, C.J. 1991. Professors Feel Conflict Between Roles in Teaching and Research, Say Students Are Badly Prepared. *Chronicle of Higher Education* May 8, A15–17.

Moore, L.V. 1990. Evolving Theoretical Perspectives on Students. *New Directions for Student Services* no. 51. San Francisco: Jossey-Bass.

Perry, W.G. 1970. *Forms of Intellectual and Ethical Development in the College Years*. New York: Holt, Rinehart, and Winston.

Perry, W.G. 1981. Cognitive and Ethical Growth: The Making of Meaning. In A.W. Chickering and Associates, eds. *The Modern American College*. San Francisco: Jossey-Bass.

Prince, J.S., Miller, T.K., and Winston, R.B. 1974. *Student Development Task Inventory Guidelines*. Athens, Ga.: Student Development Associates.

Roark, M. 1989. Challenging and Supporting College Students." *NASPA Journal* 26(4): 314–19.

Sanford, N., ed. 1962. *The American College*. New York: John Wiley and Sons.

Scarr, S. 1992. Developmental Theories for the 1990s: Development and Individual Differences. *Child Development* 63: 1–19.

Selman, R. 1976. Social-Cognitive Understanding. In T. Lickona, ed. *Moral Development and Behavior* New York: Holt, Rinehart, and Winston.

Stage, F.K. 1989. College Outcomes and Student Development: Filling in the Gaps. *Review of Higher Education* 12(3): 293–304.

Stage, F.K. 1991. Common Elements of Theory: A Framework for College Student Development. *Journal of College Student Development* 32: 56–61.

Strange, C. 1994. Student Development: The Evolution and Status of an Essential Idea. *Journal of College Student Development* 35: 399–412.

Tinto, V. 1993. *Leaving College: Rethinking the Causes and Cures of Student Attrition*. 2d ed. Chicago: University of Chicago Press.

Vesey, L.R. 1965. *The Emergence of the American University*. Chicago: University of Chicago Press.

Vygotsky, L. 1968. *Thought and Language*. Cambridge, Mass.: MIT Press.

Vygotsky, L.S. 1978. *Mind in Society: The Development of Higher Psychological Processes*. Cambridge: Harvard University Press.

Wiggins, G. 1993. *Assessing Student Performance*. San Francisco: Jossey-Bass.

Wingspread Group on Higher Education. 1993. An American Imperative: Higher Expectations for Higher Education. Racine, Wisc.: Johnson Foundation.

Personal Growth and the College Student

The Seven Vectors

Our model does not portray development as one predominant
challenge or crisis resolution after another, each invariably linked
to specific ages. Development for college students, which today
includes persons of virtually all ages, is a process of infinite complexity. Just as students are notorious for not proceeding through
the institution according to schedule, they rarely fit into over-
simplified paths or pigeonholes. We propose the seven vectors
as maps to help us determine where students are and which way
they are heading. Movement along any one can occur at different rates and can interact with movement along the others. Each
step from "lower" to "higher" brings more awareness, skill, confidence, complexity, stability, and integration but does not rule
out an accidental or intentional return to ground already tra-
versed. We assume that "higher" is better than "lower," because

in adding the skills and strengths encompassed by these vectors, individuals grow in versatility, strength, and ability to adapt when unexpected barriers or pitfalls appear.

We also recognize that developmental patterns described by psychosocial theorists may have been skewed by the exclusivity of their samples, as was the case for cognitive theorists. Women were less prominent in Erikson's thinking, and males were initially excluded from Loevinger's sample. Nontraditional students and members of minority groups often were left out altogether. These deficiencies are now being corrected. For example, there have been studies on identity formation for women (Josselson, 1987), on nonwhite students (Cross, 1971; Helms, 1990, Sue and Sue, 1971; Martinez, 1988; Johnson and Lashley, 1988; Atkinson, Morten, and Sue, 1983; Ho, 1987; Branch-Simpson, 1984), and on homosexual students (Cass, 1979; Coleman, 1981–1982; Dank, 1971; Minton and McDonald, 1983–1984; Plummer, 1975; Troiden, 1979). Many of these studies seem to be turning up variations in style and sequence, but the fundamental themes reappear and continue to serve as foundations for the seven vectors.

The vectors describe major highways for journeying toward individuation—the discovery and refinement of one's unique way of being—and also toward communion with other individuals and groups, including the larger national and global society. We propose that while each person will drive differently, with varying vehicles and self-chosen detours, eventually all will move down these major routes. They may have different ways of thinking, learning, and deciding, and those differences will affect the way the journey unfolds, but for all the different stories about turning points and valuable lessons, college students live out recurring themes: gaining competence and self-awareness, learning control and flexibility, balancing intimacy with freedom, finding one's voice or vocation, refining beliefs, and making commitments.

Since we refrained from describing development in terms of Erikson's age-specific crises, we are hesitant to portray it as movement from one stage or position to the next. Rest (1979) differentiated between "simple-stage models" and "complex-stage models." Using simple-stage models, a typical assessment question was, "What stage is a person in?" Assuming one stage at a time with no overlapping, no skipping of stages, and no steps backward, it should be easy to pinpoint where a student is and design challenges to foster the next step. Loevinger, Perry, and Kohlberg, following Piaget's lead, envisioned cognitive structures that evolved in an orderly fashion. Like windows built into a house, they became relatively fixed lenses for interpreting reality and screening input. Major remodeling was needed to change the windows. Once the new model was installed, it was as hard to go back to the old structure as to replace stained glass with a plain windowpane. Furthermore, the brain would not move from windowpane to stained glass in one leap. A sliding glass door had to come next, and then beveled, leaded designs, perhaps with inset mirrors and magnifying glasses. Perry differed from his colleagues in allowing for escape, retreat, and delay in his theory of intellectual development. For others, it was onward and upward, and while it was easy for a student to look back with disdain on an earlier way of thinking, it was hard to see beyond the next level of complexity, let alone understand an instructor who was teaching two or more stages ahead.

King (1990, pp. 83–84) warns against an overly simplified description of cognitive processes, which are inconsistent with many research findings. "For example, people don't seem to change from the exclusive use of one set of assumptions to the exclusive use of those of the next adjacent stage; rather, the use of assumptions characteristic of several stages at once often has been found. Stage usage seems to be influenced by a variety of individual factors (e.g., consolidation of existing structures, fatigue, readiness for change) and environmental factors (e.g., whether one is asked to create one's own solution to a problem or to critique someone else's solution, explaining one's beliefs verbally or in writing)." Different test characteristics and demands call forth different cognitive structures. Rest (1979, p. 63) proposes that instead of trying to assess what stage the person is in, we should ask, "To what extent and under what conditions does a person manifest the various types of organizations of thinking?"

A linear perspective may also frustrate those who want to help students achieve the upper reaches of stage theories. Pascarella and Terenzini (1991, p. 35) found no evidence of college students functioning at any of the final three stages of Loevinger's model. Kohlberg (1972) found that stage 4 (law and order) was the predominant stage in most societies. Perry (1970) was more optimistic, saying that perhaps 75 percent of the seniors in his study had reached positions 7 and 8. Subsequent research found Perry position scores ranging from 2 to 5, with no students scoring at the committed positions (Kurfiss, 1975; Pascarella and Terenzini, 1991, p. 30). This does not mean that higher levels are not present or possible. In fact, as our student populations diversify, the likelihood that all the stages will be represented increases. It may mean that the strategies for assessing developmental levels still need refining, or it may mean that the journey is a more logical priority than the destination.

Given the limitations of sequential models, we have proposed a sequence in order to suggest that certain building blocks make a good foundation (see Figure 1.4). Some tasks are more likely to be encountered early in the journey. College students, regardless of age, will be challenged to develop intellectual competence. If the college does nothing else, it will try to move students along this vector. If it requires physical education or encourages athletics and if it supports participation in music, art, drama, or dance, it will foster physical and manual competence. Unless the new student makes a serious effort to remain isolated, the experience of meeting new people inside and outside of class will stimulate interpersonal competence. Whether leaving home for the first time or returning to college late in life, students will face loneliness, anxiety, frustration, and conflict. They will be required to make decisions, set goals, and develop greater autonomy. While younger students may be more obsessed with sex and romance, older students may be forming new relationships and perhaps reexamining earlier ones in light of what they are reading and whom they are meeting. Therefore, it is likely that a college will move students along these first four vectors, and growth in each area helps construct identity. Most students also experience greater clarity about purposes, values, and ways

5

Table 1.2. The Seven Vectors: General Developmental Directions.

From	To
Developing Competence	
Low level of competence (intellectual, physical, interpersonal)	High level of competence in each area
Lack of confidence in one's abilities	Strong sense of competence
Managing Emotions	
Little control over disruptive emotions (fear and anxiety, anger leading to aggression, depression, guilt, and shame, and dysfunctional sexual or romantic attraction)	Flexible control and appropriate expression
Little awareness of feelings	Increasing awareness and acceptance of emotions
Inability to integrate feelings with actions	Ability to integrate feelings with responsible action
Moving Through Autonomy Toward Interdependence	
Emotional dependence	Freedom from continual and pressing needs for reassurance
Poor self-direction or ability to solve problems; little freedom or confidence to be mobile	Instrumental independence (inner direction, persistence, and mobility)
Independence	Recognition and acceptance of the importance of interdependence
Developing Mature Interpersonal Relationships	
Lack of awareness of differences; intolerance of differences	Tolerance and appreciation of differences
Nonexistent, short-term, or unhealthy intimate relationships	Capacity for intimacy which is enduring and nurturing
Establishing Identity	
Discomfort with body and appearance	Comfort with body and appearance
Discomfort with gender and sexual orientation	Comfort with gender and sexual orientation
Lack of clarity about heritage and social/cultural roots of identity	Sense of self in a social, historical, and cultural context
Confusion about "who I am" and experimentation with roles and lifestyles	Clarification of self-concept through roles and lifestyle
Lack of clarity about others' evaluation	Sense of self in response to feedback from valued others
Dissatisfaction with self	Self-acceptance and self-esteem
Unstable, fragmented personality	Personal stability and integration

Table 1.2. The Seven Vectors: General Developmental Directions, Cont'd.

From	*To*
Developing Purpose	
Unclear vocational goals	Clear vocational goals
Shallow, scattered personal interests	More sustained, focused, rewarding activities
Few meaningful interpersonal commitments	Strong interpersonal and family commitments
Developing Integrity	
Dualistic thinking and rigid beliefs	Humanizing values
Unclear or untested personal values and beliefs	Personalizing (clarifying and affirming) values while respecting others' beliefs
Self-interest	Social responsibility
Discrepancies between values and actions	Congruence and authenticity

of thinking. If they are lucky, they will discover interests and people they care deeply about and will make lasting commitments. And they will expand their awareness of who they are and of how valuable they are.

Few developmental theories have paid much attention to emotions and relationships. More work has been done on thoughts and values. Our theory assumes that emotional, interpersonal, and ethical development deserve equal billing with intellectual development.

How does this revision differ from the earlier version of *Education and Identity?*

1. The fifth vector, *freeing interpersonal relationships,* had been retitled *developing mature interpersonal relationships* and moved back in sequence, prior to *establishing identity.* We did this primarily to recognize the importance of students' experiences with relationships in the formation of their core sense of self.
2. The chapter on the *Managing Emotions* vector has been broadened beyond the earlier focus on aggression and sexual desire to address anxiety, depression, anger, shame, and guilt, as well as more positive emotions.

7

3. We have placed more emphasis on the importance of in-
    terdependence, while not denying the significance of learn-
    ing independence and self-sufficiency. Instead of retaining
    the term *developing autonomy,* we have renamed this vector
    Moving through autonomy toward interdependence.
4. More emphasis has been placed on the intercultural aspects
    of tolerance as a component of developing mature inter-
    personal relationships, which also entails a growing capac-
    ity for intimacy.
5. We have added more complexity to the *developing identity*
    vector. We have noted issues raised by recent researchers
    concerning differences in identity development based on
    gender, ethnic background, and sexual orientation.
6. More current research findings have been cited as they re-
    late to the vectors (although this book is not meant to con-
    tain a thorough review of the literature).
7. We have added illustrative statements from students to
    reflect greater diversity. Where earlier statements reinforce
    the text, they have been left in.

Like many humanistic models, this one is founded on an
optimistic view of human development, assuming that a nurturing, challenging college environment will help students grow
in stature and substance. Erikson believed in an epigenetic principle. Rogers saw a benign pattern at work in human beings,
similar to the process that turns acorns into oak trees. The ancient Greeks had a concept alien to our modern-day emphasis
on specialization and fragmentation between body and mind,
between the physical and the spiritual. It is called *aretê.* According
to the Greek scholar H.D.F. Kitto (1963, pp. 171–172), it was
their ideal:

> When we meet it in Plato we translate it "Virtue"
> and consequently miss all the flavour of it. "Vir-
> tue," at least in modern English, is almost entirely
> a moral word; *aretê* on the other hand is used in-
> differently in all the categories and means simply
> "excellence." It may be limited of course by its con-

text; the *aretê* of a race-horse is speed, of a cart-horse strength. If it is used, in a general context, of a man it will connote excellence in the ways in which a man can be excellent — morally, intellectually, physically, practically. Thus the hero of the *Odyssey* is a great fighter, a wily schemer, a ready speaker, a man of stout heart and broad wisdom who knows that he must endure without too much complaining what the gods send; and he can both build and sail a boat, drive a furrow as straight as anyone, beat a young braggart at throwing the discus, challenge the Phraecian youth at boxing, wrestling, or running; flay, skin, cut up, and cook an ox, and be moved to tears by a song. He is in fact an excellent all-rounder; he has surpassing *aretê*.

Kitto says that "this instinct for seeing things whole is the source of the essential sanity in Greek life" (p. 176). Institutions that emphasize intellectual development to the exclusion of other strengths and skills reinforce society's tendency to see some aspects of its citizens and not others. Just as individuals are not just consumers, competitors, and taxpayers, so students are not just degree seekers and test takers. To develop all the gifts of human potential, we need to be able to see them whole and to believe in their essential worth. In revising the seven vectors, we hope to offer useful tools to a new generation of practitioners who want to help students become "excellent all-rounders." We also hope to inspire experienced faculty, administrators, and student services and support staff to recommit to the mission of nurturing mind, body, heart, and spirit.

The Seven Vectors:
An Overview

Lasting personality changes may not occur in a blinding flash. As Dylan Thomas (1939, pp. 29–30) said, "Light breaks where no sun shines . . . Dawn breaks behind the eyes . . . Light breaks on secret lots . . . On tips of thought. . . . " While some epiphanies are dramatic and sudden, most occur gradually and incrementally. We may not know for years that a single lecture or conversation or experience started a chain reaction that transformed some aspect of ourselves. We cannot easily discern what subtle mix of people, books, settings, or events promotes growth. Nor can we easily name changes in ways of thinking, feeling, or interpreting the world. But we can observe behavior and record words, both of which can reveal shifts from hunch to analysis, from simple to complex perceptions, from divisive bias to compassionate understanding. Theory can give us the lenses to see these changes and help them along.

The challenges students, faculty, and administrators face today can be overwhelming. While the 1960s brought protest marches, drug busts, demands for curricular relevance, and students insisting on shared power, it was also an era of expanding budgets, new construction, and innovative programs. The boom lasted through the 1970s, and longer in some states. The resources were there to support adequate staffing, burgeoning specialization, and bold experiments. Perhaps we should have foreseen the pendulum swinging backward. Now administrators spend a great deal of time stretching dollars, consolidating services, and managing crises. Faculty are teaching larger classes or worrying about too few enrollees, fretting about retirement, relying on adjunct instructors, scrutinizing contracts, and going to union meetings. Students are facing higher tuition, longer lines, and fewer seats in the classroom. With higher costs, bleaker job prospects, and more evident crime statistics, students may focus more on security than on self-improvement.

Student development theory must apply to this generation of students as well as to future ones. It must be useful to institutional leaders as they cope with retrenchment as well as expansion. Without a developmental philosophy at the core of the college, it can become a dispensary of services, a training ground for jobs that may not exist, or a holding tank for those not sure what to do next. Institutions that impart transferable skills and relevant knowledge, bolster confidence and creativity, and engender social responsibility and self-directed learning are needed more than ever. To be effective in educating the whole student, colleges must hire and reinforce staff members who understand what student development looks like and how to foster it.

The seven vectors provide such a model. Though they were originally proposed as major constellations of development during adolescence and early adulthood, we have attempted to apply the vectors to adults as well. We have tried to use language that is gender free and appropriate for persons of diverse backgrounds. The vectors have stood the test of time as conceptual lenses. They have enabled higher education practitioners to view their students, their courses, and their programs more clearly and to use them as beacons for change. Those who have kept up to date on research, or who want more specificity and complexity, may be frustrated by our level of generality. Yet we believe that the original version of the model has been useful precisely because of its broad conceptual nature, leaving practitioners the options of putting their own understanding and interpretation into it and applying it within their own contexts.

We have also attempted to tie this model to student perceptions of their experience. We have drawn excerpts from student self-assessments, short reflection exercises, and papers on developmental theories where autobiographical examples were included. Over a period of three years, I (Reisser) invited students in my classes and professionals attending my presentations to complete a "developmental worksheet" by writing anonymous responses to the following:

1.   Briefly describe a change in yourself that had a major impact on how you lived your life. What was the "old" way of thinking or being, vs. the "new" way? What did you move *from* and what did you move *to?* How did you know that a significant change had occurred?

2.   What were the important things (or persons) that *helped* the process? What did the person *do?* What was the experience that catalyzed the shift? Were there any *feelings* that helped or accompanied the process?

In all, 120 worksheets were collected, and though they were not based on carefully designed sampling procedures, the statements excerpted from them bring to life the potentially dry formality of theory. When students' research or reflection papers included relevant examples; I (Reisser) asked to keep copies for future writing projects on student development. Students' statements from the 1969 edition were also used here to illustrate developmental stages.

The seven vectors are summarized below.

1. *Developing competence.* Three kinds of competence develop in college — intellectual competence, physical and manual skills, and interpersonal competence. Intellectual competence is skill in using one's mind. It involves mastering content, gaining intellectual and aesthetic sophistication, and, most important, building a repertoire of skills to comprehend, analyze, and synthesize. It also entails developing new frames of reference that integrate more points of view and serve as "more adequate" structures for making sense out of our observations and experiences.

13

Physical and manual competence can involve athletic and artistic achievement, designing and making tangible products, and gaining strength, fitness, and self-discipline. Competition and creation bring emotions to the surface since our performance and our projects are on display for others' approval or criticism. Leisure activities can become lifelong pursuits and therefore part of identity.

Interpersonal competence entails not only the skills of listening, cooperating, and communicating effectively, but also the more complex abilities to tune in to another person and respond appropriately, to align personal agendas with the goals of the group, and to choose from a variety of strategies to help a relationship flourish or a group function.

Students' overall sense of competence increases as they learn to trust their abilities, receive accurate feedback from others, and integrate their skills into a stable self-assurance.

2. *Managing emotions.* Whether new to college or returning after time away, few students escape anger, fear, hurt, longing, boredom, and tension. Anxiety, anger, depression, desire, guilt, and shame have the power to derail the educational process when they become excessive or overwhelming. Like unruly employees, these emotions need good management. The first task along this vector is not to eliminate them but to allow them into awareness and acknowledge them as signals, much like the oil light on the dashboard.

Development proceeds when students learn appropriate channels for releasing irritations before they explode, dealing with fears before they immobilize, and healing emotional wounds before they infect other relationships. It may be hard to accept that some amount of boredom and tension is normal, that some anxiety helps performance, and that impulse gratification must sometimes be squelched.

Some students come with the faucets of emotional expression wide open, and their task is to develop flexible controls. Others have yet to open the tap. Their challenge is to get in touch with the full range and variety of feelings and to learn to exercise self-regulation rather than repression. As self-control and self-expression come into balance, awareness and integration ideally support each other.

14

More positive kinds of emotions have received less attention from researchers. They include feelings like rapture, relief, sympathy, yearning, worship, wonder, and awe. These may not need to be "managed" so much as brought into awareness and allowed to exist. Students must learn to balance self-assertive tendencies, which involve some form of aggressiveness or defensiveness, with participatory tendencies, which involve transcending the boundaries of the individual self, identifying or bonding with another, or feeling part of a larger whole.

3. *Moving through autonomy toward interdependence.* A key developmental step for students is learning to function with relative self-sufficiency, to take responsibility for pursuing self-chosen goals, and to be less bound by others' opinions. Movement requires both emotional and instrumental independence, and later recognition and acceptance of interdependence.

Emotional independence means freedom from continual and pressing needs for reassurance, affection, or approval. It begins with separation from parents and proceeds through reliance on peers, nonparental adults, and occupational or institutional reference groups. It culminates in diminishing need for such supports and increased willingness to risk loss of friends or status in order to pursue strong interests or stand on convictions.

Instrumental independence has two major components: the ability to organize activities and to solve problems in a self-directed way, and the ability to be mobile. It means developing that volitional part of the self that can think critically and independently and that can then translate ideas into focused action. It also involves learning to get from one place to another, without having to be taken by the hand or given detailed directions, and to find the information or resources required to fulfill personal needs and desires.

Developing autonomy culminates in the recognition that one cannot operate in a vacuum and that greater autonomy enables healthier forms of interdependence. Relationships with parents are revised. New relationships based on equality and reciprocity replace the older, less consciously chosen peer bonds. Interpersonal context broadens to include the community, the society, the world. The need to be independent and the longing for inclusion become better balanced. Interdependence means respecting the autonomy of others and looking for ways to give and take with an ever-expanding circle of friends.

4. *Developing mature interpersonal relationships.* Developing mature relationships involves (1) tolerance and appreciation of differences (2) capacity for intimacy. Tolerance can be seen in both an intercultural and an interpersonal context. At its heart is the ability to respond to people in their own right rather than as stereotypes or transference objects calling for particular conventions. Respecting differences in close friends can generalize to acquaintances from other continents and cultures. Awareness, breadth of experience, openness, curiosity, and objectivity help students refine first impressions, reduce bias and ethnocentrism, increase empathy and altruism, and enjoy diversity.

In addition to greater tolerance, the capacity for healthy intimacy increases. For most adolescent couples, each is the pool and each the Narcissus. Satisfying relationships depend on spatial proximity, so that each can nod to the other and in the reflection observe himself or herself. Developing mature relationships means not only freedom from narcissism, but also the ability to choose healthy relationships and make lasting commitments based on honesty, responsiveness, and unconditional regard. Increased capacity for intimacy involves a shift in the quality of relationships with intimates and close friends. The shift is away from too much dependence or too much dominance and toward an interdependence between equals. Development means more in-depth sharing and less clinging, more acceptance of flaws and appreciation of assets, more selectivity in choosing nurturing relationships, and more long-lasting relationships that endure through crises, distance, and separation.

5. *Establishing identity.* Identity formation depends in part on the other vectors already mentioned: competence, emotional maturity, autonomy, and positive relationships. Developing identity is like assembling a jigsaw puzzle, remodeling a house, or seeking one's "human rhythms," a term that Murphy (1958) illustrated by photic driving. A person watching an instrument that emits flashes at precise intervals eventually hits a breaking point—the point at which the rhythm induces a convulsion. If, for example, the number is sixteen, the observer may rapidly

lose consciousness as this number is presented in the standard time interval. Seventeen and fifteen, however, are safe numbers. It is not until thirty-two or some other multiple of sixteen is reached that a breakdown recurs. Like the piano wire that hums or like the glass that shatters, we all have our critical frequencies in a variety of areas. Development of identity is the process of discovering with what kinds of experience, at what levels of intensity and frequency, we resonate in satisfying, in safe, or in self-destructive fashion.

Development of identity involves: (1) comfort with body and appearance, (2) comfort with gender and sexual orientation, (3) sense of self in a social, historical, and cultural context, (4) clarification of self-concept through roles and life-style, (5) sense of self in response to feedback from valued others, (6) self-acceptance and self-esteem, and (7) personal stability and integration. A solid sense of self emerges, and it becomes more apparent that there is an *I* who coordinates the facets of personality, who "owns" the house of self and is comfortable in all of its rooms.

College student concern with appearance is obvious. Though gowns no longer prevail except at Oxford and Cambridge, town residents recognize students, especially younger ones who don emblems of student culture. Whatever the limitations or prescriptions, experimentation occurs. With clarification of identity, however, it diminishes. By graduation, most of the early creative — or bizarre — variations are given up. Experimentation with dress and appearance herald pathways to sexual identity. Looking at old high school yearbooks confirms the evolution of hairstyles. Macho, androgynous, or femme fatale "looks" come and go, but identity hinges on finding out what it means to be a man or a woman and coming to terms with one's sexuality.

Establishing identity also includes reflecting on one's family of origin and ethnic heritage, defining self as a part of a religious or cultural tradition, and seeing self within a social and historical context. It involves finding roles and styles at work, at play, and at home that are genuine expressions of self and that further sharpen self-definition. It involves gaining a sense of how one is seen and evaluated by others. It leads to clarity and stability and a feeling of warmth for this core self as capable, familiar, worthwhile.

6. *Developing purpose.* Many college students are all dressed up and do not know where they want to go. They have energy but no destination. While they may have clarified who they are and where they came from, they have only the vaguest notion of who they want to be. For large numbers of college students, the purpose of college is to qualify them for a good job, not to help them build skills applicable in the widest variety of life experiences; it is to ensure a comfortable life-style, not to broaden their knowledge base, find a philosophy of life, or become a lifelong learner.

Developing purpose entails an increasing ability to be intentional, to assess interests and options, to clarify goals, to make plans, and to persist despite obstacles. It requires formulating plans for action and a set of priorities that integrate three major elements: (1) vocational plans and aspirations, (2) personal interests, and (3) interpersonal and family commitments. It also involves a growing ability to unify one's many different goals within the scope of a larger, more meaningful purpose, and to exercise intentionality on a daily basis.

We use the term *vocation* in its broadest sense — as specific career or as broad calling. Vocations can include paid work, unpaid work, or both. We discover our vocation by discovering what we love to do, what energizes and fulfills us, what uses our talents and challenges us to develop new ones, and what actualizes all our potentials for excellence. Ideally, these vocational plans flow from deepening interests, and in turn, lend momentum to further aspirations that have meaning and value. Considerations of life-style and family also enter the equation. As intimate relationships increasingly involve the question of long-term partnership and as formal education and vocational exploration draw to a close, next steps must be identified. It is difficult to construct a plan that balances life-style considerations, vocational aspirations, and avocational interests. Many compromises must be made, and clearer values help the decision-making process.

7. *Developing integrity*. Developing integrity is closely related to establishing identity and clarifying purposes. Our core values and beliefs provide the foundation for interpreting experience, guiding behavior, and maintaining self-respect. Developing integrity involves three sequential but overlapping stages: (1) humanizing values — shifting away from automatic application of uncompromising beliefs and using principled thinking in balancing one's own self-interest with the interests of one's fellow human beings, (2) personalizing values — consciously affirming core values and beliefs while respecting other points of view, and (3) developing congruence -- matching personal values with socially responsible behavior.

Humanizing values involves a shift from a literal belief in the absoluteness of rules to a more relative view, where connections are made between rules and the purposes they are meant to serve. Thus, the rules for a ball game can change to accommodate limited numbers of players or other unusual conditions; rules concerning honesty, sex, or aggressiveness can vary with circumstances and situations, while overriding principles (such as the Golden Rule) become more important. This change has also been called "liberalization of the superego" or "enlightenment of conscience"— the process by which the rigid rules received unquestioned from parents are reformulated in the light of wider experience and made relevant to new conditions (Sanford, 1962, p. 278).

Students bring to college an array of assumptions about what is right and wrong, true and false, good and bad, important and unimportant. Younger students may have acquired these assumptions from parents, church, school, media, or other sources. When others' values are internalized, most behavior conforms even when the judge is absent. Disobedience produces either diffuse anxiety or specific fear of discovery and punishment. Most of the values are implicit and unconsciously held; therefore, they are hard to identify or explain. With humanizing of values, much of this baggage comes to light. The contents are examined. Many items are discarded on brief inspection, sometimes with later regret. Some items are tried and found unsuitable. A few are set aside because they still fit and can be incorporated into a new wardrobe.

Personalizing of values occurs as the new wardrobe is assembled. Ultimately, the items selected are those required by the characteristics of the wearer, by the work expected to be done, by the situations to be encountered, and by the persons who are seen as important. In short, individuals select guidelines to suit themselves and to suit the conditions of their lives. In time, the components of this wardrobe are actively embraced as part of the self and become standards by which to flexibly assess personal actions.

Personalizing of values leads to the development of congruence — the achievement of behavior consistent with the personalized values held. With this final stage, internal debate is minimized. Once the implications of a situation are understood and the consequences of alternatives seem clear, the response is highly determined; it is made with conviction, without debate or equivocation.

These, then, are the seven major developmental vectors for college students. Each has additional components, and more detailed study reveals further ramifications. This overview, however, suggests the major configurations. The following chapters consider research and theory relevant to each vector in more detail.

2

Rita Preszler Weathersby

Ego Development

Ego development is an implicit aim of higher education and can be one of its most significant results. Stages of ego development constitute qualitatively different frames of reference for perceiving and responding to experience. Each successive stage represents a major reorganization of ways of understanding and reacting to situations, people, and ideas—a watershed change in patterns of thinking and feeling about oneself, others, authority, ethics, knowledge, and the central concerns that hold a life together. As a corollary, these stages reflect distinct views of the meaning and value of education, as well as characteristic styles of coping with the tasks of lifelong learning. Development through these stages parallels many other goals of higher education and tacitly informs our judgments about "what's good" and "what's next" for students in their intellectual journeys.

Higher education has a great deal to gain from recognizing these patterns of ego development as the framework of consciousness within which learning occurs. Educators are traditionally present at turning points in students' lives, whether the students are 18 or 80 and whether the curriculum is undergraduate, graduate, traditional, nontraditional, liberal arts, or vocational. A knowledge of ego development provides a "map for growth," which can help us find the best ways to reach our students. Equally important, our own stage of ego development is the frame of reference out of which we learn and teach. To be aware of the biases underlying our pedagogy, we need to know our own inner maps. The root word of *education* means to elicit or lead forth. This chapter offers ego development as a guide to understanding the personal and transformative meaning of education and explores its validity as an explicit aim for higher education.

Definition of Ego Development

By *ego,* students of ego development do not mean what is popularly called to mind by the term *ego,* such as one's self-concept or self-esteem, nor Freud's familiar idea of the ego in unconscious conflict with superego and id. Instead, they mean that aspect of personality that "keeps things together" by striving for coherence and assigning meaning to experience. The term *ego development* thus refers to a sequence, cutting across chronological time, of interrelated patterns of cognitive, interpersonal, and ethical development that form unified, successive, and hierarchical world views. Each stage or world view is a qualitatively different way of responding to life experience, which can be illustrated by representative types of individuals from Archie Bunker to Mahatma Gandhi.

Many psychologists have studied aspects of ego development as independent phenomena. Jane Loevinger and her associates (1970, 1976) have articulated a synthesis of their findings by linking insights from philosophical and humanistic psychology with psychoanalytic ego psychology and with contemporary stage-type notions of personality. She draws upon the conceptualizations of such diverse researchers as Alfred Adler, David Ausubel, Erik Erikson, Erich Fromm, Kenneth Isaacs, Lawrence Kohlberg, Abraham Maslow, George Herbert Mead, Jean Piaget, Carl Rogers, and Harry Stack Sullivan. At present, her scheme of ego development is the most inclusive of all developmental stage theories applicable to adolescents and adults. It has the added advantage of a measuring instrument (a projective test calling for sentence completions) and a scoring manual that makes explicit the experiential worlds of each stage.

Loevinger (1970, p. 7) traces her use of the term *ego development* to Adler's concept of "style of life," which at various times he equated with self, or ego, unity of personality, one's method of facing problems, and one's whole attitude toward life. Harry Stack Sullivan called this the *self-system* and advanced a theory of selective inattention to explain why an individual's ego stage is stable, or changes only slowly. According to this theory, a person tends to pay attention only to what is in accord with his or her already-existing perceptual framework. Discordant observations cause anxiety and give rise to the ego's major task: searching for coherent meanings in experience. The important point here is that one's ego stage is a pervasive, self-reinforcing frame of reference for experiencing. Additionally, it is the personality framework in which learning of any kind is embedded. What is learned is selectively assimilated to one's current patterns of cognition, introspection, interpersonal relations, and motivation. However, some learning is of such magnitude that it changes these patterns unalterably, giving rise to the next stage of development.

Piaget (in Tanner and Inhelder, 1960; see also Kohlberg, 1973) has identified the fundamental features of a concept of developmental stages. Stages are usually thought of as having an invariant sequence (no stages can be skipped), with each stage building on, incorporating, and transforming the elements of the previous one. Each stage has an inner logic that accounts for equilibrium and stability. Loevinger's conceptualization does not necessarily entail so strict a notion of a stage; it is possible to see progressions of ego development as gradations along a qualitative continuum. If one sees discrete stages, the focus is on broad character orientations. If one sees a continuum, the focus is on the dynamics of transition from one stage to the next.

In either case, ego development is considered by Loevinger to be not just *a* personality trait: it is a *master trait* second only to intelligence in determining an individual's pattern of responses to situations. Ego development is marked by a succession of turning points called *milestone sequences,* which represent broad patterns of change involving many aspects of personality. Thus, the presence, absence, or intensity of a single personality trait is best interpreted in the context of how that characteristic fits into an interrelated sequence of development. For example, concern for achievement is most pronounced at a stage of ego development midway in the sequence. A woman with little apparent urgency about achieving may be at lower stages—or may have gone beyond to higher stages in which concern for individual fulfillment transcends conventional notions of achievement. Loevinger's concept of milestone sequences (a trait develops, peaks in importance, and then reappears in a new context) allows us to place this woman's "lack of achievement motivation" in perspective.

Stages of Ego Development

Table 1 presents in summary form Loevinger's (1976) description of the milestone sequences of ego development. The descriptive phrases in the table identify milestones in character development, interpersonal relations, conscious concerns, and cognitive style associated with general stages of ego development. Reading down the columns, one sees successive levels of complexity in each facet of development; reading across, one sees the broad character patterns of each stage. Granted that this is only one way to label complex phenomena, there is substantial empirical evidence to support this formulation (Loevinger, 1970, 1976). Moreover, to most people the progressions make intuitive sense. It is obvious that change in one aspect of ego development is likely to stimulate change in another. Conversely, if there is little change in one facet, further development is necessarily restricted. Consider, for example, how difficult it would be to have a deeply held respect for the individuality and autonomy of others—a salient concern at the Autonomous Stage—if appearance and social acceptability were predominant life themes and one thought in stereotypes and clichés—characteristics of the Conformist Stage, which is earlier in the sequence.

It is helpful to have a more solid sense of these stages before considering their relevance to education (for a more complete description, see Loevinger, 1976, pp. 18-28). The earliest stages are usually thought of as childhood stages. Adults who remain in them are often marginal to society and usually the targets of other's efforts at socialization. A student at the *Self-Protective Stage,* for example, would be concerned with control and advantage in relationships; would follow rules opportunistically; would reason illogically and think in stereotypes; would tend to see life as a zero-sum game; and would externalize blame to other people or to circumstances.

A major step in ego development is the transition from the Self-Protective Stage to the series of essentially conventional stages in which individuals with increasing self-awareness identify with social rules and society. Kohlberg (1969) divides his stages of moral reasoning into preconventional, conventional, and postconventional world views; although the parallel with ego development stages is not exact, this distinction is useful in identifying the major differences in perspective across stages. A student at the *Conformist Stage* would be concerned with appearances and social acceptability; would tend to think in stereotypes and clichés, particularly moralistic ones; would be concerned about conforming to external rules; and would behave with superficial niceness. Emotions would be described in undifferentiated terms that betray little introspection. Group differences would be perceived in terms of obvious external characteristics such as age, race, marital status, and nationality. There would be almost no sensitivity to individual differences.

At the *Conscientious-Conformist Transition,* or *Self-Aware Stage,* an individual develops an increasing self-awareness and the ability to think in terms of alternatives,

Table 1. Some Milestones of Ego Development

Stage	Impulse Control, Character Development	Interpersonal Style	Conscious Preoccupations	Cognitive Style
Impulsive	Impulsiveness, fear of retaliation	Receiving, dependent, exploitative	Bodily feelings, especially sexual and aggressive	Stereotyping, conceptual confusion
Self-Protective	Fear of being caught, externalization of blame, opportunism	Wary, manipulative, exploitative	Self-protection, trouble, wishes, things, advantage, control	
Conformist	Conformity to external rules, shame, guilt for breaking rules	Concerned with belonging, superficially nice	Appearance, social acceptability, banal feelings, behavior	Conceptual simplicity, stereotypes, clichés
Conscientious-Conformist (Self-Aware)	Differentiation of norms, goals	Aware of self in relation to group, helping	Adjustment, problems, reasons, opportunities (vague)	Multiplicity
Conscientious	Self-evaluated standards, self-criticism, guilt for consequences, long-term goals and labels	Intensive, responsible, mutual, concerned with communication	Differentiated feelings, motives for behavior, self-respect, achievements, traits, expression	Conceptual complexity, idea of patterning
Individualistic	*Add:* Respect for individuality	*Add:* Dependence as an emotional problem	*Add:* Development, social problems, differentiation of inner life from outer	*Add:* Distinction of process and outcome
Autonomous	*Add:* Coping with conflicting inner needs, toleration	*Add:* Respect for autonomy, interdependence	Vividly conveyed feelings, integration of physiological and psychological, psychological causation of behavior, role conception, self-fulfillment, self in social context	Increased conceptual complexity, complex patterns, toleration for ambiguity, broad scope, objectivity
Integrated	*Add:* Reconciling of inner conflicts, renunciation of unattainable	*Add:* Cherishing of individuality	*Add:* Identity	

Note: "*Add*" means in addition to the description applying to the previous level.

Source: Adapted from Loevinger, 1976, pp. 24-25.

exceptions, and multiple possibilities in situations. Students at this stage are sometimes painfully aware of their separateness in relation to social groups; they are concerned primarily with taking advantage of opportunities, solving problems, finding reasons for the way life works, and adjusting to situations and roles.

At the *Conscientious Stage,* an individual lives according to self-evaluated standards. Rules are not absolute; exceptions and contingencies are recognized, and reasoning is more complex and based on analytical patterns. A student at this stage would be concerned about responsibility and mutuality in relationships; would see individuals as having real choices in life; would value achievement highly and be concerned with self-respect; would have long-term goals and ideals, and a tendency to look at events in societal terms, or in a broad social context. Individuals at the Conscientious Stage understand psychological causation and development over time; they also have a deeper and more differentiated self-understanding.

The *Autonomous Stage* represents yet another restructuring of personality. This world view is postconventional; one can analyze one's own social group and other social systems, and make choices and commitments despite an awareness of the complexity and social forces at work. An ability to acknowledge inner conflict is the hallmark of this stage. The autonomous individual also respects others' autonomy (for example, being willing and able to let one's children make their own mistakes) while valuing interdependence. The *Individualistic Stage* is a transition to this stage, characterized by a heightened respect for individuality and a concern for development, social problems, and differentiating one's inner and outer life. A student at the Autonomous Stage would take an expanded view of life as a whole; would tend to be realistic and objective about himself and others; would respond to abstract ideals such as social justice; would be able to unite and integrate ideas that appear as incompatible opposites to those at lower stages; and would have a cognitive style characterized by complexity and a high tolerance for ambiguity. Self-fulfillment would become an important concern, partly supplanting the importance of achievement at earlier stages. Feelings would be expressed vividly and convincingly, including sensual experiences and the kind of existential humor that shows a recognition of life's paradoxes.

The highest stage, the *Integrated Stage,* intensifies the characteristics of the Autonomous Stage and adds reconciliation of inner conflicts in a more consolidated sense of identity. Identity is a conscious preoccupation, and interpersonal relations reflect a cherishing of individuality within the broadest possible context of human life. Loevinger finds this stage rare and therefore difficult to study. Maslow's (1971) description of self-actualizing persons is an approximation of these higher stages.

Education's Role in Promoting Ego Development

From this brief review it should be clear that ego development is not a trivial, easily accomplished personality change. What conditions are propitious for ego development? Erikson (1968) says, "Ego identity gains real strength only from wholehearted achievement that has meaning in our culture" (p. 135). Sanford (1962) goes into more detail: "Anything that increases the likelihood that the sense of self will be based on personal experience rather than on outside judgment favors the stabilization of ego identity. Being placed in social roles that require new responses, having to make decisions concerning what roles one is going to take, learning from experience that some roles are suited and others not suited to one's interests and needs—any situation that brings awareness to one's real preferences and inner continuities helps to establish sound ego identity.

So, too, does the condition of being relatively free from circumstances, whether unconscious drives or external pressures, that force one to cling to an earlier inadequate identity" (p. 281). In short, there seem to be three basic conditions that foster ego development: (1) varied direct experiences and roles, (2) meaningful achievement, and (3) relative freedom from anxiety and pressure.

It is instructive to examine the progressions of cognitive style embedded in ego development. At the earliest stages, thinking is stereotyped and characterized by conceptual confusion. At the Conformist Stage, thinking is simplistic, and stereotypes and clichés abound. With the Conscientious Stage come conceptual complexity and the idea of patterns among causal relationships, along with awareness of alternatives, exceptions, and contingencies and a broader time perspective based on long-term goals and ideals. Next is added the crucial ability to distinguish between process and outcome—between a sequence of events and the results that follow. The highest stages are distinguished by increased conceptual complexity, complex patterns of thought and feelings, objectivity, an ability to tolerate ambiguity, and a broad perspective.

These progressions lie at the heart of a liberal arts education and reflect some of the central aims of higher education. They are highly relevant to increased capacity to function effectively in multiple and sometimes conflicting adult roles, and as citizens in a complex world community. They are also central to an individual's ability to learn from experience, in that each person's ego stage places constraints on understanding and action that ultimately determine how much he or she can gain from an education environment. Although higher ego stages do not necessarily mean greater personal goodness or happiness, they do enable individuals to respond more adequately to progressively deeper and more complex issues and problems, both intellectual and personal.

William Perry (1970, see Chapter Three), working independently from Loevinger, derived a compatible progression from longitudinal interviews with Harvard undergraduates. As students advanced from freshmen to seniors, they were asked, "What stood out in your experience?" Students' answers showed a progression along a series of intellectual and ethical positions from simple dualistic thinking, in which the sources of knowledge and authority are viewed in polar terms of "we-right-good" and "other-wrong-bad," through various positions in which multiple views and diversity of opinion are considered legitimate, to a contextual and relativistic view of knowledge in which personal commitment is required in assuming responsibility for the framework within which one's opinions and actions are taken. This research, having started with students and not statements of the purpose of education, lends credence to the claim that colleges are unwittingly engaged in the creation of settings that promote basic personality change. This is not to say that colleges are primarily in the business of psychological education but only to note unequivocally that the experience of being a college student can alter fundamentally the *structures* in which an individual thinks, feels, and acts.

Here, we must discard the outworn rhetorical dichotomies between intellect and emotion and between personal growth and academic achievement, for these very dichotomies embody a thought process characteristic of middle levels of development. There is a unity postulated among all facets of ego development. If higher education induces major changes in students' cognitive style, it is likely to induce change in other aspects of personality as well. According to Piaget's notion of *horizontal décalage,* a change in one dimension requires assimilation and "filling in" across other aspects of functioning. If the changes are significantly widespread and irreversible, a new stage of development may be reached. This potential impact of learning on personality may be one reason why the process of education and its intended result, learning, are almost inevitably accompanied by anxiety. It is also the reason that most educational institutions can be said to be in the business of promoting ego development, even if they merely conceive of themselves as providing students with opportunities to gain intellectual skills and mastery of a discipline or profession.

Ego Development Research in Higher Education

At what stages of ego development are we likely to find our students—and, for that matter, faculty and administrators? Loevinger's research (1970) puts the majority of late adolescents and adults at the Conformist or Conscientious Stages, or squarely between them. (See her sentence completion test, 1970.) Loevinger estimates that this transition (the Self-Aware Level) is the modal stopping place for adults in our society. This also appears to be a transition made by many traditional-age students in their first two years of college. A longitudinal study still in progress (Loevinger, at Worcester Polytechnic Institute) shows that traditional-age students go from about the Self-Aware Stage to about the Conscientious Stage between the beginning of their freshman and the end of their sophomore year. At the end of their senior year they test the same as at the end of their sophomore year.

Data for faculty and administrators are more scarce than for students; my data (Weathersby, 1977) for a very small sample suggest that scores of faculty and administrators are slightly higher than students' scores but, interestingly, cover the same range, omitting the preconventional stages.

Nancy Goldberger, at Simon's Rock Early College (enrolling students 16 to 20 years old), has compiled comparative data on college freshmen from Simon's Rock, an Ivy League college, an urban university, an engineering school, and a teacher's college and juxtaposed them with ego development scores from a national survey of college and non-college youth conducted by Daniel Yankelovich. The data show that most, but clearly not all, college freshmen are at the Conformist Stage or beyond, and that the proportionate mix of stages in any student group varies with age and with type of institution. Table 2 reproduces Goldberger's data (Goldberger, 1977), adding data from adult undergraduates at Goddard College (Weathersby, 1977) and unpublished data from students enrolled in an external degree program of the Vermont State College System.

The data in Table 2 suggest provocative differences by age and institution. For example, the proportion of traditional-age freshmen at the Ivy League college scoring beyond conformist stages of ego development is more than double that of their general peers. One possible hypothesis is that ego development accounts for their presence at an elite institution—that this is an implicit basis upon which they were admitted. Other hypotheses are possible—for example, social class or alumni bias in recruiting. However, one has only to recall the folklore in higher education about the different kinds of students who attend different types of institutions to gain an appreciation of the validity of these figures as both descriptors of students and of educational milieus.

In Table 2, it is instructive to examine the proportion of students who score at the Conscientious Stage and higher, across age and institutions. Again, for traditional-age students, the Ivy League school and the urban university have the larger proportions. In general, 18-year-olds score higher than 16-year-olds, and undergraduate adults score still higher. Thus, age makes a global difference, at least up to middle levels of development. Additionally, the two adult programs sampled had substantial proportions of students (38 to 49 percent) who scored at the Individualistic, Autonomous, and Integrated Stages. These scores are rare for students of traditional college age. These data are suggestive

Table 2. Ego-Stage Scores of College Students of Varying Ages
at Different Types of Institutions

Traditional-Age High School Students (16 years old)	Preconformist Stages (2)[a]	Conformist Stages (3, 4)	Conscientious Stage and Above (5, 6, 7, 8)
National Survey	32%	61%	7%
Simon's Rock Early College	14%	60%	20%
Selective Prep School	3%	78%	19%
Traditional-Age College Freshmen (18 years old)			
National Survey	16%	52%	31%
Ivy League College	7%	25%	68%
Urban University	8%	45%	47%
Engineering School	13%	48%	39%
Teacher's College	10%	56%	34%
Adult Undergraduates (21-81 years old)			
Goddard College Adult Degree Program	3%	16%	81%
Vermont State Colleges External Degree	—	30%	70%

[a]These codes refer to the stages listed in Table 1. In this formulation, the Self-Protective Stage (2) is preconventional, the Conformist (3) and Self-Aware (4) Stages are conventional, and the Conscientious Stage (5) is above conformity but still conventional in the terms described in this chapter. The Individualistic (6), Autonomous (7), and Integrated (8) Stages are postconventional stages.

Sources: Data for the upper portions of this table were compiled by Nancy Goldberger at Simon's Rock Early College (Goldberger, 1977). The national survey data were supplied by Daniel Yankelovich and Robert Holt and drawn from a 1975 Yankelovich survey of college and noncollege youth. The figures here represent college youth only. Data on adult undergraduates are drawn from Weathersby, 1977, and from an ongoing study of adult learners in the Vermont State Colleges External Degree Program, sponsored by the Fund for the Improvement of Postsecondary Education/DHEW.

rather than conclusive because of differences in sampling and scoring methods among the studies cited. Nonetheless, they raise questions concerning appropriate institutional responses to students' diversity or homogeneity, and also the differential impact of different kinds of college environments upon students' development.

To summarize, we can expect most traditional-age college students to start out at the Conformist or Self-Aware Stage and then move beyond, although probably not past the Conscientious Stage. Some students will still be at preconventional stages; they can be expected to have serious trouble making their way in any college environment. Those at the Conscientious Stage and beyond should tend to perform better academically and function better socially, although this relationship may not necessarily be apparent in individual grade-point averages.

An extraordinarily interesting question is how far beyond conventional stages adult students have ventured. Data from adult students in nontraditional undergraduate programs suggest that they have moved far beyond indeed, much farther than is believed representative of the general adult population. Although the proportion of students at each stage will vary across programs and institutions, most groups of students will exhibit a wide range of individual differences in ego levels. Adult students, taken as a group, probably exhibit both the highest stages and the greatest range of diversity.

We can hypothesize that adults who return to school have progressed along these dimensions as a result of life choices and nonformal learning. Furthermore, many adults "go back to school" in response to deeply felt inner imperatives. That is, their decision to enroll is dictated less by convention than that of traditional-age students. Hence this decision may in itself bespeak a radical personal transformation, or readiness to undergo such a transformation.

Data are scarce for a further and potentially promising use of these statistics: that is, to compare the range and mix of scores across age, sex, and institutions. For example, Goldberger has found sex differences in ego development scores among students at Simon's Rock. The girls who enroll tend to score higher than the boys. In Goddard's Adult Degree Program, women in their twenties tended to score higher than males in the same age group, and also higher than women in other age groups. Women in their forties, many of whom were making the transition from a career in the home to work roles in the larger society, tended to score lower than women in other age groups. Assuming these differences are generalizable past small groups at single institutions, we can account for them by hypothesizing different trajectories of development influenced by sex-related structures of opportunity.

Informally, we acknowledge that different "types" of students appear in different "types" of institutions, giving each its unique character and potential social mission. The findings reported earlier suggest individual differences in ego development may be related to choice of college and to educational outcomes. If this is so, we can employ the concept of ego development to gain a greater understanding of students' reasons for enrolling, and the meaning for them of their educational experiences. There are implications here for admission and attrition, and for brokering services that will help students of all ages find settings in which they can succeed.

Conceptions of Education at Different Ego Levels

Individuals at different stages of ego development have different conceptions of what education is, why it is valuable, and how closely tied education is to what is taught or required by a college faculty. College faculty and administrators exhibit the same diversity of views as students. Our conceptions of education are crucial because they guide our objectives and actions. Nearly everyone says education is valuable; however, across stages the source of value shifts from concern with the practical benefit of getting a job, or a more desirable job, to a means of developing one's skills and capacities for advancement and personal growth, to help in coping with life and involvement in a lifelong learning process that has intrinsic value for self-fulfillment. Table 3 illustrates these differences in one-sentence responses characteristically given to the sentence stem "Education," which appears on most forms of Loevinger's sentence-completion test.

People at the lowest stages tend to view education as external to the self, something that one gets in school and then has. At the Conformist Stage, education is equated with school attendance and the socially defined number of necessary years of schooling. This view is both practical and idealized. Education is "an essential requirement in acquiring a good job" and "the greatest thing on earth." At the Self-Aware Stage, education becomes important as an investment in one's life or future. There is a shift away from thinking of education as a concrete entity toward thinking of it as a goal and an asset. Education becomes "a very important step in life" and "is the best investment anyone can make."

At the Conscientious Stage, education is usually seen as an experience that affects a person's inner life. It is no longer merely a number of years of useful schooling. Its importance lies in intellectual challenge and in potential enrichment for the individual. It

Table 3. Perceptions of Education by Ego Stages

Ego Stage	Characteristic Responses to Sentence-Completion Stem "Education"
Impulsive and Self-Protective Stages	Education . . .
Education is viewed as a *thing* that you get in school and then have. Positive remarks are undifferentiated. There are also expressions of distaste for education, or of not getting along in school.	. . . is fun and hard.
	. . . is a very good thing.
	. . . is OK.
	. . . is very nice to have if you ain't got it you can't get a job.
	. . . and me don't get along too good.
	. . . is useless and a lot of bother.
	. . . is good for finding a job.
	. . . is a drag but important.
	. . . is good, although I hate it, because where would the world be without it?
Conformist Stage	
Education is generally interpreted as school attendance, which has practical usefulness; one can get a better job with it than without it. An uncritical, idealized view of education is expressed, in which the current number of years of schooling is considered necessary for everyone.	. . . is of the utmost importance.
	. . . is a very important and useful thing today.
	. . . is a necessity for all U.S. citizens.
	. . . is very important for children.
	. . . I think everyone should graduate high school.
	. . . is an essential requirement in acquiring a good job.
	. . . helps everyone.
	. . . is the greatest thing on earth.
	. . . I had ten and one half years of schooling and someday I will get that last year. Because that's important.
Self-Aware Stage	
Education's importance is viewed in terms of one's life or future. There is a shift away from thinking of education as a concrete entity toward thinking of it as a goal and an asset.	. . . is a very important step in life.
	. . . is a preparation for life.
	. . . is very important and invaluable to one's future.
	. . . should be a prized possession.
	. . . is very desirable and a goal for all members of my family.
Conscientious Stage	
Education is viewed as an experience that affects a person's inner life. It is no longer merely a prescribed number of years of useful schooling. Its importance lies in intellectual stimulation and enrichment. It influences a person's whole life, making it more worthwhile and enjoyable. Education is an opportunity that should be available to everyone. It is seen as being a significant force in improving society, though the educational system may be seen as needing improvement as well.	. . . is the standard for a strong America.
	. . . seldon lives up to its goals.
	. . . will get quite poor if the type and quality of teachers does not improve.
	. . . is not just what they teach at school.
	. . . is very important, and worth working for.
	. . . is a privilege and not a right.
	. . . should be provided with equal opportunity for all.
	. . . is a challenge but also a necessity.
	. . . is a constant process not limited to a classroom.

Table 3 *(Continued)*

Ego Stage	Characteristic Responses to Sentence-Completion Stem "Education"
Conscientious Stage (Continued)	Education . . . . . . is a source of satisfaction in the present and for the future. . . . is essential in gaining maturity. . . . helps one acquire insight into problems. . . . is the most important thing along with being able to love. . . . is the foundation for a socially and secure life.
Individualistic Stage This view has an element of both the conscientious and autonomous perspectives; conscientious themes are more fully elaborated, and the focus is shifting to education as a lifelong process essential for a full life.	. . . is a lifelong process. . . . you can never have enough of it. Life should be a process of learning as much as you can about anything at all. . . . opens new avenues of thought and produces more joy in living. . . . is a must because the more I learn, the more I enjoy life. . . . is necessary now but the general trend of education should be training for life not a profession. . . . is necessary. What we learn is not as important as the fact that we are learning to think for ourselves.
Autonomous and Integrated Stages Education is seen as leading to a deeper understanding of oneself and others, as helping to cope with life, as leading to creativity, self-fulfillment, and deeper values; hence, education is intrinsically valuable. It is not a thing one has or gets, once and for all, nor is it identified solely with school and intellectual achievement apart from interpersonal relations and emotional involvements.	. . . seems valuable in itself. . . . will help me through life. I am not being educated because I have to, but education is a wonderful thing. . . . can be a means or an end depending on other characteristics of those who pursue it. . . . is learning to solve problems in a better way—to know what needs doing and when and how to do it. . . . means a lot to me, I'll stagnate if I never do anything creative. . . . is a necessary part of my development as a unique individual. . . . is the development of the entire man, mental, physical and spiritual. . . . is rewarding only if you learn to see things in a variety of ways and can have feelings for other people's beliefs.

(continued on next page)

Table 3 *(Continued)*

Ego Stage	Characteristic Responses to Sentence-Completion Stem "Education"
Autonomous and Integrated Stages (Continued)	Education . . . . . . *is both a stimulation to growth and method for accumulating knowledge for future use.* . . . *is a many splendored thing. It is also a necessity, a responsibility and at times a trouble, a sadness.*

Note: The left column gives scoring guidelines; the right column gives characteristic responses to the sentence stem "Education . . . ," which appears on the standard form of the sentence-completion test for ego development.

Source: Material in this table is abstracted from the scoring manual for *Measuring Ego Development* (Loevinger, Wessler, and Redmore, 1970, Vol. 2), pp. 97-107.

influences a person's entire life, making it more worthwhile and enjoyable. Education "broadens and enlightens the view," and "helps one acquire insight into problems." Education is seen in social terms as a privilege or opportunity that should be available to everyone. Education is also seen as a significant force in improving society, and individuals at this level often express definite opinions about ways in which the educational system needs improvement. At the Individualistic Transition, these themes are more fully elaborated as the time horizon stretches to a view of education as a lifelong process essential for full life. Education is "a lifetime pursuit," "an ongoing experience," and "a never-ending process." Some responses are slightly clichéd, as if overemphasizing the discovery of one's own role in this process. For example, one enthusiastic student at this stage commented that education is "a never-ending daily life growth experience."

At the Autonomous and Integrated Stages, education has intrinsic value apart from the goal-orientation of earlier stages. It is not a thing one has or gets, nor is it identified with schooling or intellectual achievement apart from interpersonal relationships and emotional involvements. Education is seen primarily as leading to a deeper understanding of oneself and others, as helping to cope with life, and as leading to creativity and deeper values. It is part of an individual process of growth and development seen in broad social perspective. Education is "the means of new ideas and knowledge that can be tools of change and growth in the context of any life-style." It is "a many-splendored thing: it is also a necessity, a responsibility, and at times a trouble, a sadness."

These statements are not isolated responses: they represent pervasive assumptions that influence how students respond to educational settings. Consider, for example, two students in Goddard's individualized, external Adult Degree Program (ADP) who are within two years of the same age and at opposite ends of the continuum of ego development. Philip (age 24), an entering student whose sentence-completion test is scored at the Self-Protective Stage, explains his reasons for enrolling in concrete terms. His view of education is seemingly external to his inner life; a degree is necessary for job security and fulfilling family obligations. "I enrolled so that I can get a degree in Art, since I have been involved in Art most of my life." Philip explains that his father has died recently and that, as the oldest son, he "gets the responsibilities with the family." The major issue in his work right now is "to be able to work in the U.S. and in Canada"; the major issue in his personal life is to "get my degree and help my family get an education." In response to the "Education" sentence-completion stem, he writes that education "is a necessity."

In contrast, Mark (age 26), whose ego development score falls between the Auton-omous and Integrated Stages, describes his reasons for enrolling in the abstract terms of personal integration. He writes that "education is traditionally a matter of knowing but is much more powerful when it includes understanding and using." He describes being frus-trated in a conventional undergraduate program, where he took shelter from what he described as "bone-chilling mediocrity" by taking advantage of opportunities to study in unconventional ways. Mark chose Goddard as a positive alternative "because it seemed to emphasize skills I thought were important, but which I was not confident in, and do so within a structure which I thought I would find challenging but not impossible." The major issue in his work is to define a career after eight years of many different jobs—"I am using my time in the ADP not to prepare myself for a career but to help me get the intellectual background to choose a field. I am preparing to prepare for a career, if you wish. I see an appropriate career as being an outgrowth of my personal concerns." Like Philip, Mark notes that Goddard's individualized instructional mode matches his style of learning reasonably well. However, the reasons are different. Mark comments on the qual-ity of the instructional system: "One of the important aspects of the ADP is that the style of instruction and modes of learning are open to wide variation and considerable negotiation as long as sufficient rigor is maintained."

The patterned differences in perspective between these two men illustrate the wide range of individual differences within a single sex and age group, as well as different concerns at the extremes of ego development. Philip thinks of frustration as external to himself, whereas Mark is explicit about his responsibility for making use of what he de-scribes as "an incoherent environment characterized by the tremendous amounts of energy which individuals invest in finishing and evaluating their six months' studies and planning the next." When each was asked what was frustrating or missing in the learning environment, Philip replied, "a basketball court" (which, in fact, would be a useful addi-tion). Mark spoke of inner frustration—"The greatest frustrations are the ones I bring on myself when my self-discipline fails, and I get bogged down by my own confusion." The difference in individualizing education for these two students is obvious. Loevinger's scheme permits these differences to be viewed as positions on a continuum describing interrelated patterns and not merely as individual idiosyncrasies.

Students' Motives and Values

The important point is that individuals at different stages of ego development have very different capacities for framing educational goals, for using the structure of a college program (whether teaching is individualized or in lecture format), and for develop-ing relationships with faculty and peers. For some students, the intellectual task is to develop mastery of logical and contextual reasoning; others need help in choosing among authorities and commitments. One use of ego development as a map is to clarify the themes and central issues around which students' struggles take place. This requires pay-ing close attention to what students are doing and thinking while learning and how they are reacting. The next two sections of this chapter illustrate differences in students' inner structuring of experience. The examples are from a participant-observation study of adult undergraduates at Goddard College (Weathersby, 1977). Students' reasons for enrolling and the outcomes of study they value most become multidimensional when superimposed upon the matrix of ego development.

I asked adult students in the Goddard study, "Why did you enroll?" Then I asked whether there was a critical incident or realization leading to this decision. Seven basic reasons emerged: (1) a degree was necessary for work or career goals, either current or anticipated (22 percent); (2) it was important to continue or finish one's education, in many cases to pursue career plans but also to complete "unfinished business" with respect to one's education (16 percent); (3) enrollment came at a time when outside resources were sought for a reorientation or redirection of both work and personal concerns (16 percent); (4) enrollment made it possible to study valued interests in depth and in an individualized manner not permitted by other modes of study (14 percent); (5) studying was a means of seeking personal growth and fulfilling one's potential (12 percent); (6) studying provided an enjoyable challenge and intellectual stimulation (10 percent); and (7) this seemed to be the appropriate time in one's life to enroll (10 percent). Many people, particularly those at higher ego levels, mentioned several reasons.

The content of these "basic reasons for enrolling" changed somewhat systematically by ego level. Even generalized statements of individuals' reasons for enrolling, robbed of their nuances of wording and experiential contexts, seem to cluster at particular ego levels, forming "milestone sequences" similar to those outlined in the theory of ego development. Reorientation and redirection are most salient at the Conscientious Stage and below; the importance of getting a degree or finishing one's education peaks at the Conscientious Stage (which is noted for its focus on achievement), as does the importance of intellectual challenge and stimulation. No one at the Self-Aware Stage or below gave in-depth study or wanting to pursue one's own pressing interests as a reason for enrolling. The importance of being able to study valued interests in depth becomes salient at postconventional stages, as do personal growth and fulfillment. Responses at the lower ego levels are often flat and one-dimensional; beginning at the Individualistic Stage people give multifaceted reasons that reflect their personal goals and life experience. Thus, in the reasons given for enrollment there is a clear progression of themes, which peak in salience and then become transformed. At successively higher ego levels the "same" motives may assume significantly different meanings.

I have observed a similar phenomenon in reviewing application forms and evaluation questionnaires for other adult programs. Lasker (1978), in a study of achievement motives across ego levels, found that at lower ego levels the motivation to achieve often seems linked to a sense of correcting deficiencies or fixing something that is wrong. At middle levels, achieving seems related to the sense of crossing a self-set goal line. At higher levels, goals for achievement are related to an ongoing process of personal growth and social concern. Several examples will illustrate these points. For one man (age 29) at the Self-Aware Stage, getting a degree was clearly related to tangible benefits now denied him. Being laid off at work as the result of not having the B.A. degree was a critical incident that led to enrollment.

> I felt that time was running out. I wanted the benefits of a B.A. while I still had time to use it.

A woman at the Conscientious Stage described her desire for a degree as a means to meet specific, personal goals within a long-term time perspective. This woman (age 44) says:

> I enrolled in the ADP because my last child is about ready to leave home, and I wanted to prepare myself for some satisfying work. My goal is to go into library science, and in that you need a degree. Also, I liked the way ADP functions. . . . There was also the added thought that I need some mind stimulation now.

In contrast, a man (24) at the Individualistic Stage experiences his need for credentials in terms of the undesirable emotional dependency this lack creates in his work.

> I want to finish my undergrad work so that I can get my graduate degrees. I'm presently doing the work I would do after earning graduate degrees, but without proper academic credentials I'm dependent on others. . . . So, even though I'm left with not much time to do ADP work, I'm feeling almost urgent about finishing college so that I can be more independent in my work.

These responses illustrate Lasker's observations that at lower stages there is often a sense of compensating for a lack ("time is running out") and at middle levels a sense of crossing a goal line ("My goal is to go into library science"). At higher ego levels, there is a clear recognition that motives and goals for education are interconnected with the ongoing process of learning how to live one's life. The degree is important but is often mentioned as an afterthought, or as a natural outgrowth of other concerns. A woman (age 26) at the Individualistic Stage says:

> I am a seeker—in this case, seeking knowledge with enough discipline and supervision as well as personal contact to keep me on course, and enough freedom and self-direction to keep me interested. ADP was the only place I could find allowing both. I'm also career-oriented, and I find that the jobs I'm interested in require degrees.

Another woman at this level, an artist with a strong sense of what she wants to study to improve work already in progress, says:

> I have a very strongly developed learning program of my own, and it is extremely important to me that this not be truncated by any outside force. . . . [However,] having a college degree will help me to make my program of study into a career.

Personal growth is understood differently at different ego levels. One man at the Self-Aware Stage gives as his reason for enrolling:

> I need to have some organization in my growth. I also need to get credit (reinforcement) for the work I do.

Here the source of organization and reinforcement is external. By contrast, an internal orientation is displayed by a woman at the Autonomous Stage, who explains:

> For a long time now I have been searching for integration—growth—"profession"—calling in life. Here I am.

She experiences the program structure as a catalyst, a sequence of experiences, compressed in time, in which she can work out the personal integration she is seeking.

There are implications here for education. Some of these students have concrete goals for which training and skill development are important. Others have more general concerns regarding professional or vocational development and the clarification of work and values. Still others seek greater independence, self-definition, recognition, and validation. How the institution responds to these motivational differences deriving from variances in ego development will significantly affect the educational and developmental outcomes for each student. Students who are seeking personal growth at different ego levels need something else than the traditional educational setting, with its predominant focus on cognitive training and skills.

Implicit in ego development is an increasing ability to understand and articulate one's own motivation. Adults at higher ego levels make more conscious use of educational settings for clearly articulated ends. Those at lower ego levels may desire some of the same results as those at higher levels but be unable to articulate them. At postconventional stages there is greater apparent congruency between one's personal motives and one's articulated reasons for study (see Tarule, 1978).

Most Valued Outcomes of Study

Goddard students were also asked to identify the most valued outcomes of study and to comment on any changes in their lives, perspective, or sense of self that they would attribute wholly or in part to their experience of being a student. From the diverse responses given, many of which reflected individual differences that could not be attributed to ego development, there emerged, nevertheless, a clear patterning by ego stage of the perceived benefits of college. At the Self-Aware Stage, the orientation was to interpersonal relationships; this shifted to achievement themes at the Conscientious Stage, and to a series of more individually expressed concerns and realizations at the Individualistic Stage and beyond. Often the outcomes reported as most valued are changes that characterize the next steps in ego development. The differences lie in both the *content* of what an individual values and the *context* in which he or she experiences the impact of education. For example, almost everyone in the program wanted and expected some kind of certification of competency for valued social roles as a result of "getting a degree." Similarly, almost everyone at some point referred to the importance of supportive interpersonal relationships in easing the anxieties of study. However, these same themes have differential saliency as *the* most valued outcomes at different ego stages, and these shifts in emphasis describe a milestone sequence from validation by others to self-validation. This is central to the learning process, as the locus of authority is first seen as external, and then internalized, in conjunction with increasingly differentiated cognitive capacities. Perry describes this, as does Gilligan.

Table 4 summarizes characteristic responses concerning the most valued outcomes of study. Responses at the Self-Protective Stage deal with externalities, tangible results hoped for as an outcome of study—a "job possibility" and "my learning and the degree." The only response at the Conformist Stage is focused on interpersonal relationships—"Having met people in my field through the ADP, and the resulting interactions."

A common quality in answers at the Self-Aware Stage is, appropriately enough, a

Table 4. Most Valued Outcomes of Study by Ego Stage

Self-Protective Stage
. . . My learning and the degree
. . . Job possibility

Conformist Stage
. . . Having met people in my field through ADP, and the resulting interactions.

Conscientious-Conformist or Self-Aware Stage
. . . Exposure to new people and new ideas
. . . Focusing of goals, guidance and supervision as I work on them.
. . . I have had a place to take risks personally-professionally-academically. I have come to majority . . . As an individual I am more open and trusting. My self-worth has increased. I like myself.
. . . ADP has provided me with the confidence in myself to believe in myself and my abilities. I find that I am a "challenger" and a leader.
. . . Validation by others

Table 4 *(Continued)*

Conscientious Stage

... That my life does not stay limited to a few areas. That I'm experiencing or at least mulling over new interests which keep me rolling. My main objective of getting my B.A. and eventually M.A. in psych. has not changed, though.

... 1. sense of achievement, 2. B.A. (closer all the time), 3. New relationships, 4. more knowledge.

... The most important result is the ADP has helped me learn to try new areas, follow through on commitments and discover myself.

... Probably the rise in my self-concept as I see myself doing work that is recognized by others as well as myself, that what I do is not "magic" but the result of real and chosen effort.

Individualistic Stage

... The educational experience, itself. The options it will create for me.

... A wish to continue to read and to study and grow and learn and share: a wish to be in and of life.

... The increase in my ability to learn, to know I can approach many different topics and problems ... it has greatly broadened my style of learning ... and helped me appreciate my abilities more. . . . . Changes in confidence, ability to relate to others, pleasure in intellectual pursuits.

... I have become more inquisitive, questioning, observant and have learned that I am a creative person.

Autonomous and Integrated Stages

... Feeling more complete and whole as a person; Getting in touch with how, what I *really* think I want; Optimistic view towards others' realities, personal and worldly; Helping other people emotionally and intellectually; Integrating past confusements, decisions, reflections and feelings.

... Re-excitement in the learning process and new respect for concentrated effort in a field or endeavor.

... Continued growth re philosophy and science—personal satisfaction. Additionally, I find it gratifying working in a setting with such varying ages, ideas, backgrounds, and so on.

... For the first time in my life I am learning how to study something. I am particularly pleased about this as 2½ years of traditional University study failed to even start the process.

Note: These are answers to a questionnaire (Weathersby, 1977) that asked, "What is the most important result or outcome for you of your participation in the Goddard Adult Degree Program" and "In addition to what you said previously, have you experienced any other changes in your life, your perspective, or your sense of yourself which you attribute wholly or in part to your experience in the program?"

freshly experienced self-awareness. This is conceptualized as "exposure to new people and new ideas," better skills in relationships, and greater self-confidence. There is a poignancy to the answers of some women at midlife who are experiencing this self-awareness simultaneously with difficult life periods. For example, one woman (age 49), who entered the program after a long series of life changes and as a "last chance effort to pull myself together," reports upon graduating:

> I feel that I have grown to be a better person. . . . My daily life is more exciting and interesting. I'm happier now. I am more conscious of my own actions. I am growing more aware of how I see the world around me and the people in it. My sense of confidence has returned. I am happy to see each new day begin.

Another woman (age 56), attending her first residency, reports that the outcome of the two weeks was "validation by others" and "experiencing myself as valuable." The outcome here may not be change from one stage of ego development to another; it may be restabilization and revitalization within one's current personality structure.

As mentioned previously, there is a negative cast to the responses of many subjects near or below the Conformist Stage, as if the subjective purpose of education were to make up for a serious lack in one's life. One man (age 30) at the Self-Aware Stage identified the most important result of study for him as "my getting a teaching certification and my pursuing and persevering in my desires without regard to others' expectations." He explains:

> Throughout my previous education, force was applied externally. I hated school. The ADP was (is) an opportunity to do it myself, to prove that I didn't need to be pushed, to prove that in fact it was the pushing itself that caused my intellect to atrophy.

A woman near the same age and also at the Self-Aware Stage of ego development says "I don't feel right now, as I usually do, that I'm working in isolation or that my goals are futile." The coauthor of a successful book, she explains her reasons for enrolling in terms of making up for a lacking sense of herself as a successful student.

> I think it's important now because I seem to be going through a period of rapid growth. I finally have some work I'm proud of. I'm earning a good salary at work I can respect, if not love. . . . One of the two things still missing for me is a sense of myself as a successful student. It frustrates me very much that I don't have my degree. It frustrates me very much that I don't have *several* degrees. So, I'm here to prove to myself that I can be a successful student.

This sense of lack also appears at higher stages, but there is a greater sense of ease with oneself.

At the Conscientious Stage, the most valued outcomes mentioned are the degree itself, a sense of achievement, new ideas, increased self-esteem, and learning to follow through on commitments. Goals are personally set, and time is seen in long-term perspective in relation to goals. Responses tend to be more abstract—for example, "concretization of certain ideas" and "greater awareness of potential" (man, 22). One woman (age 41) speaks for a noticeable group whose goal is to find meaningful work. In response to the question about the result she most valued, she joked, "I don't know what it will be. One might be having to take gainful employment (as opposed to wife, mother, and maid) in order to pay back money borrowed!" Then she explains:

> I am ready to run the risk now. I have heard such glowing accounts of the ADP program that I am convinced I have to try it. My perspective of the world and my place in it is changing. I understood Goddard was quite selective in its students, so my acceptance indicated they thought I could do their work. Perhaps there is other work in the world for me to do and this will prepare me to accept the challenge.

Here the emphasis is on direction toward a goal, on crossing the finish line in a race set according to the individual's internalized standards.

At the Individualistic Stage, the most valued outcomes of study are often described as differentiated, personally relevant learning: an increased sense of competence, learning how to learn as well as mastering a body of knowledge, commitment to à personal and career-oriented learning process, the assumption of responsibility for one's perceptions and actions, and the integration of past experience with present and future agendas for growth. Responses tend to be elaborated and to describe a critical insight that has ramifications for other areas of life. For example, a woman of 25 observed:

> It took me the best part of a cycle [a six-month academic term] to fully realize that it was really up to me to determine what I wanted and needed and what would and would not be worth the effort. . . . That piece of learning added a major new feature to my perspective on my whole life.

The word *growth* appears more frequently, along with expressions of the intrinsic pleasure of study. One woman (age 56) whose most valued outcome was the opportunity to study and "enjoy it while doing so" reported realizing that "an interesting study can be done just for the joy of doing it—and it does not have to be 'justified.' Next time I'd like to try a totally different study—say, in the interrelated arts just to see what I might create."

Overall, many people at this level report a richly articulated sense of discovery about their own learning processes, and make a point of identifying their own responsibility in those processes. For example:

> My experience in the ADP has cultured my willingness to assume full responsibility for my perceptions and my actions. Having developed a greater "sense of self" and a greater self-confidence, I have also developed my capacity to honestly try to accept self-responsibility.

This same woman (age 27) also talked of developing her capacities to give others "the space and support they need for their own growth and development." There is a clear difference in perspective between this response and that of the man (age 30) at the Self-Aware Stage, quoted earlier, who sees the program as "an opportunity to do it myself, to prove that I didn't need to be pushed," as well as that of the woman (age 56) at the same stage who sought "validation by others." The link point in this progression is the discipline and goal-orientation of the Conscientious Stage—"I hope to learn how to do a better job learning more" (woman, age 52)—and the concomitant sense of control over one's destiny—"the result being an alive sense of discovery that what I do is not 'magic' but the result of real and chosen effort" (woman, 41).

A more explicit appropriation of the learning process appears at the Individualistic Stage. One man (age 25) views his increasing resourcefulness in solving problems and increased assertiveness in all aspects of his life as the result, in part, of Goddard's instructional process:

> It has helped me to grow a great deal, both intellectually and personally. Even more important than the sizable body of knowledge I have acquired is the increase in my ability to learn, to know I can approach many different topics or problems and understand or appreciate them. It has greatly broadened my style of learning and approach to learning. It has also helped me appreciate my abilities more.

This implies a kind of mastery of the process of "learning how to learn" that is probably the hallmark of self-directed learners. This self-conscious awareness of one's own *process* of learning is undoubtedly heightened by the program's instructional mode. However, a differentiated knowledge of one's own learning process and an increasing sense of personal agency and effectiveness in learning are characteristic of this stage of ego development.

At the Autonomous and Integrated Stages, the valued outcomes of study are expressed in terms of pleasure in the process of studying. No one at this level mentioned a degree as the most valued outcome, neither did anyone mention increased self-confidence or self-esteem. Instead, respondents mentioned valued pursuits or personal learning—for example, "feeling more complete and whole as a person, getting in touch with how, what I *really* think or want" (woman, 24) and "re-excitement in the learning process or new respect for concentrated effort in a field or endeavor" (woman, 26). Also noted were increased commitment to one's self and one's chosen work—"I am beginning to take myself and my work much more seriously. I am less quick to judge other people's lives and more willing to accept my own responsibilities" (woman, 27), and increased satisfaction from pursuing valued interests in a setting with people of different backgrounds. A businessman (40) reports as outcomes "continued growth re philosophy (and) science—personal satisfaction. Additionally, I find it gratifying working in a setting with such varying ages, ideas, and backgrounds."

Increases in self-confidence are often cited as a valued outcome of study, and there is a progression across ego levels in the manner in which this concept is understood. Mentions of increased self-confidence are proportionately more frequent at the Self-Aware and Conscientious Stages; at the Individualistic Stage the concept seems to disappear and become reworded as an increased sense of competence or an increase in self-esteem. Often at this level it appears as one of a series of items rather than the major and most valued outcome. At the Self-Aware Stage, the source of self-confidence appears to be experienced as external to oneself. For example, "ADP has provided me with the confidence in myself to believe in myself and my abilities." One woman reports that her self-confidence has returned, and another values the validation by others that she has received. Adults at the Conscientious Stage tend to see their increased capacities and ability to meet their goals as the source of their self-confidence. For example, one observes, "I feel very good about myself; where I am, how I am getting there. I feel like all the parts of myself are working together." Self-evaluated standards are important as well as recognition by others. A student reports, for example, a "rise in my self-concept as I see myself doing work that is recognized by others as well as myself as being well done." At the Individualistic Stage, the source of self-confidence is related to greater awareness, a greater sense of self, and acknowledged responsibility for one's choices, as this statement by a 34-year-old woman reveals:

> My anticipated results of the ADP are an increase in knowledge, but even more important, an increase in self-esteem as the result of completing something I want very much to do. Fourteen years as a housewife have left me with a lack of confidence in my abilities.

Ego Development as an Outcome of Study

In the Goddard Adult Degree Program, awareness of students' ego development provided a background against which to understand their aspirations and dilemmas. The most convincing evidence of the relevance of ego development appeared in students' accounts of their exciting experiences and their frustrations. They reported critical incidents, realizations, and changes in perspective that were consistent with the direction of ego development. For example, "validation from others" as one moves away from the Conformist Stage is a necessary foundation for the self-confidence in internalized standards and goals inherent in the achievement-orientation of the Conscientious Stage. This, in turn, is a necessary foundation for exploring one's learning preferences and personal patterns of achievement at the Individualistic Stage, and for exploring possible conflicts between achievement and self-fulfillment at the Autonomous and Integrated Stages.

One respondent at the Self-Protective Stage volunteered that "It is a new experience for me to be in such a program with so many different kinds of adults." For a student at this stage, being in the program means exposure not only to people of different backgrounds but also to people further along in ego development; if he feels accepted and supported, the effect may be to facilitate movement to the Conformist Stage. A businessman (age 42) who is probably at the Self-Aware Stage commented with surprise that he never would have expected to have anything in common with a roommate who labels himself a Communist. However, his much younger roommate in the residency did call himself a Communist, and the businessman found they had some common interests in history and politics. This man said that his ability to relate to people beyond stereotyped group labels had increased as a result of his Goddard experience. This is at least a move beyond conformist thinking into the realm of multiplicity. Similarly, a 43-year-old woman who described herself as "a traditional mother of six children" and felt she did not want to apologize for believing in the institution of marriage, being chairperson of her local school board, or belonging to a formal religion said:

> The Goddard experience has helped me to understand my own children better. It has also given me the opportunity to identify with many people of different life-styles that I would not have had the opportunity to meet. It has given me more tolerance to meet problems head on and a better discipline to my life. I see the absolute need for the two-week residency. It is mind-boggling at times but does provide for intensive situations, which I found I can cope with.

Her sentence-completion score placed her at the Individualistic Stage. Her ability to identify with diverse life-styles and increased tolerance for the ambiguities of an intensive group residency are characteristics that distinguish the Individualistic Stage from the Conscientious Stage. She reports them as new; this is perhaps a reflection of ego development over the two years of her experience in the program.

Implications for Instruction

I have shown how ego development forms the framework in which learning and teaching take place, and have traced qualitative differences across stages in individuals' experience of educational settings. Now the question of application arises. Now that we can label the progressions and classify, approximately, students and groups of students, what do we do differently? This is a tough question for any psychological theory, especially one that describes sequences of development. I do not propose that we use measures of ego development like intelligence tests, as sorters of students or indicators of program effectiveness. Nor do I believe we should try to force ego development. After all, it represents a major personality change and, as such, takes time. An assignment, a semester, or even four years of college may not substantially alter an individual's frame of reference, although clearly some students do move rapidly and sometimes explosively along these progressions. Every student will not move along these progressions, and our institutions per se may have relatively little influence in this regard. We do not yet have enough knowledge of the dynamics of transition, or the conditions that promote development, or the impact of college, to establish highly structured programs geared toward ego development. However, exposure to higher-level reasoning, opportunities to take others' roles and perspectives, discomfiting discrepancies between one's actual experiences in a situation and one's current explanations and beliefs—these are basic elements of the transition process. It is possible, therefore, to open doors and to help students open doors for themselves. But it is their choice to walk through.

Thus, the major use of this body of theory is, as suggested in this chapter, as a map or matrix that can help us identify the next steps in development. It can also heighten our appreciation for shared patterns of differences among students. If we tune our ears so that we can hear students across different frameworks of meaning, we are more likely to communicate effectively and to respond with an appropriate form of support or challenge. Familiarity with the patterns of ego development can create simple and profound differences in our perceptions, attitudes, and behavior as we approach teaching, administration, and counseling. For example, we are more likely to be humbled by the task of facilitating learning, and less likely to be judgmental of students who do not fit our molds or our institutions. We are more likely to listen to students' frames of references, to *ask* for their reasons and feelings about a situation, to expect patterns of diversity, and to value responses that represent advances in development regardless of our norms of expected levels of achievement. We are likely also to have some humility about grading, realizing that for some students what is asked for may not yet be comprehensible, and that what is being graded may not be simply gains in knowledge or competence, seriousness of purpose or effort expended, but, at least in part, responses made more or less difficult by a student's stage of development. We will be more aware that faculty play different roles with different students, and that these roles become more complex as the range of developmental stages broadens. Corresponding to the major stage-related orientations, faculty roles can range from authoritative transmitters of knowledge and agents of socialization, to role models helping develop cognitive skills and mastery, to facilitators of personally relevant, transformative learning. Goal setting and evaluation are present whatever the role, but in different degrees of colleagueship with students. Finally, we are more likely to recognize causes of soul searching and confusion inherent in the material we teach, or the methods we use, and to offer support.

It is possible to design assignments and curriculums that more directly facilitate development, although other schemes such as Perry's lend themselves more easily to direct application. The basic principle is to create a course structure in which the assignments and interpersonal interactions foster ego development. Often diversity of perspectives is involved. For example, in the introductory behavioral science course at the University of New Hampshire's School of Business and Economics, students work in groups to analyze cases, develop arguments for and against managerial decisions, study group dynamics, and participate in experiential exercises designed to simulate the effects of divergent leadership styles. Each work group is responsible for evaluating its own members. The students are mostly traditional-age undergraduates; many are at the Self-Aware Stage in ego development, while some are above and some are below this stage. The course structure employs a group setting—especially suitable for students at the Self-Aware Stage—to encourage complex and contingent thinking, to support the validity of diverse viewpoints, and to avoid group thinking and conformity. Many students report learning that there is no right or wrong way of thinking about a management problem and that others' viewpoints, although different, deserve consideration. Although this course was not designed to promote ego development (the intent was to create an effective teaching environment), it is a developmental intervention in students' lives, aimed intellectually and emotionally at higher-stage thinking and action.

Arthur Chickering (1976), adapting materials developed by Harry Lasker primarily from studies of ego development, has sketched out broad correspondences between stages of ego development and various conceptualizations of faculty and student roles, institutional functions, and teaching practices such as lectures, discussions, programmed instruction, and contract learning. Generally speaking, an instructional system based on lectures and exams fits the orientation of a Conformist Stage or lower, in which the teacher is the transmitter of knowledge and functions as a judge and certifier of the students' mastery. This is teaching to the lowest common denominator. Instructional methods that involve discussion and other forms of active participation, and require individuals to make decisions around goals, activities, and standards or methods of evaluation are more suited to students at the middle and higher stages; they are also more likely to create the interpersonal interactions and self-questioning that facilitate development. This accounts for the sometimes powerful unleashing of energy associated with these teaching practices. The issue at hand is not a narrow argument about teaching methods. A skilled teacher can use almost any method with success and find ways to create an environment that fosters development for some students. Correspondingly, no curriculum or method will suit every student. Miller (1978) describes some adults as dependent learners for whom the individualized learning contracts employed in most external degree programs are as highly frustrating as they are rewarding to other adult students seeking the opportunity for self-direction.

The central issue is that of creating teaching practices that are congruent with the developmental orientations of students. Knowledge of ego development suggests teaching practices that honor students' multiple frames of references and allow multiple levels of progress. Ego development theory also provides a framework for examining the curriculum for intended or unintended emphases. For example, very little of our current formal education is designed to help students reorganize past conceptions on the basis of new experience and develop personally generated insights and paradigms, although these are learning processes that reflect higher stages of ego development. Any methodology conveys underlying messages; if the message is that education consists only of providing individuals with access to certification, information, and increased cognitive skill, this is far too narrow a conceptualization.

Education as a Support for Lifelong Development

Chickering and Havighurst's perspective on the adaptive tasks of the life cycle (Chapter One) adds dimensions of lifelong learning to the picture. Reasons for enrolling in educational programs and outcomes of study may vary not only according to one's ego development but also according to one's place in the life cycle and the developmental tasks associated with each life period. Both perspectives help explain the amount and nature of developmental change that can accompany higher education—the intrapsychic work necessitated or stimulated by the academic process. Traditional-age college students are certainly in a major life cycle transition. Many adults also enroll in academic programs, or other programs in higher education, at transition points in their lives, or as a help in coping with new adaptive tasks. If the combination of new life tasks and education stimulates ego development as well, the amount of inner stress and disequilibrium can be considerable. Expanding Erikson's (1968) idea of a "developmental crisis" to include simultaneous changes in one's life structure *and* one's framework of coping, we can predict that some students will be "at risk" in the face of life transitions. They may experience heightened anxiety in the course of their studies but will also have the opportunity to emerge with new personality strengths forged in the educational process.

We must not forget that educational institutions serve a certifying and credentialing function in society. Traditional-age students are more or less required to attend college by virtue of the opportunity structure in society. Adults choose to attend, at varying life periods and for varying reasons, but the social functions of accrediting learning and providing access to opportunity remain. In a society in which lockstep patterns of schooling and careers are being broken and education is becoming an intrinsic as well as a practical good, educational institutions can be a support structure, encouraging ego development for individuals of all ages. This outcome can be enhanced while the certifying and accrediting function is also maintained. To do so creates implications for program design, curriculum planning, teaching effectiveness, and counseling and support services—for designing higher education in ways that legitimize and facilitate our continuing need to grow.

The possibility of developmental change as an outcome of study raises the all-important question of the purposes of education. One's stage of ego development is a framework for experiencing education and assigning to it both value and meaning. Ego development is quite probably an unintended consequence for many students as well as a good many teachers. Should it be an intentional goal? On the one hand, it is doubtful that students enrolling in college to "better their opportunities" or "get an education" have in mind learning tolerance for ambiguity, relativism, and greater acceptance of responsibility for creating their perceptual worlds. And in the end, students are the final arbiters of educational purposes and results. But on the other hand, institutions can unwittingly put ceilings on development. For those students whose aim is a greater ability to deal with complex problems—a greater mastery of the learning process, by means that constantly push the limits of their current ways of thinking and living—colleges can and ought to support ego development. Society needs individuals who can cope with a world of uncertainty, rapid change, and global interrelationships, which means people at the higher stages of ego development. These same people, of course, are apt to view society's rules with a critical eye—including the cherished values and procedures of academic institutions. Discussions of educational policies and procedures can perhaps be approached with greater humility if we recognize that everyone involved—students, faculty, administrators, and legislators—understands educational goals and outcomes within the legitimate context of his or her own stage of development.

For my own part, I believe that ego development is an inextricable goal of higher education. The very process of education invites and enforces developmental change. Acknowledging ego development as a conscious purpose gives us a multidimensional map that unites intellect and emotion, helps us interpret students' difficulty with subject matter and self-esteem, highlights the need for courage and community, and points to the necessity of providing support and challenge with teaching practices that take students beyond their current ways of constructing useful knowledge.

References

Chickering, A. W. "Developmental Change as a Major Outcome." In M. T. Keeton and Associates, *Experiential Learning: Rationale, Characteristics, and Assessment.* San Francisco: Jossey-Bass, 1976.

Erikson, E. *Identity: Youth and Crisis.* New York: Norton, 1968.

Goldberger, N. "Breaking the Educational Lockstep: The Simon's Rock Experience." Great Barrington, Mass.: Simon's Rock Early College, 1977.

Kohlberg, L. "Stage and Sequence: The Cognitive-Developmental Approach to Socialization." In D. A. Goslin (Ed.), *Handbook of Socialization Theory and Research.* Chicago: Rand McNally, 1969.

Kohlberg, L. "Continuities in Childhood and Adult Moral Developmental Revisited." In P. B. Baltes and K. W. Schaie (Eds.), *Life-Span Developmental Psychology: Personality and Socialization.* New York: Academic Press, 1973.

Kohlberg, L., and Mayer, R. "Development as the Aim of Education." *Harvard Education Review,* November 1972, *42* (4), 449-496.

Landa, A., and others. "Towards a Developmental Curriculum: Principles and Applications." Plainfield, Vt.: Goddard College, 1977.

Lasker, H. "Ego Development and Motivation: A Cross-Cultural Cognitive-Developmental Analysis of Achievement." Unpublished doctoral dissertation, University of Chicago, 1978.

Loevinger, J. *Ego Development: Conceptions and Theories.* San Francisco: Jossey-Bass, 1976.

Loevinger, J., Wessler, R., and Redmore, C. *Measuring Ego Development.* 2 vols. San Francisco: Jossey-Bass, 1970.

Maslow, A. H. *The Farther Reaches of Human Nature.* New York: Viking, 1971.

Miller, M. R. "Retaining Adults: New Educational Designs for a New Clientele." In L. Noel (Ed.), *New Directions for Student Services: Reducing the Dropout Rate,* no. 3. San Francisco: Jossey-Bass, 1978.

Perry, W. G., Jr. *Forms of Intellectual and Ethical Development in the College Years.* New York: Holt, Rinehart and Winston, 1970.

Piaget, J. "The General Problem of the Psychobiological Development of the Child." In J. M. Tanner and B. Inhelder (Eds.), *Discussions on Child Development.* Vol. 4. New York: International Universities Press, 1960.

Sanford, N. "The Developmental Status of the Entering Freshman." In N. Sanford (Ed.), *The American College.* New York: Wiley, 1962.

Tarule, J. "Patterns of Developmental Transition in Adulthood: An Examination of the Relationship Between Ego Development Stage Variation and Gendlin's Experiencing Levels." Unpublished doctoral dissertation, Graduate School of Education, Harvard University, 1978.

Weathersby, R. "A Synthesis of Research and Theory on Adult Development: Its Implications for Adult Learning and Postsecondary Education." Special Qualifying Paper, Graduate School of Education, Harvard University, 1976.

Weathersby, R. "A Developmental Perspective on Adults' Uses of Formal Education." Unpublished doctoral dissertation, Graduate School of Education, Harvard University, 1977.

Cognitive and Ethical

3

William G. Perry, Jr.

Cognitive and Ethical Growth:
The Making of Meaning

Have you received the latest "printout" of your students' evaluation of your teaching from the computer? If so, I trust you are properly encouraged. But my intent is to raise the possibility that those comfortable "means" and "standard deviations" may conceal unexamined educational riches. In the usual form of such evaluations, the shortness of the scale (commonly five or seven points, from superb to awful), the neatness of the standard deviations, and the comfort of the mean inspire in us all a confidence that further analysis would tell us little. Indeed, our friends assure us that even those vagaries in our students' opinions that prevent the mean ratings from being as high as we had hoped can be chalked up to our credit under the rubric, "The best teacher never pleases *everybody*."

Surely it seems reasonable enough to average check marks on items like

	1	2	3	4	5
Organization of assignments:	Excellent	Good	Fair	Poor	Very Bad

and to print 1.9 as the mean. But if you have ever given your students an opportunity to be more expansive, you can never again be wholly comforted. What can you do with such unaverageable judgments as "This course has changed my whole outlook on education *and life*! Superbly taught! Should be required of all students!'' and "This course is falsely advertised and dishonest. You have cheated me of my tuition!''

Over the years I have received just such comments at the end of a noncredit course on Strategies of Reading, when I asked, "What did you expect of this course?" (big space) and "What did you find?" (big space). I do not ask the students for their names, just for their scores on pre- and post-tests. Twenty years ago I reported on the course in a faculty meeting (Perry, 1959) and read one student's comment as my punch line. Since the student had scored 20 percent comprehension at 120 words per minute on pre-test and 90 percent comprehension at 600 words per minute on post-test, I had looked forward to some flattery. What I found was, "I expected *an organized effort to improve my reading,*" followed by, "This has been the most sloppy, disorganized course I've never taken. Of course I *have* made some improvement (arrow to the scores), but this has been due *entirely to my own efforts.*" This got a good laugh from the faculty, largely, I suspect, owing to the realization that "evaluations" threaten not only the vanity of teachers but their very sanity as well.

At the time, no one, myself included, stopped to inquire whether this student's outrage bespoke more than some comical aberration. It took my colleagues and me twenty years to discover that such comments reflect coherent interpretive frameworks through which students give meaning to their educational experience. These structurings of meaning, which students revise in an orderly sequence from the relatively simple to the more complex, determine more than your students' perception of you as teacher; they shape the students' ways of learning and color their motives for engagement and dis-engagement in the whole educational enterprise. Teachers have, of course, always sensed this and have tried to teach accordingly.

This chapter illustrates, in students' own words, the typical course of development of students' patterns of thought. Twenty years ago, a small group of us, counselors and teachers, were so puzzled by students' varied and contradictory perceptions of ourselves and their other teachers that we set out to document their experience. We invited volunteers to tell us, at the end of their freshman year, what had "stood out" for them. We encouraged them to talk freely in the interview without preformed questions from us, and the diversity of their reports exceeded even our own expectations. After the manner of the time, we supposed the differences arose from differences in "personality types." However, as the same students returned to report their experience year by year, we were startled by their reinterpretations of their lives. Then these reinterpretations seemed to fall into a logical progression. Each step represented a challenge to the student's current view of the world. Different students might respond differently, with courage or defeat, but all faced the same basic challenges to making meaning in a complex world (Perry, 1970).[1]

We found that we could describe the logic or "structure" of each of these succes-sive reinterpretations of the world and identify the challenges that precipitated them. We made a map of these challenges—a "Pilgrim's Progress" of ways of knowing, complete with Sloughs of Despond—giving each of the successive interpretations a numbered "Posi-

[1] *Forms of Intellectual and Ethical Development in the College Years: A Scheme* (New York: Holt, Rinehart and Winston, 1970; first published Cambridge, Mass.: Bureau of Study Counsel, Harvard University, 1968). It embarrasses me that in the argot of the field this ponderous title has been shortened, inevitably, to "The Perry Scheme"; the evo-lution of the scheme required teamwork involving more than thirty people over a span of fifteen years—six to eight counselors at any one time, working in a small office without formal provisions for research.

tion." We then put the map to a test by giving raters a number of interviews and asking them to state for each interview that Position which seemed most congruent with the pattern of the student's thought. Since the raters agreed strongly with one another, we knew that the developments that we had seen were there for others to see. This map of sequential interpretations of meaning, or *scheme of development,* has since been found to be characteristic of the development of students' thinking throughout a variety of educational settings (see this chapter's reference section). This chapter makes this developing sequence of interpretations explicit. Along the way, I shall suggest what I see to be the general implications of this sequence for educational practice. Readers interested in the ways these implications have found particular expression in various educational contexts can then consult the work of those researchers and practitioners whom I cite.

Scheme of Development

One naturally thinks of any scheme of development in terms of its "stages"—or "Positions," as we called them in our own scheme. In summarizing our students' journey for the reader of this chapter, I therefore first excised from all our students had told us a quotation or two to illustrate each Position. To my dismay, the drama died under the knife.

Then I realized that Positions are by definition static, and development is by definition movement. It was therefore the Transitions that were so fresh and intriguing. Each of the Positions was obvious and familiar in its delineation of a meaningful way of construing the world of knowledge, value, and education. The drama lived in the variety and ingenuity of the ways students found to move from a familiar pattern of meanings that had failed them to a new vision that promised to make sense of their broadening experience, while it also threatened them with unanticipated implications for their selfhood and their lives. I thus decided to select quotations illustrating for each step the breakup of the old and the intimations of the new. (Perhaps development is all transition and "stages" only resting points along the way.)

But this expansion of the summary puts severe strains on the boundaries of this chapter and on the reader. I can surely trust the reader to remember that each simple quotation stands for many intriguing variants in the ways students gave meaning to the unfolding landscapes of the journey. But we have more to do than trace the journey. I have promised to note some further thoughts on these developmental progressions—thoughts that have arisen in a decade of dialogue with others who have used our scheme as a starting point for explorations of their own. Had my briefest summary of the scheme sufficed, I could have moved on directly to commentary on other researchers' work and on our own recent thinking about particular passages or issues in the scheme. After the more expanded summary, however, the reader and I would find ourselves too far away from the data relevant to such commentary. It has seemed best, therefore, to digress occasionally as relevant points emerge.

If the reader is to tolerate lengthy digressions at dramatic moments—as happens in early Victorian novels—I should at least give evidence in advance that I know where I am going. Figure 1 gives a synopsis, in bare bones, of our scheme of cognitive and ethical development—the evolving ways of seeing the world, knowledge and education, values, and oneself. Notice that each Position both includes and transcends the earlier ones, as the earlier ones cannot do with the later. This fact defines the movement as *development* rather than mere changes or "phases." Figure 2 gives a map of this development. Following are definitions of the key terms, abstractions to which the students' words will subsequently give life:

Figure 1. Scheme of Cognitive and Ethical Development

Dualism modified→	Position 1	Authorities know, and if we work hard, read every word, and learn Right Answers, all will be well.
	Transition	But what about those Others I hear about? And different opinions? And Uncertainties? Some of our own Authorities disagree with each other or don't seem to know, and some give us problems instead of Answers.
	Position 2	True Authorities must be Right, the others are frauds. We remain Right. Others must be different and Wrong. Good Authorities give us problems so we can learn to find the Right Answer by our own independent thought.
	Transition	But even Good Authorities admit they don't know all the answers *yet*!
	Position 3	Then some uncertainties and different opinions are real and legitimate *temporarily,* even for Authorities. They're working on them to get to the Truth.
	Transition	But there are *so many* things they don't know the Answers to! And they won't for a long time.
Relativism discovered→	*Position 4a*	Where Authorities don't know the Right Answers, everyone has a right to his own opinion; no one is wrong!
	Transition *(and/or)*	But some of my friends ask me to support my opinions with facts and reasons.
	Transition	Then what right have They to grade us? About what?
	Position 4b	In certain courses Authorities are not asking for the Right Answer; They want us to *think* about things in a certain way, *supporting* opinion with data. That's what they grade us on.
	Transition	But this "way" seems to *work* in most courses, and even outside them.
	Position 5	Then *all* thinking must be like this, even for Them. Everything is relative but not equally valid. You have to understand how each context works. Theories are not Truth but metaphors to interpret data with. You have to think about your thinking.
Commitments in Relativism developed→	Transition	But if everything is relative, am I relative too? How can I know I'm making the Right Choice?
	Position 6	I see I'm going to have to make my own decisions in an uncertain world with no one to tell me I'm Right.
	Transition	I'm lost if I don't. When I decide on my career (or marriage or values) everything will straighten out.
	Position 7	Well, I've made my first Commitment!
	Transition	Why didn't that settle everything?
	Position 8	I've made several commitments. I've got to balance them—how many, how deep? How certain, how tentative?
	Transition	Things are getting contradictory. I can't make logical sense out of life's dilemmas.
	Position 9	This is how life will be. I must be wholehearted while tentative, fight for my values yet respect others, believe my deepest values right yet be ready to learn. I see that I shall be retracing this whole journey over and over—but, I hope, more wisely.

Dualism. Division of meaning into two realms—Good versus Bad, Right versus Wrong, We versus They, All that is not Success is Failure, and the like. Right Answers exist *somewhere* for every problem, and authorities know them. Right Answers are to be memorized by hard work. Knowledge is quantitative. Agency is experienced as "out there" in Authority, test scores, the Right job.

Multiplicity. Diversity of opinion and values is recognized as legitimate in areas where right answers are not yet known. Opinions remain atomistic without pattern or

Figure 2. A Map of Development

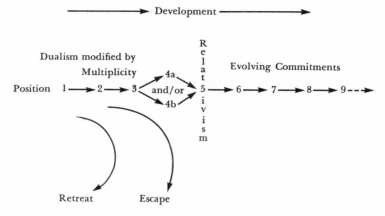

Retreat   Escape

system. No judgments can be made among them so "everyone has a right to his own opinion; none can be called wrong."

Relativism. Diversity of opinion, values, and judgment derived from coherent sources, evidence, logics, systems, and patterns allowing for analysis and comparison. Some opinions may be found worthless, while there will remain matters about which reasonable people will reasonably disagree. Knowledge is qualitative, dependent on contexts.

Commitment (uppercase *C*). An affirmation, choice, or decision (career, values, politics, personal relationship) made in the awareness of Relativism (distinct from lowercase *c* of commitments never questioned). Agency is experienced as within the individual.

Temporizing. Postponement of movement for a year or more.

Escape. Alienation, abandonment of responsibility. Exploitation of Multiplicity and Relativism for avoidance of Commitment.

Retreat. Avoidance of complexity and ambivalence by regression to Dualism colored by hatred of otherness.

I shall now let the students speak for themselves as they spoke in interviews in which we asked unstructured questions (such as "what stands out for you as you review the year?") in order to allow the students freedom to structure their own meanings. I shall report our sense of the import of their words for the development we trace, and I shall digress on occasion to consider implications for teaching and educational policy.

Positions 1 Through 5

Position 1: Basic Duality. This is the Garden of Eden, with the same rules. Here the student is embedded in a world of We-Right-Good (Other-Wrong-Bad is "out there"). We called this Basic Duality. Right Answers for everything exist in the Absolute, and these are known to Authorities, whose role is to mediate (teach) them. Knowledge and goodness are perceived as quantitative accretions of discrete rightnesses to be collected by hard work and *obedience* (including the requirement to read *all* assigned books word by word from the beginning). We held our interviews in May and June, and no freshman still spoke from this Position in its purest form. A few, however, saw themselves in retrospect as having come to college with this view intact. This student's words show how hard it is to articulate an embeddedness so complete that it offered no place from which to observe it:

> Student: I certainly couldn't—before I was, you know, I wouldn't ask. /Yeah/ I wouldn't have—I wouldn't be able to *talk* on this subject at *all* . . . that what I had just—well, was *there* you know.

Only a dim sense that there is a boundary somewhere beyond which lies Otherness provides Eden with shape:

> Student: Well I come, I came here from a small town. Midwest, where, well, ah, everyone believed the same things. Everyone's Methodist and everyone's Republican. So, ah, there just wasn't any . . . well that's not quite true . . . there are some Catholics, two families, and I guess they, I heard they were Democrats, but they weren't really, didn't seem to be in town really, I guess. They live over the railroad there and they go to church in the next town.

But obedience is the Way:

> Student: Well the only thing I could say to a prospective student is just say, "If you come here and do everything you're supposed to do, you'll be all right," that's just about all.

But such innocence is short-lived:

Transition from Position 1 to Position 2. The first challenge often comes from peers:

> Student: When I went to my first lecture, what the man said was just like God's word, you know. I believe everything he said, because he was a professor, and he's a Harvard professor, and this was, this was a respected position. And, ah, ah, people said, "Well, so what?" . . . and I began to, ah, realize.

And especially in the dorm:

> Student: So in my dorm I, we've been, ah, [in] a number of discussions, where there'll be, well, there's quite a variety in our dorm, Catholic, Protestant, and the rest of them, and a Chinese boy whose parents, ah, follow the teachings of Confucianism. He isn't, but his folks are . . . And a couple of guys are complete, ah, agnostics, agnostics. Of course, some people are quite disturbing, they say they're atheists. But they don't go very far, they say they're atheists, but they're not. And then there are, one fellow, who is a deist. And by discussing it, ah, it's the, the sort of thing that, that really, ah, awakens you to the fact that, ah . . .

Diversity, experienced among peers and again in the classroom, must now be accounted for. Difference of opinion surely cannot exist in the Absolute. If earthly Authorities disagree, perhaps some are mere pretenders? Or do They put all the complexities in there just to exercise our minds? Such interpretations of diversity deny it a full legitimacy and preserve the simplicity of Truth:

Position 2: Multiplicity Prelegitimate. True authority may perform its proper role of direct mediation while complexities confuse pretenders:

> Student: For one thing, Professor Black who taught us [in First Term] . . . Christmas! you couldn't lose him on one point. Man, he wouldn't, you couldn't, you couldn't *find* a question *he* couldn't answer. I doubt. And you respected him for it. Not that you're trying to trick the, the section man, but you, when you come up with any kind of a reasonable question, he [Prof. Black] can answer it

for you, and he can answer it *well*. Whereas the section men dwiddle around and, and talk a lot of nonsense.

Or if True Authorities offer complexities, they enable us to learn the way to truth:

Student: I found that you've got to find out for yourself. You get to a point where you, ah, see this guy go through this rigamarole and everything and you've got to find out for yourself what he's talking about and think it out for yourself. Then try to get to think on your own. And that's something I never had to do, think things out by myself, I mean. In high school two and two was four; there's nothing to think out there. In here they try to make your mind work, and I didn't realize that until the end of the year.

Interviewer: You kept looking for the answer and they wouldn't give it to you?

Student: Yeah, it wasn't in the *book*. And that's what confused me a lot. *Now* I know it isn't in the book for a purpose. We're supposed to think about it and come *up* with the answer!

So in Position 2, the student has given meaning to diversity, uncertainty, and complexity in Authority's realm by accounting for them as unwarranted confusion in poorly qualified Authorities or as mere exercises set by Authority "so we can learn to find The Answer for ourselves."

Transition from Position 2 to Position 3. This last concession—that answers sometimes must be *searched for* by students—can lead directly to a generalization that fatefully includes Authority itself. The issue may be avoided temporarily by dividing disciplines into the definite and the vague:

Student: I'll tell you the best thing about science courses: Their lectures are all right. They sort of say the facts. But when you get to a humanities course, especially—oh, they're awful—the lecturer is just reading things into the book that were never meant to be there.

But in the end even Science fails:

Student: That seems to be the, the excuse that natural science people give for these courses: They're supposed to teach you to arrive at more logical conclusions and look at things in a more scientific manner. Actually, what you get out of that course is that science is a terrifically confused thing in which nobody knows what's coming off anyway.

Position 3: Multiplicity Legitimate but Subordinate. If even Scientific Authority does not yet know all Truths in its own domain, one must, presumably, settle for less, at least for now:

Student: I'd feel [laughs] rather insecure thinking about these philosophical things all the time and not coming up with any definite answers. And definite answers are, well, they, they're sort of my foundation point. In physics you get definite answers to a point. Beyond that point you know there *are* definite answers, but you can't reach them.

That is, as many students said, "you can't reach them *yet*." Uncertainty is temporary. The Truth is still there to be found in the Laplacean Universe. Some diversity of opinion, therefore, is legitimate, but temporary.

Transition from Position 3 to Position 4. The concession, "but you can't reach them [yet]," contains the seeds of destruction for the major structural assumptions of Positions 1 through 3. Human uncertainty has been accorded a legitimacy that has the potential of spreading from a temporary case to the whole of human knowledge. The tie between Authority and the Absolute has been loosened. Uncertainty is now unavoidable, even in physics.

> Student: Here was this great [physics] professor and *he* was groping *too*!

This realization can raise a severe procedural problem. How, in an educational institution where the student's every answer is evaluated, are answers judged? Where Authority does not know *the* answer yet, is not any answer as good as another?

So far, Authority has been perceived as grading on amount of rightness, achieved by honest hard work, and as adding an occasional bonus for neatness and "good expression." But in the uncertainty of a legitimized Multiplicity, coupled with a freedom that leaves "amount" of work "up to you" and Authority ignorant of how much you do, rightness and hard work vanish as standards. Nothing seems to be left but "good expression," and Authorities are suspected of different or obscure standards for that:

> Student: If I present it in the right manner it is well received. Or it is received . . . I don't know, I still haven't exactly caught onto what, what they want.

Authority's maintenance of the old morality of reward for hard work is called into serious question, and disillusion is imminent:

> Student: A lot of people noticed this throughout the year, that the mark isn't proportional to the work. 'Cause on a previous paper I'd done a lot of work and gotten the same mark, and on this one I wasn't expecting it . . . I just know that you can't, ah, expect your mark in proportion to the amount of work you put in . . . In prep school it was more of a, more, the relationship was more personal and the teacher could tell whether you were working hard, and he would give you breaks if he knew you were working. It wasn't grading a student on his aptitude, it was grading somewhat on the amount of work he put in.

This uncertain relationship between work and rewards can lead to bitterness:

> Student: This place is all full of bull. They don't want anything really honest from you. If you turn in something, a speech that's well written, whether it's got one single fact in it or not is beside the point. That's sort of annoying at times, too. You can put things over on people around here; you're almost given to try somehow to sit down and write a paper in an hour, just because you know that whatever it is isn't going to make any difference to anybody.

> Hence, an intellectual question has led to a precarious ethical dilemma:
> Student: It looks to me like it's [laughs] kind of not very good, you know? I mean you can't help but take advantage of these things.

Here, as in every transitional phase, the issues of development hang in the balance. The students have not yet distinguished between legitimate abstract thought and its counterfeit, "bull."[2] They see the "bullster" winning honors while they themselves work hard and receive C's. They feel tempted. Their dilemma may appear false, looked at from the vantage point of later Positions, which transcend it, but at the moment it is bitter and poignant. In their disillusion they find cynicism and opportunism inviting indeed. The students are struggling in a moral battle, blind to the possibility that its resolution is intellectual.

[2]For a discussion of the relation of "bull" and "cow" in academia see Perry, 1969.

In this moment, then, the students are confronting two closely related perceptions incongruent with their construal of the world from Position 3: (a) the spread of uncertainty and diversity into Authority's domain of the known and (b) Authority's insistence on grading even in the domain of uncertainty. Our interviews reveal that a student's attitude toward Authority is crucial at this point. If the student is intensely resentful (Oppositional, as we called it), the temptation may be strong to take refuge in alienation (which we called Escape) or in the simplistic dualism of Position 2 (which we called Retreat), from which otherness, differentness, and complexity can be righteously hated.

In contrast, students whose opposition to Authority was less intense, and those whose trust in Authority we called Adherence, moved forward, but along a different path. The structure of the meaningful world constructed by the moderately Oppositional students requires attention first:

Position 4a: Multiplicity (Diversity and Uncertainty) Coordinate with the "known."

> Student: I mean if you read them [critics], that's the great thing about a book like *Moby Dick.* [Laughs] *Nobody* understands it!

Students such as this seize on the notion of legitimate uncertainty as a means of creating, out of personalistic diversity of opinion, an epistemological realm equal to and over against the world of Authority in which certain Right Answers are known. In this new realm, freedom is, or should be, complete: "Everyone has a right to his own opinion; they have no right to say we're wrong!"

This new structure, by dividing the world into two domains, preserves the fundamentally dualistic nature of earlier structures. To replace the simple dualism of the right-wrong world of Authority, these students create the double dualism of a world in which the Authority's right-wrong world is one element and personalistic diversity (which we labeled Multiplicity) is the other. The students have thus succeeded in preserving a dualistic structure for their worlds and at the same time have carved out for themselves a domain promising absolute freedom. In saying in this domain, "Everyone has a right to his own opinion," students are also saying, "Where Authorities do not know the Answer, any opinion is as good as any other."

> Interviewer: Can you say that one point of view is better and another worse?
> Student: No, I really can't on this issue [creation versus evolution of man]. It depends on your beliefs. Since there's no way of proving either one.
> Interviewer: Can you say that one is more accurate than the other?
> Student: No, I can't, I believe they're both the same as far as accuracy.
> Interviewer: Would you go so far as to say your opinion is the right one?
> Student: No.
> Interviewer: But yet you believe so strongly in it; that's why I'm asking . . .
> Student: I'm the type of person who would never tell someone that their idea is wrong—even if they have searched, well, even if they haven't searched, even if they just believe it—that's cool for them.
> Interviewer: Can you say that one opinion is better and one opinion is worse?
> Student: No, not at all. It's better for them and like their opinion would probably be worse for me.

I am indebted to King (1977a) for this vivid excerpt from her interviews. We have found few students who would defend this personalism so nobly against an interviewer's probes; under pressure most students move ahead into concessions, albeit still epistemologically quantitative: "Well, maybe some opinions might have more facts." The pure statement that, in the domain of uncertainty, to "have" an opinion makes it as "right" as any other expresses an egocentric personalism that we called *Multiplicity*. The students, as they moved on, were emphatic about the distinction between this outlook and that of disciplined Relativism (discussed later).

This personalism that we called Multiplicity Coordinate serves many purposes besides that of a hoped-for freedom from the tyranny of Authority. It makes sense in the midst of a diversity which can only appear chaotic until some reasoned qualitative distinctions can be discerned. Moreover, its egalitarian spirit provides a haven of ultimate peace at the end of dormitory bull sessions. At a deeper level, it expresses a respect for others through a respect for their views. (Others as persons are not yet differentiated from the opinions they *hold*; they *are* their opinions, as I am mine). As a stepping stone, then, Multiplicity is not to be dismissed as mere license or as a simple misapplication of religious tolerance to epistemological and ethical realms.

Yet in this structure all debatable propositions remain atomistic. An opinion is related to nothing whatever—evidence, reason, experience, expert judgment, context, principle, or purpose—except to the person who holds it. Even the relation of the opinion to the person is limited to the fact that the person "has" it. All that Authority cannot prove to be Wrong is Right. This structuring of meaning is therefore still dualistic; the world so construed is not yet open to Relativism's analysis, rules of evidence, disciplines of inference, and concern for the integrity of interpretations and systems of thought.

Unfortunately, the unconsidered statement, "Anyone has a right to his own opinion," is popularly thought to be the heart of Relativism, and its implication of moral license has given Relativism a bad name. King herself labels the excerpt quoted above as an illustration of "relativism," and such a veteran as Kohlberg has been perilously slow to acknowledge the distinction. I shall remark later in this chapter (see also Gilligan in her chapter) on the difficulties that have followed on such conflation in such crucial matters as evaluation of the moral development of women. Perhaps some simpler-sounding word than Multiplicity (Personalism, for example) would have helped distinguish this more simplistic structure.

In any case, the students, having construed diversity of opinion as a realm for personalistic rightness, are poised at the edge of a fateful moment in their destinies. Major incongruities face them. In their academic work, teachers insist on continuing to grade the students' opinions in such debatable areas as sociology and literature. On what grounds? What teacher has not experienced despair in trying to explain to a student at this level of development that grades depend, not on the *quantity* of work and "facts" and, especially, unsupported "opinions," but on the quality of the relationships between data and interpretations? Such a freshman, winner of a national prize in history in senior year of high school, once complained to me: "They told me here to 'Describe the theory of monarchy assumed in Queen Elizabeth's speech to the Commons in 1601.' I said what her main points were, but my section man says to look between the lines for her theory of monarchy! And I look between the lines and I can't see anything there!"

The capacity for *meta*-thought, for comparing the assumptions and processes of different ways of thinking, has not yet emerged. This is perhaps the most critical moment in the whole adventure for both student and teacher.

Transition from Position 4a (Multiplicity) to Position 5 (Relativism). Before taking up the smoother movement of the more Adherent students through Position 4b, I wish to note the special difficulty of transition into Relativistic thought experienced by the students who have embraced Multiplicity with greatest enthusiasm. I have suffered too many defeats by the ingenuity of Multiplistic Libertarians to offer any handy-dandy pedagogical devices for helping students in this transition. Together with the teacher-researchers, mentioned later in the chapter, who have focused their experimentation on this problem, I have found all solutions to be relative to the subject matter. The work of these researchers contains rich ore for any prospector. Here I wish to report our students' experience of first discovery, so vital and usually so explicit, of qualitative epistemological structures and complex relations.

Sad to say, the very spunk with which our most Oppositional students invented the realm of Multiplicity (to set against the Right-Wrong world they attributed to Authority) seemed to lead them into a stalemate. Entrenched in this Position, they found it difficult to abandon the slogan, "Every opinion is right," for the qualitative analyses and appraisals of Relativism to which the best of their instructors would try to introduce them. Most did find ways, as I shall suggest shortly in discussing the general mechanisms of transition, but some were cornered into a choice between leaving the field and outright capitulation. Most fortunate were those for whom the demand to substantiate opinion came from more advanced peers.

Those less entrenched in opposition moved more easily:

> Student: [Reading written statement handed him by interviewer] "In areas where experts disagree, everyone has a right to his own opinion"—Yeh, sure. I mean, if the answers aren't in, like in lots of things, then sure, anyone's opinion.
> Interviewer: So really you're saying that here, anyway, no opinion can be *wrong*, sort of, so one opinion is really as good as any other?
> Student: Yeh, ah, well—no, not really—I, well I hadn't thought of that before. No—I mean you've got to have some facts *under* the opinion, I guess.

"Some facts" is still a quantitative criterion, but it opens the door to the qualitative notion of "better" (rather than right-wrong) opinions. Though the student may still have much to learn about the relations of "facts" and "opinions," that learning has now a real potential. Here, the transition seems initiated by the interview itself. It is easy to imagine, however, a variety of experiences other than the interviewer's question that would have set the same process in motion.

Position 4b: Relativism Subordinate. The more trusting Adherent students seemed to find a smoother path. Their integrity seemed less entrenched in Multiplicity's fortress: "They have No Right to Call Me Wrong." Trusting in Authority to have valid grounds for grading even in areas of uncertainty, they set themselves to discover those grounds. Laurence Copes recently pointed out to me that some students may sensibly find their way out of the impass of Position 4a via the discovery of Position 4b as described later. A review of the data supports this proposition, namely that a path through Position 4a and 4b can be sequential. In some one course or another—or in some other particular context —they perceived relativistic thinking as a special case of "what They want":

> Student: Another thing I've noted about this more concrete and complex approach—you can get away without . . . trying to think about what they want—ah, think about things the *way* they want you to think about them. But if you try to use the approach the course outlines, then you find yourself thinking in *complex terms*: weighing more than one factor in trying to develop your own opinion. Somehow what I think about things seems to be more—oh—it's hard to say right or wrong—but it seems [pause] more *sensible.*

58

Here the correction from *"what* they want" to "the *way* they want you to think" signals the discovery of the articulation of the "concrete" with the "complex" in "weighing" relationships—a mode of thought that is the structural foundation of Relativism. The weighing of "more than one factor," or, as this student later explained, "more than one *approach* to a problem," forces a comparison of patterns of thought—that is, a thinking about thinking. The person, previously a *holder* of meaning, has become a *maker* of meaning. For most students, as for this student, the event seems to be conscious and explicit; that is, the *initial* discovery of meta-thought occurs vividly in foreground, as figure, against the background of previous ways of thinking, and usually as an assimilation to the old paradigm—that is, as an item in the *context of* "what They want."

Now, the capacity to compare different approaches to a problem in "developing one's own opinion" is presumably the ordinary meaning of *independent thought.* The paradox for liberal education lies in the fact that so many of our students learned to think this way because it was "the way They want you to think"—that is, out of a readiness to conform. The challenge of a more genuine independence then confronted these students later in the revolutionary perception of the general relativism of *all* knowledge, *including* the knowledge possessed by Authority itself (Position 5).

Transition from Position 4b (Relativism Subordinate) to Position 5 (Relativism). The first steps in the direction of Relativism are articulated by the same student just quoted:

> Student: I don't know if complexity itself [he has been speaking of relativistic analysis] is always necessary. I'm not sure. But if complexity is *not* necessary, at least you have to find that it *is* not necessary before you can decide, "Well, this particular problem needs only the simple approach."

Although this transitional statement implies that relativistic thinking will be required more *frequently* than "simple" (dualistic) solutions, the student does not yet recognize that even the "simple" case owes its simplicity to a complex context of assumptions, rules, and contingencies. That is, this same student, quoted in the illustration of Position 4b, first saw relativistic thought as a special case in the context of "what They want." This present statement catches him halfway to the perception of relativistic thought as general *context* and "what They want" as a special case. I shall refer to this transformation of a special case into a context later in considering the forms of transitions in general.

We found it rare to catch this momentous revolution in the act. By the next year this student simply took the whole matter for granted, with a kind of amnesia for the deep reorganization involved. Indeed, in senior year he had this to say on hearing himself as sophomore:

> Student: [scornfully] You can't even *talk* about taking a simple approach to something. I mean it's just a way of looking at things that is complex—it's not a conscious policy, it's just something that's been absorbed into you.

I recall, without the precise reference, that Piaget once remarked on this curiosity of cognitive growth: *assimilations*—the attributions of meaning to objects or events that reduce their dissonance with the person's extant structures of meaning—tend to be remembered; *accommodations*—the subsequent reorganizations of basic structures to achieve congruence with dissonant assimilations—tend to be forgotten (perhaps because memory's own filing system is, in the very process, in flux). Could it be that we teachers require special exercise in the recall of our own accommodations in order to understand some students' apparent density?

In any case, an understanding of the forms that such transitions take would seem fundamental to curriculum design and teaching strategies. The transitions we have noted so far appear to start with assimilation of some incongruity to an extant paradigm. In the transition just traced, for instance, the student first perceived relativistic thinking simply as a special case in the general dualistic frame of "what They want." But this assimilation turned out to be a Trojan Horse, its inner forms emerging to overwhelm its simplistic host and force an accommodation of fundamental assumptions. Education has thus changed from collecting "what They want" to developing a way of thinking shared by both teacher and student.

Here, then, the accommodation takes the form of a radical reversal of part and whole, detail and context: the task of generating and comparing several interpretations of a poem, for example, may first be assimilated as a special case into the larger context of "what They want." In short, contextual relativism is perceived as if it were similar to "right answers." And yet it is also perceived as not quite similar: "As soon as I saw what they wanted . . . well, no, not *what* they wanted but the *way* they wanted you to think. . . ." The shift from "what" (content) to "way" (generalized process), being a move to a higher level of abstraction, frees the "way" to become context, displacing the "what" and relegating it to the status of a particular. In other instances, accommodation appears to be brought about by the sheer weight of quantitative expansion of the assimilated incongruity: uncertainties or diversities multiply until they tip the balance against certainty and homogeneity, precipitating a crisis that forces the construction of a new vision of the world, be it one marked by cynicism, anxiety, or a new sense of freedom.

The use of analogy—what Piaget called *décalage*—is doubtless involved in these processes and will become more evident in the remaining steps of the journey. *Vertical décalage* manifests itself in the "lifting" of a pattern of meaning from a concrete experience and using it as an analogue for meaning at a level of greater abstraction. For example, one student, terrified after making an error on his job, was astounded by the calmness of his employer's quiet suggestion that he plan things more carefully next time. He reported that the experience freed him to think more creatively in his studies and to affirm his opinions more confidently, relieved of irrational anxiety about impending judgment. Likewise, there are many areas of life in which students have learned at early ages patterns of qualitative and contextual judgment, as opposed to all-or-none quantitative and absolutistic judgment. For example, they have moved in early years from "What's your *favorite* color, ice cream, friend, sport, and so on" to considerations of what color with what other colors, what ice cream with what other foods, what friend in what activity or sharing. These contextual schema provide ready analogies in concrete experience that the student may "lift" to provide patterns for abstract thought itself. Ideas can then be conceived as contextual, relativistic, and better or worse, rather than right or wrong.

This comparison of interpretations and thought systems with one another introduces *meta-thinking*, the capacity to examine thought, including one's own. Theories become, not "truth," but metaphors or "models," approximating the order of observed data or experience. Comparison, involving systems of logic, assumptions, and inferences, all relative to context, will show some interpretations to be "better," others "worse," many worthless. Yet even after extensive analysis there will remain areas of great concern in which reasonable people will reasonably disagree. It is in this sense that relativism is inescapable and forms the epistemological context of all further developments.

Position 5: Relativism. Let us now examine the reactions of students to the simultaneous discovery of disciplined meta-thought and irreducible uncertainty.

> Student: It's a method that you're dealing with, not, not a substance. It's a method, a purpose—ah, "procedure" would be the best word, I should imagine, that you're looking for. And once you've developed this procedure in one field, I think the important part is to be able to transfer it to another field, and the example that I brought up about working with this, this crew of men. It's probably, ah, the most outstanding, at least one of the achievements that I feel that I've been able to make as far as transferring my academic experience to the field of everyday life.

This process of drawing an analogy between different areas of experience *(horizontal décalage)* highlights the fact that individuals mature their cognitive structures at different rates in different areas of their lives. They can thus transfer the more advanced patterns of thought learned in one area to areas in which they have been thinking more simplistically. The student just quoted has used relativism learned in academic work to broaden his understanding of others and expand his social skills. No doubt this has increased his potential for empathy. However, the salient initial experience is usually one of expanded competence:

> Student: Besides your meeting people, it's—it's the way of thinking—I mean just by the process of going through school, the courses are lined up so they make you think, especially when you come to, say, hour exams and you have to take them. This rubs off—when you meet people and have to talk to them, the process is in your mind and then you can think about things and be able to come up on your feet.

Relativistic consideration has already grown somewhat beyond its value as a practical tool, and its epistemological implications soon become explicit.

> Student: So here were all these theorists and theories and stuff in [economics] and psychology and historiography—I didn't even take any straight philosophy—and hell, I said, "These are *games,* just *games* and everybody makes up their own rules! So it's gotta be bullshit." But then I realized "What else have we got?" and now every time I go into a thing I set out to learn all its rules cold—'cause that's the only way I can tell whether I'm talking bullshit.

In this powerful statement, the responsibility and initiative that used to be the domain of Authority (leaving that of obedience to the student), have been internalized. This sense of agency as a learner is expressed first, appropriately enough, in a care for precision of thought within given contexts. Indeed, the student's redefinition of "bullshit" encapsulates his momentous revision of his epistemology and his self-definition in it. It is hardly surprising that there is still no hint in the protocol of a further responsibility to choose among contexts or "games." In Position 5 students seem much taken up with expansion of their new skills, exploring alternative perspectives in many disciplines and areas of life. Their explorations may occupy them for more than a year before they sense a necessity to orient themselves in a relativistic sea through their own Commitments (see the discussion of Positions 6-9). It is not really fair to describe the typical suspension of development at this point as Temporizing, since there is evidence of "lateral growth" (Perry, 1970, p. 175). This factor may help explain the findings of recent experiments (Knefelkamp, 1978c) that "developmental instruction" is more successful in facilitating students' movements from Dualism into Relativism than from Relativism into Commitments, at least within the limits of a semester.

Needless to say, many students react to the discovery of relativistic thinking with profound anxiety.

> Student: You know, in the past months, it's been a matter of having really ... having reduced to the level where I really wasn't sure there was anything in particular to follow. I, you do begin to wonder on what basis you'd judge *any* decision at all, 'cause there really isn't, ah ... too much of an absolute you can rely on as to ... and even as to whether ... there are a lot of levels that you can tear it apart, or you can base an ethical system that's a, presupposes that there are men who ... or you can get one that doesn't presuppose that anything exists ... and try and figure out of what principles you're going to decide any issue. Well, it's just that right now I'm not sure that ... of what the, ah, what those de-, how to make any decision at all. When you're here and are having the issues sort of thrust in your face at times ... that is, just seeing the thinking of these men who have pushed their thought to the absolute limit to try and find out what was their personal salvation, and just seeing how that fell short of an all-encompassing answer to, for everyone. That those ideas really are individualized. And you begin to have respect for how great their thought could be, without its being absolute.

I picture this student standing beside Sisyphus (Camus' embodiment of the human predicament in the *Myth of Sisyphus*) and gazing in dismay at the rock of reason, which has turned on itself and rolled once again to the foot of the mountain. He sees, in wonder and terror, Sisyphus' wry smile bespeaking his awareness that he must again resume the quest for certainty of meaning, a labor that forever ends in the same defeat. Is this vision tolerable?

Deflections from Growth

We shall leave our students poised in their journey at this realization that even the most careful analytical thought and logical reasoning will not, in many areas vital to their lives, restore the hope of ultimate rightness and certainty promised by Authority in the Eden they have left behind. "I'm not sure how to make any decision at all." At this moment, the potential for apathy, anxiety, and depression may appear alarming clinically, and the potential for cynicism equally alarming educationally.

Looking back to the dualistic worlds of Positions 1-3, we can observe that the students and much of the environment were conspiring to maintain the illusion that meaning existed "out there," along with rightness, power, and sound advice. One should, of course, try to "think for oneself," but when such efforts end in uncertainty and confusion, one naturally appeals to external authority, secure in the expectation of an answer. Students in this frame of mind present themselves to "career counselors" expecting to be told "the right job" or even to be "placed" in it. "What do the tests say my interests are?"

When all knowledge is revealed to be relativistic, probabilistic, and contingent, Authority appears as limited authority, uncertain even in its specialties, and ignorant beyond them. In this collapse, the agency for making sense, originally supposed to exist "out there," may vanish entirely. We should note here, therefore, the reactions of those students (happily a small minority of our informants) who reacted with postponement, apathy, or rage. Against the background of their experience we can then better appreciate the transcendence of those who found a more positive resolution.

Temporizing. Some students simply waited, reconsigning the agency for decision to some event that might turn up:

> Student: I'll wait and see what time brings, see if I pass the foreign service exam. Let that decide.

Or even more passively:

Student: It, ah . . . Well, I really, I don't know, I just, I don't get particularly worked up over things. I don't react too strongly. So that I can't think. I'm still waiting for the event, you know, everyone goes through life thinking that something's gonna happen, and I don't think it happened this year. So we'll just leave that for the future. Mainly you're, you're waiting for yourself to change, see after you get a good idea, continued trial and effort, exactly how you're going to act in any period of time, once you get this idea, then you're constantly waiting for the big chance in your life. And, it certainly didn't happen this year.

Students speaking this way often expressed a sense of guilt or shame—an uneasiness about a failure of responsibility with which they felt helpless to cope.

Retreat. In the late sixties and early seventies, some students found in the far extremes of political positions, both of the right and of the left, a way of preempting the absolutism that "wishy-washy" authorities had abandoned. The structure of thought to which they returned was that of Position 2, but with an added moralistic righteousness and righteous hatred of Otherness: "The others are so wrong they should have *no rights,* even to speak." Academically, however, this Retreat to the all-or-none of Position 2 often took the form of childlike complaints and demands:

Student: I mean, when I talk, as I say, I like to be out in the open. I mean I like to just, just come out with the facts and have them say, "Here's the information I want you to learn. This is the way I want you, this is what I want you to get out of the course when you come out." If I know what I want . . . I'm expected from a teacher . . . and what kind of questions he might ask, how thoroughly he wants you to read this material. . . . The big things are to get the basic principles. But he doesn't give you these! He ought to line them up right at the beginning; right at the first lecture he ought to tell you exactly what you're going to go over and what he wants us to basically get out of that course.

Escape. More complex reactions of alienation we labeled Escape. I shall not attempt to categorize or analyze their variants here; a few samples will speak for themselves —perhaps all too well:

Student: But, ah, I just, I don't, don't, don't have any, ah, consuming interest or burning desire or anything. And I just, just drift along, I guess you might say.

On the one hand, I, I—am, um, having an, an, ah . . . ah, an extremely comfortable life here. But, ah, perhaps later, I'm, I may find out that I'm ah . . . drifting and, and that I'm not happy in my drift.

And I was wondering if I might not be headed in that direction and, and it might turn out that when I get older I, I'll find that . . . umn . . . I am living a, a hollow life.

Is Relativism the road to Escape or the precondition of Commitment?

Student: I know that I had trouble, ah, first of all in just listening to the lectures, trying to make out what they meant . . . These, ah, ah, the pursuit of the absolute first of all . . . And then I . . . [laughs] sort of lost the absolute, and stuff like that. I think that gradually it sunk in, and, I don't know, maybe it's just . . . Well, it came to me the other night: if relativity is true on most things, it's an easy way out. But I don't think that's . . . maybe that's just the way I think now . . . Well, in, in a sense I mean that you don't have to commit yourself. And maybe that's just the push button I use on myself . . . right now, because I am uncommitted.

Does the purity of detachment preclude meaningful involvement?

Student: I've thought quite a bit about this: I've never really identified myself with anything. I hadn't permitted myself to so far as grades were concerned or as far as friends—particularly in a few isolated cases. I had just a sort of "I'm me, and I just like to stand out there and look things over" attitude, and I don't know whether this is good or bad.

But there's always impulse:

Student: So the best thing I have to do is just forget about deciding, and try to ... I mean, not give up on any scheming or any basic set of ideas ... that'll give myself, they'll give me a direction. Just give up completely, and when it comes down to individual choices, make them on what I feel like doing emotionally at the moment.

Not all the students who spoke this way left such statements with us as their final words. Many reported a resurgence of vitality and involvement:

Student: Emotionally I think I was trying to find some sort of rationalization for my feeling that I wasn't going to achieve anything. These are certainly not the values I have now. They're not the goals I want now. I don't think I'm going to be happy unless I can feel I'm doing something in my work.

Student: I think I've, to some extent, not perhaps as well as I like, have risen up to be able to accept it [academic work], and the responsibility that goes with it, but it's one little change.

Student: I was sort of worried when I came back, wondering if, "Well, shucks, am I just going to lie down on the job or am I going to do it because it has to be done?" I found out that I wasn't doing it because it *had* to be, but because things interested me. Some things didn't interest me so much, but I felt I couldn't let them slide and I took them as best I could, in what order I could.

We know from everyday observations and from studies of adults (Keniston, 1960; Vaillant, 1977; Salyard, in progress) that the alienation we called Escape can become a settled condition. For the students reporting their recovery of care, however, their period of alienation appears as a time of transition. In this time the self is lost through the very effort to hold onto it in the face of inexorable change in the world's appearance. It is a space of meaninglessness between received belief and creative faith. In their rebirth *they experience in themselves the origin of meanings, which they had previously expected to come to them from outside.*

Development Resumed

Position 6: Commitment Foreseen. Students who were able to come more directly to grips with the implications of Relativism frequently referred to their forward movement in terms of commitments.

Student: It took me quite a while to figure out that if I was going for something to believe in, it had to come from within me.

Many students foresaw the challenge:

Student: I would venture a guess that this problem bothers everybody except for, ah, a very, very small few, this, this constant worry about whether you can face up to it, and, and I think the earlier you find out that you can ... I think the more important it is ... A sense of responsibility is something which, I don't think ... you're necessarily are born with, it's, ah ... something that you're aware of ... but ... it's never very pronounced until you're on your own and until you're making your own decisions, more or less, and then you realize how very important it really is.

As a generalized realization, lacking as yet a focus in some specific content, the vision seems to derive from the felt exigency of "action":

> Student: Once you get to be past twenty-one or twenty-two, if you haven't begun to get control of yourself, you can't, if you haven't begun to get a certain amount of direction, you can't expect these internal evolutions to just develop and then suddenly bloom, you've got to work at it, I think.
> You've got to do something, you've got to act. You've got to act these things ... if you have these thoughts, and you don't act on them ... nothing happens.

But how to begin? The same student goes on to imagine that the first steps may require an almost arbitrary faith, or even a willing suspension of disbelief:

> Student: You just have to jump into it, that's all, before it can have any effect on you. And the farther in you force yourself to get in the first place, the more possibilities there are, the more ideas and concepts there are that can impinge on you and so the more likely you are to get involved in it. Actually you have to make some kind of an assumption in the first place that it's worthwhile to get into it, but ... and that you're capable of doing something once you get into it.

Commitments and choices are apprehended as "narrowing"—there are so many potentialities and alternatives to let go of. Yet the sustaining energy is the awareness of some sort of internal spiritual strength. Such an explicit affirmation as this one is rare:

> Student: I wasn't *deploring* the fact that my interests were narrowing, I was just simply *observing* it. I don't see how I could get by without it. You know what Keats says in one of his letters, he says when he's sitting in a room and everybody is talking brilliantly and he's sitting in the corner and he's sulking and everybody is whispering to each other, "Oh that poet Keats is sitting over there like a wallflower," he says in moments like that, he doesn't care about that because he's aware of the, the resource in his breast. I think that's the expression he uses. And what goes along with this narrowing of the purpose is the greater and greater sense of, that resource in my breast which is, I don't suppose that everybody needs it, but I need it. You know, it just, it just puts a center and a focus into your life, into what you're doing. And it hasn't really anything to do with where you would like to think that it would go on, this "inner life" (which I think is really bad to call it) that will go on no matter what you're doing, whether you're traveling around the world or whether you're sitting in your stack in Widener. So I know that it must seem like a disparity, but I don't feel it that way.

> More usually:
> Student: There are all kinds of pulls, pressures and so forth ... parents ... this thing and that thing ... but there comes a time when you've just got to say, "Well, ... I've got a life to live ... I want to live it this way, I welcome suggestions. I'll listen to them. But when I make up my mind, it's going to be me. I'll take the consequences."

So far I have chosen statements that are "contentless" in the sense that no specific value or activity is named as the investment of commitment. My object has been to allow the students to convey the sense and "feel" of commitment as an internal disposition through which one apprehends the possibility of orienting oneself and investing one's care in an uncertain and relativistic world. The next step, of course, is one of choice and action (see Positions 7, 8, and 9), as for example in one's academic work:

> Student: This year I'm beginning to see that you don't ever get anywhere unless you do work. You, you just can't sort of lie back and expect everything to come to you. That's the way I was trying to let it work, but that doesn't work.

That these emerging Commitments call upon a *new kind* of investment from within (as compared with unquestioned commitments—lowercase *c*—of the past) is evident in this student's report of her new sense of her religion. She has just reported that she had always "taken it for granted" that she would join the ministry:

> Student: The thing is, when you have a bunch of beliefs sort of handed to you, you don't really do that much thinking. I mean I was never even concerned with philosophy. I never read a single thing. I didn't have to. I mean, I accepted the Christian faith because my parents were Christians and I believed that, well, you know I never even thought, well, maybe there isn't any God. I mean it doesn't enter your mind. You just think, well, there's a God, you know, and he has a purpose for everybody's life. . . . But the thing is, I didn't know what I was really gonna do with my life. My life just sort of seemed, well, the main purpose was just telling everybody else that they had to believe in Jesus or they weren't going to go to heaven. . . . It's just that I was always going to be . . . working with the church, you know, but, I, I never really thought about what is my, you know, place in the universe, or anything. And, but the thing is, it really hasn't been unsettling, because . . . ahh . . . well, I don't know, now I'm more . . . somehow now I feel . . . I don't know, just more honest about, about my beliefs, now that I'm sort of getting them on my own.

Positions 7-9: Evolving Commitments. Our students, at sea in Relativism, now realized that they must choose, at their own risk, among disparate systems of navigation. What star to steer by? Many felt that once "I know what I'm going to do," all other problems would be solved—or at least fall in line. Then they made their first Commitment (Position 7), whether to a set of values ("This may sound sort of silly, but I've developed a sense of, ah, a set of morals") or to a person ("I started dating this girl"), or, most usually, to a career ("Right now I'd like to go into pediatrics; I'm really set on this deal"). In any case, the sense of "claiming" is vivid:

> Student: Then, by a few months or a few weeks ago, feeling new kinds of resolve, you know, just grabbing hold of myself and saying, "This I want, that I don't want, this I am, that I'm not, and I'll be solid about it."
>
> I'd never believed I could do things, that I had any power, I mean power over myself, and over effecting any change that I thought was right. I'd artificially try to commit myself to something, intellectually understand that I was this way, and then a few months later, the realization would come that yes, I really *am* that way. They're two different things. One's intellectual and comes fairly easily; one is emotional and is a process of absorbing something—the things inside just sort of slowly shifting around and there's a lot of inertia there.

The difference between such Commitments, made after doubt, and those unquestioned childhood beliefs that Erikson calls "foreclosed identity" was dramatized for us by a doctor-to-be who, after years of struggle, received notice of his admission to medical school. He reacted with panic: "But I've never *decided* to be a *doctor*!" He decided, and then had to decide if his decision was real or simply a way of justifying his investment. Such is the nature of Commitments.

Yet one Commitment does not, after all, order all one's life:

> Student: I don't think it reduces the number of problems that I face or uncertainties, it just was something that troubled me that I thought was—I always thought it was an unnecessary problem and based on my limited experience with a broadened world . . . [Now] I don't see it as something that is passed; it is something that I have to decide continually.

So when further Commitments are affirmed (Positions 8 and 9) it becomes necessary to balance them—to establish priorities among Commitments with respect to energy, action, and time. These orderings, which are often painful to make, can lead to periodic experiences of serenity and well-being in the midst of complexity—moments of "getting it all together":

> Student: Well, ah . . . I don't know exactly if there's any one thing that's central . . . this is the whole point that, ah . . . there are factors in the whole . . . you group all these facts . . . I don't know that there's one thing about which everything revolves . . . but it's rather just a circle.
> Interviewer: It's the constellation that, ah . . . you try to maintain?
> Student: Yeah. Right. Yeah, you think of the old, ah . . . the balance of powers, you know . . . you know it's not . . . north and south or black and white . . . it's . . . it's not a simple thing. It comes in any given occasion . . . and . . . it's different . . . This is what makes things exciting—it offers a challenge.

Another senior has been groping to describe the new sense of living with trust even in the midst of a heightened awareness of risk:

> Interviewer: And I take it, part of this mellowness that you speak of is being able to live in peace with this complexity . . . if it isn't so simple . . .
> Student: It's not as frightening as it may have been. . . . If you feel that, ah, whatever you do there's going, there's going to be much more to do, more to understand, you're going to make mistakes . . . but you have a certain sense of being able to cope with a specific, or rather, a small fragment of the general picture and, ah, doing a job, getting the most out of it, but never, never giving up, always looking for something.

Order and disorder may be seen as fluctuations in experience:

> Student: I sort of see this now as a natural thing—that you constantly have times of doubt and tension—a natural thing in existing and being open, trying to understand the world around you, the people around you.

In the loneliness or separateness implicit in these integrations and reintegrations, students seek among their elders for models not only of knowledgeability but of courage to affirm commitment in full awareness of uncertainty.

> Student: That was just about what it was. Somehow I wanted to emulate [such people] because they seemed in some way noble people, and what they were doing seemed somehow noble and lofty—a very moral and superior type of thing. I think I fastened on this.

Yet the same student must come to see that it is the nobility of their care that he wishes to emulate, not the content of their Commitments. At the level of "what they were doing," even the model must be transcended:

Student: One thing I have found *since* is that it's not really *right* to make decisions on this basis, because you may come out doing something you don't find yourself suited for. It's really strange.

Dialectical Logic of Commitments

If one knows one's Commitments are to flow and fluctuate and conflict and reform, is one committed at all? This is the first of the many paradoxes the students encountered in working out their Commitments. Allport (Allport, 1955) observed the paradoxical necessity to be both wholehearted and tentative—attitudes that one cannot "compromise" but must hold together, with all their tensions. The students wrestled with logic to express this paradox:

Student: Well, "tentative" implies ... perhaps uncertainty and, and, I mean readiness to change to anything, and, ah, it's not that. It's openness to change, but, but not looking for change, you know, ah ... At the same time, ah, believing pretty strongly in what you do believe, and so it's not, you know, it's not tentative.

In reporting the original study, I pointed to an array of such polarities in the account of a single student in his senior year (Perry, 1970, pp. 167-176). They included certainty versus doubt, focus versus breadth, idealism versus realism, tolerance versus contempt, internal choice versus external influence, action versus contemplation, stability versus flexibility, and own values versus others' values. Because a polarity of this kind does not represent the poles of a continuum, it cannot be resolved simply by finding some balance point or compromise. Instead, our most mature students saw that the tension must be embraced and somehow transcended. To do so, they appealed to dialectical logic, without actually calling it by name.

[Speaking of the necessity of trusting in a professional healer even when evidence contradicts]: See, this is the way you get educated [laughs] ... that's the big surprise. See I'm still sort of ironical about it, 'cause that's about the only way you can be—'cause ironic—being ironic handles both values at once.

At the time of the original study, I sensed that the term *dialectical thought* meant many things to many people, and I was troubled by the absence of a sense of its limits in the works of Hegel, Nietzsche, and Marx. Various recent writers (Riegel, 1973; Fowler, 1978; Basseches, 1978) have delimited more clearly the reference of the term and write convincingly of the central role of dialectical processes in thought characteristic of the higher ranges of human development.

Basseches (1978) has recently delineated twenty-four characteristics of dialectical thought. He proposes that these analytical tools will distinguish, in the present scheme, between those persons whose Commitments involve forward transcendent movement and those whose Commitments represent more a regression into dualism. By way of analogy, he points to Fowler's Paradoxical-Consolidative stage in the development of faith:

[This stage] affirms and incorporates existential or logical polarities, acting on a felt need to hold them in tension in the interest of truth. It maintains its vision of meaning, coherence, and value while being conscious of the fact that it is partial, limited, and contradicted by the visions and claims of others.

It holds its vision with a kind of provisional ultimacy: remembering its inadequacy and open to new truth but also committed to the absoluteness of the truth which it inadequately comprehends and expresses.

Symbols are understood as symbols. They are seen through in a double sense: (1) their time-place relativity is acknowledged and (2) their character as relative representations of something more nearly absolute is affirmed [Fowler, 1978, p. 22].

Again, Basseches quotes Fowler regarding the *costs* of this "identification beyond tribal, racial, class, or ideological boundaries. To be genuine, it must know the cost of such community and be prepared to pay the cost" (Fowler, 1978, pp. 6-7). Basseches' distinction regarding this cost is trenchant: "The cost of this openness to universal community of identification surely includes having to embrace viewpoints in conflict with and contradictory to one's own, rather than avoiding those conflicts with 'separate but equal' or 'live and let live' attitude." In short, it is in one's way of affirming Commitments that one finds at last the elusive sense of "identity" one has searched for elsewhere, fearful lest Commitments might narrow and compromise the very self that only the investment of care can create. It is in the affirmation of Commitments that the themes of epistemology, intellectual development, ethics, and identity merge. Knowing that "such and such is true" is an act of personal commitment (Polanyi, 1958) from which all else follows. Commitments structure the relativistic world by providing focus in it and affirming the inseparable relation of the knower and the known.

In the poignant realization of our separateness and aloneness in these affirmations, we are sorely in need of community. Our mentors can, if they are wise and humble, welcome us into a community paradoxically welded by this shared realization of aloneness. Among our peers we can be nourished with the strength and joy of intimacy, through the perilous sharing of vulnerability.

A graduating senior, shaken by the questioning of values he thought he had so firmly established, said to his interviewer, "Now I know I'll never know how many times I'm going to be confronted." Indeed, the development we have traced in college students reveals itself now as "age-free."

Development as Recursive

Fowler's words, which speak of the paradoxical dialectic of holding absolutes in symbols acknowledged to be relativistic, reveal also the limits of the linear structure embedded in the metaphor of our journey. We have followed our students in their cumulative expansion of the meanings of their worlds. Our map of their adventure has required only two dimensions, for in the time at the students' disposal they could traverse this "Pilgrim's Progress" only once. But any adults who have perused the diaries of their teens know well that growth and discoveries are recursive. We are shocked at finding we "knew" at sixteen what we just discovered yesterday. Have we just been going around in circles? Yet the "same" issues, faced over and over again, may not really be the same.

Perhaps the best model for growth is neither the straight line nor the circle, but a helix, perhaps with an expanding radius to show that when we face the "same" old issues we do so from a different and broader perspective (Perry, 1977b). I have before me a letter from a professor:

I thought you might be interested in a small example of passing through your series of stages more than once. Two years ago I spent three months working on a Danforth Faculty Fellowship Grant on a topic in faculty development, which was a new area for me. For many years I have been confident about skimming, picking and choosing within, and even abandoning books in my own discipline. When reading in faculty development materials, however, I found it necessary to struggle constantly against the impulse to dutifully examine and finish anything that was recommended to me whether it seemed fruitful or even bore on my problem or not.

The old "impulse" was there, but the new person was not "subject" to it.

Further Explorations with the Scheme

After the graduation of our last sample of volunteers in the original study, eight years passed before our small office found the energies to follow another class through its experience of college. Even then, since our daily work of counseling had doubled, we were unable to afford the systematic rating of the interviews necessary to formal research and had to rely on the informal consensus of our impressions. The average Harvard-Radcliffe freshman of 1970-71 seemed a full Position in advance of his or her predecessor in 1959-60—in fact, beyond the developmental crisis of Position 5. We wondered if this accounted in part for the relative "flatness" we felt characterized most of these students' four-year reports (Perry, 1974). Their concerns with Commitments, too, seemed to focus more narrowly on careers, usually with less sense of permanence of investment (reflecting the slackening in economic growth? post-Vietnam depression?). The overall progression, however, appeared congruent with that traced in the original study. We would say the same of our present sample of the class of '79. The course of cognitive and ethical development outlined in our scheme appears to be a constant phenomenon of a pluralistic culture.

However, we could not subject our impressions to objective testing. Furthermore, the data, as in the original study, are provided by students in a single institution. It has therefore remained for other researchers to show that the scheme provides a useful description of students' development of meaning in other settings, to refine the scheme further, to design more economical measurements, and to illustrate its power for the improvement of teaching and counseling in higher education. James Heffernan was the first to use the scheme for research in his study of the outcomes of the Residential College at Michigan (Heffernan, 1971). Heffernan subsequently developed a cumulative bibliography of research and commentary relating to the scheme, a task currently under the direction of Laurence Copes.[3] This bibliography of over 100 entries (as of April 1980) is included in the references for this chapter.

Here I shall mention briefly the work of those researchers and practitioners most familiar to me, hoping only to show the direction of their explorations. Readers interested in more detailed reviews should start with Heffernan, 1975. Until September of 1975, I was unaware that anyone had taken up the study of our scheme—other than Heffernan and also Joanne Kurfiss (1975), to whose work I shall refer later. To be sure, I had received many requests for a quick pencil-and-paper rating scale to be used for all purposes from admissions to the evaluation of faculty. In the face of my doubts about the reliability of a quick checklist, my friend Eugene Hartley, of the University of Wisconsin at Green Bay, made one from brief illustrative quotations from the original study, which students were to check "acceptable" or "unacceptable" (Hartley, 1973). This prodded

---

[3] In compiling this bibliography, Laurence Copes has received assistance from L. Lee Knefelkamp, Katherine Mason, John Griffith, and others. Clyde Parker at the University of Minnesota has contributed library facilities and supported the distributions of a newsletter of which Copes is editor. Interested persons may address Copes at the Institute for Studies in Educational Mathematics, 1483 Hewitt Ave., St. Paul, Minn. 55104.

me into making an "improved" version myself to demonstrate that no such things would work. In this exercise I was so successful that my null hypothesis was unequivocally confirmed (unpublished study).

Then, at the Annual Conference of the American Psychological Association (APA) in 1975, Clyde Parker's students came forward with the fruits of three years' research on our developmental scheme. Carol Widick examined the scheme's theoretical structure. L. Lee Knefelkamp and Widick reported on college-level courses taught through "Developmental Instruction" based on the scheme. They adjusted four instructional variables to their students' Positions on the scheme: (1) diversity, (2) learning activity, (3) degree of structuring of assignments, and (4) personalism. Pre-post measures demonstrated superior substantive mastery and developmental progress in students in this special program, compared with those in a comparable course taught traditionally. A measuring instrument developed by Knefelkamp and Widick included sentence-completion and paragraphs susceptible of reliable rating. At the same meeting, Pierre Meyer reported on the uses of the scheme in a study of religious development (Meyer, 1977); Ron Slepitza and Knefelkamp demonstrated its contribution to a model of career counseling making salient the shift from external to internal locus of control (Slepitza and Knefelkamp, 1976); and Stephenson and Hunt confirmed Knefelkamp and Widick's pedagogical methods for furthering college students' movements from dualism to relativistic thinking (Stephenson and Hunt, 1977).

The outlines of this symposium delineated the types of studies that other researchers and teachers were already conducting with reference to our scheme and that later workers would also pursue: (1) elaborations and extensions, (2) use of the scheme to illuminate particular aspects of development, (3) validations in various settings, (4) design of curriculums, instruction, and advising in the light of the scheme, and (5) instrumentation.

Elaborations and Extensions. Blythe Clinchy and Claire Zimmerman at Wellesley College have been engaged in a longitudinal study (1975) in which they first assumed the general validity of the original scheme in order to explore it in greater depth. Their interviews are therefore more focused than those of the original study, with interviewers offering the students groups of statements from which to start their thinking, and following with probes. In 1978-79 they will have thirty complete four-year sequences of rich data. Movement along the scale is already evident, regression rare. They have elaborated on several Positions, especially 3-5, in which they find substages. They are especially interested in exploring the process and contents of Commitment in women. In this regard, they found differential development of girls in a "traditional" and a "progressive" high school (Clinchy, Lief, and Young, 1977) and plan follow-up studies with alumnae. In exploring linguistic and other differences in the "voices" of women and men, they are presently collaborating with Ann Henderson of our office and with Carol Gilligan.

Referring to this scheme as an initial framework, Patricia King (1977a) analyzed the forms of "Reflective Probabilistic Judgment" evident in various levels of development, especially the later ones. Her labeling of Multiplistic thought as "Relativistic" (see the distinction made earlier between these modes of thought) led her to refer to the reasoning she examined as "beyond relativism" (King, 1977b, pp. 12, 17), whereas it would seem in the terms of this scheme to articulate relativistic processes themselves. However, her analysis and scoring procedures, together with those of her colleague Karen Kitchener (1977), provide an invaluable contribution to the understanding of the development of disciplined relativistic thought.

I have already mentioned Basseches' contribution to the identification and analysis of dialectical logic in the upper stages of development.[4] King (1977a) documents a decline in strictly Piagetian formal operations from high school through graduate school, remarking that such logic, so necessary to solutions of "puzzles" in physics, is inadequate for addressing "problems" in life. I would add that a premise common to most formal logic, namely that nothing can be A and not-A at the same time, is too humorless to live by. As one of our students said, "Irony gets both sides."

Joanne Kurfiss, in her early study (Kurfiss, 1975), examined in depth the conceptual properties of the developmental scheme and individuals' comparative rates of development in different areas. She compared five areas—(1) Moral Values, (2) Counseling and Advice, (3) Evaluation of Essays, (4) Responsibility of the Professor, and (5) the Nature of Knowledge—using as a measure the person's capacity to paraphrase statements characterizing various Positions of development in each area. She found considerable disparity in levels of development within individuals. Correlations were found between the areas of Moral Values and The Nature of Knowledge, and also among the other three areas, but not across these two groups. She surmised that the former pair are each relatively abstract and the later trio more concrete.

Use of the Scheme to Illuminate Particular Areas of Education. Confirming the usefulness of our scheme in respect to development of women, Carol Gilligan reports in the present volume on the consequence of rescoring Kohlberg ratings on the basis of the distinction we made between Multiplicity (anything-goes personalism) and contextual Relativism. The rescoring reverses Kohlberg's previously reported differences in rates and achievements of moral development between men and women at the upper levels (see also Gilligan and Murphy, 1979; Murphy and Gilligan, in press). Women appear less interested than men in the issues of conflict of rights presented in Kohlberg's dilemmas; rather, they develop contextually relativistic thinking in their search for the loci of care and responsibility in human relationships. Where this concern has been rated as personalistic "relativism" (Multiplicity), it has been devalued developmentally. The findings of Murphy and Gilligan (1980) are therefore of first-order import in the study of moral development. Their work also rescues sophomores from the condition of anomalous regression to which the earlier scoring had consigned them.

I have mentioned the work of Knefelkamp and Slepitza in career development and of Pierre Meyer in religion. Nowakowski and Laughney (1978) are working with Knefelkamp on the uses of the scheme in the design of training in health careers.

Clyde Parker initiated a Faculty Consultation Project with the College of Agriculture at Minnesota (Parker, 1978b). Interviews revealed the faculty's purposes to be couched in terms proper to our Positions 5 to 9:

> *Professor C:* One criticism I've had is that I ask questions that don't have absolute answers . . . I give them these kinds of questions because that's what life is. There aren't nice clean answers. They must come up with alternatives, weigh things, and make a decision.

Students were responding with plaints characteristic of Positions 2 to 3:

> *Student A:* In biology, there's really not two ways you can look at it. A bird has two feet. That's pretty conclusive.

These are brief samples of findings that are proving seminal in many undertakings in fac-

---

[4]For a study of the whole developmental progression itself in dialectical terms, see Heffernan and Griffith, 1979.

72

ulty development throughout the country in which the present scheme forms a point of reference (Chickering, 1976).

Design and Evaluation of Curriculums, Instruction, and Advising. In May of 1976, researchers and teachers interested in the uses of our scheme for improvement of instruction met at Ithaca College on the initiative of Laurence Copes (Copes, 1974) and Frances Rosamond, both assistant professors of mathematics. (I shall remark near the end of this chapter on an incident in this conference linking students' growth in sophistication in mathematics with their experience of loss—a connection I had never imagined.) The patterning provided an opportunity to share the validations and expansions under review and to derive a sense of their momentum.

Heffernan (1975) has this to say of the work of Laurence Copes and also Jack K. Johnson:

> The process in teaching college-level mathematics and their relationships to students' concepts of knowledge, per the Perry framework, have recently been examined by Laurence C. Copes, in a Ph.D. dissertation at Syracuse University. Copes' contention is that the presentation of the relativistic nature of mathematics is conducive to students' developing concepts of knowledge, and that certain teaching methods may be employed which reveal the creative and transcendent aspects of mathematics. He also has examined the theoretical potential of a number of teaching models for creating environments supportive of such conceptual development. His work and a dissertation by Jack K. Johnson relating Positions to open versus closed learning styles and a proposed study on teaching effectiveness in terms of the Perry scheme at the University of Wisconsin-Whitewater represent promising new directions in the improvement of teaching practices by conceptual rather than experiential guidelines [p. 497].

At the conference in Ithaca and subsequently, Knefelkamp and Widick have reported on continued elaboration of their model of Developmental Instruction (Widick and Simpson, 1978; Knefelkamp and Cornfeld, 1977). Others have extended its implications into peer training (Clement, 1977), career education (Touchton, 1978), graduate curriculum in counseling (Knefelkamp and Cornfeld, 1978), and the teaching of history (Widick and Simpson, 1978) and English drama (Sorum, 1976).

Most promising, too, is Knefelkamp's cross-cutting of this developmental scheme with the personality typology of John Holland. Given their choice among six approaches to an assignment centering on the same content, students regularly choose the style designed for their type and level of development (Knefelkamp, personal communication, 1978).

The uses of the scheme in the design of curriculums (Kovacs, 1977) and individual advising of adult learners, as at Empire State (Chickering, 1976), have been elaborated beyond my ability to document here.

Instrumentation. Some economical way of estimating the levels of students' thinking in given areas is central to the scheme's usefulness. Knefelkamp has carried this work furthest in company with Widick in 1975, and Slepitza in 1976. She is presently establishing the reliability of two instruments, both consisting of sentence-completions and short essays. The measure centering on students' thinking about their careers correlates .78 with expensive full-length interviews. Knefelkamp has a rating manual in manuscript.

The probing procedures of Clinchy and Zimmerman (1975) and the paraphrase method used by Kurfiss (1975) need further investigation. The former is economical in assuming the scheme's validity, thus bypassing the diffuseness of our original open interviews. The latter assumes that students can adequately paraphrase short paragraphs where the complexity is not more than a step beyond the forms in which they characteristically think but will misperceive the meaning of paragraphs in which the structure of thought is more advanced.

Two standards apply to all such instrumentations. Experimenters will naturally require quite precise assessments.[5] For ordinary teaching purposes, however, rough-hewn groupings of students evidencing dualistic thinking, multiplistic thinking, and relativistic thinking will provide ample base for such differential instruction as is economically possible in most classes. For ourselves, we use two estimates. In one we ask for a short essay on "How I learn best." In the other we ask students to grade, with reasons, two students' answers to an essay question on familiar material. One essay, full of facts, is chosen as superior by students honoring memorization but blind to relevance; the other is designed to be chosen as superior by students alert to the issue of interpretation of data in reference to the issue posed in the question. For such rough purposes as selecting those who most stand to benefit from our course in strategies of learning, these measures suffice.

Pending the further development of measurements, it is encouraging to note that in classes with up to forty students, teachers who have simply tuned their ears to the distinctions among modes of thought outlined in this chapter have found themselves able to distinguish students in the major levels of development *in vivo*. Following Knefel-kamp's model, they have then been able to create two or three combinations of different supports and challenges appropriate to the major groupings in the class.

Cognitive Styles, Learning Strategies, and Development

The attempts to gear strategies of teaching to students' modes of learning raise the issue of the mutability or immutability of cognitive and learning styles. (See Johnson, 1975; Messick, 1976; Witkin, 1967; Kagan and Kogan, 1970; Whitla, 1978; Santostefano, 1969; and Kolb, in this volume. For a review of contradictory findings see Danserau, 1974, and also Letteri, 1978.)

Hardly any of the studies dealing with this issue (except Johnson's) seem to relate observations and measurements of cognitive or learning styles to a student's development of perceived meaning of learning tasks. Yet when students radically revise their notions of knowledge, would they not be likely to change their ways of going about getting it?

Here, for example, a student recounts the radical change in his ways of learning:

> Student: *Then* it was just the weight of the thing. *Now* it's, it's not so much how many pages there are on the reading list, it's more what the books are worth. What sort of ideas do they have. I mean, I can read a book now, without regard for the pages. And read it pretty rapidly and get the ideas. That is, I'm looking for the ideas rather than plodding over the words and, . . . well, the ideas

[5]There is a problem inherent in making finer measurements with such an ordinal scale. The Positions are coherent *gestalten* in a hierarchical sequence. The scheme says nothing about the "distance" between Positions. If a student is rated as structuring the world from Position 5 three times out of four and from Position 4 once in four, is the rating 4.75 meaningful? The difficulty is compounded in averaging such ratings for groups of students and finding the "modal student" to be at, say, Position 3.83. We ourselves are among those who have committed this sin against parametric statistics. Whether the ends justify the means is a nice problem in contextual ethics, but the act should be deliberate and explicit. The use of parenthetical notation of secondary and tertiary patterns evident in a student's thought—for example, 4(5) or 3(2)(4)—is now a popular and effective way to express location on such ordinal schemes.

are what count, and unless it's a particularly well-written book, you're not going to get that much pleasure out of how the words are put together. And after all, I've finally decided that you don't read a book just to say you've read it, just to say that you've gone through it. But you read the book for what it's worth, for what it has in it. And this, this doesn't count on any, for exam purposes, that is, it's a broad outlook really. I mean, before maybe I was reading, whereas *now* I tend to generalize the things and get the main ideas and concepts, and then pick up a few illustrations here and there, and amplifications when it seems worthwhile. But it's the broader picture. It's just not reading to have read, but reading to learn something, perhaps.

Since this student has perceived anew the nature of knowledge and of Authority's relation to it, he has discarded obedience in favor of his own agency as a maker of meaning. He dares to select, to judge, to build. As he studies, his intent is now not simply to conciliate Authority, external or internalized, but to learn on his own initiative.

In keeping with this revolution, he tells us that his entire manner of studying has undergone profound change. Judging from what he says, this change should be evident in his observable behavior, all the way from his manner of searching library shelves to his eye movements in scanning a page. These surface changes will, of course, express changes in his altered modes of learning and cognition.

Let us suppose that we had the opportunity to observe this student at work before his restructuring of the meaning of his world and that we had set out to draw inferences about his cognitive and learning styles, selecting our categories from such sources as the glossary of cognitive styles provided by Messick (1976) and the related array explored by Whitla (1977). From the student's literal interpretation of his assignments and his undifferentiated word-by-word reading, we might guess that he would be rated as stylistically *field-dependent* rather than *field-independent*. The probable flatness of his notes and the inevitable confusion among cumulative details in his memory would be congruent with a *leveling* rather than *sharpening* manner of cognition. We would rate him more *cautious* than *risk-taking*, more *constricted* than *flexible* in control, more *receptive* than *perceptive*, more *narrow* than *broad* in scanning, more *data-minded* than *strategy minded*, and more *descriptive* than *analytical* conceptually.

Were we then to observe him again after his conversion, we would of course be led to the opposite inference in every case. Even at the perceptual level, he might report that those words that developmental reading teachers are fond of calling *signposts*—words like *however, moreover, first of all, in sum,* and the like—are beginning to "jump off the page" at him, just as faces hidden in pictures of trees emerge for *field-independent* people.

Granted, this hypothetical observation contradicts the impressive research demonstrating that an individual's "cognitive styles" are remarkably stable over time. Yet it speaks to the present-day concern about the "matching" and "mismatching" of learning styles with teaching styles and the structures of various academic disciplines. Are students' learning or cognitive styles enduring characteristics of the person, subject only to minor and uncomfortable adjustment to uncongenial teaching or subject matter? Kolb's suggestion, in this book, that higher education tends to increase specialization of styles rather than to broaden them has recently been supported by Whitla's findings (Whitla, 1977).

Stability and Mutability of Learning Styles. As a person whose daily work is directed toward increasing the range of students' learning styles to enable them to construct strategies appropriate to different contexts, I have reason to question whether learning styles are as stabile as some measures have made them seem. Allow me to introduce my "evidence."

Over the past thirty years we have in our office counseled over 15,000 students. If I estimate that only one in three of these consulted us explicitly and directly about ways of learning, the sample is still 5,000. In addition, we have provided direct instruction in strategies of learning to another 15,000 students in classes enrolling 80 to 200 at a time. Of this combined sample of 20,000 students (mostly bright undergraduates and graduate students with a scattering of advanced high school students, middle-aged students, and professors) I would say that a minimum of 40 percent reported to us, and demonstrated for us, the same kind of revolution in purpose and strategies of learning reported by the student just quoted; another 30 percent, who seemed already to have attained such a vision of meaning and purpose, used the time with us simply to extend and refine their range of strategies and skills; another 10 percent left us with inconclusive evidence; and 15 percent had a very hard time indeed.

Will the reader be content with that 40 percent figure—800 vivid instances of workaday observation as a substitute for some laboratory-type hard data? I am bargaining; the reader may make a much smaller concession and still share in the dilemma I wish to present. What I feel should concern all educators is the kind of contrast illustrated by the gap between those who experienced this "revolution" and those 15 percent who had a very hard time indeed. What can account for this difference in their response, at a given moment in their lives, to an invitation to alter certain strategies of learning?

Allow me to back up a moment and describe the nature of our instructional effort. Thirty years ago we inherited a conventional "developmental speed-reading" program, including instruction in preliminary scanning of reading material, asking oneself questions, watching for signposts, and all the rest, together with instructional films for pacing and increasing "eye-span." We had not a clue as to how "developmental" such instruction was going to turn out to be, but we did learn in our one-to-one counseling that ways of reading were often integrally embedded in assumptions about purpose, authority, and morals. Students who read word by word often told us that our recommendation to "look ahead" was commending to them a form of "cheating" in which they refused to participate. We found that these students had invested their courage in "concentrating" (that is, *not thinking* of other things) for long hours, and we could not help them to concentrate *on* thinking about what an author was saying until they could reinvest their courage in the risks of judgment.

Such findings led us to dramatize for the students in our large "reading course" the contrasting constellations of meaning, feeling, ethics, and risk that surround the more passive and more active strategies of reading. We created illustrative dramatic monologues of what it felt like to be studying in one's room and then asked the students to engage in reading exercises based on such contrasting assumptions. At the same time, we learned how necessary it was to continue daily the conventional exercises and visual aids as a "support."

Nowadays we regularly provide on the students' work sheets for each day a space for comment, and the next day we may read two or three to the class, anonymously. Recently, in about the middle of the eighteen-day program, I read this comment among others:

> Why does the instructor waste so much time *ranting*? We should be doing more exercises and films. All that ranting takes up time that could be *used.*

This provoked some laughter and many "comments" on the next day's sheets. These comments fell into four types, of which the following are representative:

Type 1. The "ranting" fellow is *right!* You're very funny *sometimes,* but when are you going to teach us to *read faster?*

Type 2. I don't think you're "ranting." I understand what you're saying, but I can't seem to *do* it, damn it.

Type 3. Hey! Rant away! I'm *getting* it! I've *got* it! Last week I did a research paper in half the time and got an A! More! More!

Type 4. Well, it isn't "ranting," but why do you go on repeating yourself? All you've been saying all along is, "think while you read," and I knew that in high school. (But it's still a good course! Courage!)

In the early 1950s, in keeping with much thinking of the time, we would have seen these comments as emanating from different "types" of students. Indeed, when we started out on the study I am summarizing in this chapter, we intended to document the experience of these different types—the "authoritarian," the "dogmatic," the "intolerant of ambiguity," and their opposites. Then, as we listened year by year, it was the students who turned us into developmentalists.

We now see comments of Types 4, 3, and 1 as follows:

- Type 4: Students commenting in this way have come to college construing the academic world in meanings characteristic of at least Position 5 in our scheme. Their capacity to sense the instructor's predicament ("Courage!") suggests that they perceive at these levels in their social worlds as well.
- Type 3: Students making such comments have just discovered (constructed?) the meanings we locate at Position 5 and beyond and have begun to use new strategies of learning and communicating appropriate to these meanings.
- Type 1: Students making such comments are construing the academic world through meanings we characterize as Position 2 or 3. Since I am offering alternatives at Position 5+, two Positions beyond their level of development, the students cannot hear me. Instead, they assimilate my behavior to their own structures by seeing it as "ranting," in which Authority is failing in its duties.

I shall return to the plight of students making comments of Type 2 in a moment. First, I wish to consider students of Types 4 and 1. Apparently, I was boring the former and had so far failed to "reach" the latter. The tone of the former is one of mild frustration, while the latter convey a sense of mounting anxiety and anger. In an early experiment in "matching and mismatching" of teaching-learning styles, Gordon Allport and Lauren Wispe gave instruction congruent and incongruent with students' preferred styles (Wispe, 1951). The experimenters assigned students judged to "want more direction" to one pair of sections and students judged to "want more permissiveness" to another pair of sections. In each of these pairs of sections, one section received its preferred style of teaching and the other received the opposite. The results in terms of students' satisfaction and frustration were as predicted. What startled the experimenters was the intensity of anxiety and hostility expressed by the students who desired precise directions and failed to receive them. In contrast, those who were disappointed of their desired freedom simply reported feeling frustrated.

If we consider "want more direction" and "want more permissiveness" in terms of our scheme, the parallel to our comment sheets is striking. Students thinking in the forms of advanced Positions can understand earlier meanings and procedures and be impatient; students thinking in earlier forms cannot understand the assumptions of advanced Positions. The fear of abandonment evident in Type 1 comments is understandable.

Toward the end of our course there are always some Type 1 comments still coming to us, ever more urgent, and we redouble our efforts to reach these students, mainly through individual counseling. This context makes these results possible: (a) Some students, encouraged to speak freely about their experience and concerns, will suddenly hit upon the very approach they missed in class and exclaim, "Oh, is that what you've been saying in class?" (b) Other students will respond to the counseling session as they did to the course; they give the impression that their emotional controls are so bound up with an internalization of the all-or-none, authority-oriented structures of Positions 2 and 3 that they cannot contemplate change without overwhelming anxiety. Whether their stylistic predispositions could allow them to act on new meanings if they could generate them cannot be determined. (c) The remaining students will make the same discoveries as the first group but not be able to make use of their discoveries. They will then report back with comments of Type 2 ("I understand you, but I can't do it").

We take it that students speaking to us through Type 2 comments have come to construe their educational worlds in ways that make the strategies we offer meaningful and desirable, especially for their approach to reading and research in expository materials characteristic of so much of higher education. Granted the academic performance they have demonstrated in their primary and secondary schooling, their measured "aptitude," and their evident emotional resilience, their sense of incapacity to "do" these strategies suggests strongly that their particular "styles" of cognition, information processing, or learning may be relatively resistant to change and of a kind that do not support the skills required by the strategies we invite them to learn.

Cognitive "Styles" Versus "Strategies." The questions with which I began this digression had to do with the stability and mutability of learning "strategies" and cognitive "styles." I have tried to indicate how this question is embedded in a fabric patterned by developmental status, emotional readiness to develop new interpretations of the world, "dynamics" and traits of personality, and the contexts of teaching and counseling. It should be clear why the researches on "strategies" and "styles" often appear contradictory. Despite the importance of all these threads to higher education, not even the terms of the question are stable; what for one writer is "style" is "strategy" for another.

Educators would be greatly aided in their efforts to make use of these vital researches if the investigators could come to some rough consensus about terms. I would propose that cognitive *style* be used to refer to the relatively stable, preferred configuration of tactics that a person tends to employ somewhat inflexibly in a wide range of environmental negotiations. The word *strategy* could then be used to refer to a configuration of tactics chosen or constructed from an array of available alternatives to address a *particular kind* of environmental negotiation. In short, a strategy would be dominant over "style."

Against this background, I can now say that cognitive styles have been demonstrated to be in many instances highly stable generalized traits often ill-fitted to the cognitive task at hand. However, I can also say that many people demonstrate (both rapid and gradual) acquisition of alternative styles, which then become available to strategies adaptable to the character of different tasks. The stability and mutability of styles are therefore both characteristics in need of explication. The apparently contradictory findings reported by Danserau (1974), for example, may reflect the interests and methods of the researchers. Such is the present state of the art. As practitioners in higher education, meanwhile, we must keep the stability of styles in mind while we also design instruction to maximize the probability that students will develop appropriate strategies.

Kolb, in this book, brilliantly summarizes the development of styles of "experiential learning," positing stages (phases) of *acquisition, specialization,* and *integration.* Acquisition is complete in adolescence. Specialization, the strengthening of one's preferred style, continues through higher education and into midlife. Integration, "the reassertion and expression of the nondominant adaptive modes or learning styles," which makes possible the exercise of what I call strategies, emerges in later life. Kolb's study at M.I.T. documenting the specialization process is paralleled by Whitla's (1977) contemporaneous study at three colleges: students with certain styles who major in subjects with structures congruent with these styles tend to be happy in their work and to become even more specialized in their styles.

These findings concern tendencies or differences statistically significant but "small" (Whitla, 1978). In order to obtain these differences, also, many measurements of "style" must be made under conditions in which the student is put under such stringent time limits that the possibility to exercise choice among procedures is virtually eliminated (Whitla, 1978). These studies, then, have documented the existence of individual differences in styles at certain levels, using large samples under limiting conditions. As educators, however, we stand to learn as much from the minority in the sample as from the majority. What would those students have to tell us who *have* developed a wider range of strategies, instead of specializing?

I suggest that further researches into cognitive and learning styles must include a consideration of the different meanings and purposes that the learners ascribe to learning in different contexts and at different times in their lives. This consideration remains primary to the whole problem of relating strategies and styles of teaching to strategies and styles of learning.

Values and Costs

From all that has been published, written but unpublished, in process of being written, and "personally communicated," I conclude that our scheme of development can be of more practical use to educators than I first supposed (Perry, 1970). Not only did I assume a substantial gap to exist between the scheme and the actual curriculum or classroom but also I felt a deep aversion to "application" in the sense of transforming a purely descriptive formulation of students' experience into a prescriptive program intended to "get" students to develop (Perry, 1974). Lee Knefelkamp took the initiative in challenging me on both these matters, and I joined in a battle that I have found edifying to lose.

Confronting the issues of values and ethics first, Knefelkamp pointed to my agreement that the values inherent in the scheme itself were indeed congruent with the commonly stated objectives of liberal education; there was a sense, then, in which progression toward these general values was inherently prescriptive. But in what sense? Surely educators cannot coerce students into intellectual and ethical development, even if it were ethical to do so. What was prescriptive was that the teaching and curriculums be optimally designed to invite, encourage, challenge, and support students in such development. Our scheme, therefore, is helpful to the extent that it contributes to the ability of planners and teachers to *communicate* with students who make meaning in different ways and to provide differential opportunities for their progress. Within the limits of institutional resources and teachers' energies, a better understanding of where different students are "coming from" can save wasted effort and maximize the effort expended. Knefelkamp has convinced me not only by this logic but by her demonstrations (see, for example, Knefelkamp, 1975).

At the same time, I am impressed by the extent of the revolution in our own thinking—a change that has been forced upon all of us who have become involved over time in what might be called *developmental phenomenology*. We seem so unconsciously immersed in the dregs of the Lockean tradition that we still suppose that there is at least some space in students' heads where a *tabula rasa* awaits the imprint of our wisdom. We observe in ourselves that there seems to be a developmental process involved in coming to understand development. We begin to feel strange and lonely.

I want to burst out to you, my reader, "Look! Do I sound crazy in saying that the *students* are the source of the meanings they will make of you? All right, so you feel that you are making meaning for them; you know your subject, they do not. But it is the meanings they make of your meanings that matter!" Obviously. Why am I shouting? After all, it is the meanings you make of my meanings that matter, and shouting will not help. It is not simply that I have forgotten the long trail of my own accommodations. Our common enemy is that Lockean heritage:

I find hope in the confluence of developmental studies. I do not mean parallelism in their "stages," which would be a dubious virtue in theories that should be complementary. I mean that whether the investigator starts from empirical observations made largely from outside (as did Loevinger with observations of sequential integrations of concerns; or Kohlberg with observations of sequential criteria in moral reasoning) or starts with empathic participation in the phenomenal experience of individuals (as we did in this study) the end products tend to converge. Weathersby, in the second chapter of this book, extends the rating cues of Loevinger's scale to reveal the patterning of individuals' construction of meaning in their lives and learning. Gilligan, in her chapter, does the same with the cues for Kohlberg's scoring, as Kegan (1977, 1979) has also done in an extraordinary reinterpretation of acute depression as a concomitant of transition. This confluence suggests that the centrality of the individual learner as a maker of meaning may be a radical notion but quite likely congruent with the facts.

I have spoken of development of meaning-making as a good thing, at least in our complex world. I have implied, too, in tracing the transitions of the scheme, that development has its costs. I want to end, therefore, with the educator's responsibility to hear and honor, by simple acknowledgment, the students' losses.

I have remarked elsewhere (Perry, 1978) on the importance we have come to ascribe to a student's "allowing for grief" in the process of growth, especially in the rapid movement from the limitless potentials of youth to the particular realities of adulthood. Each of the upheavals of cognitive growth threatens the balance between vitality and depression, hope and despair. It may be a great joy to discover a new and more complex way of thinking and seeing; but yesterday one thought in simpler ways, and hope and aspiration were embedded in those ways. Now that those ways are to be left behind, must hope be abandoned too?

It appears that it takes a little time for the guts to catch up with such leaps of the mind. The untangling of hope from innocence, for example, when innocence is "lost," may require more than a few moments in which to move from despair through sadness to a wry nostalgia. Like all mourning, it is less costly when "known" by another. When a sense of loss is accorded the honor of acknowledgment, movement is more rapid and the risk of getting stuck in apathy, alienation, or depression is reduced. One thing seemed clear: Students who have just taken a major step will be unlikely to take another until they have come to terms with the losses attendant on the first.

"Hearing" a student at such a moment may be best expressed simply by a nod or a respectful silence. We have been accustomed to these suspended moments in our counseling hours. But now we ask ourselves more broadly, "What is the responsibility of teachers, including ourselves, as we help our students to transcend their simpler ways of knowing?" Jesse Taft, a follower of Otto Rank, once wrote that "the therapist becomes the repository of the outworn self" (Taft, 1933). Perhaps the metaphor is too passive. Perhaps, in moments of major growth, the instructor can serve as a bridge linking the old self with the new: "He knew me when, and he knows me now."

There may be no subject matter in which teachers are wholly immune to the responsibilities of such moments. I was told of an extreme instance by a professor of mathematics who remarked to me after a meeting that he now understood the breakdown of a freshman to whom he insisted that there were indeed three equally good ways of finding the answer to a given problem. "I didn't even tell him there were other answers— just three ways of finding *the* answer—and he went all to pieces." The story made poignant for me a moment in the conference at Ithaca: I was attending the last minutes of a workshop "On Relativism in the Teaching of Mathematics," and on the board was an algebraic proof such as a student might find in an advanced junior class in high school. Under it was another proof, as offered in senior year in calculus, which revealed the false assumptions of the first. Discussion was lively and highly philosophical. The moderator was smiling and saying over and over, "Yes, ladies and gentlemen, but you haven't told me what *happened* to that *first* proof? It was a certainty, wasn't it? I want to know: where did it *go*?" The participants were sobered by their evident reluctance to address this question and finally remarked that it was after all, the same question Gödel has invited us to ask ourselves of all proofs. They wondered, since the question is painfully devoid of an answer, if we are refusing to hear the students ask it.

It is now clear to me that a teacher's confirmatory offering of community is necessary even in the highest reaches of development. Here, where both formal logic and even "reflective probabilistic judgment" fail to support the tensions of life's paradoxes, the students' development is at risk. Even if students do achieve a sense of irony, it may drift into a bitter alienation. Many institutions of higher learning have succeeded, sometimes through careful planning, sometimes through the sheer accident of their internal diversity, in providing for students' growth beyond dualistic thought into the discovery of disciplined contextual relativism. Many would hope to encourage in their students the values of Commitment, and to provide in their faculties the requisite models. To meet this promise, we must all learn how to validate for our students a dialectical mode of thought, which at first seems "irrational," and then to assist them in honoring its limits. To do this, we need to teach dialectically—that is, to introduce our students, as our greatest teachers have introduced us, not only to the orderly certainties of our subject matter but to its unresolved dilemmas. This is an art that requires timing, learned only by paying close attention to students' ways of making meaning.

I have before me the senior thesis of a student who survived an accident in his freshman year that led to the medical prediction that he could never read again or return to academic work. His defiance of the prediction, in the midst of his acceptance of it, led five years later to this honors thesis on the subject of Hope. His preface ends:

> I would define hope as a human self-transcending movement. Hope rests on a foundation of antithesis, particularly the dialectic of possibility and limitation. It serves a centering function within this dialectic; the hoping person at once acknowledges finitude and limitation, and with and within these limitations affirms the power to move forward in time and to create. With the affirmation of this power, hope is not just a mode of being in the world, but brings a world into being. The dialectical character of hope creates the possibility that, in acknowledging limitation and affirming creative possibility, the centered self may transcend its elements [Holmes, 1974].

References

Adams, H. B. *The Education of Henry Adams.* New York: Modern Library, 1931. (Originally published 1907.)

Allport, G. W. *Becoming.* New Haven, Conn.: Yale University Press, 1955.

Baron, J. "Some Theories of College Instruction." *Higher Education,* 1975, *4,* 149-172.

Basseches, M. "Beyond Closed-System Problem-Solving: A Study of Meta-Systematic Aspects of Mature Thought." Unpublished doctoral dissertation, Harvard University, 1978.

Blake, L. "A Measure of Developmental Change: A Cross-Sectional Study." Paper presented at 84th annual meeting of the American Psychological Association, Washington, D.C., September 1976.

Boyd, D. "Some Thoughts on a Comparison of Perry and Kohlberg." Unpublished manuscript, Harvard University, 1972.

Broughton, J. M. "The Development of Natural Epistemology in Adolescence and Early Childhood." Unpublished doctoral dissertation, Harvard University, 1975.

Buerk, D. "Women and Math Anxiety/Avoidance: A Developmental Approach." Doctoral dissertation proposal, State University of New York at Buffalo, 1979.

Camus, A. *The Myth of Sisyphus.* New York: Knopf, 1955.

Chandler, M. J. "Relativism and the Problem of Epistemological Loneliness." *Human Development,* 1975, *18,* 171-180.

Chickering, A. W. "Developmental Change as a Major Outcome." In M. T. Keeton and Associates, *Experiential Learning: Rationale, Characteristics, and Assessment.* San Francisco: Jossey-Bass, 1976.

Chickering, A. W. "A Conceptual Framework for College Development." Unpublished manuscript, Empire State College.

Chickering, A. W. "The Developmental and Educational Needs of Adults." Unpublished manuscript, Empire State College.

Clement, L., and others. "Paraprofessionals—Development of Our Systems and Our Human Resources—a Model for Training." Paper presented at the Maryland Student Affairs Conference, University of Maryland, March 1977.

Clinchy, B., Lief, J., and Young, P. "Epistemological and Moral Development in Girls from a Traditional and a Progressive High School." *Journal of Educational Psychology,* 1977, *69* (4), 337-343.

Clinchy, B., and Zimmerman, C. "Cognitive Development in College." Unpublished paper, Wellesley College, June 1975.

Connell, C. W. "Attitude and Development as Factors in the Learning of History: The Work of William Perry." Paper presented to the annual meeting of the American Historical Association, San Francisco, 1978.

Copes, J. "Forms and Patterns: A Book Review." *The Herald.* Geneva, New York: Hobart and William Smith Colleges, 1979.

Copes, L. "Teaching Models for College Mathematics." Unpublished doctoral dissertation, Syracuse University, 1974.

Copes, L. "Mathematics Education—or Vice Versa?" Paper presented at meeting of Seaway Section, Mathematical Association of America, 1976a.

Copes, L. "Musings on Growing." Unpublished manuscript presented to the Ithaca College faculty as an invitation to the Ithaca Perry Conference, 1976b.

Copes, L. "Mathematics and the Perry Development Scheme." Paper presented at 3rd International Conference on Educational Mathematics, 1978.

Copes, L. "College Teaching, Mathematics, and the Perry Development Scheme." Unpublished paper, Institute for Studies in Educational Mathematics, St. Paul, Minn., 1980.

Copes, L. "The Perry Development Scheme and the Teaching of Mathematics." In D. Tall (Ed.), *Proceedings of the Third International Conference for Psychology in Mathematics Education.* Warwick, England: University of Warwick, in press.

Cornfeld, J., and Knefelkamp, L. "Application of Student Development Theory to Graduate Education Sequence. The Developmental Instruction Design of a Year-Long Counselor Education Curriculum." In *Integrating Student Development Services and Professional Educations. The Maryland Approach.* A Commission XII sponsored presentation at the American College Personnel Association National Convention, Denver, 1977.

Danserau, D. *Learning Strategies: A Review and Synthesis of the Current Literature.* US AFHRL Technical Report 74-70, December 1974.

Entwistle, N., and Hounsell, D. "How Students Learn: Implications for Teaching in Higher Education." In N. Entwistle and D. Hounsell (Eds.), *How Students Learn.* Lancaster, England: Institute for Research and Development in Post-Compulsory Education, University of Lancaster, 1975.

Fowler, J. W. "Mapping Faith's Structures: A Developmental Overview." In J. W. Fowler, S. Keen, and J. Berryman (Eds.), *Life-Maps: The Human Journey of Faith.* Waco, Tex.: Word Books, 1978.

Froberg, B., and Parker, C. A. "Progress Report on the Developmental Instruction Project." Minneapolis: College of Agriculture, University of Minnesota, 1976.

Gilligan, C. "In a Different Voice: Women's Conceptions of Self and of Morality." *Harvard Education Review,* 1977, *47,* 481-517.

Gilligan, C., and Murphy, J. M. "The Philosopher and the 'Dilemma of Fact': Evidence for Continuing Development from Adolescence to Adulthood." In D. Kuhn (Ed.), *New Directions for Child Development: Intellectual Development Beyond Childhood,* no. 5. San Francisco: Jossey-Bass, 1979.

Goldberger, N. "Developmental Assumptions Underlying Models of General Education." Paper presented at Conference on General Education, William Patterson College, 1979a.

Goldberger, N. "Meeting the Developmental Needs of the Early College Student: The Simon's Rock Experience." Unpublished manuscript, Simon's Rock Early College, 1979b.

Goldberger, N., Marwine, A., and Paskus, J. "The Relationship Between Intellectual Stage and the Behavior of College Freshmen in the Classroom." Unpublished manuscript, Simon's Rock Early College, 1978.

Goldsmith, S. "Application of the Perry Schema in a College Course on Human Identity." *Pupil Personnel Services Journal,* Minnesota Department of Education, 1977, *6* (1), 185-196.

Hartley, A. "Contexts for Learning." *Bulletin* of the Office of Educational Development, University of Wisconsin at Green Bay, September 1974.

Hartley, A. "Contexts for Academic Achievement." *Bulletin* of the Office of Educational Development, University of Wisconsin at Green Bay, August 1973.

Heffernan, J. "Identity Formation, Identity Orientations, and Sex Differences Related to College Environment Features: A Comparative Study of Conventional and Innovative Undergraduate Programs." Unpublished doctoral dissertation, University of Michigan, 1971.

Heffernan, J. "An Analytical Framework for Planning and Research in Higher Education." *Liberal Education,* 1975, *61,* 493-503.

Heffernan, J., and Griffith, J. "Implications of a Dialectical Model for Extending the Perry Scheme of Development." Paper presented at the Association for the Study of Higher Education, Syracuse University, 1979.

Holden, J. C. "Structures of Ego Development in the College Student: An Interdisciplinary Approach." Unpublished doctoral dissertation, University of Wisconsin at Madison, 1978.

Holmes, L. "The Nature of Hope." Senior honors thesis, Harvard College, 1974.

Hursh, B. A., and Barzak, L. "Toward Cognitive Development Through Field Studies." *Journal of Higher Education,* 1979, *50,* 63-78.

Johnson, J. "Freshman Responses to Autonomous Learning: A Study of Intrinsic Versus Extrinsic Dispositions to Learn." Unpublished doctoral dissertation, University of Minnesota, 1975.

Kagan, J., and Kogan, N. "Individual Variation in Cognitive Processes." In P. H. Mussen (Ed.), *Carmichael's Manual of Child Psychology.* Vol. 1. New York: Wiley, 1970.

Kaul, T. J. "Students' Schemes and Harvard Dreams." *Contemporary Psychology,* 1971, *16,* 657-658.

Kegan, R. G. "Ego and Truth: Personality and the Piaget Paradigm." Unpublished doctoral dissertation, Harvard University, 1977.

Kegan, R. G. "The Evolving Self: A Process Conception for Ego Psychology." *The Counseling Psychologist,* 1979, *8* (2), 5-34.

Keniston, K. *The Uncommitted.* New York: Harcourt Brace Jovanovich, 1960.

King, P. M. "Perry's Scheme of Intellectual and Ethical Development: A Look at Assessment." Unpublished manuscript, University of Minnesota, 1975.

King, P. M. "The Study of Commitment: Pursuing an Ambiguous Construct." Paper presented at 84th annual meeting of the American Psychological Association, Washington, D.C., September 1976.

King, P. M. "The Development of Reflective Judgment and Formal Operational Thinking in Adolescents and Young Adults." Unpublished doctoral dissertation, University of Minnesota, 1977a.

King, P. M. "Taking a Stand with Yourself: Making Commitments in a Relativistic World." Unpublished manuscript, University of Minnesota, 1977b.

King, P. M. "William Perry's Theory of Intellectual and Ethical Development." In L. Knefelkamp, C. Widick, and C. A. Parker (Eds.), *New Directions for Student Services: Applying New Developmental Findings,* no. 4. San Francisco: Jossey-Bass, 1978.

King, P. M., and Parker, C. A. "Assessing Intellectual Development in the College Years." A report from the Instructional Improvement Project, University of Minnesota, 1978.

Kitchener, K. S. "Intellect and Identity: Measuring Parallel Processes in the Perry Scheme." Unpublished manuscript, University of Minnesota, 1976a.

Kitchener, K. S. "The Perry Scheme: A Review and Critique." Paper presented at 84th annual meeting of the American Psychological Association, Washington, D.C., 1976b.

Kitchener, K. S. "Intellectual Development in Late Adolescents and Young Adults: Reflective Judgment and Verbal Reasoning." Unpublished doctoral dissertation, University of Minnesota, 1977.

Kitchener, K. S. "Reflective Judgment: Concepts in Justification and Their Relationship to Age and Education." Unpublished manuscript, University of Minnesota, 1979.

Kitchener, K. S., and King, P. M. "Intellectual Development Beyond Adolescence: Reflective Judgment, Formal Operations, and Verbal Reasoning." Unpublished manuscript, University of Minnesota, 1978.

Knefelkamp, L. L. "Developmental Instruction: Fostering Intellectual and Personal Growth in College Students." Unpublished doctoral dissertation, University of Minnesota, 1974.

Knefelkamp, L. L. "Developmental Instruction: Fostering Intellectual and Personal Growth of College Students." Paper presented at 83rd annual meeting of the American Psychological Association, Chicago, August 1975.

Knefelkamp, L. L. "Training Manual for Perry Raters and Rater Training Cue Sheets." Unpublished mimeograph, University of Maryland, 1978.

Knefelkamp, L. L., and Cornfeld, J. L. "Counselor Education Basic Survey." Unpublished mimeograph, University of Maryland, 1975.

Knefelkamp, L. L., and Cornfeld, J. L. "Application of Student Development Theory to Graduate Education: The Developmental Instruction Design of a Year-Long Counselor Education Curriculum." Paper presented at the American College Personnel Association National Convention, Denver, 1977.

Knefelkamp, L. L., and Cornfeld, J. L. "The Developmental Issues of Graduate Students: A Model of Assessment and a Model of Response." Paper presented at the American Personnel and Guidance Association National Convention, Washington, D.C., 1978.

Knefelkamp, L. L., and Cornfeld, J. L. "Combining Student Stages and Style in the Design of Learning Environments: Using Holland Typologies and Perry Stages." Paper presented to the American College Personnel Association, Los Angeles, March 1979.

Knefelkamp, L. L., and Slepitza, R. "A Cognitive-Developmental Model of Career Development: An Adaptation of the Perry Scheme." *The Counseling Psychologist,* 1976, *6* (3), 53-58. Reprinted in C. Parker (Ed.), *Encouraging Development in College Students.* Minneapolis: University of Minnesota Press, 1978a.

Knefelkamp, L. L., and Slepitza, R. A. Comments made in Perry Rater Training Seminar, University of Maryland, 1978b.

Knefelkamp, L. L., Widick, C., and Parker, C. A. (Eds.). *New Directions for Student Services: Applying New Developmental Findings,* no. 4. San Francisco: Jossey-Bass, 1978.

Knefelkamp, L. L., Widick, C., and Stroad, B. "Cognitive-Developmental Theory: A Guide to Counseling Women." *The Counseling Psychologist,* 1976, *6* (2), 15-19.

Kohlberg, L. "The Concepts of Developmental Psychology as the Central Guide to Education: Examples from Cognitive, Moral, and Psychological Education." In M. C. Reynolds (Ed.), *Proceedings of the Conference on Psychology and the Process of Schooling in the Next Decade: Alternative Conceptions.* Washington, D.C., 1975.

Kohlberg, L., and Kramer, R. "Continuities and Discontinuities in Childhood and Adult Moral Development." *Human Development,* 1969, *12,* 93-120.

Kovacs, I. D. "Development of Cognitive, Coping, and Relational Abilities Through the Study of Participation in the University." Paper presented at 3rd International Conference on Improving University Teaching, Newcastle-on-Tyne, England, 1977.

Kroll, M., and Associates. *Career Development: Growth and Crisis.* New York: Wiley, 1970.

Kurfiss, J. "A Neo-Piagetian Analysis of Erikson's 'Identity' Formulation of Late Adolescent Development." In S. Modgil and C. Modgil (Eds.), *Piagetian Research: Compilation and Commentary.* New York: Humanities Press, 1974.

Kurfiss, J. "Late Adolescent Development: A Structural Epistemological Perspective." Unpublished doctoral dissertation, University of Washington, 1975.

Kurfiss, J. "What Makes Students Grow? A Survey and Theoretical Integration of Literature on College Student Development." Unpublished manuscript, Eastern Oregon State College, 1976.

Kurfiss, J. "Sequentiality and Structure in a Cognitive Model of College Student Development." *Developmental Psychology,* 1977, *13,* 565-571.

Lawson, J. M. "Review of the Literature on Perry Research." Unpublished manuscript, University of Minnesota, 1978.

Letteri, C. A. *Research Report of the Center for Cognitive Studies.* University of Vermont, 1978.

Mason, K. E. "Effects of Developmental Instruction on the Development of Cognitive Complexity, Locus of Control, and Empathy in Beginning Counseling Graduate Students." Unpublished master's thesis, University of Maryland, 1978.

Messick, S., and Associates. *Individuality in Learning: Implications of Cognitive Styles and Creativity for Human Development.* San Francisco: Jossey-Bass, 1976.

Meyer, P. "Intellectual Development: Analysis of Religious Content." *The Counseling Psychologist,* 1977, *6* (4), 47-50.

Meyerson, L. "Conception of Knowledge in Mathematics: Interaction with and Applications to a Teaching Methods Course." Unpublished doctoral dissertation, State University of New York at Buffalo, 1977.

Murphy, J. M. "Intellectual and Moral Development from Adolescence to Adulthood." Unpublished manuscript, Harvard University, 1979a.

Murphy, J. M. "Moral Judgment Coding Based on Perry's Scheme." Unpublished manuscript, Harvard University, 1979b.

Murphy, J. M., and Gilligan, C. "Moral Development in Late Adolescence and Adulthood: A Critique and Reconstruction of Kohlberg's Theory." *Human Development,* in press.

Nowakowski, L., and Laughney, J. "Health Education: Theory of Curriculum Design—Developmental Implementation." Unpublished manuscript, School of Nursing, Georgetown University, 1978.

Orr, C. J. "Communication, Relativism, and Student Development." *Communications Education,* 1978, *27* (2), 80-98.

Parker, C. A. (Ed.). *Encouraging Development in College Students.* Minneapolis: University of Minnesota Press, 1978a.

Parker, C. A. "Individualized Approach to Improving Instruction." *National Association of Colleges and Teachers of Agriculture Journal,* 1978b, *22,* 14-28.

Parker, C. A. "Teaching Students to Cope with Complexity and Uncertainty." Unpublished manuscript, University of Minnesota, 1979.

Parker, C. A., and Lawson, J. M. "From Theory to Practice to Theory: Consulting with College Faculty." *Personnel and Guidance Journal,* 1978, *56,* 424-427.

Perry, W. G., Jr. "Students' Use and Misuse of Reading Skills: A Report to the Faculty." *Harvard Educational Review,* 1959, *29* (3), 193-200.

Perry, W. G., Jr. "Examsmanship and the Liberal Arts: An Epistemological Inquiry." In M. Eastman and others (Eds.), *The Norton Reader.* New York: Norton, 1969.

Perry, W. G., Jr. *Forms of Intellectual and Ethical Development in the College Years: A Scheme.* New York: Holt, Rinehart and Winston, 1970.

Perry, W. G., Jr. "Counseling." In *Annual Report of the Bureau of Study Counsel, Harvard University, 1973-74.* Cambridge, Mass.: Harvard University Press, 1974.

Perry, W. G., Jr. "On Advising and Counseling." In *Annual Report of the Bureau of Study Counsel, Harvard University, 1974-75.* Cambridge, Mass.: Harvard University Press, 1975.

Perry, W. G., Jr. "A Study of Learning." In *Annual Report of the Bureau of Study Counsel, Harvard University, 1975-76.* Cambridge, Mass.: Harvard University Press, 1976.

Perry, W. G., Jr. "Comments, Appreciative and Cautionary." *The Counseling Psychologist,* 1977a, *6* (4), 51-52.

Perry, W. G., Jr. "Intellectual and Ethical Forms of Development." In *Pupil Personnel Services Journal,* Minnesota Department of Education, 1977b, *6* (1), 61-68.

Perry, W. G., Jr. "Sharing in the Costs of Growth, and Comments on Chapters 2, 3, 5, and 6." In C. A. Parker (Ed.), *Encouraging Development in College Students.* Minneapolis: University of Minnesota, 1978.

Perry, W. G., Jr., and Whitlock, C. P. "Of Study and the Man." In *Harvard Alumni Bulletin,* 1958.

Perry, W. G., Jr., and others. *Patterns of Development in Thought and Values of Students in a Liberal Arts College: A Validation of a Scheme.* United States Department of Health, Education, and Welfare, Office of Education, Bureau of Research, Final Report, Project No. 5-0825, Contract No. SAE-8973, April 1968.

Polanyi, M. *Personal Knowledge: Towards a Post-Critical Philosophy.* Chicago: University of Chicago Press, 1958.

Riegel, K. F. "Dialectic Operations: The Final Period of Cognitive Development." *Human Development,* 1973, *16,* 346-370.

Rust, V. "Review of *Forms of Intellectual and Ethical Development in the College Years: A Scheme,* by William G. Perry, Jr." *Teachers College Record,* December 1970, *72,* 305-307.

Salyard, A. "The Educated American: A Study of Intellectual Development in Adulthood." Doctoral dissertation in progress, University of California at Los Angeles.

Santostefano, S. "Cognitive Controls v. Cognitive Styles: Diagnosing and Treating Cognitive Disabilities in Children." *Seminars in Psychiatry,* 1969, *1,* 291-317.

Slepitza, R. A., and Knefelkamp, L. L. "Perry's Scheme of Intellectual Development: An Adaptation to Career Counseling." Paper presented at 83rd annual meeting of the American Psychological Association, Chicago, August 1975.

Slepitza, R. A. "The Validation of Stage Model for Career Counseling." Unpublished master's thesis, University of Maryland, 1976.

Slepitza, R. A., and Knefelkamp, L. L. "A Cognitive Developmental Model of Career Development: An Adaptation of the Perry Scheme." *The Counseling Psychologist,* 1976, *6* (3), 53-58.

Solt, L. F. "Comments about Connell and Rosenzweig Papers Concerning Perry and Kohlberg Schemes, Respectively." Presented to annual meeting of the American Historical Association, San Francisco, 1978.

Sorum, J., and Knefelkamp, L. L. "Developmental Instruction in the Liberal Arts: A Dialogue." Presentation at the Bureau of Study Counsel, Harvard University, 1976.

Stephenson, B. W., and Hunt, C. "Intellectual and Ethical Development: A Dualistic Curriculum Intervention for College Students." *The Counseling Psychologist,* 1977, *6* (4), 39-42.

Strange, C. C. "Intellectual Development, a Motive for Education and Learning During the College Years: A Comparison of Adult and Traditional-Age Students." Unpublished doctoral dissertation, University of Iowa, 1978.

Syracuse Rating Group. "Rater's Manual: Guide to Assessing 'Position.' " (Working draft.) Syracuse University, 1978.

Taft, J. *The Dynamics of Therapy in a Controlled Relationship.* New York: Macmillan, 1933.

Touchton, J. G. "Developmental Programming at a University Career Center—the Maryland Experience." A Commission XII sponsored presentation at the American College Personnel Association National Convention, 1977.

Touchton, J. G., and others. "Career Planning and Decision Making: A Developmental

Approach to the Classroom." In C. A. Parker (Ed.), *Encouraging Development in College Students.* Minneapolis: University of Minnesota, 1978.

Trabin, T., and Parker, C. A. "Evaluation Report for the Instructional Development Consultation Project." Unpublished manuscript, University of Minnesota, 1978.

Vaillant, G. E. *Adaptation to Life.* Boston: Little, Brown, 1977.

Valiga, T. M. "The Cognitive Development and Views about Nursing as a Profession of Baccalaureate Nursing Students." Doctoral dissertation proposal, Columbia University, 1979.

Welfel, E. R. "The Development of Reflective Judgment: Its Relationship to Year in College, Major Field, Academic Performance, and Satisfaction with Major among College Students." Unpublished doctoral dissertation, University of Minnesota, 1979.

Wertheimer, L. "A New Model and Measure for Career Counseling: Incorporating Both Content and Processing Aspects of Career Concerns." Unpublished master's thesis, University of Maryland, 1976.

Whitla, D. K. *Value Added: Measuring the Outcome of Undergraduate Education.* Cambridge, Mass.: Office of Instructional Research and Evaluation, Harvard University, 1977.

Whitla, D. K. Personal communication, 1978.

Widick, C. "An Evaluation of Developmental Instruction in a University Setting." Unpublished doctoral dissertation, University of Minnesota, 1975.

Widick, C. "The Perry Scheme: A Foundation for Developmental Practice." *The Counseling Psychologist,* 1977, *6* (4), 35-38.

Widick, C., Knefelkamp, L. L., and Parker, C. "The Counselor as a Developmental Instructor." *Journal of Counselor Education and Supervision,* 1975, *14,* 286-296.

Widick, C., and Simpson, D. "Developmental Concepts in College Instruction." In C. A. Parker (Ed.), *Encouraging Development in College Students.* Minneapolis: University of Minnesota, 1978.

Wispe, L. G. "Evaluating Section Teaching Methods in the Introductory Course." *Journal of Educational Research,* 1951, *45,* 161-186.

Witkin, H. A., Goodenough, D. R., and Karp, S. A. "Stability of Cognitive Style from Childhood to Young Adulthood." *Journal of Personality and Social Psychology,* 1967, *7* (3), 291-300.

Women's Ways of Knowing

ON GAINING A VOICE

NANCY RULE GOLDBERGER
BLYTHE McVICKER CLINCHY
MARY FIELD BELENKY
JILL MATTUCK TARULE

Nancy Rule Goldberger is currently a Visiting Scholar at the Research Center for Mental Health at New York University. She coauthored the book *Women's Ways of Knowing: The Development of Self, Voice, and Mind,* with Belenky, Clinchy, and Tarule (Basic Books, 1986). She has been a Research Associate and Psychotherapist at the Austen Riggs Center in Stockbridge, MA. Her interest in developmental epistemology began during her years as Director of Research on Adolescent Development at Simon's Rock of Bard College, an innovative B.A. program for high school-age students.

Blythe McVicker Clinchy is Professor of Psychology at Wellesley College. Her research concerns the development of "natural epistemologies"— conceptions of knowledge, truth, and value—in children and adults, and the implications of epistemological development for education from the preschool through college years.

Mary Field Belenky is an Associate Professor of Psychology at the University of Vermont, where she directs Listening Partners, a program designed to promote the epistemological development of isolated rural women who are raising children alone. She conducted a study of abortion decisions with Carol Gilligan and wrote a doctoral dissertation on the role of conflict in development.

Jill Mattuck Tarule is an Associate Professor at the Lesley College Graduate School and is Director of the Weekend Learning Community. She has devoted her career to faculty development and educational programs designed to sponsor the development of adult students. She is a former dean of the graduate program at Goddard College.

We do not think of the average person as preoccupied with such difficult and profound questions as, "What is truth?" "What is authority?" "What counts for me as evidence?" "How do I know what I know?" Yet, to ask ourselves these questions and to reflect on our answers is more than an intellectual exercise, for our basic assumptions about the nature of truth and the origins of knowledge shape the way we see the world and ourselves as participants in it. In this chapter we describe five different perspectives from which women view reality and draw conclusions about truth, knowledge, and authority. Our description is based on extensive interviews with rural and urban American women of different ages, class and ethnic backgrounds, and educational histories. We examine how women's self-concepts and ways of knowing are intertwined. We describe how women struggle to gain a voice and claim the power of their own minds.[1]

In the course of our prior work on student development (Belenky, Tarule, & Landa, 1979; Clinchy, Lief, & Young, 1977; Clinchy & Zimmerman, 1975, 1982, 1985a, 1985b; Goldberger, 1978, 1981, 1985; Tarule & Weathersby, 1979), we became concerned about why women students spoke so frequently of problems and gaps in their learning and so often expressed doubts about their intellectual competence. We observed that women often felt alienated in academic settings and experienced formal education as peripheral or irrelevant to their central interests and development. Although men, particularly members of minority groups, may also find the educational process alienating, anecdotal reports as well as research on sex differences point to special factors in the alienation of women. Girls and women tend to have more difficulty than boys and men in asserting their authority or considering themselves as authorities (Clance & Imes, 1978; Clinchy & Zimmerman, 1982; Cross, 1968; Maccoby & Jacklin, 1974; Piliavin, 1976; West & Zimmerman, 1983), in expressing themselves in public so that others will listen (Aries, 1976; Eakins & Eakins, 1976; Piliavin, 1976; Sadker & Sadker, 1982, 1985; Swacker, 1976; Thorne, 1979), in gaining respect of others for their minds and their ideas (Hagen & Kahn, 1975; Hall & Sandler, 1982; Serbin, O'Leary, Kent, & Tonick, 1973) and in fully utilizing their capabilities and training in the world of work (Gallese, 1985; Kanter, 1977; Ruddick & Daniels, 1977; Sassen, 1980; Treichler & Kramarae, 1983).

In private and professional life, as well as in the classroom, women often feel unheard even when they believe that they have something important to say. Most women can recall incidents in which they or their female friends were discouraged from pursuing some line of intellectual work on the grounds that it was unwomanly or incompatible with female capabilities. Many female students and working women are painfully aware that men succeed better than they in getting and holding the attention of others for their ideas and opinions. All women, like it or not, grow up having to deal with historically and culturally engrained definitions of femininity and womanhood—one common theme being that women, like children, should be seen, not heard.

We believe that education, as it is traditionally defined and practiced, does not adequately serve the needs of women students and is unresponsive to women's doubts about their competence and worth. Most of our major educational institutions were originally founded by men for the education of men. Even girls' schools and women's colleges have been modeled after male institutions to give women an education "equivalent" to men's (Horowitz, 1984). In spite of the increase in the number of women students in higher education and professional schools, faculties, usually predominantly male, have argued against a special focus on women students and resisted open debate on whether women's educational needs are different from men's. Even when the content of coursework includes issues of concern to women, strategies of teaching and methods of evaluation are rarely examined by faculty to see if they are compatible with women's preferred styles of learning. Usually faculty assume that pedagogical techniques developed by and for men are suitable for women.

Conceptions of knowledge and truth that are accepted and articulated today have been shaped throughout history by the male-dominated majority culture. Up until recently women have played a relatively minor role as theorists in philosophy, the sciences, and social sciences. Indeed, recent feminist writers have convincingly argued that there is a masculine bias at the very heart of most academic disciplines, methodologies, and theories (Bernard, 1973; Gilligan, 1979, 1982; Harding & Hintikka, 1983; Jansen-Jurreit, 1980; Keller, 1978, 1985; Langland & Grove, 1981; Sherman & Beck, 1979). Yet, our accepted concepts of truth, knowledge, and the nature of proof have been left unexamined by most social scientists and educators and have had consequences for how we all, male and female alike, learn, establish criteria and methods for unearthing "truth," and evaluate those who claim to know. It is likely that the commonly accepted stereotype of women's thinking as emotional, intuitive, and personalized has contributed to the devaluation of women's minds and contributions, particularly in Western, technologically oriented cultures that value rationalism and objectivity (Sampson, 1978). It is generally assumed that intuitive knowledge is more primitive, therefore less valuable, than so-called objective modes of knowing. In general, both men and women are taught to value what is assumed to be the objective "male mind" and to devalue "female intuition."

Even after the onset of the women's movement, research studies and critical essays on gender and intelligence have tended to focus more on the demonstration of women's intellectual comparability to men and have minimized gender differences. By and large, these studies have shown that women are the equals of men in intellectual aptitude and academic performance (for reviews of this literature, see Maccoby & Jacklin, 1974; Rosenberg, 1982). However, relatively little attention has been given to modes of learning, knowing, and valuing that may be especially common among women. As Gilligan has pointed out (1979), women have been missing even as research subjects at the formative stages of our psychological theories. If and when scientists turn to the study of women, they typically look for ways in which women conform to or diverge from patterns found in the study of men. Thus psychological theory has established men's experience and competence as a baseline against which both men's and women's development is judged, often to the detriment or misreading of women. From past research, we have learned a great deal about the development of autonomy and independence, abstract critical thought, and the unfolding of a morality of rights and justice in both men and women. We have learned less about the development of attributes typically associated with the female: interdependence, intimacy, nurturance, and contextual thought (Bakan, 1966; Chodorow, 1978; Gilligan, 1979, 1982; McMillan, 1982).

When the woman's voice is included in the study of human development, women's lives and qualities are revealed and the maps that chart the life cycle can be redrawn. Once these qualities are observed and acknowledged, we are more likely to observe their unfolding in the lives of men as well. The power of the woman's voice in expanding our conceptions of epistemology and development is amply illustrated in Gilligan's (1982) work, which influenced our own thinking. By listening to girls and women resolve serious moral dilemmas in their lives, Gilligan has traced the development of a morality organized around notions of responsibility and care. This conception of morality contrasts sharply with the morality of rights described by Piaget (1965) and Kohlberg (1984), which is based on the study of the evolution of moral reasoning in boys and men. In recent work, Gilligan and Lyons (Lyons, 1983) have extended their study of gender-related differences in moral perspectives to the area of identity development. They have shown that a responsibility orientation tends to be more central to those whose conceptions of self are rooted in a sense of connection and a caring concern for others whereas a rights orientation is more common to those who experience relationships in terms of objective fairness between separate individuals. Lyons found that many more women than men define themselves in terms of their connected relationships to others, a point that has also been made by Chodorow (1978) and Miller (1976).

In addition to Gilligan's work, the work of Perry (1970, 1981) on developmental epistemology influenced our thinking. Based on interviews gathered each spring from male students as they moved through their undergraduate years at Harvard, Perry describes how students' conceptions of the nature and origins of knowledge evolve and how their understanding of themselves as knowers changes over time. Perry depicts a passage through a sequence of epistemological perspectives that he calls "positions." It is through these coherent interpretive frameworks that students give meaning to their educational experience. Perry traces a progression from an initial position, which he calls *basic dualism*— where the student views the world in polarities of right/wrong, black/white, we/they, and good/bad—through a position called *multiplicity*—in which the student perceives multiple perspectives on truth— to a position at which the *relativism* of all knowledge is recognized. Perry does not claim that his positions represent an invariant developmental sequence or stages; however, he does believe that each position "both includes and transcends the earlier ones" (1981, p. 78).

The Perry scheme stimulated our interest in modes of knowing and provided us with our first images of the paths women might take as they develop an understanding of their intellectual potential, as well as providing a description of the routes most often taken by men. Our work uncovers themes, epistemological perspectives, and catalysts for development that are prominent among women, but sketchy or missing in Perry's version of male development.

In summary, two major concerns led us to our current research on women's epistemology: (1) women appear to have difficulties in assuming authority and valuing their own minds, and (2) women's modes of thought and experience as knowers have been inadequately investigated. We believe that, until there is a better understanding of how women think and experience themselves as developing beings, families, educators, employers, and others who live and work with women will continue to be ill-informed about what women know and need to know.

THE ANALYSIS OF THE WOMEN'S INTERVIEWS

Our data consist of extensive interviews with 135 women of varied class and ethnic backgrounds drawn from three private liberal arts colleges, an inner-city community college, an urban public high school, a B.A. program for adults, and three rural human service agencies. The women ranged in age from 16 to 65; some were single or divorced, others married; many had borne and raised children.

Our open-ended interview was designed to investigate the respondent's structure of thought as well as her attitudes. The interview is similar in form to the Piagetian clinical interview that has been adopted in the research of many cognitive-developmentalists such as Perry (1970), Kohlberg (1984; Colby et al., 1983), and Gilligan (1977, 1982). Interviews were tape-recorded and transcribed; they ran from two to five hours in length. Because of our prior research at some of the sites, we had more than one interview with 40 women in our sample, obtained anywhere from one to five years apart.

We told each participant that we were interested in her experience— and in women's experience—because it had been so often excluded as people sought to understand human development. We told her that we wanted to hear what was important about life and learning from her point of view. Each interview began with a question adapted from Perry's research—"Looking back, what stands out for you over the past few years?"—and proceeded gradually at the woman's own pace to questions concerning self-image, relationships of importance, education and learning, real-life decision making and moral dilemmas, accounts of personal change and growth, perceived catalysts for change and impediments to growth, and visions of the future. Embedded in the interview were also standard questions adapted from Kohlberg and Gilligan to elicit moral reasoning and concepts of self, and questions we developed for eliciting epistemological assumptions.

We used two approaches in analyzing the interviews. First, we separated out the section of the interview that was designed to yield information on epistemology. This section was scored by coders who were unaware of the woman's age, ethnicity, social class, institutional base, and other factors. We found that the women's thinking did not fit so neatly into Perry's positions. After much discussion about disagreements in scoring, and then about Perry's classification system itself, we decided to regroup and rename the epistemological perspectives to capture more adequately women's ways of knowing. We identified, in our group of women, five major epistemological perspectives or positions that are built upon Perry's, but also diverge from them. They are (1) Silence, (2) Received Knowledge, (3) Subjective Knowledge, (4) Procedural Knowledge, and (5) Constructed Knowledge. These will be described in the next section.

The question of why and when women shift from one mode of knowing to another, as many of our women evidently did at points in their life, is an important one, but is not answered conclusively with our data, which are, for the most part, limited to single interviews with individuals. Nevertheless, based on the repeated interviews available to us and the retrospective accounts of the women, it appears that, when context is held constant (for example, women of similar backgrounds studying at similar institutions), there is a developmental progression across the last four positions in the order we describe them. We believe, however, that it is premature to consider our five positions as stages, particularly as our data suggest that many women do not seem to follow this developmental sequence.

Our second approach to data analysis was what we called the *contextual analysis*. After coding the interviews for epistemological perspective, we reassembled the interviews and read and reread them in their entirety. Gradually we developed a number of additional coding categories (see Belenky et al., 1986, for a description), designed to capture the ways in which women construe their experience of themselves as developing beings and experience their learning environment. During this part of the interview analysis, we stayed alert to the socioeconomic realities of each woman's life. We tried to enter the woman's world so that we might get close to her experience. We asked ourselves, "What problems is this woman trying to solve? What is adaptive about the way she is trying to accommodate to the world as she sees it? What are the forces—psychological or social—that expand or limit her horizons? What are the growth metaphors that she uses to depict her experience of development?"

One growth metaphor in particular reverberated throughout the women's stories of their intellectual and ethical development. Again and again the women spoke of "gaining a voice," by which they meant gaining a sense of having something worthwhile to say and feeling the security within themselves to say it. As these women described their struggle to gain a voice, they also told us much about silence and listening, often using phrases such as "being silenced," "not being heard," "really listening," "words as weapons," "feeling deaf and dumb," "having no words," "saying what you mean," "listening to be heard," and so on in an endless variety of connotations all having to do with sense of authority and self-worth and feelings of isolation from or connection to others.

The tendency we observed for women to ground their epistemological premises in metaphors suggesting speaking and listening is at odds with the visual metaphors—such as equating knowledge with illumination, knowing with seeing, and truth with light—that scientists and philosophers most often use to express their sense of mind. Keller and Grontkowski (1983), tracing the metaphorical uses of vision in the history of Western intellectual thought, argue that such analogies have led to a favored cultural model for truth and the quest for mind. Visual metaphors, such as "the mind's eye," suggest a camera passively recording a static reality and promote the illusion that disengagement and objectification are central to the construction of knowledge. Visual metaphors encourage standing at a distance to get a proper view, removing—it is believed—subject and object from a sphere of possible intercourse.

By holding close to women's experience of voice, we have come to understand conceptions of the mind that are different from those held by individuals who find "the mind's eye" a more appropriate metaphor for expressing their experience with the intellect. For women, a sense of voice and a sense of mind appear to be intricately intertwined.

THE EPISTEMOLOGICAL POSITIONS: WOMEN'S WAYS OF KNOWING

Silence

Only a few women fell into this category at the time of the interview. None of these women was currently in school; all were minimally educated. Although the designation "silence" is not parallel to the terms we have chosen for other epistemological positions, we selected it because the absence of voice in these women is so salient. This position, though rare, at least in our sample, is an important anchoring point for our epistemological scheme, representing an extreme in denial of self and dependence on external authority for direction.

Women at this position are utterly subject to the power and aggression of others. They are dwarfed by authority. Whereas they experience themselves in the world as passive, reactive, and dependent, they see all authorities as being powerful, if not omnipotent. Blind obedience to authorities is seen as being of utmost importance for "keeping out of trouble" and ensuring one's survival. One woman, who grew up in a family with a physically and sexually abusive father, said, "I spent my life, until recently, keeping quiet and looking for a safe place to hide."

96

Although these women view authorities, generally male, as omnipotent, the power that they see authorities as holding is not communicated through words imbued with shared meanings. Authorities seldom tell you what they want you to do. They apparently expect you to know in advance. If authorities do tell you what is right, they never tell you why it is right.

The references these women make to language suggest that words are not perceived as a means of communication, but as weapons. Authorities have used words to attack them, to denigrate, or to keep them in place. Using words to protest the actions of others—that is, "speaking out"—is to court danger and retaliation. Silence is the best policy. There is little evidence that these silent women actively listen to the content of authorities' voices. It is as if command and action are undifferentiated: to hear is to obey. One woman explained why her abusive husband ruled the roost: "You know, I used to hear his words, and his words kept coming out of my mouth. He had me thinking that I didn't know anything."

These women are not preverbal. Each has developed language. Yet their experience using language has been so limited they have not explored the power that words have for expressing or developing thought. To look for meaning in the words of others or to share one's experience with words seems impossible. Trying to talk to others typically leaves them feeling "deaf and dumb." They may sense that truth is passed from one person to another in the form of words, but they feel left out of the process and incapable of understanding what others know. Seeing themselves as incapable of receiving and retaining truths from others' words, or of having ideas of their own, they are dependent on the continual presence of authorities to guide their actions if they are not to be ruled by impulse. New situations evoke paralysis and the need to cling to others, too often to violent and deprecatory men. Some women speak of clinging to other women—mothers, aunts, friends— whom they feel have lived through similar experiences and share their plight.

Learning in traditional educational settings has been traumatic for them and only reinforced their image of themselves as stupid. They claim that only demonstration helps them to learn: "Someone has to show me—not tell me—or I can't get it." Their thought is utterly dependent on concrete everyday actions and experience. Even their self-definition is embedded in concrete action. In response to our question, "How would you describe yourself to yourself?" they tended to describe themselves in terms of geographic space (if they could answer at all): "I am a person who likes to stay home. Before I got pregnant, I used to describe myself as not being home."

The world of the silent or silenced seems a static and unchangeable place to those within it. With language and thought so limited to the immediate and concrete, they have little ability to anticipate a different future. That anyone should emerge from their childhood years, into a modern society, with so little confidence in their meaning-making and meaning-sharing abilities signals the failure of the community to nurture all those entrusted to its care. To us, the situation of these women seemed to be in part the result of a cultural stereotype of femininity gone awry and at its most pernicious. These are women living in the worst imaginable social conditions as victims of physical abuse, incest, and neglect. Although the silent are by no means the only women in our sample who have experienced sexual and physical abuse, they are notable for their inability to speak out in protest.

Received Knowledge: Learning
Through Listening to Others

At this position women are also oriented to authority outside themselves but believe that close attention to the words and wisdom of others is central to the knowing process. They conceive of themselves as capable of receiving, but not of creating, knowledge. The origins of knowledge lie outside the self. Because these women are subject to the standards, directions, and authority of others, they are conventional in the sense that they adhere to the prevailing cultural stereotypes and expectations of women. They rely on the words of others for self-knowledge; thus self-concept is organized around social expectations and roles. Approximately 9% of our sample are in this category. This perspective was held by some of the youngest women in the sample; many of the older women, in particular those who had returned to school after spending years as homemakers, retrospectively describe themselves in these terms, even though their epistemological outlook may have recently shifted.

When striving to comprehend new ideas, the person at this position discounts the importance of her own experience and actions in the process of knowing. Truth is sought and found in the words of authorities. The woman does not really try to understand or evaluate new ideas. She has little notion of understanding as a process taking place over time. She collects facts, but does not develop opinions. Receiving, retaining, and returning the words of authorities are seen as synonymous with learning. Teachers are always right because ultimately "they can always look up the right answer in a book." Thus even authorities lack the capacity for constructing knowledge. Authorities must receive Truths from the words of even higher authorities.

These women (like Perry's dualists) divide the world into distinctive, polarized categories: true and false, good and evil, black and white, right and wrong. They assume that there is only one right answer to any question. All other answers and all contrary views are automatically wrong. There are no gradations of truth—no grey areas. When faced with controversy, there is for them a category of good authorities who have the right answers and bad ones who are either confused or misled (Perry, 1970, p. 68). Paradox is inconceivable as several contradictory ideas are never imagined to be simultaneously in accordance with fact. Ambiguity is intolerable. To impose oneself in the process of learning is improper: One reads the lines and follows the plot, but one should not read between the lines. People who see things between the lines are making them up. By dichotomizing the world, women at this position appear to value the objective over the subjective. Truth is thought to have a concrete, tangible existence independent of the mind.

From other studies we know that there are males who also see the world from this dichotomized, authority-oriented perspective (Knefelkamp, Widick, & Parker, 1978; Perry, 1970). However, we believe that there may be a major difference in the way men and women think about authority at this position. Men are taught that they can expect ultimately to join the authorities by virtue of their gender, whereas women do not identify with authority or anticipate being included. Even today it is still relatively rare for women to find authorities of their own sex to serve as models. Leadership in public life still rests predominantly on male shoulders. The schools that these women attend have often ignored the works and achievements of women in developing the curriculum. Their male classmates are more likely to have gotten and held the floor in the classroom. In fact, as Hall and Sandler (1982) have pointed out, the classroom may be experienced as a "chilly" place to women who sense that many teachers do not welcome their words or ideas.

The belief that there is a single right answer and that one can hear it in the words of others encourages women to become aware of and appreciative of their own listening skills. Wanting to do the right thing, but having no opinions of their own to give guidance, they listen to others and shape their behavior to fulfill the expectations and exhortations of others. They come to believe that a good woman listens and lets others do the talking. They listen closely and react to authorities and peers in their immediate community more readily than remote authority. We heard in the stories of our women a theme identified by Gilligan (1982) as characteristic of conventional female morality: that women should devote themselves to the care and empowerment of others while remaining selfless. Many of the women we interviewed had devoted a large part of their lives listening to others, stilling their voices so that others could be heard. Most felt a sense of pride in their response to the needs of others and indeed seemed quite attuned to the nuances and demands of human relationships.

Subjective Knowledge: The Inner Voice

At this position there is an emphasis on the authority within the self, on listening to the inner voice. The words, directives, and admonitions of external authorities fade and lose their power. Truth is defined as personal, private, and subjectively known or intuited.

Most women at this position have a difficult time identifying the source of their knowing, other than that it is within. It is like an inner conviction, a process that bypasses awareness. As one woman said, "I just know. I try not to think because if you trust yourself, you just know the answer." It is clear that these women do not see thought as central to the process of knowing. They do not experience themselves as constructors of truth, but as conduits through which truth emerges. The criterion for truth most often referred to is "what satisfies me" or "what feels right to me." Occasionally women distinguish between truth as feelings that come from within versus ideas that come from without. This differentiation between thinking and feeling may be a consequence of their belief that thinking is not womanly or that thought will destroy the capacity for feeling. Ideas are thus relegated to male authority and as such may or may not have relevance to one's life.

Truth, then, is not universal. Women at this position claim that each person's experience makes her see a different reality from that of any other person. What is more, truth is necessarily a private matter, known only to oneself, and should not be imposed on others. Convergence of truths is possible; however, in the case of disagreement, one's own experience and inner voice are the final arbiters. Another person's opinion may be misguided or disagreeable but there is a tolerance for differences because others "must obviously believe in their opinion." These women recognize that others may disagree with them but seem less concerned than men in persuading others to their point of view, in part because they want to avoid battles that threaten to disrupt relationships. Whereas men claim they "have a right to their opinion" (Perry, 1970), women tend to state more cautiously, "It's just my opinion."

Many women at this position distrust logic, analysis, abstraction, and even language itself, perceiving these as alien territory belonging to men. They tend to argue against and stereotype those experts and remote authorities whom society promotes as holding the keys to truth—teachers, doctors, scientists, men in general. It is as if, after turning inward, they deny strategies for knowing that they perceive as belonging to the masculine world. Some seem never to have learned to use logic and theory as tools for knowing; others imply that they have and have rejected it. Generally they have vague and untested prejudices against a mode of thought that they believe is impersonal, inhuman, or unfeminine and possibly detrimental to their capacity for feeling. They prefer to rely on direct sensory experience and on real interactions and connections with real people—and ultimately on gut response—as a way of informing themselves about the world. Some of these women express a distrust of books and the written word, calling them instruments of oppression that are too often used against women. They prefer to express themselves nonverbally or artistically so as to bypass the categorizing and labeling that language implies.

In our sample, there were a large number of women who viewed reality from the position of subjectivism—46% of all we interviewed. They appeared in every educational and agency setting included in this study and cut across class, ethnic, age, and educational boundaries. What is most remarkable in the stories of our women is that the shift in perspective from adhering to external authority to knowing from the inside is not tied to any specific age or phase. We found that it was the predominant perspective on knowing in women as young as 16 and as old as 60, many of whom claimed that they had only come to this way of knowing very recently.

Women's discovery of the power of inner knowing is experienced as a liberation, and greatly affects changing definitions of the self. Openness to change and novelty is the fulcrum around which their new identity revolves. Many women use the imagery of birth or rebirth to describe their experience of a nascent self.

We believe that a shift into subjectivism is a particularly significant reconceptualization of knowledge for women when and if it occurs. Women's emergent reliance on their intuitive processes is an important move in the service of self-protection, self-assertion, and self-definition. Over half of our large group of subjectivists had recently taken steps to end relationships with lovers or husbands, to reject further obligations to family members, and to move out and away on their own. For these women, subjectivism is a way of knowing that is safe from the dictates of others. It provides the space for a birth of the self without the constraints of social convention and it provides them with a reassuring sense of personal power and authority.

One woman in her 30s described her recent liberation this way:

> Now I only know with my gut. It helps me and protects me. It is perceptive and astute. My gut is my best friend—the one thing in the world that won't let me down or lie to me or back away from me.

Procedural Knowledge: The Voice of Reason

Most of the women in this category—24% of the sample—were attending or had recently graduated from prestigious colleges. Most were privileged, bright, white, and young, ranging in age from late teens to mid-twenties. One can hear in the stories of women in this category how they acquire the tools of reason and attitudes about knowledge that are valued in most of our esteemed institutions of higher education. These are women striving to join the academic elite and the professional public world of men.

All of the women at this position are absorbed in the business of acquiring and applying procedures for obtaining and communicating knowledge. Some seem passionately involved in the process, whereas others seem to treat it as a "game," but the emphasis on procedures, skills, and techniques is common to all. Developing procedures for knowing—such as critical thinking, textual analysis, and scientific method—becomes paramount, as does an emphasis on "learning the way they want you to think" (Perry, 1970, p. 100).

The woman at this position recognizes that some events are open to interpretation, and that some interpretations make better sense than others. Because one's ideas must "measure up" to certain objective standards, one must speak in measured tones, or not speak at all. It is not sufficient to parrot the authorities' words or to blurt out the first thing that comes to mind. One should systematically muster support for one's opinions and be careful not to jump to conclusions.

For most of the women at this position, form predominates over content. It matters less what you think than that you have thought it through thoroughly. The women pride themselves on the skills they acquire. Asked what she valued most about her college education, one woman named her philosophy course.

> I couldn't tell you right now the philosophies of most of the people we studied, but I can tell you how I would set about criticizing their arguments and what types of things you should look for.

Most women in this category retain or regain some trust in authority; authorities are perceived as relatively benign, neither dictatorial nor attacking. Authorities do not offer answers, only techniques for constructing answers. And, most important to the women, they judge, not opinions per se, but the procedures one uses to substantiate opinions. Authorities apparently do not seek to silence but to teach a new language.

However, some of these women, even as they go about developing their intellectual competence and authority, begin to express a deep ambivalence about the institutionalized pressure to conform to normative ideals about the right ways to learn and think. In the process of learning the new academic language, women do come to understand that we can know things that we have never seen or touched, that truth can be shared, and that expertise can be respected. They learn, too, that intuition can deceive and that gut reactions can be irresponsible. They are often told that first-hand experience has no place in the classroom. They are taught to look for general laws, for universal trends, and to avoid personalizing. They are taught that they isolate events and people from contexts in order to arrive at objective evaluations. They are taught to pay attention to objects in the external world, that is, for instance, to the painting itself rather than the feelings a painting arouses in oneself. Most of the women in our sample of procedural knowers have learned these lessons well and have demonstrated that they can excel in academic circles and adversarial debate. Some pride themselves, as the philosopher Sara Ruddick once did, on their "male minds" (Ruddick, 1984, p. 143).

But others speak of a sense of fraudulence about their proven academic abilities and success, feeling that, although they can perform adequately, they have lost a sense of their true selves. They talk about feeling like imposters who no longer aspire to having a male mind. Truth, for them, seems to lie somewhere outside the academy. The voice of reason that they have acquired, though it serves them well, is not necessarily their voice. Nor are the questions asked in academic circles necessarily their questions.

Some of these women have begun to experiment with more "feminine" procedures for knowing, procedures that are more personal and empathic. They speak of learning how to "open oneself up to ideas." The women in the next section have developed these procedures more fully.

Constructed Knowledge: Integrating the Voices

The women in this final category (18% of our sample) are all articulate and reflective people, some quite young, others among the oldest in our sample. All of them were attending or had graduated from college. At some time in their past, they said, they had felt deadened to their inner experience and inner selves; thinking and feeling were split asunder. They told us that their current way of knowing and viewing the world—the way of knowing we call *constructed knowledge*—began as an effort to reclaim the self by attempting to integrate knowledge that they felt intuitively was important with knowledge and methods of knowing that they had learned during their formal education. They had "moved outside the givens" of their social and intellectual world by removing themselves psychologically, and at times even geographically. Their stated intention was to take time out to get to know the self and to reflect on the contexts that confined and defined them. They described the development of a new way of thinking that emphasized not the extrication of the self in the process of knowing but a "letting the inside out and the outside in."

The central insight that distinguishes this position is that all knowledge is constructed and the knower is an intimate part of the known. The woman comes to see that the knowledge one acquires depends on the context or frame of reference of the knower who is seeking answers and on the context in which events to be understood have occurred. One woman put it this way:

> We can assume that something exists out there—but "something" is thinking that something exists. Our consciousness is part of the world. We are creating the world at the time.

Recognizing that everything is relative, these women concern themselves with the basic assumptions that govern the kinds of questions being asked and the methods being used for getting answers. They are aware that even personal truths are a matter of history, circumstance, and timing, and are subject to change. Theories are seen not as truth but as models for approximating experience; theories are "educated guesswork."

Women at this position overcome the notion that there is One Right Answer or a Right Procedure in the search for truth. They see that there are various ways of knowing and methods of analysis. They feel responsibility for examining, choosing, questioning, and developing the systems that they will use for constructing knowledge. Question-posing and problem-posing become prominent methods of inquiry, strategies that some researchers have identified with the "fifth" stage of thought beyond formal-operational or logical thought (Arlin, 1975; Kitchener, 1983; Labouvie-Vief, 1980). The woman tends not to rely as readily or exclusively on hypothetico-deductive inquiry, which posits an answer (the hypothesis) prior to data collection. She prefers to examine the basic assumptions and the conditions in which a problem is cast. She can take, and often insists upon taking, a position outside a particular context or frame of reference and looks back on "who" is asking the question, "why" the question is asked at all, and "how" answers are arrived at.

The way of knowing prized by most constructivist women is anything but detached. For these women, intimate knowledge of the self not only precedes but always accompanies understanding. They are intensely aware of how perceptions are processed through the complex web of personal meaning and values; they resist excluding the self from the process of knowing for the sake of simplicity or "objectivity." They strive to find a way of weaving their passions and their intellectual life into some meaningful whole. All the old polarities—self and others, thought and feeling, subjective and objective, public and private, personal and impersonal, love and work—lose their saliency. The constructivist mode of thought, in women at least, stresses integration and balance and inclusion rather than exclusion and parsimony.

As we noted in the last section, "opening oneself up to ideas" (or people or poems) is stressed by some women as a procedure for knowing, but the relative lack of self-knowledge prevents the procedural knower from finding points of connection between that which she is trying to understand and her own experience. At the position of constructed knowledge, women often describe themselves in terms that denote passionate or "connected knowing"—a union of the knower with that which is to be known. Empathic seeing and feeling with the other is a central feature in the development of connected knowing. The empathic potential—the capacity for what Weil (1951) calls "attentive love" and Ruddick (1980) identifies with "maternal thinking"—is particularly characteristic of constructivist women. They use the language of intimacy and care to describe relationships with ideas as well as with people. Communion and communication are established with that which one is trying to understand. Women use such images as "conversing with nature," "getting closer to ideas," "having rapport with my reading matter," and "communicating with an author" in order to understand, rather than more masculine images such "pinning an idea down," "getting on top of ideas," or "seeing through an argument."

Dialogue is at the center of this way of knowing. A balance is found between speaking and listening. The women here are able to listen to others without silencing their own voice, whereas at other positions they attend to only one or the other. They make a distinction between conversing and what they call "really talking" by which they mean a reciprocal drawing out of each other's ideas and meanings. "Really talking" requires careful listening; it implies a mutually shared agreement that together you are creating the optimum setting so that emergent ideas can grow. This mode of talk is something similar to what Habermas (1973) has called "the ideal speech situation." "Real talk" reaches deep into the experience of each; it also draws on the analytical abilities of each. It is as important in the public as the private sharing of knowledge. To this end, the women strive for an exploration of assumptions and intersubjective reality rather than a one-way didactic stating of views. Domination is absent; reciprocity and cooperation predominate.

These women strive to gain a public as well as a private voice. They want to communicate to others the complexities of the world as they experience it. However, even among women who have found a voice, problems of voice abound. In a society such as ours that values the words of male authority and often dismisses the woman's voice as soft or misguided, constructivist women are no more immune to the experience of feeling silenced than any other group of women.

Needless to say, the women at this position set themselves a difficult task. They want always to be sensitive to context, to include rather than exclude, to listen as often as to speak, to stay open to the ideas of others, to engage in "real talk," and to reevaluate continually their basic assumptions as they acquire knowledge. They do not claim that they always succeed at this task. Most of the women learn to live with compromise and to soften ideals that they find are unworkable. Nevertheless, they set an example of a refreshing mixture of idealism and realism. More than any other group of women, they are seriously preoccupied with the moral or spiritual dimension in their lives. They actively reflect on how their judgments, attitudes, and behavior coalesce into some internal experience of moral consistency. For most of these women, the moral response is a caring response; an opinion is a commitment, something to live by. Further, they strive to translate their moral commitments into action, both out of a conviction that "one must act" and out of a feeling of responsibility to the larger community in which they live.

IMPLICATIONS FOR HUMAN DEVELOPMENT

The epistemological taxonomy that we describe is, at this point in our work, a beginning attempt to understand the variety of perspectives from which women know and view the world. Our descriptive scheme provides a framework for further research on gender similarities and differences in ways of knowing and on life experiences that shape thought. Our study, based on interviews with women, represents both an extension and modification of Perry's scheme of developmental epistemology, which was derived primarily from interviews with Harvard men. We recognize that the five ways of knowing we identify are not necessarily fixed or exhaustive categories; that they are abstract categories that will not always capture the complexities and uniqueness of an individual woman's thought and life; that other people might organize their observations differently; and that the scheme itself awaits further study and validation. The addition of new populations of women might extend the number of categories or lead to their modification. And it will only be with the study of men and women from equally mixed class, ethnic, and educational backgrounds that comparisons between the sexes can be made.

In spite of these cautions, we believe that our study does allow us to raise important questions about women's development and thought and to draw some conclusions. It also provides a firmer grounding than existed before for speculation about when and why women's concepts of self and ways of knowing change.

Because we approached this study with questions about women's sense of competence and authority, we paid particular attention to that part of their stories that dealt with their experience in two of the major social institutions that affect human development: families and schools. In their struggle to develop their voices and minds and hold onto their values in a society that tends to devalue women and their ideas, many women falter, deny their potential and values, accommodate to the views and expectations of others, and suffer from feelings of inauthenticity and/or powerlessness. Some women find their way out of the morass of accommodations, retreat, and self-denial largely on their own initiative, but sometimes with the help of perceptive, responsive families and schools or social agencies.

The women's interviews were, of course, quite diverse, but as we read and reread their accounts of what they had learned and failed to learn, of how they liked to learn and were forced to learn, some common themes emerged, themes that may be distinctly, although surely not exclusively, feminine. We shall touch briefly on some of these themes here; we develop them more fully elsewhere (Belenky et al., 1986).

Confirmation of the Self as a Knower

Our interviews have convinced us that every woman, regardless of age, social class, ethnicity, and academic achievement, needs to know that she is capable of intelligent thought, and needs to know it sooner rather than later. Many women told us of personal incidents of being doubted, overlooked, and teased for their intellectual efforts even in well-intentioned families and schools. Several women spoke of the ambiguity inherent in male professors' praise for women students, of the "games" into which male professors and female students fall. They wonder, "Am I a student or a flirtation? Am I smart or does he want something else from me?"

Women who attended the more prestigious colleges in the sample and who had a history of privilege and achievement were still uncertain of their abilities. Achievement did not protect them from self-doubt. The need for confirmation was even more prominent among the less privileged women, many of whom had grown up being told they were stupid. Their views of themselves began to change when they came across "maternal" social agencies that refused to treat them as dumb. What these women needed and what the agencies provided—perhaps more clearly, consistently, and sincerely than any other institutions we sampled—was confirmation that they could be trusted to know, to learn, and to share this knowledge with others. For these women to discover that they had opinions and experience of value to others was a lesson that they had missed during all their years of formal education. Most of the women we interviewed, rich and poor, educated or not, made it clear that they did not wish to be told merely that they had the "capacity" or the "potential" to become knowledgeable or wise. They needed to know that they already knew something (though by no means everything), that there was something good inside. They worried that there wasn't.

In the masculine myth, confirmation comes not at the beginning of education but at the end. Confirmation as a thinker and membership in a community of thinkers come as the climax of Perry's (1970) story of intellectual development in the college years. The student learns, according to Perry, that "we must all stand judgment" and must earn "the privilege of having [our] ideas respected" (p. 33). Having proved beyond reasonable doubt that he has learned to think in complex, contextual ways, the young man is admitted to the fraternity of powerful knowers. Certified as a thinker, he becomes one of Them (now dethroned to lower-case them). This scenario may capture the "natural" course of men's development in traditional, hierarchical institutions, but it does not work for women. For women, confirmation and community are prerequisites rather than consequences of development.

Collaboration, Community, and Trust

Most women say they learn best in groups and prefer collaborative work. When they are isolated from those who know by a wall of silence or status, their talents for learning through the drawing out of others are left untapped. Opportunities to match experiences, reveal insecurities and obtain reassurance, and try out ideas without fear of ridicule are possible where trust exists. And trust exists in classrooms and groups in which the "believing" rather than "doubting" game is played (Elbow, 1973). As Elbow says, the doubting game involves "putting something on trial to see whether it is wanting or not" (p. 173). The teacher or student playing the doubting game looks for something wrong—a loophole, a factual error, a logical contradiction, an omission of contrary evidence. Good teachers and good parents, according to women, are believers. They trust their students' or children's thinking and encourage them to expand it.

But in the psychological literature concerning the factors promoting cognitive development, doubt has played a more prominent role than belief. People are said to be precipitated into states of cognitive conflict when, for example, their ideas are challenged by some external event, and the effort to resolve conflict leads to cognitive growth. We do not deny that cognitive conflict can act as an impetus to growth; all of us can attest to such experiences in our own lives. But in our interviews only a handful of women described a powerful and positive learning experience in which the teacher aggressively challenged their notions. Because so many women are already consumed with self-doubt, doubts imposed from outside seem at best redundant ("I'm always reprimanding myself") and at worst destructive, confirming women's own sense of themselves as inadequate knowers. The doubting model of teaching, then, may be particularly inappropriate for women, although we are not convinced that it is appropriate for men either.

Firsthand Experience

In considering how to design an education appropriate for women, suppose we were to begin by asking, simply: What does a woman know? Traditional courses do not begin there. They begin not with the student's knowledge but with the teacher's knowledge. Most of the women we interviewed, however, were drawn to the sort of knowledge that comes from firsthand observation, whereas most of the institutions they attended emphasized abstract out-of-context learning. The women spoke as often of the way students interacted in classes as of the course content; they were often more concerned about another's pride or shame than whether he or she supplied good answers; they were relieved when they could find some connection between the course material and their own experience.

For many women, the most powerful learning experiences took place out of school. The mothers usually named childbearing or child-rearing. The kind of knowledge that is gained in child-rearing is typical of the kind of knowledge that women value and schools do not. Ruddick (1980) has argued that "maternal thought" has rules of evidence and criteria for truth, just as do more esteemed modes of thought accepted within academic disciplines. The knowledge of mothers comes not from words but from action and observation, and much of it has never been translated into words, only into actions. As the philosopher Carol McMillan (1982) has noted, this kind of knowledge does not necessarily

110

lead to general propositions. Good mothering, for instance, requires adaptive responding to changing phenomena; it is tuned to the concrete and particular. Mothers are understandably hesitant about "concocting theories about how other people should bring up their children" (McMillan, 1982). Most women are not opposed to abstraction per se. They find concepts useful as ways of making sense of their experiences, but they balk when the abstractions precede the experiences or push them out entirely. Even the women who were extraordinarily adept at abstract reasoning preferred to start with personal experience.

It should come as no surprise that the courses most often mentioned by women as powerful learning experiences were those that helped them translate private experience into a shared public language (for instance, courses on feminist theory or courses requiring the sharing of journals) and courses that provided experiential opportunities (for instance, collecting interviews from old-timers in the study of small-town life or comanaging a student theatrical group).

Models for Learning: Sharing and Listening

There is considerable evidence that parents who enter into a dialogue with their children, who draw out and respect their children's opinions, are more likely to have children whose intellectual and ethical development proceeds rapidly and surely (Baumrind, 1971; Haan, Smith, & Block, 1968; Hauser et al., 1984; Lickona, 1983). Among our women, only the constructivists and a few procedural knowers described both parents as good listeners. Most women at the other positions came from families in which relationships among family members were hierarchical, with talking and listening unevenly divided between the members. Typically the husband spoke, the women and children listened. In these conventionally ordered families, fathers were depicted as being more like conventional teachers—bent on handing out truths; mothers were more like students—listening and trying to understand. The daughters from such families described themselves as students in much the same terms—obediently attentive students before all-wise lecturers. Constructivists, however, painted a different picture of their families and had a different vision of what makes a good teacher. They noticed and valued mothers who had gained a voice and fathers who had developed a listening ear. So, too, these women valued teachers who showed that they could both think and feel, that they could both speak and listen, that they could both teach and learn.

It can be argued, of course, that students need models of impeccable reasoning, that it is through imitating such models that students learn to reason. Perhaps. But none of the women we interviewed named this sort of learning as a powerful experience in their own lives. They did mention deflation of authority as a powerful learning experience. Women have been taught by generations of men that males have greater powers of rationality than females have. When a male professor presents only the impeccable products of his thinking, it is especially difficult for a woman student to believe that she could have produced such a thought. And it must be remembered that in spite of the women's movement, most of the teachers are still male, although more than half of the students are now female. Female students need opportunities to watch how female professors solve (and fail to solve) problems and male professors fail to solve (and succeed in solving) problems. They need role models of thinking as a human activity—as imperfect, yet attainable.

GROWTH AND CHANGE

Based on our research, it appears that women's intellectual growth and shifts in self-concept and worldview are often tied to events beyond classroom and parental teaching—events such as child-bearing and child-rearing, crises of self-doubt and feelings of inauthenticity, value conflicts in relationships, and the failure of male authority on whom the woman has depended. The fact that even well-intentioned families and teachers can hinder, as well as support, women's development has led us to question conventional assumptions about the education of women. In this chapter, we have touched on some correctives to educational practice that would benefit women, and perhaps men as well.

Significant developmental change, according to women's retrospective accounts, often occurs in middle adulthood. These transition points are accompanied by major shifts in the woman's assessment of her value, options, goals, and responsibilities. Most women experience a tremendous sense of growth as they begin to move away from silence and social stereotypes and rely on inner resources for knowing. For some, subjective knowing may be a stopping point and the predominant epistemology for much of their lives because reliance on inner authority provides a security that they need and hold on to. Other women, who have also come to value the power of rational and objective thought, gain a new sense of internal cohesion when they can find ways to balance subjective/intuitive and objective/rational knowledge. It is clear from our data that women's sense of self and voice flourish when they become what we call connected and passionate knowers. We argue that educators can help women develop their minds and authentic voices if they emphasize connection over separation, understanding and acceptance over assessment, collaboration over competition, and discussion over debate, and if they accord respect to and allow time for the knowledge that emerges from first-hand experience. We have learned these things by listening to the woman's voice.

NOTE

1. This chapter is adapted from our book, *Women's Ways of Knowing: The Development of Self, Voice, and Mind* (Basic Books, 1986). An earlier version of the chapter was presented in July 1985 at the Eighth Biennial Meeting of the International Society of Behavioral Development in Tours, France. The research was supported by a grant (#G008005071) from the Fund for the Improvement of Post Secondary Education, Department of Education.

REFERENCES

Aries, E. (1976). Interaction patterns and themes of male, female, and mixed groups. *Small Group Behavior, 7,* 7-14.
Arlin, P. (1975). Cognitive development in adulthood. *Developmental Psychology, 11,* 602-606.
Bakan, D. (1966). *The duality of human existence.* Boston: Beacon Press.
Baumrind, D. (1971). Current patterns and parental authority. *Developmental Psychology Monographs, 4,* (1, Pt. 2).
Belenky, M., Clinchy, B., Goldberger, N., & Tarule, J. (1986). *Women's ways of knowing: The development of self, voice, and mind.* New York: Basic Books.
Belenky, M., Tarule, J., & Landa, A. (Eds.). (1979). *Education and development.* Washington, DC: National Teachers Corp.
Bernard, J. (1973). My four revolutions: An autobiographical history of the American Sociological Society. *American Journal of Sociology, 78,* 773-791.
Chodorow, N. (1978). *The reproduction of mothering.* Berkeley: University of California Press.
Clance, P. R., & Imes, S. A. (1978). The imposter phenomenon in high achieving women: Dynamics and therapeutic intervention. *Psychotherapy: Theory, Research, and Practice, 15,* 241-247.
Clinchy, B., Lief, J., & Young, P. (1977). Epistemological and moral development in girls from a traditional and a progressive high school. *Journal of Educational Psychology, 69,* 337-343.

Clinchy, B., & Zimmerman, C. (1975). *Cognitive development in college.* Unpublished manuscript, Wellesley College.

Clinchy, B., & Zimmerman, C. (1982). Epistemology and agency in the development of undergraduate women. In P. Perum (Ed.), *The undergraduate woman: Issues in educational equity.* Lexington, MA: D. C. Heath.

Clinchy, B., & Zimmerman, C. (1985a). *Connected and separate knowing.* Paper presented at the Eighth Biennial Meeting of the International Society of Behavioral Development, July, Tours, France.

Clinchy, B., & Zimmerman, C. (1985b). Growing up intellectually: Issues for college women. *Work in Progress,* #19. Wellesley, MA: Stone Center for Developmental Services and Studies.

Colby, A., Kohlberg, L., Candee, D., Gibbs, J. C., Hewer, R., Kaufman, K., Power, C., & Speicher-Dubin, B. (1983). *Assessing moral judgments: A manual.* New York: Cambridge University Press.

Cross, P. (1968). College women: A research description. *Journal of the National Association of Women Deans and Counselors, 32,* 12-21.

Eakins, B., & Eakins, G. (1976). Verbal turn-taking and exchanges in faculty dialogue. In B. L. Dubois & I. Crouch (Eds.), *The sociology of the language of American women.* San Antonio, TX: Trinity University.

Elbow, P. (1973). *Writing without teachers.* London: Oxford University Press.

Gallese, L. R. (1985). *Women like us.* New York: Morrow.

Gilligan, C. (1977). In a different voice: Women's conceptions of self and of morality. *Harvard Educational Review, 47,* 431-446.

Gilligan, C. (1979). Woman's place in man's life cycle. *Harvard Educational Review, 49,* 431-446.

Gilligan, C. (1982). *In a different voice: Psychological theory and women's development.* Cambridge, MA: Harvard University Press.

Goldberger, N. (1978). Breaking the educational lockstep: The Simon's Rock experience. In P. E. Kaylor (Ed.). *The early college in theory and practice.* Great Barrington, MA: Simon's Rock.

Goldberger, N. (1981). *Meeting the developmental needs of college students.* Final report to The Fund For the Improvement of Post Secondary Education (FIPSE). Great Barrington, MA: Simon's Rock of Bard College.

Goldberger, N. (1985). *Women's epistemology: An empirical scheme.* Paper presented at the Eighth Biennial Meeting of the International Society of Behavioral Development, July, Tours, France.

Haan, N., Smith, M. B., & Block, J. (1968). The moral reasoning of young adults: Political-social behavior, family background, and personality correlates. *Journal of Personality and Social Psychology, 10,* 183-201.

Habermas, J. (1973). *Legitimation crisis.* Boston: Beacon Press.

Hagen, R. I., & Kahn, A. (1975). Discrimination against competent women. *Journal of Applied Social Psychology, 5,* 362-376.

Hall, R., & Sandler, B. R. (1982). *The classroom climate: A chilly one for women?* Project on the Status and Education of Women. Washington, DC: Association of American Colleges.

Harding, S., & Hintikka, M. B. (Eds.). (1983). *Discovering reality: Feminist perspectives on epistemology, metaphysics, methodology, and philosophy of science.* Dordrecht, Holland: Reidel.

Hauser, S., Powers, S. I., Noam, G., Jacobsen, A. M., Weiss, B., & Follansbee, D. J. (1984). Familial contexts of adolescent ego development. *Child Development, 55,* 195-213.

Horowitz, H. L. (1984). *Alma mater.* New York: Knopf.

Janssen-Jurreit, M. (1980). *Sexism: The male monopoly on history and thought.* New York: Farrar, Straus, & Giroux.

Kanter, R. M. (1977). *Men and women of the corporation.* New York: Basic Books.

Keller, E. (1978). Gender and science. *Psychoanalysis and Contemporary Thought, 1,* 409-433.

Keller, E. (1985). *Reflections on gender and science.* New Haven, CT: Yale University Press.

Keller, E., & Grontkowski, C. R. (1983). The mind's eye. In S. Harding & M. Hintikka (Eds.), *Discovering reality.* Dordrecht, Holland: Reidel.

Kitchener, K. (1983). Cognition, metacognition, and epistemic cognition: A three-level model of cognitive processing. *Human Development, 26,* 222-232.

Knefelkamp, L. L., Widick, C., & Parker, C. A. (Eds.). (1978). *New directions for student services: Applying new developmental findings* (no. 4). San Francisco: Jossey-Bass.

Kohlberg, L. (1984). *The psychology of moral development.* New York: Harper & Row.

Labouvie-Vief, G. (1980). Beyond formal operations: Uses and limits of pure logic in life-span development. *Human Development, 3,* 141-161.

Langland, E., & Gove, W. (Eds.). (1981). *A feminist perspective in the academy.* Chicago: University of Chicago Press.

Lickona, T. (1983). *Raising good children: Helping your children through the stages of moral development.* New York: Bantam.

Lyons, N. (1983). Two perspectives on self, relationships and morality. *Harvard Educational Review, 53,* 125-145.

Maccoby, E., & Jacklin, C. (1974). *The psychology of sex differences.* Stanford, CA: Stanford University Press.

McMillan, C. (1982). *Women, reason, and nature.* Princeton, NJ: Princeton University Press.

Miller, J. B. (1976). *Towards a new psychology of women.* Boston: Beacon Press.

Perry, W. G. (1970). *Forms of intellectual and ethical development in the college years.* New York: Holt, Rinehart & Winston.

Perry, W. G. (1981). Cognitive and ethical growth: The making of meaning. In A. Chickering (Ed.), *The modern American college.* San Francisco: Jossey-Bass.

Piaget, J. (1965). *The moral judgment of the child.* New York: Free Press. (Original work published 1932)

Piliavin, J. A. (1976). On feminine self-presentation in groups. In J. I. Roberts (Ed.), *Beyond intellectual sexism.* New York: McKay.

Rosenberg, R. (1982). *Beyond separate spheres: Intellectual roots of modern feminism.* New Haven, CT: Yale University Press.

Ruddick, S. (1980). Maternal thinking. *Feminist Studies, 6,* 70-96.

Ruddick, S. (1984). New combinations: Learning from Virginia Woolf. In C. Asher, L. DeSalvor, & S. Ruddick, *Between women.* Boston: Beacon Press.

Ruddick, S., & Daniels, P. (Eds.). (1977). *Working it out.* New York: Pantheon Books.

Sadker, M. P., & Sadker, D. M. (1982). *Sex equity handbook for schools.* New York: Longman.

Sadker, M. P., & Sadker, D. M. (1985, March). Sexism in the schoolroom of the 80's. *Psychology Today,* 54-57.

Sampson, E. E. (1978). Scientific paradigm and social value: Wanted—a scientific revolution. *Journal of Personality and Social Psychology, 36,* 1332-1343.

Sassen, G. (1980). Success anxiety in women: A constructivist interpretation of its source and its significance. *Harvard Educational Review, 50* (1), 13-24.

Serbin, L. A., O'Leary, K. D., Kent, R. N., & Tonick, I. J. (1973). A comparison of teacher response to pre-academic and problem behavior of boys and girls. *Child Development, 44,* 796-804.

Sherman, J., & Beck, E. (Eds.). (1979). *The prism of sex.* Madison: University of Wisconsin Press.

Swacker, M. (1976). Women's verbal behavior at learned and professional conferences. In B. L. Dubois & I. Crouch (Eds.), *The sociology of the languages of American women.* San Antonio, TX: Trinity University.

Tarule, J., & Weathersby, R. (1979, Fall). Adult development and adult learning styles: The message for non-traditional graduate programs. *Alternative Graduate Education: The Journal of Non-Traditional Studies, 4.*

Thorne, B. (1979). *Claiming verbal space: Women, speech, and language in college classrooms.* Paper presented at the Research Conference on Educational Environments and the Undergraduate Woman, Wellesley College, Wellesley, MA.

Treichler, P., & Kramarae, C. (1983). Women's talk in the ivory tower. *Communication Quarterly, 31,* 118-132.

Weil, S. (1951). Reflections on the right use of school studies with a view to the love of god. In S. Weil, *Waiting for God.* New York: Harper Colophon Books.

West, C., & Zimmerman, D. H. (1983). Small insults: A study of interruptions in cross-sex conversations between unacquainted persons. In B. Thorne, C. Kramarae, & N. Henley, *Language, gender and society.* Rowley, MA: Newbury House.

116

The Review of Higher Education
Spring 1992, Volume 15, No. 3
Pages 265-87
Copyright © 1992 Association for the
Study of Higher Education
All Rights Reserved
(ISSN 0162-5748)

Students' Epistemologies and Academic Experiences: Implications for Pedagogy

Marcia B. Baxter Magolda

Recent dialogue about higher education is characterized by words like "revitalization," "search for renewal," and "realization of potential." One predominant theme emerging from this dialogue is community. The Carnegie Foundation for the Advancement of Teaching offered six principles to guide the development of a learning community. The first speaks directly to teaching: "First, a college or university is an educationally purposeful community, a place where faculty and students share academic goals and work together to strengthen teaching and learning on the campus" (1990, 7). The authors argued that teaching should extend beyond the transmission of information to stimulate active learning and creativity. The NIE Study Group emphasized the need for students to be more involved in learning "to extend their abilities in critical thinking and analysis, and to develop their capacities to synthesize, imagine and create" (1984, 28). Ernest Boyer, president of the Carnegie Foundation for the Advancement of Teaching, concurred: "The undergraduate experience, at its best, involves active learning and disciplined inquiry that leads to the intellectual empowerment of students" (1987, 151).

Marcia B. Baxter Magolda is an associate professor of educational leadership at Miami University and author of a book on assessing intellectual development.

Reshaping pedagogy in these terms requires dialogue on another level: teachers' and students' epistemologies. I use epistemology here to refer to assumptions about the nature, certainty, and limits of knowledge (Kitchener 1983). This article describes students' epistemologies as a foundation for reshaping pedagogy.

Parker Palmer, a senior associate for the American Assocation of Higher Education and a sociologist, eloquently articulated the overriding epistemology of higher education and its role in creating educational communities that foster mutual exchange and complex thinking. He identified higher education's dominant epistemology, or mode of knowing, as objectivist. Seeking to avoid subjectivity, objectivism distances knowledge from knowers; what is to be known becomes an object. This object can then be analyzed and manipulated to form a world divorced from knowers' personal lives. This mode of knowing, Palmer argued, breeds competitive individualism, a characteristic he described as "essentially anticommunal" (1987, 24). He observed three exceptions to this mode of knowing—feminist, black, and Native American scholarship—which replace objectivism with a relational epistemology. This relational mode of knowing requires a connection between the knower and what is being known, an interactive weaving together of one's story with the one being told. Such an approach stands in stark contrast to the abstract, objectivist epistemology. Judy Rogers (1988), in her work on leadership, also described the strong relational aspects of new epistemologies and noted that these modes of knowing are consistent with the relational values of the female ethos. Certainly the epistomologies themselves are not new. The female ethos, characterized by relationships and values of duty, love, and care, has coexisted with the more masculine world of competition, manipulation, and destruction for millennia. Similarly, Native American epistemology, which blurs the line between perceiver and perceived, has developed over millennia. What is new is the increasing acceptance of these relational epistomologies with their accompanying values into the scholarly world.

Unfortunately, conventional pedagogy is not consistent with these new relational modes of knowing. Instead, most of our current models about teaching stem from and validate the objectivist epistemology; they focus on the individual as a knower, on the transmission of knowledge from instructor to individual, on distance between knowers and the knowledge they seek, and on "success" as the ability to reproduce and manipulate that knowledge. Palmer defines pedagogy based on a relational epistemology as requiring "a continual cycle of discussion, disagreement, and consensus over what has been seen and what it all means" (1987, 25). Beyond this, he suggests two crucial components of this process: creative conflict and support. Teachers and learners must share their perspectives, grow through the process of encountering contradictory perspectives, and support one another sufficiently to allow the risk-taking necessary for expressing, discussing, and forming perspectives.

If we are to create a pedagogy that promotes communal learning and complex thinking, then we must not only deal with the teachers' epistomologies but also with those of the students. Nona Lyons, a noted researcher in the area of moral and epistemological development, incorporates this side of the equation in her concept of "nested knowing" (1990, 162), which considers the teacher's epistemology, the student's epistemology, and the teacher's insight into the student's epistemology. Students' epistemologies affect students' interpretations of community, involvement in learning, and the pedagogies aimed at creating both.

When students derive their ways knowing from their teachers' objectivist epistemology and conventional pedagogy, they view knowledge as certain, see the teacher as the authority, and define learning as individual mastery. Student involvement then becomes a matter of engaging with teachers and peers to demonstrate one's learning prowess or refusing to engage with others to avoid the competition. Students with this orientation are likely to resist—or at least feel confused by—new pedagogies based on mutual sharing, creative conflict, and consensus. Perhaps this explains the frustration many teachers encounter when they initiate classroom discussions, only to find that no meaningful exchange takes place.

Under these circumstances, changing teachers' epistemologies and pedagogy alone will not bring the communal, or relational, approach to learning that Palmer and Boyer suggest. Instead, student epistemologies and their effect on the learning process must be a central consideration in designing pedagogy. Toward that end, I offer one description of college students' epistemologies and of the students' perceptions of how these ways of knowing have affected their academic experiences. Using their perceptions as a basis, I have designed a pedagogy that promotes communal learning and complex modes of knowing.

Epistemological Development: Students' Ways of Knowing

Jean Piaget (1926) defined intellectual development as the evolution of thought structures characterized by qualitatively different assumptions about knowledge. These assumptions were later labeled epistemic because they focused on the limits and certainty of knowledge and the criteria for knowing (Kitchener 1983). Numerous models describe the evolution of epistemic assumptions, or epistemological development, in college student populations. The most prominent models have described male (Perry 1970) and female (Belenky et. al. 1986) development separately, or have described gender-inclusive models without specifically tracking gender differences (Kitchener and King 1981, 1990). All of these models depict an overall trend; epistemic assumptions move from certainty and accepting authority's knowledge to uncertainty and developing a personal perspective. I view variations in the models as due to the populations from which they were developed.

I conducted a four-year longitudinal study of both women's and men's epistemological development during college to further explore the possibility of gender differences. Two sets of data emerged from the study. The first describes students' epistemological perspectives and gender-related patterns within them. The second describes students' perceptions of specific academic experiences. Although this article focuses on the second set, a brief overview of students' epistemologies will help clarify their perceptions of their academic experiences.

The annual, open-ended interviews allowed students to discuss six areas defined in previous models as relevant to epistemological development: the role of the learner, peers, and instructor in learning; evaluation of learning; educational decision making; and the nature of knowledge. The interview format had previously identified significant differences in epistemological levels between freshmen, seniors, and graduate students (Baxter Magolda 1987). To determine epistemological levels, I compared students' reasons for their responses to the Measure of Epistemological Reflection rating manual (Baxter Magolda and Porterfield 1988). This manual described epistemological levels and also reasons students used within levels; I had developed these categories from an empirical study of 752 students' responses to short essay questions about the same six areas. I then averaged the epistemological level for each of the six areas to obtain an overall level rating. The validity of this rating system is based on consistent differences across levels of education (Baxter Magolda and Porterfield 1988), .80 reliability between two independent raters (N = 752), and agreement between raters ranging from 70 to 80 percent (Baxter Magolda and Porterfield 1985). The manual also provided for new reasoning structures that emerged from the interview data in the present study.

Table 1 overviews the three epistemological levels, or ways of knowing (absolute knowing, transitional knowing, independent knowing), that emerged from the eighty sets of four-year interviews. Each is defined by qualitatively different epistemic assumptions. In

TABLE 1
EPISTEMOLOGICAL REFLECTION MODEL

Domains	Absolute Knowing	Transitional Knowing	Independent Knowing
Role of learner	Obtain knowledge from instructor	Understand knowledge	Think for oneself Share views with others Self-authored knowledge
Role of peers	Share materials Explain what they have learned to each other	Active exchanges	Share views Source of knowledge Self-authored knowledge
Role of instructor	Communicate knowledge appropriately Insure that students understand it	Use methods aimed at understanding Methods tha help apply knowledge	Promote independent thinking Promote exchange of opinions
Evaluation	Provide vehicle to show instructor what was learned	Measure student's understanding of the material	Reward independent thinking
Nature of knowledge	Certain or absolute	Partially certain and partially uncertain	Uncertain, everyone has own beliefs

121

addition, gender-related patterns emerged in the reasoning structures used within these epistemological levels. I labeled reasoning structures with 20 percent (or more) differences in the use patterns between men and women as gender-related patterns. (For a more detailed discussion of the development of the model and reasoning patterns, see Baxter Magolda 1991.)

Absolute Knowers

Absolute knowers' core assumption about knowledge was that it is certain. They defined learning as obtaining knowledge from the instructor. The teacher's responsibility was to communicate knowledge appropriately and insure that students understood it. The peers' role included asking questions, sharing materials, and explaining what they had learned to each other. These students saw evaluation as a tool to show the teacher what they had learned. Despite these shared basic assumptions, some absolute knowers focused on receiving knowledge, while others focused on mastering knowledge.

The receiving pattern, used more often by women than by men, involved learning through listening and recording information. These students adjusted their listening and note-taking efforts to whatever instructional style they encountered to record as much information as possible. They expected peers to be quiet, share notes, and ask questions to relieve pressure in the class; and they valued getting to know others in the class. These students preferred evaluation opportunities in which they could express what they had learned and/or provide evidence that they had received knowledge.

Mastery pattern knowers, who are more likely to be men than women, described their role as participating in interesting activities and showing the teacher their interest. They expected peers to engage in a mutual effort to master the material, including arguing and quizzing each other in and out of class. Mastery of the material took precedence over comfort in the learning environment for them. They also expected instructors to make learning interesting and defined evaluation as opportunities for feedback from the instructor to help improve their performance.

Transitional Knowers

Transitional knowers shared the epistemic assumption that knowledge was partially certain and partially uncertain. Subsequently they defined learning as understanding rather than acquisition. They expected instructors to show students how to apply knowledge to aid understanding and expected peers to take active roles in exploring material. Evaluation, they felt, should measure their understanding.

Students in this category could also be grouped into one of two subcategories by approach—interpersonal learning and impersonal learning, the first more used by women and the second more used by men. Students with an interpersonal approach to learning (more often women), collected others' ideas, were involved in learning, and valued practical material. Students described this approach as listening to peers and relating their ideas to personal experience. They expected rapport with the instructor and wanted instructors to base their evaluations of students' work on individual differences. They tended to focus on the uncertain portion of knowledge, suggesting that personal judgment would resolve uncertainty.

Proponents of the impersonal approach (more often men) stressed understanding rather than memorizing material, being forced to think, and exchanging ideas through debate. These students expected challenge from instructors and evaluations that were fair and practical. They demonstrated an equal focus on certainty and uncertainty and used logic and research to resolve uncertainty.

Independent Knowers

Independent knowers' core epistemic assumption was that knowledge is uncertain. This assumption allowed for a variety of beliefs but largely defined learning as thinking for oneself and sharing viewpoints with others. They expected both the instructor and the evaluation of students' work to encourage independent thinking and exchange of opinions. Both genders demonstrated a self-authored knowledge at this level, indicating that they generated their own perspectives for the first time.

Gender-related patterns were less evident (perhaps because fewer students were independent knowers than were transitional or absolute knowers), but they emerged in answers to questions about the nature of knowledge and the role of peers. For some students, usually men, the source of knowledge shifted from authority to self. As a result, these students wanted to hear peers' views to help them learn and wanted the chance to challenge peers with their own views. For other students, usually women, the source of knowledge shifted from collecting others' ideas as one's own to thinking independently. These students enjoyed hearing others' views but relished more their new-found voices. They stressed being open to others' views rather than challenging them.

These three epistemologies and the gender-related patterns within them serve as a backdrop for this examination of students' descriptions of their academic experiences.

METHOD

I chose a qualitative research approach for the academic experiences portion of the study. I assumed that students' perceptions of their academic experiences would be complex and that their epistemologies would interact with the epistemologies of their teachers. Recognizing that multiple realities would result from such interactions, I sought to understand possible connections between students' academic experiences and their epistemological development.

I conducted the four-year interview study at one institution, and my findings are specific to that context. The detailed extensive description of the students and the institution should help readers judge the transferability (Lincoln and Guba 1985), or applicability, of these findings to other contexts.

Participants

I randomly selected participants from among first-year students at a midwestern, public, four-year institution. Although random selection is not essential in qualitative research, I hoped it would help me acquire students from a variety of majors and backgrounds. The 101 participants included fifty males and fifty-one females with similar academic ability. Three were members of nondominant racial or ethnic groups. The mean ACT score of the population was 25.8, the average high school grade-point average was 3.4, and 70 percent of the participants ranked in the top 20 percent of their high school class. The mean age of participants was eighteen. Of the original 101 students interviewed the first year, ninety-five returned for the sophomore interview, eighty-six for the junior interview, and eighty for the senior interview. Students' majors represented all six institutional divisions and the honors program.

Seventy-five percent of the institution's 16,000 students are state residents. The liberal arts focus in the institution's mission is evident in a core requirement aimed at developing informed citizens: twenty-four required credits from English composition and literature, humanities, social science, and natural science and eighteen credits from outside the student's major. Students are encouraged to meet these requirements during the first two years of enrollment. Approximately 130 majors are offered in six divisions: arts and science, education, business administration, fine arts, applied science, and interdisciplinary studies. The school has twenty students to each instructor, and women comprise 27 percent of the full-time faculty.

The institution's main campus is situated in a small community approximately forty-five minutes away from the nearest metropolitan area. Of 16,000 students, 8,500 students live in university housing, and most of the remainder live within a two-mile radius of the campus. Because of the university location and the typical high level of high school involvement of entering students, most students participate in campus activities. The institution offers over 200 student organizations in forty fields, student-edited publications, and student government. One-third of the students belong to Greek organizations.

Procedures

The annual interview invited students to talk freely about their role as learners, the role of instructors and peers in learning, their perception of evaluations of their work, the nature of knowledge, and educational decision-making. I selected these six areas hoping to reveal epistemic assumptions, but the students also gave me rich descriptions of their actual academic experiences and their judgments about those experiences. The question in each area introduced the topic but did nothing beyond that to frame the response. For example, the question for the role of peers was, "Tell me about the interactions you have with other students that help you learn." The question, "What observations do you have about instructors who you think are effective?" prompted discussion about the role of instructors. The nature of knowledge was introduced with "Have you ever encountered a situation in which you heard two explanations for the same idea?" Students who had encountered such experiences were asked to describe the experience and their reaction to it. Follow-up questions clarified the students' responses and helped me understand their perspective. I routinely summarized their responses to make sure I understood their perspective accurately. The interviews were tape-recorded and transcribed verbatim.

Two independent readers (a trained graduate student and I) read the interview transcripts. We used Yvonna Lincoln and Egon Guba's 1985 version of the constant comparative method of processing naturalistic data. We defined units as any student's comment that described a personal academic experience and his or her reaction to it. Working separately, we recorded these comments on index cards. Next we compared our entries. If one of us recorded a comment that the other did not, we reread the interview transcript to decide if the comment met our criteria for a unit and included or excluded it on that basis.

When we completed this step, we had two identical sets of cards. Independently we sorted the cards, grouping those with similar ideas and labeling those categories. We then reviewed the categories for overlap, rearranged them to best describe the data, and recorded subsets of similar cards within each category as themes, or recurrent patterns of the same subject or emphasis. At this point, we compared our categories and themes. When we encountered a discrepancy, we reread the cards in question to reach consensus about how best to interpret the data. Finally, we jointly reread the cards in each category and theme to be sure that they accounted for all the data assigned to each. We used this same process annually, separating data by epistemological level and gender.

Qualitative data collection and processing requires purposeful effort to assure the trustworthiness, or truth value, of the findings. I used Lincoln and Guba's (1985) techniques of prolonged engagement and triangulation here to enhance the credibility of the findings. The continued contact I had with the students over a four-year period (prolonged engagement) enabled me to build trust with them and to see their experiences through their eyes rather than my own. I also used the member checking technique to some extent when I summarized student interview responses to check my understanding with the students. I used triangulation, or checking the interpretations with another source, when two of us interpreted the interview transcripts.

STUDENTS' PERCEPTIONS OF THEIR ACADEMIC EXPERIENCES

The students' collective academic experiences yielded the following categories: professor attitude, professor-student interaction, teaching strategies, class structure (format and atmosphere), evaluation techniques and systems, and knowledge discrepancies. Knowledge discrepancies occurred when students encountered inconsistent explanations of the same phenomenon. In this discussion, I explain the themes from each developmental level in students' experiences and their perceived effect.

Absolute Knowers' Experiences

Absolute knowers' experiences were drawn from the sophomore-year interviews. Although many students were absolute knowers during their first year, their perception of the college environment was very limited; I conducted the interview during the first semester. Too few students remained absolute knowers in their junior year to identify themes; but there were twenty-six sophomore women and nineteen sophomore men—enough that we could identify thematic patterns of topics or emphases prevalent for women and/or men.

Professor attitude was a salient category for both women and men in the "absolute knowledge" category. Women said they appreciated professors who enjoyed teaching and cared about students; however, with one exception, they did not report going to professors for help. Men appreciated professors with a helping attitude and also solicited (and got) help. Both men and women complained about professors who were arrogant and intimidating.

Women and men reported different experiences when discussing interaction with professors. Women reported no interaction with their professors, except one student who went to her professor for help because the course was so difficult that she was in danger of failing. Men, on the other hand, reported interactions in class and some that extended beyond class, including friendships and invitations to accompany professors to class-related events. Despite these interactions, men expressed an interest in knowing professors better but women did not.

In discussing teaching strategies, both men and women frequently mentioned how much they valued interesting activities in the classroom. This usually meant that the professor did demonstrations or opened the time for questions from the students. Most students reported only occasional "interesting" classes; more common were lectures with little student interaction. Male students additionally expected professors to explain the material being studied. They appreciated professors who explained effectively and complained about those whose presentations were confusing.

When I asked students to comment about class structure the answers involved class format (lecture or discussion) and class atmosphere (intimate or impersonal). From that point, however, men and women emphasized different aspects of class structure. Women emphasized atmosphere, advocating an intimate, relaxed atmosphere to foster learning. Getting to know classmates was the main advantage of this type of atmosphere. Men emphasized class format, reporting that most of their classes were large lecture classes with minimal interaction. They preferred the few experiences they had in small classes, also wanted to get to know peers, and expressed a desire for more interaction and debate. Women expressed no desire for debate and clearly placed more emphasis on getting acquainted with others than men. Both genders reported more large classes than small ones and liked the chances they had for interaction.

Students' comments on the topic of evaluation techniques were often reports of the types of exams they had taken rather than opinions on whether the exams effectively assessed their learning. Still, they pointed out a few areas of concern. Men disliked subjective grading. Women were concerned with what instructors wanted and whether they curved grades. Students seemed to take testing and grading for granted except when they became problematic.

The question, "Have you ever encountered a situation in which you heard two explanations for the same idea?" was designed to get at knowledge discrepancies. The most startling finding here was the absence of discrepancies. They also reported minimal encounters with contradictions; the examples were limited mostly to reports that they discovered something they had thought was true was false and that different instructors amplified different aspects of the material. Given these descriptions, it seems that sophomore absolute knowers perceived very little contradiction in their encounter with various areas of knowledge.

To summarize, absolute knowers' perceptions of their experiences indicate that the professor played a central role in the learning process. The professor's attitude could determine the student's ability to learn, as could professor-student interactions when they occurred. A professor's classroom demonstrations could promote more interest than a straightforward lecture. Minimal peer interaction was a common theme; most class time seemed to be spent with the professor lecturing or demonstrating. Absolute knowers encountered very few, if any, contradictory views. If they did encounter contradictory perspectives, they clearly did not interpret them as such.

The gender-related emphases in this area corroborate the mastery (usually male) and receiving (usually female) patterns described earlier. Men's desire to have professors explain effectively and help them is consistent with their interest in mastering knowledge. Women's focus on the professor's interest in the subject and care for the students harmonizes with the value women place on a comfortable learning atmosphere. Women also expressed greater interest than did men in knowing peers, undoubtedly for the same reason. Although both men and women reported similar professor attitudes, women reported no interaction with professors. Perhaps men received help from professors because they asked for it, as part of their attempt at mastery. Men also wanted more interaction and debate with the other students and instructors, again consistent with the mastery pattern.

Transitional Knowers' Experiences

The sheer numbers of transitional knowers (twenty-one women and twenty-nine men as sophomores; thirty-one women and thirty-seven men as juniors; and forty-three women and twenty-eight men as seniors) provided a rich array of information about their experiences. In some categories, themes remained consistent over the three years; in others, variations occurred in a particular year.

Both women and men appreciated professors who were "interested" in students. However, the two groups defined "interest" differently. For women, interest was personalized—the professor, as an individual, cared for students and their learning. For men, "interest" meant that the professor cared about the teaching process—he or she treated students courteously as learners, related to them, wanted students to learn, and enjoyed teaching. Both men and women had encountered professors with negative attitudes; they defined these teachers as impersonal, arrogant, intentionally intimidating, dismissive of student abilities, not receptive to student questions and needs, and not concerned about student learning. Although this theme was clearly evident each year, positive student experiences always outweighed the number of negative attitudes.

Two gender differences were evident in the themes for professor-student interaction. First, sophomore women reported minimal interaction with their professors, while their male counterparts reported professors who were receptive and engaged in helpful interactions with students. Second, junior men reported both positive and negative interactions with professors, while junior women reported only positive interactions. Junior men complained that professors had criticized their ability, questioned their integrity, and hurried them out during office-hour conferences. Junior men also reported trying to avoid contact with their teachers because they didn't understand the material but didn't want to admit it.

Both women and men reported helpful interactions in and out of class in the junior and senior years. Professors helped them with course work, invited classes to their homes, played sports with students, helped students with internship applications and resumes, and actively helped seniors with job searches. For students, such in- and out-of-class interactions increased their interest in learning and their ability to learn.

The overriding theme for teaching strategy was student involvement. Sophomores and juniors described involvement to promote thinking, application, and understanding. Junior men emphasized forming their own ideas. Senior women placed greatest value on experiences in which they could actually do something, such as student teaching or group projects where the products were actually used. In contrast, senior men described how forced involvement (being "put on the spot" by a professor's question) furthered their learning. The contrast between these two definitions of involvement implies that women preferred first-hand experiences, while men found talking about the material sufficient for learning.

Transitional knowers also preferred teaching strategies that prompted them to think rather than simply requiring them to repeat their instructors' ideas. Juniors and seniors also emphasized application; to understand and use what they had learned, they needed to relate the material to real life. Juniors, seniors, and sophomore men commonly noted a number of ineffective teaching strategies such as not connecting lecture and reading material, presenting material poorly, not involving the students, miscalculating student needs and abilities, going through the motions without concern for genuine learning, and not relating to the students' level.

Three additional teaching strategies that helped learning were the teacher's organization (junior and senior men), enthusiastic delivery (senior men), and a "straightforward approach" to teaching (senior women), by which they meant that they knew what to expect and that the teacher worked through the material explicitly. Senior women preferred this approach for difficult courses.

The most important element of class structure in all three years for both genders was peer involvement—a theme that is consistent with the importance of student involvement to teaching strategies. Reports of peer involvement group themselves into two subcategories: participation (talking to understand) and discussion (talking to hear others' views). In participation, the talking itself—rather than interest in others' views per se—was valuable and helpful to learning. In discussion, however, students reported that others' views had an effect on their own. Knowing peers emerged as a prevalent theme for juniors of both genders and for senior women. Knowing peers furthered learning, made learning more fun, and provided support in the learning process. Most freshman and sophomore classes were lecture courses, and few students commented on the value of lectures beyond contrasting this format unfavorably to smaller classes that allowed more involvement. Sophomores described lectures as impersonal, juniors rarely mentioned it in any detail, and senior men labeled lectures as boring.

As students discussed evaluation techniques, the predominant theme that emerged was the value of promoting understanding, application, and thinking instead of memorization. Common secondary themes for women included repeating an authority's views on exams (juniors and seniors), peer critique (juniors and seniors), and constructive feedback from professors (seniors). Repeating authority's views was a matter of identifying what a professor was looking for or wanted to hear; and women felt that teachers who wanted them to do it were unfair. Peer critique and instructor feedback were both viewed as ways to enhance learning.

Secondary themes for men were showing one's knowledge in evaluation (juniors and seniors), professor attitudes and expectations regarding evaluation (juniors), and fairness (juniors and seniors). Men noted that any type of evaluation was appropriate if the student had to know the material to respond. They felt that professor attitudes and expectations could enhance or hinder learning, that tests should be on material covered in class, and that questions should be fair. Predetermined plans of grade distribution and tests on which the majority of students performed poorly were judged as unfair.

Both men and women agreed about two general criticisms of evaluation. Senior men and women felt that much evaluation was ineffective because it did not reflect what they had learned. Junior men and women often wanted more frequent testing so that each exam carried less weight.

All of the themes that emerged from the section on evaluation harmonize well with the primary focus of transitional knowers: understanding, thinking, and application. For women, feedback aided this process. They wanted access to instructors' views on tests. Men expected flexible evaluations that truly reflected their ability to understand, think, and apply.

Unlike the previous categories, knowledge discrepancies showed more differences than similarities between women and men. The only area in common was the agreement of sophomore men and women that they had not encountered contradictory views. (A few sophomore men did report some encounters with contradictions, but the number was not significant.) Juniors and seniors both reported encountering contradictory views regularly, but their responses differed. Women emphasized that diverse views made them aware of new ideas that expanded their thinking; however, they did not mention exploring these ideas. They seemed to encounter these contradictory views during group work, where they often focused on resolving the differences. Men were more interested in exploring contradictions and deciding on their own what they thought about them, while women frequently added the new idea to their current view or replaced their current view with the new idea without serious exploration.

Collectively, the transitional knowers' responses once again identified student involvement as the key to learning. They defined learning as understanding, thinking, and applying material. The individual student's involvement promoted learning as he or she talked about the material; talking led to thinking, which led, in turn, to understanding. Listening to the views of peers also helped a student think and understand. These students wanted the instructor to use teaching strategies that promoted involvement, thinking, and real-life application, and evaluation techniques that measured understanding, thinking, and application. Students encountered knowledge discrepancies regularly, often through peers' views in group discussion. Junior and senior transitional knowers reported more opportunity for involvement in their classes than did sophomore transitional knowers.

Gender-related themes for transitional knowers match the gender divisions between interpersonal and impersonal approaches described earlier. The distinction is most evident in women's preference for instructors who care about students and men's preference for instructors who care about teaching. It is also inherent in seniors' definitions of student involvement. Senior women endorsed hands-on learning, describing an actual experience as far more effective than a discussion of it. Men conversely described being forced to discuss an issue as effective. Personal involvement, so necessary for women, did not seem necessary for men. Relationships with others were important to both genders, but women sometimes emphasized them more than men. When knowledge discrepancies occurred, women wanted to hear others' views and, in groups, wanted to resolve differences. Men often described hearing others' views in a debate context and focused on exploring the ideas, then forming their own ideas. Women preferred feedback from peers and professors, whereas men were concerned with accurate ways to measure their knowledge.

Independent Knowers' Experiences

The themes in this section are less detailed than those in the previous one because a smaller number of students were independent knowers. Independent knowing occurred in the junior year (three women, two men) and senior year (three women, five men).

In this group of independent knowers, only women commented on professors' attitudes. Women wanted professors to be open-minded, to listen to students, to consider their points of view, and to avoid condescension. Women valued their status as knowers and wanted the instructor to acknowledge that value. A few students made explicit comments about interactions with professors, all of them positive. However, interaction was inherent in the teaching strategies independent knowers preferred. Active involvement best characterizes this theme for both genders. Students described active interchanges between instructors and students that acknowledged and valued students' contributions. It is no surprise that independent knowers found this type of activity preferable; it reinforced their view of themselves as knowers with their own voices.

Independent knowers placed equal emphasis on learning from peers. The class structure they most often preferred was an exchange of views among peers. Their descriptions implied that something further developed from peer exchange than would have been possible without it and that peers' views sometimes helped students express their thoughts.

Complex thinking was an element of class structure on which only men commented. Men described effective classes as those that required students to think about material, to sort out ideas, and to look at them from different perspectives. For all of the men advocating this theme, the instructor was the key to creating this value or environment in the classroom.

The most distinct gender differences emerged in the evaluation techniques category. Women emphasized the importance of techniques that allowed them to express their own opinions, an idea similar to their emphasis on instructors listening to students. Although some women found opportunities for self-expression, others did not. Those who felt restricted had negative feelings about learning. Senior men emphasized techniques that acknowledged different perspectives. This theme initially seemed similar to women's focus on self-expression but actually focused more on appreciating a variety of perspectives rather than one's own.

Encounters with contradictory views were foundational to independent knowers. Every theme in every category hinged on the existence of different perspectives and the acceptance of contradictory views. Both men and women emphasized how important they felt it was that instructors listened to students' views and avoided swaying students' views, that peers appreciated each other's views, that they themselves thought critically about material, questioned it, and expressed opinions freely in discussion and evaluation. No gender differences were evident in the knowledge discrepancy category.

At first glance, the thread that connects the independent knowers' perspectives seemed to be active involvement. However, it had a different purpose from the involvement described by transitional knowers, and I would conceptualize this central element as independent thinking. Involvement was the major activity through which this took place. Independent knowers collectively conveyed that they had their own perspectives to contribute to their learning and to that of their peers. Other views, from instructors or peers, helped them assess their own ideas. The exchange of views with peers and instructors enriched the individual student's ability to think through her or his own perspective.

Independent knowers had few gender differences, perhaps in part because there were fewer of them. Women were more insistent than men about having opportunities to express themselves. Perhaps expression was necessary in being able to truly view themselves as knowers or to convince authorities that women can be knowers. Men's lack of emphasis on self-expression may result from feeling (and getting reinforcement for the feeling) that they were legitimate knowers all along. Men's emphasis on critical thinking and acknowledging different perspectives seems to be mastery moved to a new level. They seemed still focused on achieving as knowers rather than being satisfied with expressing their own opinions.

IMPLICATIONS OF STUDENTS' PERCEPTIONS FOR PEDAGOGY

The three epistomologies of absolute, transitional, and independent ways of knowing produced striking differences in academic experiences for these students. They emphasized different key elements in learning and different definitions of learning. For absolute knowers, instructors were the key element in learning, and learning meant knowing the material. Instructors' attitudes, teaching strategies, interactions with students, classroom structures, and evaluation methods all determined the success of student learning. Knowledge discrepancies did not exist. Variations in students' reactions to academic experiences were consistent with receiving or mastery approaches.

Transitional knowers turned to student involvement as the key to learning, which they defined as the ability to understand, apply, and think about material. The individual student's own involvement, as well as that of peers, was aimed at understanding. Thus, peers' views became new ways to think about material and hence to further one's own understanding. Evaluation became increasingly complicated as knowledge discrepancies became more common. These students' responses were also consistent with the interpersonal and impersonal patterns. Independent knowers, who defined learning primarily as thinking, took student involvement one step further; a full exchange of views with all parties involved in the learning task was central to enhancing thinking for oneself. Balancing one's own and others' views differed slightly for women and men.

These data suggest that students' perceptions about their academic experiences stemmed from their underlying epistemologies and the gender-related patterns within them. When academic experiences matched their epistemology and pattern, they were more invested in learning. For example, when transitional knowers were actively involved in classes, they reported heightened interest and ability to learn. Interpersonal-pattern transitional knowers wanted to share ideas collectively, while impersonal-pattern transitional knowers preferred to debate ideas.

In short, students learned better when the process matched their way of knowing. A pedagogy/epistemology match thus seems an important step in promoting communal learning (Palmer 1987) and epistemological growth (Perry 1970; Piaget 1926). However, this match should include both support *and* challenge. Mere support seems only to reinforce the student's existing epistemology (Rodgers 1983; Sanford 1967). It is possible to challenge students' knowledge and epistemic assumptions enough to prompt them to question and reshape both while still supporting their ability to know and respecting their epistemic assumptions. Challenge is also a component of Palmer's definition of learning: encountering conflict and taking risks to express, discuss, and form perspectives. Challenge and support can be balanced if we connect pedagogy to students' epistemologies. In this sense, "connecting" means providing degrees of challenge and support that place learning opportunities within the range of students' ways of knowing.

Some of the stories students told contained information about how to connect pedagogy to students' epistemology. Because instructors were the central element in absolute knowers' learning, absolute knowers' ideas on professor attitude offer important advice. Fran described her calculus professor as caring: "He knows my name and makes me feel like he cares [enough] to go out of his way. He says, `Come to office hours or call for an appointment if you can't come to hours.' He is not against you." Spencer described his physics professor as caring about teaching: "He gives letter grades for homework. He hands it back and goes over it so you can see your mistakes. He offers a help session once a week. He goes the extra mile for you." Both quotes show that it does not take extraordinary measures to provide support for absolute knowers.

Anita, describing how teachers could involve students and get to know them simultaneously, said, "We've had projects and exercises where we've been put in groups with other people. Having to work with other people, you get to know them pretty well. You can work it out together." Her experience would seem to work for mastery knowers as well; they could test each others' understanding in this setting. Group work would also address the preference absolute knowers expressed for more interaction in class. Implementing these attitudes and teaching strategies would provide enough support to introduce more challenges. The challenge missing for this group of students was looking at topics from more than one perspective. Such a challenge could be introduced by having groups work on a topic from two perspectives or having each group focus on a different perspective and later share their findings.

Transitional knowers enjoyed professors who were more personal and excited about teaching. Megan liked instructors who "get to know you. You can go to their offices and they'll tell you more about themselves and ask more about you. It makes them human." Andrew liked instructors who "express enthusiasm in class. They live and breath what they teach. They take it seriously, so students do too." Again, this type of support would be fairly easy for most teachers to provide. Transitional knowers' advice about involvement is particularly important because that was the key issue in their learning. Candace recommended discussion: "We do groups. The discussion aids understanding and application. There is a more open atmosphere. I don't feel inferior anymore if I don't understand. Discussion causes you to change opinions when you hear others' perspectives." Tracy gave a more detailed description of one type of discussion: "The professor encouraged us to critique theory. He made it comfortable to do this because he was down to earth. He gave us real-life examples to relate to. He played devil's advocate. He rewarded us for challenging him, and we learned more." Chuck explained a similar experience in a political science class: "We question the teacher. They want you to get a wide base of knowledge, to think for yourself. It helps to know how others think. Students who take the class know we are going to be debating." These students suggest that offering opportunities for students to question the knowledge being studied and to hear others' perspectives reduces feelings of inferiority, promotes learning, and results in better-developed opinions. These attitudes and class formats apparently provide sufficient support for the challenge of considering diverse perspectives.

Transitional knowers described how this same balance of challenge and support could be created in evaluation. In Valerie's business law class, the instructor offered an opportunity for students to explain their multiple choice answers, especially when a student thought two answers might be right. Valerie consequently felt that the instructor respected her thoughts. Getting feedback on her ideas was important to Marge, who said, "I like essays where I can voice my opinion and see what the teacher thinks about what I'm thinking." Journals also provided a mix of challenge and support. Kris liked how her instructor graded a class journal: "She would write comments on just about every page. Some were critical and offered things to think about and some were praise. She offered suggestions." Transitional knowers were able to accept criticism of their ideas when it was presented supportively.

Independent knowers' interest in exchanging views was facilitated by a professorial attitude Marla described as "open minded."

She said, "Someone will bring up something and the instructor will say, 'Oh, I never thought of that' or 'That's a good point.' Just honest, no pretenses." This attitude allowed peer interaction in the classroom. Dawn described becoming "instructors for each other. We work closely together, we know one another, we're all learning at the same level. I admire the opinion of everyone in my class because I think we all know something, maybe from different aspects and in different areas." Kurt offered another version of this idea:

> Interactions with peers are important to my learning experience. It's important to be able to disagree with your peers, and to not be defensive about that, to be open-minded when somebody disagrees with what you said. It provides you with a different perspective you can take to something. It also makes me look more into the perspective that I am taking. When peers make me defend my position, then I have to analyze it more for myself.

Teaching strategies and evaluation techniques also encouraged students to establish their own views. Tracy reported simply accepting whatever she read until one of her professors said, "Stop and think a minute about this. Don't just accept everything we tell you as true. Critically evaluate this." Her professor's support made meeting this challenge possible. Marla's open-minded teacher gave students a blank paper with their multiple choice tests so they could explain answers they thought were ambiguous. As a result, Marla concluded that the teacher "cares what I have to say; she thinks I have a brain and that I may not put the thing she wanted me to put, but at least I have my own reason for why I did it." Again, the instructor's support made it possible for the student to state an independent opinion. For independent knowers, instructors who acknowledge the limits of their knowledge, appreciate students' knowledge, and give students opportunities to explore and exchange views helped students develop their own independent views.

These students would like a more central role in learning. Their comments show that a professor who values them would initially be receptive to them and eventually get to know them and exchange ideas with them. Student desire for more responsibility is inherent in the suggestions about active involvement in class and increased responsibility in exploring knowledge and forming opinions. Giving students opportunities to explain themselves in evaluation is another form of additional responsibility. Setting up class formats which help students get to know each other and using both sharing/debating techniques also support students in undertaking these challenges. In fact, these students suggest that they could handle more challenge than they are sometimes offered, particularly in entertaining different perspectives.

Translating their ideas to new forms of pedagogy entails changing traditional pedagogical assumptions. We must start with students' knowledge rather than teachers' knowledge, recognizing that helping students think about their perspectives is more useful than having them memorize those of others. Helping students struggle together to sort out their perspectives seems less efficient than providing them with a good summary of the material. However, the difference in impact for these students makes it clear that helping them struggle is the best option for promoting complex thinking. Perhaps pedagogy should balance a focus on the thinking process with a focus on learning specific content. Finally, the students' stories show that the learning process is richly laced with emotion. Learning across all epistemological perspectives was more effective when professors expressed regard for students as learners and knowers.

Students' reactions to their academic experiences speak clearly to the value of a relational rather than objectivist pedagogy. When students felt valued, involved (by their definitions), and able to relate to teachers and when they felt that teachers related to them, they were more satisfied and perceived themselves as learning more effectively. Although the receiving and interpersonal patterns emphasized these characteristics most clearly, the mastery and impersonal patterns also contained these basic elements. Themes that described ineffective teaching strategies or negative professor attitudes invariably contained elements of distance between knowledge and the student's personal life and between the teacher and student. Renewal in higher education could be achieved through relational pedagogy guided by listening, valuing, and engaging with students' epistemologies.

BIBLIOGRAPHY

Baxter Magolda, Marcia B. "Comparing Open-ended Interviews and Standardized Measures of Intellectual Development." *Journal of College Student Personnel* 28 (September 1987): 443-48.

Baxter Magolda, Marcia B. "Epistemological Reflection: A Gender Inclusive Model." Miami University, Oxford, Ohio. Manuscript submitted for publication.

Baxter Magolda, Marcia B., and William Porterfield. *Assessing Intellectual Development: The Link Between Theory and Practice.* Alexandria, Va.: American College Personnel Association, 1988.

_____. "A New Approach to Assess Intellectual Development on the Perry Scheme." *Journal of College Student Personnel* 26 (July 1985): 343-51.

Belenky, Mary F., Blythe M. Clinchy, Nancy R. Goldberger, and Jill M. Tarule. *Women's Ways of Knowing.* New York: Basic Books, 1986.

Boyer, Ernest L. *College: The Undergraduate Experience in America.* New York: Harper and Row, 1987.

Carnegie Foundation for the Advancement of Teaching. *Campus Life: In Search of Community.* Princeton, N.J.: Princeton University Press, 1990.

Kitchener, Karen. "Cognition, Metacognition, and Epistemic Cognition." *Human Development* 26 (1983): 222-32.

Kitchener, Karen S., and Patricia M. King. "Reflective Judgment: Concepts of Justification and Their Relationship to Age and Education." *Journal of Applied Developmental Psychology* 2 (Summer 1981): 89-116.

_____. "The Reflective Judgment Model: Ten Years of Research." In *Adult Development Volume II: Models and Methods in the Study of Adolescent and Adult Thought,* edited by Michael Commons, Cheryl Armon, Lawrence Kohlberg, Francis Richards, T. A. Grotzer, and Jan Sinnott. New York: Praeger, 1990.

Lincoln, Yvonna, and Egon Guba. *Naturalistic Inquiry.* Beverly Hills, Calif: Sage, 1985.

Lyons, Nona Plessner. "Dilemmas of Knowing: Ethical and Epistemological Dimensions of Teacher's Work and Development." *Harvard Educational Review* 60 (May 1990): 159-80.

NIE Study Group. *Involvement in Learning: Realizing the Potential of American Higher Education.* Washington D.C.: U.S. Government Printing Office, 1984.

Palmer, Parker J. "Community, Conflict, and Ways of Knowing." *Change,* September/October 1987, 20-25.

Perry, William G. *Forms of Intellectual and Ethical Development in the College Years: A Scheme.* New York: Holt, Rinehart, and Winston, 1970.

Piaget, Jean. *The Language and Thought of the Child.* Translated by M. Gabian. London: Routledge & Kegan Paul, 1926.

Rodgers, Robert F. "Using Theory in Practice." In *Administration and Leadership in Student Affairs,* edited by Theodore K. Miller, Roger B. Winston, Jr., and William R. Mendenhall, 111-14. Muncie, Ind.: Accelerated Development Inc., 1983.

Rogers, Judy L. "New Paradigm Leadership: Integrating the Female Ethos." *Initiatives* 51 (1988): 1-8.

Sanford, Nevitt. *Where Colleges Fail.* San Francisco, Calif.: Jossey-Bass, 1967.

The Reflective Judgment Model: Transforming Assumptions About Knowing

Karen S. Kitchener
Patricia M. King

For years, educators have emphasized the importance of helping children, adolescents, and young adults become critically reflective in problem solving. Mezirow, in his introduction to this book, offers a definition of critical reflection that emphasizes questioning the assumptions with which individuals typically begin problem solving. These assumptions range from beliefs about the self as an effective problem solver to beliefs about whether and when problems are solvable. Transformative learning is aimed at helping the individual become more aware and critical of assumptions in order to actively engage in changing those that are not adaptive or are inadequate for effective problem solving.

Our own writing and research has been on the development of reflective judgment. Based on the work of Dewey (1933), who identified reflective thinking as a goal of education, our

Note: The material in this chapter on developmental instruction using the reflective judgment model is based primarily on work done by Patricia M. King, Tammy M. Gocial, and Jonathan Dings at Bowling Green State University in 1987.

141

work defines a reflective thinker as someone who is aware that a problematic situation exists and is able to bring critical judgment to bear on the problem. In other words, a reflective thinker understands that there is real uncertainty about how a problem may best be solved, yet is still able to offer a judgment about the problem that brings some kind of closure to it. This judgment, which Dewey refers to as a "grounded" or "warranted" assertion, is based on criteria such as evaluation of evidence, consideration of expert opinion, adequacy of argument, and implications of the proposed solution.

Our research suggests that the ability to make reflective judgments is an outcome of a developmental sequence that both limits learning and can be influenced by learning. Our work has focused primarily on validating the sequence and understanding the relationship between it and other aspects of development, such as moral and ego development. As a result, the emphasis of this chapter will differ somewhat from other chapters in this book. First, we will describe the reflective judgment model. Second, we will identify several developmental parameters, based on research, that influence learning to be reflective. Third, we will suggest possible methods that educators can use to promote reflective judgment at two developmental points. Last, we will briefly describe a program that was designed to promote development.

The Reflective Judgment Model

The reflective judgment model (Kitchener and King, 1981; Kitchener and King, forthcoming) describes changes in assumptions about sources and certainty of knowledge and how decisions are justified in light of those assumptions. In other words, the model focuses on describing the development of epistemic assumptions and how these assumptions act as meaning perspectives (see Chapter One) that radically affect the way individuals understand and subsequently solve problems. Initially, the model was influenced by the work of Perry (1970) and Broughton (1975) on epistemological development.

At each step in the model, there are sets of assumptions that develop at about the same time, apparently because they are logically interrelated. As already noted, each set includes assumptions about what can be known and how certain one can be about knowing; it also includes assumptions about the role of evidence, authority, and interpretation in the formation of solutions to problems. While most often these assumptions are not explicit, they can be inferred from how individuals approach problem solving, their expectations of instructors, their beliefs about the certainty of problem solving, and so on. For example, in the following two quotations, the students imply that they expect truth to be clear and easy to decipher, that interpretation is both unnecessary and illegitimate, and that instructors ought to provide them with the "truth" about the world.

> Example A-1. "It seems as if college examinations don't test the student on the material covered in the lecture, but on whether the student can decipher a trick question. Why can't the test come right out and ask for a simple answer?"

In other words, the student asks why tests involve interpretation and why instructors can't require students simply to repeat the facts (or the "truth") on tests.

> Example A-2. "Instead of discussing all these issues, I wish you'd [the instructor] just tell us the real reasons for the Civil War."

In other words, the instructor should simply tell students the truth rather than ask them to figure it out.

Other students have given up ever finding the absolute truth and, as a consequence, they conclude that there are no ways to evaluate any conclusion as better than another. Their assumptions are reflected in comments like those in examples B-1 and B-2.

> Example B-1. "What do you mean I got a *C?* Art can be anything you want it to be and my judgment is as good as yours. I worked hard so I think I deserve an *A.*"

Without certainty, students like this one suggest that hard work is the only way to judge merit. At least it is concrete.

Example B-2. "The instructor kept trying to force her ideas
about the poem on us . . . I mean, what makes her ideas
any better than mine, anyway?"

In other words, this student suggests that if there are no absolute criteria for evaluation, that is, no sources of certainty,
then anything goes.

The reflective judgment model regards such comments
as implicit clues to students' meaning perspectives. Our research
suggests that these perspectives are identifiable, that they are
age related, and that they change in a predictable fashion over
time. Further, our research suggests that these perspectives act
as frames of reference through which students interpret learning experiences.

In the following paragraphs, each stage in the developmental sequence will be described. We refer to each step as a
stage because we are describing a set of beliefs and assumptions
that typically develop at about the same time. Descriptions of
these stages are based on the rules for reflective judgment scoring in Kitchener and King (1985), as well as on other recent formulations of the model (Kitchener and King, forthcoming;
Kitchener, King, Wood, and Davison, forthcoming). The descriptions illustrate more precisely the sets of assumptions evident at each stage.

We should note that the grade levels to which we refer
throughout this next section have been drawn from interviews
with more than 1,000 subjects and from several studies (Kitchener
and King, forthcoming). Reflective judgment scores have consistently increased with age and education. Adult students between their mid twenties and mid fifties entering college for the
first time typically score remarkably similarly to traditional-age
undergraduates. In other words, the epistemic meaning perspectives of adult learners are, on the average, similar to those of
a traditional-age learner at a similar educational level. The adults'
scores, however, are more variable, providing a reminder of the
need to acknowledge individual differences among adult learners.

Stage One. At this stage, knowing is characterized by a
concrete, single-category belief system: What the person observes

to be true is true. Individuals assume that knowledge is both absolute and concrete, thus, beliefs do not need to be justified. Since they need only observe to know what exists, individuals do not acknowledge that problems exist for which there are no absolutely true answers. This stage in its purest form is probably only found in young children.

Stage Two. Knowing takes on more complexity at this stage since individuals assume that, while truth is ultimately accessible, it may not be directly and immediately known to everyone. Since truth is not available to everyone, some people hold "right" beliefs while others hold "wrong" ones. Perry (1970) called this belief system *dualism.* However, since the truth may ultimately be known, individuals continue to assume that all problems are solvable. As a consequence, they assume that the knower's role is to find the right answer and that the source of this answer will be an authority, for example, a teacher, priest, or doctor. Individuals holding these assumptions often make statements like those in examples A-1 and A-2. This frame of reference is most typical of young adolescents, although some college students continue to hold these assumptions (Kitchener and King, forthcoming).

Stage Three. At this stage, individuals acknowledge that in some areas truth is temporarily inaccessible, even for those in authority. In other areas, they maintain the belief that authorities know the truth. In areas of uncertainty, they maintain the belief that absolute truth will be manifest in concrete data sometime in the future and argue that, since evidence is currently incomplete, no one can claim any authority beyond his or her own personal impressions or feelings. Beliefs can only be justified on the basis of what feels right at the moment. Consequently, like the students who made statements B-1 and B-2, individuals at this stage do not understand or acknowledge any basis for evaluation beyond those feelings. Implicitly, however, they maintain the assumption that ultimately all problems have solutions and that certainty will, in the long run, be attained. Students in their last two years of high school or first year of college typically score at about Stage Three (Kitchener & King, forthcoming).

Stage Four. The uncertainty of knowing is initially acknowledged in this stage and usually attributed to limitations of the knower. Without certainty, individuals argue that knowledge cannot be validated externally; thus, they argue that it is idiosyncratic. They often appear confused about how to make claims to knowledge in light of uncertainty and without authorities to provide them the answers. In fact, individuals at this stage frequently express skepticism about the role of authorities. Example C-1 quotes one college student who was asked about how to sort out the claims about evolution and creationism.

> Example C-1. "I'd be more inclined to believe in evolution if they had proof. . . . I don't think we'll ever know because people will differ. Who are you going to ask? No one was there" [quoted in Kitchener, King, Wood, and Davison, forthcoming].

For him, uncertainty was real because people cannot go back in time to relive the event. As a result, he was at a loss to substantiate his views. Authorities were of no help because they faced similar epistemic limits.

The fact that uncertainty is clearly accepted at this stage as an intrinsic characteristic of knowing is, however, an important development. It allows individuals to distinguish between what we (Kitchener, 1983) and others (Churchman, 1971; Wood, 1983) have called well- and ill-structured problems.

Well-structured problems — for example, an arithmetic problem — can be described completely and solved with certainty. Real-world problems, such as what career path to follow or how to reduce pollution, can rarely be treated as well-structured problems since all the parameters are seldom clear or available and since it is difficult to determine when and whether an adequate solution has been identified. Therefore, we call real-world problems *ill structured.* When individuals in Stages One, Two, or Three cannot acknowledge that some problems do not have an absolutely correct solution, they cannot acknowledge the existence of real, ill-structured problems. At Stage Four, ill-structured problems are afforded legitimacy. Such reasoning is most typical of college seniors (Kitchener and King, forthcoming).

Stage Five. At this stage, individuals believe that knowledge must be placed within a context. This assumption derives from the understanding that interpretation plays a role in what a person perceives. Although these individuals move beyond the idiosyncratic justifications of Stage Four to argue that justification must be understood as involving interpretation of evidence within a particular perspective, they cannot compare and evaluate the relative merits of two alternative interpretations of the same issue. We have found that this type of reasoning is most typical of graduate students (Kitchener and King, forthcoming).

Stage Six. Individuals at this stage believe that knowing is uncertain and that knowledge must be understood in relationship to the context from which it was derived. In addition, they argue that knowing involves evaluation and that some perspectives, arguments, or points of view may be evaluated as better than others. These evaluations involve comparing evidence and opinion across contexts, which allows an initial basis for forming judgments about ill-structured problems. Such solutions are typically found among advanced graduate students (Kitchener and King, forthcoming).

Stage Seven. Although individuals at this stage believe that knowing is uncertain and subject to interpretation, they also argue that epistemically justifiable claims can be made about the better or best solution to the problem under consideration.
As with Dewey's description (1933) of reflective thinking, individuals claim that knowledge can be constructed via critical inquiry and through the synthesis of existing evidence and opinion into claims that can be evaluated as having greater "truth value" or being more "warranted" than others. Individuals argue that such views can be offered as reasonable current solutions to the problem at hand, as stated in the example that follows.

Example D-1. "[We] can argue here that one is a better argument than the other. One is more consistent with the evidence. What I am really after is a story that is . . . as intelligible as possible. . . . I don't think it's as much of a puzzle solving as it is trying to get the narrative straight" [quoted in Kitchener, King, Wood, and Davison, forthcoming].

Such reasoning is a rarity even in graduate students, although it is found in some educated adults as they mature into their thirties and beyond.

Developmental Parameters for Learning

Research on the reflective judgment model has several implications for education. First, individuals are quite consistent in their reasoning across different tasks (Kitchener and King, forthcoming; Kitchener, King, Wood, and Davison, forthcoming). Typically, when people are presented with several ill-structured problems, their assumptions about knowing and justification will best be represented by the same stage about three out of four times. On the remainder of the problems, their reasoning will seldom vary by more than one stage, even when they are tested on similar tasks drawn from disciplines as different as science and history. After identifying a student's reflective judgment stage, educators can assume that the student typically will approach most ill-structured problems with the same set of epistemic filters.

Second, recent research at the University of Denver (Lynch and Kitchener, 1989) suggests that even under conditions designed to elicit the highest stage of reasoning of which people are capable, individuals are seldom able to produce reasoning that is more than one stage above their typical response. Furthermore, the data suggest that there are age-related developmental ceilings on the highest reflective judgment stage an individual can use. These data parallel those found by Fischer and Kenny (1986) on arithmetic reasoning. The Lynch and Kitchener data and Fischer's (1980) model suggest that adolescents prior to ages nineteen to twenty are not capable of understanding the highest reflective judgment stages (Stages Six and Seven). Our own data (Kitchener, King, Wood, and Davison, forthcoming) show that even among a college-educated sample, the majority did not typically use reasoning higher than Stage Four prior to age twenty-four. In other words, educators should not assume that younger students can either understand or emulate what Dewey described as reflective thinking. On the other hand, while adult learners ordinarily reason with assumptions like those of similarly educated younger students, there may not be a ceiling on the highest reflective judgment level that adults can understand after practice and with support.

Third, our data strongly suggest that epistemic assumptions change sequentially (Kitchener, King, Wood, and Davison, forthcoming). In other words, it is not typical for individuals to move from Stage Four assumptions to Stage Seven assumptions without showing some evidence of understanding and using the assumptions of the intermediate stages. In fact, it is most typical for subjects' scores to move upward about one stage every six years. Regressions are rare.

Preliminary data from the University of Denver study (Lynch and Kitchener, 1989) also suggest that individuals have difficulty comprehending epistemic assumptions more than one or two stages higher than the stage they typically use. These data, along with the data on sequentiality, suggest that educators ought to target their interventions no more than one or two stages higher than where the student typically responds. Trying to move from *A* to *C* without attending to the meaning perspectives of *B* will probably be counterproductive.

By identifying a student's typical reasoning style and knowing the next step in the sequence, educators can identify a developmental range within which transformative learning experiences can be targeted. Learning tasks can be identified that cause critical reflection on current meaning perspectives, for example, by requiring skills more typical of the next-highest reflective judgment stage. (This point is illustrated below.)

Fourth, critical to acknowledging uncertainty is the recognition that some problems are ill structured (Davison, King, and Kitchener, forthcoming). Too often in traditional educational settings, courses are taught and textbooks are written as though they provide the absolute truth (Finster, forthcoming). By contrast, students need to struggle with ill-structured problems in many domains if they are to come to terms with the need for reflective thinking on many of life's problems.

Last, from our perspective, transformative learning that leads to developmental change does not occur without disequilibrium. Disequilibrium is frequently uncomfortable and, in some cases, can even be frightening. As Kegan (1982) has noted, giving up old frames of reference, old worldviews, or, in this case, old meaning perspectives about how and what we can know, is like losing the self. When the self is lost, individuals are often unsure that a new self or frame of reference can be found. As educators, when we accept the task of deliberately educating to promote development, we must also accept the responsibility of providing students with both an emotionally and intellectually supportive environment. In other words, we must not only challenge old perspectives but must support people in their search for new ones. Thus, we must create an educational milieu that is developmentally appropriate.

In the following section, we will describe learning objectives and the difficult learning tasks for individuals who are reasoning primarily at reflective judgment Stages Three and Five. We will then suggest the kinds of assignments that can be used to both challenge and support individuals at those stages in order to create transformative learning experiences. While these learning tasks and assignments are designed for traditional classrooms, they can be applied to nontraditional educational settings as well. It is assumed in the following examples that students are working on problems that are ill structured.

Developmental Instruction Using the Reflective Judgment Model

Challenging and Supporting Stage Three Reasoning. As noted in an earlier section of this chapter, the following assumptions are characteristic of Stage Three reasoning: Knowledge is absolutely certain in some areas and temporarily uncertain in others; conclusions are justified via authorities in areas of certainty and via intuition in areas of uncertainty; and evidence does not play a role in reasoning to a conclusion since there is no certain way to evaluate it. It is difficult for learners who hold this view to recognize legitimate sources of authority as better qualified than themselves to make judgments or to draw conclusions about ill-structured problems. They also have difficulty distinguishing between facts and opinions and do not understand the use of evidence to justify a point of view. In addition, it remains difficult for these individuals to tolerate or value multiple evidence-based perspectives on a single issue. For many, these multiple perspectives are seen simply as adding confusion to an already confusing world or as examples of false authoritative claims in areas of temporary uncertainty.

One learning objective for individuals using Stage Three reasoning is to differentiate between evidence and opinion — for example, between the use of authority to support an argument and the evidence the authority uses. A second objective is for learners to use evidence to evaluate their intuitive beliefs about a problem. Last, they need to confront and evaluate the evidence for multiple perspectives on an issue. Some possible assignments that follow from these objectives are listed below.

1. Evaluate an argument (for or against an issue) in terms of its use of evidence, dependence upon authority, and understanding of the other view of the issue.
2. Give the best evidence you can find for a specific point of view. Identify what makes it count as evidence.
3. Identify the evidence and arguments for a view that an authority in the field is presenting. What makes the evidence for the argument strong or weak?
4. Identify two or more points of view on an issue.
5. What do you believe about an issue? Is there any evidence that supports what you believe? What is the evidence that is contrary to what you believe?

As a step in the transformation of Stage Three to Stage Four perspectives, each of these assignments is designed to help students who use Stage Three reasoning to critically reflect upon their implicit assumptions about evidence and opinion, about how arguments are validated, or about the legitimacy of different points of view. It should be noted that other naturally occurring events—for example, contact with individuals with alternative life-styles and belief systems—will also contribute to the transformation of Stage Three meaning perspectives.

Although it is important to challenge implicit epistemic assumptions, it is also important to legitimize students' struggles with their feelings of being confused and overwhelmed by alternative perspectives and with questioning what counts as evidence. Educators can acknowledge the struggle explicitly as well as help peers share their confusion with each other in discussions or written assignments. Educators can also provide support by modeling good use of evidence—for example, making explicit the justification for both sides of an argument, distinguishing inapplicable evidence from relevant evidence, or explaining the rationale behind their own use of expert or authoritative opinion.

The anxiety that comes from giving up the belief that knowledge is certain may be exacerbated by the anxiety of not knowing what an instructor expects in a class. Therefore, detailed assignments with clear expectations can provide the students at this level with an environment that allows safe exploration.

Challenging and Supporting Stage Five Reasoning. To review, Stage Five reasoning is characterized by the assumption that no knowledge is certain because interpretation is inherent in all understanding. Individuals suggest that beliefs may be justified only within a given context. Within particular contexts, however, they acknowledge that some evidence can be evaluated qualitatively as stronger or more relevant than other evidence.

It is difficult for those using Stage Five reasoning to evaluate competing evidence-based interpretations that reflect different points of view on an issue. It is hard for them to identify relationships between points of view and to act as though each were discrete. These individuals also have difficulty endorsing one view as better than another, as if doing so would deny the legitimacy of other perspectives. Consequently, the most important learning objective for those at this stage is to relate alternative points of view to each other, comparing the evidence and opinion for each in order to arrive at a conclusion that integrates the alternatives or evaluates one as better or best in a limited sense. Further, individuals must acknowledge that such conclusions need not sacrifice the appreciation for multiple perspectives that is the hallmark of Stage Five reasoning.

Possible assignments that make this goal explicit are listed below.

1. Compare and contrast two competing points of view, citing and evaluating evidence and arguments used by proponents of each. Determine which author makes the better interpretation of the evidence and which conclusion is most appropriate.
2. Select a controversial issue from those discussed in class. Explain at least two points of view from which the issue has been addressed by scholars. Indicate which point of view you believe to be most appropriate and the grounds for that decision.

As with Stage Three reasoning, the transformation of one's meaning perspective can be frustrating, confusing, and sometimes frightening. Therefore, with individuals using Stage Five reasoning, it is important to legitimize the struggle to adjudicate between competing points of view as required in the above assignments. Modeling choice making by carefully explaining the evaluation process and reasons for choices provides support for the students' own struggles. For example, instructors can give relevant interpretations of evidence from different points of view and explain the reasons for choosing one interpretation over another. Because individuals who use Stage Five constructs often equate choice making with intolerance for different points of view, legitimizing inquiry from different perspectives and valuing different points of view remains important.

A Programmatic Example

As noted earlier, our work has been primarily on developing and empirically testing the reflective judgment model. While we have applied ideas such as those discussed above to our own teaching, we have not developed or tested a program designed to help students examine their own epistemic perspectives. Kroll (forthcoming), however, has developed such a program, which we describe below.

Based on our work as well as the work of Perry (1970), Kroll designed a learning experience for a literature and composition class to help freshmen college students become more thoughtful and reflective. Based on data suggesting that many college freshmen struggle with the epistemic assumptions characteristic of Stage Three, he focused the assignments on understanding that different people in positions of authority may provide discrepant accounts of the same event, a factor that makes it difficult to know what to believe.

The content of Kroll's course was taken from accounts of the Vietnam War. Students were asked to make judgments at the beginning and at the end of the course about two different accounts of a battle. Specifically, they were asked whether one account of the battle was more believable than the other, whether one was more likely to be true, and, last, what *really* happened in this battle. In other words, Kroll asked students to identify *what* they could know and *how* they could know when they were faced with an ill-structured historical problem. The questions were designed to help the instructor understand more about the students' epistemological assumptions when they entered the class and to evaluate those assumptions again when they left the class.

At the end of the semester, most students were emphatic in claiming that the course had influenced their ability to be critical in their thinking, to be cautious about what they read, and to be more skeptical about accepting what others claim to be truth. Because many students pointed to a unit on the Hue massacre as particularly influential, it seems useful to identify the key elements of that unit.

First, Kroll had students read two quite different accounts of what happened at Hue. One presented the offical view that Communist forces had systematically massacred many South Vietnamese because of their political ties to the United States. The other account took the perspective that the Viet Cong planned to execute only a few government officials and that most of the civilians died in the ruthless counterattack of the United States forces. After reading these accounts, students read thirteen more accounts of the event and viewed a documentary that depicted several interpretations of what happened at Hue. At each step, they kept an account of their thinking about the articles in journals. Instructors' comments, both in response to journal entries and in class discussion, were focused on getting students to reflect critically on what they were reading. Instructors carefully avoided endorsing one interpretation. Instead, they asked students to identify the different positions, to articulate which claims supported each, and to begin to evaluate these claims. Later, they asked students to analyze the material they had read and to present the best case they could for what really happened in Hue in 1968.

Kroll reports that when asked at the end of the course to again interpret the two accounts of the battle on which they wrote during the first week of class, students' writing reflected some differences: Students appeared to use dogmatic approaches less often and to use what he called precritical and critical strategies more often. They also expressed skepticism more frequently about what they read. While Kroll acknowledged that there was no way to clearly prove that these changes resulted only from the course work, students attributed the changes to it. Kroll also noted that while there were some differences in students' responses at the end of the course, they did not involve major changes in what we would call epistemological orientation. He notes, and we would agree, that reflective thinking develops slowly and students need more than a single-semester course to make major changes in their meaning perspectives. However, he and we would also argue that education can make a difference in epistemological perspectives if it takes into account the developmental world through which students filter their educational experiences.

Conclusions

Research on the reflective judgment model has shown that students at different ages and educational levels enter the learning environment with markedly different assumptions about what and how something can be known and how to make judgments in light of these assumptions. Some enter believing that they can know absolutely through concrete observation. They see their learning task as discovering the truth or identifying someone, an authority, who can explicate it. Others accept that there are many problems for which there are no absolutely true answers. The task for these problem solvers is to construct a solution that is justifiable after considering alternative evidence and interpretations. In this complex world, where so many of the problems adults face involve uncertainty or are ill structured, we would argue that the latter meaning perspective is more adaptive, more essential, and more consistent with the stated mission of colleges and universities.

Our data suggest that this second meaning perspective does not develop until the adult years (that is, in the late twenties or early thirties) and that it is usually tied to participation in advanced education when individuals are involved in the creation of knowledge. Since our data also suggest that those of the same age without higher education score more similarly to younger subjects of the same educational level, we believe that education does make a difference (Kitchener and King, forthcoming).

We suspect that educational experiences, whether inside or outside the classroom, can be deliberately designed to challenge meaning perspectives and that these challenges along with appropriate environmental support will promote growth. Kroll's work on improving reflective thinking through a literature and composition course supports that position. Similarly, Welfel (1982) suggests that since career counseling involves making decisions about an ill-structured problem, it can also facilitate the transformation of epistemic meaning perspectives. Undoubtedly, many other experiences, from travel to participation in reading groups, can have similar effects. On the other hand, there may be some developmental limits to how far or how fast students at a given age level can advance. Development occurs slowly; and, in our opinion, it is unlikely that young adults, even given the best educational environment, will very often use the kind of reflective judgment that Dewey idealized.

One key to developing reflective thinking is the identification and use of ill-structured problems (Davison, King, and Kitchener, forthcoming). Kroll chose an ill-structured historical problem as the content on which to base his course in literature and writing. Ill-structured problems are not, however, limited to history and literature. They can be found in the hard sciences, the social sciences, business, humanities, and the professions because they are the problems of the real world. We believe their use as educational tools is essential if critical, reflective thinking is to be advanced.

References

Broughton, J. M. *The Development of Natural Epistemology in Years 11 to 16*. Unpublished doctoral dissertation, Harvard University, 1975.

Churchman, C. W. *The Design of Inquiring Systems: Basic Concepts of Systems and Organizations*. New York: Basic Books, 1971.

Davison, M. L., King, P. M., and Kitchener, K. S. "Developing Reflective Thinking Through Writing." In R. Beach and S. Hynds (eds.), *Becoming Readers and Writers During Adolescence and Adulthood*. Norwood, N.J.: Ablex, forthcoming.

Dewey, J. *How We Think*. Lexington, Mass.: Heath, 1933.

Finster, D. "Developmental Instruction: Part 2. Application of Perry's Model to General Chemistry." *Journal of Chemical Education*, forthcoming.

Fischer, K. W. "A Theory of Cognitive Development: The Control and Construction of Hierarchies of Skills." *Psychological Review*, 1980, *87*, 477–531.

Fischer, K. W., and Kenny, S. L. "Environmental Conditions for Discontinuities in the Development of Abstractions." In R. M. Mines and K. S. Kitchener (eds.), *Adult Cognitive Development*. New York: Praeger, 1986.

Kegan, R. *The Evolving Self*. Cambridge, Mass.: Harvard University Press, 1982.

Kitchener, K. S. "Educational Goals and Reflective Thinking." *Educational Forum*, 1983, *48*, 75–95.

Kitchener, K. S., and King, P. M. "Reflective Judgment: Concepts of Justification and Their Relationship to Age and Education." *Journal of Applied Developmental Psychology,* 1981, *2,* 89–116.

Kitchener, K. S., and King, P. M. "Reflective Judgment Scoring Manual." Bowling Green, Ohio: Bowling Green State University, 1985. (Mimeographed.)

Kitchener, K. S., and King, P. M. "The Reflective Judgment Model: Ten Years of Research." In M. L. Commons, J. D. Sinnott, F. A. Richards, and C. Armon (eds.), *Adult Development: Comparisons and Applications of Adolescent and Adult Developmental Models.* New York: Praeger, forthcoming.

Kitchener, K. S., King, P. M., Wood, P. K., and Davison, M. L. "Consistency and Sequentiality in the Development of Reflective Judgment: A Six-Year Longitudinal Study." *Journal of Applied Developmental Psychology,* forthcoming.

Kroll, B. M. "Teaching English for Reflective Thinking." In R. Beach and S. Hynds (eds.), *Becoming Readers and Writers During Adolescence and Adulthood.* Norwood, N.J.: Ablex, forthcoming.

Lynch, C. L., and Kitchener, K. S. "Environmental Conditions for Optimal Performance in Reflective Judgment." Paper presented at the annual meeting of the American Educational Research Association, San Francisco, March 1989.

Perry, W. G. *Forms of Intellectual and Ethical Development in the College Years.* New York: Holt, Rinehart & Winston, 1970.

Wood, P. K. "Inquiring Systems and Problem Structure: Implications for Cognitive Development." *Human Development,* 1983, *26,* 249–265.

Moral Stages and the Development of Faith

JAMES FOWLER

INTRODUCTION

In 1974 Lawrence Kohlberg published an article entitled "Education, Moral Development and Faith."[1] Originally an address to the National Catholic Educational Association, this paper represents a rather direct statement of the central themes of Kohlbergian "faith." It expresses Kohlberg's commitment to a Platonic understanding of justice as the central and unitary moral virtue.[2] It states his claim that justice is a naturalistic virtue, emerging in children (at differing rates and with differing points of final equilibration) in all cultures as a result of their interaction with other persons and with social institutions. It affirms that the capacity for discerning the requirements of justice has an ontogenetic history, recapitulated at varying rates in individuals and their societies, but essentially common to all persons. It claims that moral education can be pursued in public schools without reference to the contents of students' particular beliefs, attitudes, or values. To fulfill this possibility, public education must meet the following imperatives: according to Kohlberg, (1) justice must be embodied in the *modus operandi* of the school; (2) moral thinking must be stimulated by attention to real and hypothetical moral dilemmas; and (3) students must be exposed to moral arguments on these issues one stage beyond their own. If these significant conditions are met, Kohlberg believes, growth in individuals' capacity to discern the requirements of justice should occur. Further, if the social environment encourages children and youth to take the personal and social perspectives of others, the expansion of moral imagination eventually required for principled moral reasoning will be nurtured.

Underlying these elements of Kohlbergian faith is a conception of moral development which Kohlberg appropriated from J. Mark Baldwin, John Dewey, Jean Piaget, and others. This tradition rejects theories of moral development centering in the teaching of multiple virtues or moral ideals. Instead, it argues that moral judgment and action arise out of a person's way of constructing (knowing) situations requiring moral choice. The key to moral development, and therefore to moral education, lies in the cognitive operations by which persons "know" their social environments. Moral development requires progress in the ability accurately to take the perspectives of others, their needs and rights, and to see one's own claims and obligations with similar balance, detachment, and accuracy. Following the path of cognitive development more generally, moral judgment—cognitive operations as applied to questions of rightness, goodness, obligation, duty, and responsibility—also exhibits a developmental trajectory.

Kohlberg's stage theory sets forth the developmental trajectory he finds in persons' moral thinking. Claiming both empirical validation and logical-philosophical justification for the stage sequence,[3] Kohlberg has provided a powerful heuristic model against which to examine patterns of moral reasoning in individuals and groups.

"Education, Moral Development and Faith"either assumes or explicitly restates most of the elements of the Kohlbergian faith I have just enumerated. But it also does more. Kohlberg begins the article in an interesting way:

While moral development has a larger context including faith, it is possible to have a public moral education which has a foundation independent of religion. We believe that the public school should engage in moral education and that the moral basis of such education centers on universal principles of justice, not broader religious and personal values.[4]

The references to "faith," "religion," and "broader religious and personal values" signal an agenda to which Kohlberg returns later in the article.

In a section headed "Moral Development and Education as Centered on Justice," he points to Socrates and Martin Luther King, Jr. as great moral teachers whose lives and teachings manifested their centering commitments to principles of justice. For Kohlberg, the principle of justice held by both these men derived from their considering "social justice, or the nature of an ideal society."[5] The principle of justice, this suggests, is a transcendent ideal, a universal norm arising from the vision of a just society. With this point Kohlberg circles back to the themes promised in his opening sentences:

> We have stressed so far the place of universal principles of human justice as central to moral development, principles which can be defined and justified without reference to a specific religious tradition. We need now to note that while Socrates and Martin Luther King died for principles of human justice, they were also deeply religious men. What, then, is the relation of the development of religious faith to the development of moral principles?[6]

At this juncture in his 1974 text, Kohlberg introduces the fledgling work on stages of faith development of his then Harvard colleague James Fowler, myself. He quoted an early version of our stage theory *in extenso,* but without any attention to what we mean by "faith." In order to discuss some of the relations between moral development and faith, and between stages of moral judgment and possible stages in faith, let me present an introduction to the focus of our work in its present form.

THE FOCUS ON FAITH

I begin with three brief case synopses.
Case Number 1:

> A woman in her mid-twenties tells her story. "The years from seventeen to twenty-two were my lost years, the years I searched and tried everything, but

accomplished nothing. I tried sex, illicit drugs, Eastern religions, the occult, everything. I filled myself with vain knowledge, but gained nothing as far as my real spiritual hunger was concerned." At twenty-two, eight months after "an extraordinary experience on L.S.D.," and after having two persons close to her witness to the lordship of Jesus Christ, she accepted him as her Lord. Her story of the next five years resembles those of many in her generation: movement from one new Christian, true church movement to another; submission to the often conflicting authority of self-appointed Christian elders and to the disciplines of neo-Christian group life. She suffered the psychological violence inflicted by newly converted folk who, in radically denying their own pasts and affirming their new beings in Christ, projected much of the horror and guilt of what they denied in themselves onto others. Her odyssey carried her through at least four such groups before she found one led by mature Christians. At the encouragement of one ill-prepared leader, she had married a man she hardly knew, and for two years "submitted" to horrendous marital anarchy and degradation. Through it all, she affirms, "The Lord never left me bereft. He was leading me, teaching me, shaping me." Though raw and hurting, her faith in the Lord more than ever occupies the center of her efforts to discern what she should do next and to know how to think of herself. "I just pray that the Lord will show me the ministry he has for me."

Case Number 2:

A small-town merchant pours six long days a week into the management of his clothing store. A kind man with a friendly and helpful attitude, his business flourishes. He belongs to a local church and contributes generously. He belongs to a local civic association and gives modestly of his time to its projects. He is a respected member of the town's Chamber of Commerce, and is admired as a progressive force in the refurbishing of Main Street. One day his son, intending it as a joke, gives the attentive observer a frightening clue: "Daddy," he says, "doesn't have a thing except Mama that he wouldn't sell if the price were right!" And this was true. It would be too extreme to speak of money in his case as a fetish, but clearly his son had named the center of the father's value system. And the other involvements and extensions of self—even to the extent of caring financially for an alcoholic brother—served this central devotion to enlarging his "estate."

Case Number 3:

The fourth of ten children born to an Irish-Italian marriage, Jack grew up in "the Projects." "There were so many of us boys that people never knew our first names. They just called us 'Seely' (not the real name). My voice sounded so much like my brothers that sometimes even I got confused." Under the influence of the Sisters in parochial school he became, during his late childhood and early adolescence, a faithful churchgoer. "One year," he said, "I made mass every day and did two novenas, which was hard. I got up early every day and went over there; I never sat on the bench, but always stayed on my knees. I felt like I was one of Jesus' special kids. I liked it, and I kind of made a bargain that I would do all this for him if he would sort of straighten my dad's drinking out a little bit. He would go out on Friday, Saturday, and Sunday nights and come back drunk. Sometimes he beat mother when they argued." At the end of his seventh grade year Sister called him up to the front of the room and publicly recognized him as the only boy who had been faithful in attending mass daily throughout the spring. "She should'na done that," he said. "They got me then, the bullies. They gave me a hard time for the next two years. I quit going to church. But I guess it was just as well. The old man didn't ease up on the drinking. In fact, he started going out on Thursday nights too!" Today, near thirty, still out of church, he lives in a nice but confining low-cost private housing project. Every thirty seconds during most of the day the large jets taking off or landing at the nearby airport shake the windows in their apartment. He and his wife lead the Tenants Association in its struggle against rent-gouging landlords. They have helped organize tenant groups all over their part of the city, and, for their troubles, have two separate $1 million suits against them initiated by landlord associations. His $12,000 per year job and her nightly work as a waitress keep them both very busy. "Blacks and poor white people need to get together here. We've been pitted against each other, to *their* advantage, for too long. I don't know much theory; I can't talk about Hegel and philosophy, and I don't know Marx too good. But I do know my class and I know we're getting stepped on. Me and my wife want to give everything we got to giving poor folks a break. And while we do it, we gotta remember that there are people under us too, people worse off. We may be in the alley fighting, but down below in the cellar somewhere they are fighting for a chance to breathe, too. We gotta be careful not to step on them."

These are vignettes on faith; windows into the organizing images and value patterns by which people live. The stories let us in on their life wagers. They give us access to the ways three persons are pouring out their life energies—spending and being spent in the service of valued projects, in light of which their own value and worth as persons seek confirmation.

In this way of thinking, faith need not be approached as necessarily a religious matter. Nor need it be thought of as doctrinal belief or assent. Rather, faith becomes the designation for a way of leaning into life. It points to a way of making sense of one's existence. It denotes a way giving order and coherence to the force-field of life. It speaks of the investment of life-grounding trust and of life-orienting commitment.

Now let us look at these matters a little more systematically. This way of approaching faith means to imply that this phenomenon is a human universal. That is to say, as members of a species burdened with consciousness and self-consciousness, and with freedom to name and organize the phenomenal world, we nowhere can escape the task of forming tacit or explicit coherent images of our action-worlds. We are born into fields of forces impinging upon us from all sides. The development of perception means a profound limiting and selection of the *sensa* to which we can consciously or unconsciously attend. The development of cognition—understood here in its broadest sense—means the construction of operations of thought and valuing in accordance with which the *sensa* to which we attend are organized and formed. Composition and interpretation of meanings, then, are the inescapable burdens of our species. Consciously or unconsciously, in this process, we invest trust in powerful images which unify our experience, and which order it in accordance with interpretations that serve our acknowledgment of centers of value and power.

We encounter this force-field of life in the presence of others. From the beginning others *mediate* in our interaction with the conditions of our existence. Somatic contact, gestures, words, rituals from other persons—all serve to link us with aspects of the surrounding environment. And before we can think with words or symbols, primitive images or pre-images of felt "sense" begin to form in us. Therefore we must think of even our earliest steps toward interpretation and meaning as shared, as social.

Reflection on this social character of even our earliest moves toward construction of meaning points to another important feature of faith. Our investment of reliance upon, or trust in, interpretative images does not occur apart from our investment of reliance upon or trust in the significant others who are companions or mediators in our acts of meaning construction. Faith involves, from the beginning, our participation in what we may call tacit, covenantal, fiduciary relationships. Put another way, our interpretations of and responses to events which disclose the conditions of our existence are formed in the company of co-interpreters and co-respondents whom we trust and to whom we are loyal. Faith is a relational matter. As we relate to the conditions of our existence with acts of interpretative commitment, we do so as persons also related to and co-involved with companions whom we trust and to whom we are loyal. This means that the interpretative images by which we make sense of the conditions of our lives inevitably implicate our companions. It also means, reciprocally, that our experiences with these companions in interpretation have decisive impact on the forming and re-forming of our interpretative images and for the values and powers they serve.

Let us designate those images by which we holistically grasp the conditions of our existence with the name *images of the ultimate environment.* And let us point out that such images of the ultimate environment derive their unity and their principle of coherence from a center (or centers) of value and power to which persons of faith are attracted with conviction. Faith then, is a matter of composing an image of the ultimate environment, through the commitment of self to a center (or centers) of value and power giving it coherence. We do this in interaction with communities of co-interpreters and co-commitants. And our commitments so made with the interpretative impacts they carry, become occasions for the re-ordering of our loves and the re-directing of our spending and being spent.

We have intended in these paragraphs on faith to present it as a dynamic phenomenon. Faith is an ongoing process. It is a way of being and of leaning into life. Crises, disclosure-events, the fulfillment or failure of hopes, betrayals and experiences of fidelity in the force-field of life continually impact a person's image of the ultimate environment and his or her commitment to the value-, or power-center(s) sustaining it. Conversion or re-conversion in small or large ways can be precipitated without conscious desire or intent. Confusion, doubt, and the conflicts of double or multiple pulls to commitment represent inherent dynamics of faith. And for most of us our controlling image of the ultimate environment is likely to be as much an aspiration to worthy and true faith as it is an accomplished and integrated reality of faith. Competing master images of the ultimate environment contend for loyalty in societies and cultures, and within individual human breasts.

Let us try to bring this introductory characterization of faith into summary focus. Faith, we may say, is
—a disposition of the total self toward the ultimate environment
—in which trust and loyalty are invested in a center or centers of value and power
—which order and give coherence to the force-field of life, *and*
—which support and sustain (or qualify and relativize) our mundane or everyday commitments and trusts
—combining to give orientation, courage, meaning, and hope to our lives, and
—to unite us into communities of shared interpretation, loyalty, and trust.[7]

FAITH AND MORAL REASONING

Before we go on to the matters of stages of faith in relation to stages of moral reasoning we should examine some conceptual and phenomenal relations between faith and moral reasoning. I am claiming that we human beings necessarily engage in constructing frames of meaning for our lives, and that we do this, with others, by making tacit and/or explicit commitments to value-and-power centers which promise to sustain our lives and meanings. This activity I call faith. Faith is a valuing and a committing; it is axiological and volitional. But it is also a knowing—a composing, a construing, an interpreting. Faith, like moral judgment, has an important epistemological dimension.[8]

Kohlberg recognizes this in the latter parts of "Education, Moral Development and Faith." There he introduces—for the only time in published form that I am aware of—reference to a metaphorical, nonmoral "stage 7." He introduces this intriguing notion after having reiterated his belief that moral principles can be formulated and justified without reliance upon faith or religion. He says:

In some sense, however, to ultimately live up to moral principles requires faith. For this reason, we believe, the ultimate exemplars of stage 6 morality also appear to be men of faith.... I believe then, like Kant, that ultimate moral principles, stage 6 morality, can and should be formulated and justified on grounds of autonomous moral rationality. Such morality, however, "requires" an ultimate stage of faith and moves men toward it. The faith orientation required by universal moral principles I call stage 7, though at this point the term is only a metaphor. This faith orientation does not basically change the definition of universal principles of human justice found at stage 6, but it integrates them with a perspective on life's ultimate meaning.[9]

In other writings Kohlberg has held that the critical question, "Why be moral?" is answered from within the logic of stages one through five. In "Moral Stages and Moralization," for example, he includes a chart which provides one of the most recent accounts of stage specific "reasons for doing right."[10] At stage 1 the person "does right" in order to avoid punishment and because of the superior power of authorities. At stage 3, one is moral because of "the need to be a good person in your own eyes and those of others. . . . " Adherence to the requirements of justice at stage 5 derives from "a sense of obligation to law because of one's social contract to make and abide by laws for the welfare of all and for the protection of all peoples' rights."[11] Kohlberg nowhere claims that these motivational factors *exhaustively* account for persons' adherence to the requirements of right or justice. But clearly he wants to avoid any suggestion that moral judgments are essentially dependent upon the particular contents of a person's or group's values, attitudes, world view, or religious orientation.

At stage 6, however, Kohlberg sees no rationale inherent in universal moral principles by which to answer the question, "Why be moral?" The answer to this question at stage 6, he has often said in public discussions, is always a religious answer. In "Education, Moral Development and Faith," he puts it this way:

I have argued that the answer to the question, "Why be moral?" at this level entails the question, "Why live?" (and the parallel question, "How face death?") so that ultimate moral maturity requires a mature solution to the question of the meaning of life. This, in turn, is hardly a moral question per se, it is an ontological or religious one.[12]

"Solutions" to these ontological or religious questions, Kohlberg points out, cannot be reached on purely logical or rational grounds.

They represent ways of seeing the human situation in relation to a more transcending framework of meaning and value. In Kohlberg's language:

> The characteristic of all these stage 7 solutions is that they involve contemplative experience of a nondualistic variety. The logic of such experience is sometimes expressed in theistic terms of union with God but it need not be. Its essential is the sense of being a part of the whole of life and the adoption of a cosmic, as opposed to a universal humanistic "stage 6" perspective.[13]

He turns then to an example of stage 7 faith constituted by the Stoic, mystical resignation of the *Meditations of Marcus Aurelius.*

In private, and in a brief published statement,[14] I have expressed my agreement with Kohlberg in his claim that moral stage 6 implies an accompanying faith vision and faith commitment. I am glad for his recognition that commitment to principled morality is part of a more comprehensive stance or disposition toward the ultimate conditions of our lives. But this recognition, I contend, does not go far enough. The question, "Why be moral?" cannot be answered adequately within the terms of *any* of Kohlberg's stages without reference to a person's commitments to a wider frame of meaning and value. There is a faith context—as I characterize the term faith—informing and supporting a person's consistent adherence to justice, the right or the good, as discerned through the logic of *any* of the stages of moral reasoning.

Let us consider a few examples. In stage 1, Kohlberg tells us, the child's reason for doing good is to avoid punishment and to be rewarded. Also there is deference—presumably a mixture of fear and respect—for the superior physical power of authorities. I am inclined to believe Kohlberg is right as regards the epistemology of moral judgment at this stage. Children do determine what is right by reference to the punishment and reward responses of parents or parentlike adults. But surely the issue of why the child wants to be good, or is interested at all, requires us to go further. My own research with children leads me to suggest that because of ties of dependence and affection, and because of the preoperational child's imitative interest in adult behaviors and values, there is already forming by stage 1 what I call a rudimentary loyalty to the *child's construction* of her or his family's "ethos of goodness." For punishment and reward to make any sense to the child, and for it to contribute to moral growth, it must be linked to a framework of shared meaning and value, no matter how primitively construed by the child. Otherwise we have no way to account for the generalization of experiences of punishment and reward into "improved behavior" across the board, or for the child's countless adoptions of desirable behavior patterns for which there have been no specific occasions of positive or negative sanction. Moral decision or choice for the preschool and early school child, I am arguing, is already beginning to be lodged in a framework of meaning and value, and is part of the child's way of participating in the faith ethos of his or her family or family surrogate.

At moral stage 2, Kohlberg tells us, persons are moral "To serve one's own needs or interests in a world where you have to recognize that other people have their interests too."[15] Stage 2's instrumental hedonism, with its reciprocity of perspectives and its recognition of others' claims, represents the child's first constructions of "fairness." Surely with these insights Kohlberg contributes something extremely valuable to our understanding of the epistemology underlying the child's conception of fairness. But as an account of why the child becomes committed to fairness as a normative principle, it is plainly incomplete. It sheds very little light on why the child feels that some ligament of the universe has been torn if he or she, or a friend, or even a stranger, is treated unfairly. Here again, I submit that the child's adherence to fairness as a valued and respected norm bespeaks a broader frame of meaning and value through which the child finds coherence in life and maintains a sense of worthy membership in a valued group.

In other writings[16] I have followed theologian H. Richard Niebuhr and philosopher Josiah Royce in claiming that any lasting human relation or association has a fiduciary or faith structure. By this I mean initially that as selves we maintain our identities through relations of reciprocal trust in and loyalty to significant others. Our mutual investments of trust and loyalty with these others, however, are deepened, stabilized, and prevented from having to bear more moral weight than they can sustain, by our shared trusts and loyalties to centers of value and power of more transcendent worth.

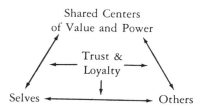

Kohlberg's stages of moral judgment, *especially* through stage 4 and the conventional level, are inexplicable as regards moral motivation and accountability apart from a self's valued membership in groups or communities joined by commitments to meaning frames centering in shared values and images of power.[17]

The stages of faith development to which I now wish to turn, represent our effort to describe a series of stagelike "styles" in which persons participate in the activity of meaning-making and in communities of shared meaning and value. From this perspective, faith stages are to be understood as formal (i.e., content-free) descriptions of the operations of knowing and valuing underlying a person's composing and maintenance of a meaning-value perspective. As such, a faith stage includes and contextualizes a form of moral reasoning such as that characterized in the corresponding Kohlberg stage. After examining the overview of faith stages, we will look briefly at some theoretically predicted and empirically determined relations between the faith stages and stages of moral reasoning.

STAGES OF FAITH

We are going to examine here stages of faith development as we have identified them in the course of seven years of research. Our research procedure has been described in detail elsewhere.[18] Briefly, we employ a semiclinical, open-ended interview of one to three hours (somewhat briefer with children) in which the respondent is asked to share aspects of his or her life history and to express in detail his or her feelings and attitudes regarding a cluster of universal life-issues with which faith must deal. (The list of issues: death and afterlife; the limits of knowledge; causation and effectance in personal and historical life; evil and suffering; freedom and determinism; power and agency; meaning of life; ideal manhood or womanhood; the future; grounding of ethical and moral imperatives; communal identifications and belongings; bases of guilt and shame; central loyalties and commitments; locus of transcendent beauty, value, or power; objects of reverence or awe; grounds of terror or dread; sin and violation; religious experiences, beliefs, and practices; specific meaningful religious symbols.) This list is uniformly pursued in each interview. Respondents are encouraged to share concrete experiences and crises out of their own lives, and to address the faith issues experientially whenever possible. Though respondents often voluntarily answer in specifically religious terms, religion as an issue and context is not explicitly introduced until the last one-third of the interview. An effort is made to test espoused beliefs, values, and attitudes against self-reports of performance and choice in actual situations.

These interviews are then transcribed. Analysis for structural features is carried out by trained scorers. The formulations of position and outlook in relation to the faith issues are regarded as the *contents* of the person's faith. A thematic or content analysis can be carried out and systematized in order to understand the person's faith or belief system. Structural analysis, however, aims to go "under" the content elements to "liberate" the deeper structural operations of knowing and valuing which underlie, ground, and organize the thematic content.

We have conducted and analyzed about 380 interviews of the type just described. The sample has been cross-sectionally balanced for age from four to eighty. It includes slightly more females than males, includes Protestants, Catholics, Jews, atheists, and agnostics (in representative numbers), several Western adherents of Eastern traditions, and has a reasonable range of educational, social class, and ethnic variations. We have begun to follow a select longitudinal sample at five-year intervals, but have only limited longitudinal data so far. We have not conducted cross-cultural investigations. Therefore the stage descriptions we offer here must still be considered as provisional.

In this context, what do we mean by the term "stage"? In contemporary usage this word has a lot of meanings. Here we intend by it the following: *one of a sequence of formally describable "styles" of composing an ultimate environment, of committing the self to centers of value and power, of symbolizing and expressing those commitments, and of relating them to the valued perspectives of others.* We speak of stages rather than of types because we believe that the stage sequence we have identified is invariant. That is, we believe the stages come in the order presented here and that persons do not skip over a stage. Please notice that we say "formally describable." This means that a stage is not defined by a particular *content* of belief or valuing. Rather, a stage is a particular *way* or organizing, composing, or of giving form to the contents of beliefs or values. Stage descriptions focus on the *how* of faith rather than on the *what* or the content of faith.

Stages are not "there" like a set of stair-steps to climb up. To make a transition from one stage to another is to undergo the often painful process of giving up one's familiar and comfortable ways of making meaning and sustaining commitment. Transition means a kind of coming apart as well as a new construction. Periods of transition can be protracted over several years.

Let me make one other potentially confusing matter clear. Many stage theories, such as Erikson's "Eight Ages of the Life Cycle,"[19] tie the movement from one stage to another directly to chronological age and biological maturation. Particularly in the earlier stages which, for Erikson, are most directly psycho-sexual stages, maturation sets the pace and precipitates the movement from one stage to another. Our stages, like Piaget's and Kohlberg's, are dependent upon age and maturation in that these factors provide some of the *necessary* conditions for stage transition. But they are not *sufficient* conditions. Other factors, such as the richness and stimulation of the environment, the availability of models of the next "place," and "catch" a subject as to correct a test-taking set to choose items on the person's encounter with crises or dilemmas which shake up his or her faith outlook, play significant roles in determining the rate and timing of stage changes. To show what this means, it is not too unusual to find normal persons who are chronologically and biologically adult, but whose patterns of faith can best be described by our stage 2. This is a stage that typically arises during the years from seven to eleven. We are suggesting that "normal" persons may equilibrate or arrest in faith growth at any of these stages from the second stage on. Certain factors in maturation must occur before the school child is ready for transition to stage 3, but maturation and age, by themselves, do not guarantee readiness for the next stage.

Now we are ready to examine an overview of this sequence of stages. The description of each stage will include a general characterization. This will be followed by a somewhat more detailed elaboration. Then, briefly, we will suggest some of the signs of transition to the next stage.[20]

Undifferentiated Faith

The preconceptual, largely prelinguistic stage in which the infant unconsciously forms a disposition toward its world.

Trust, courage, hope, and love are fused in an undifferentiated way and contend with sensed threats of abandonment, inconsistencies, and deprivations in the infant's environment. Though really a prestage, and largely inaccessible to empirical inquiry of the kind we pursue, the quality of mutuality and the strength of trust, autonomy, hope, and courage (or their opposites) developed in this phase, underlie (or undermine) all that comes later in faith development.

Transition to stage 1 begins with the convergence of thought and language, opening up the use of symbols in speech and ritual play.

Stage 1. Intuitive-Projective Faith

The fantasy-filled, imitative phase in which the child can be powerfully and permanently influenced by the examples, moods, actions, and language of the visible faith of primal adults.

The stage most typical of the child of three to seven, it is marked by a relative fluidity of thought patterns. The child is continually encountering novelties for which no stable operations of knowing have been formed. The imaginative processes underlying fantasy are unrestrained and uninhibited by logical thought. In league with forms of knowing dominated by perception, imagination in this stage is extremely productive of long-lasting images and feelings (positive and negative) which later, more stable and self-reflective valuing and thinking will have to order and sort out. This is the stage of first self-awareness. The "self-aware" child is egocentric as regards the perspectives of others. Here we find the first awarenesses of death and sex, and of the strong taboos by which cultures and families insulate those powerful areas.

The emergence of "concrete operational" thinking underlies the transition to stage 2. Affectively, the resolution of Oedipal issues or their submersion in latency are important accompanying factors. At the heart of the transition is the child's growing concern to *know* how things are and to clarify for himself or herself the bases of distinctions between what is real and what only "seems to be."

Stage 2. Mythic-Literal Faith

The stage in which the person begins to take on for himself or herself the stories, beliefs, and observances which symbolize belonging to his or her community. Beliefs are appropriated with literal interpretations, as are moral rules and attitudes. Symbols are taken as one-dimensional and literal in meaning.

In this stage the rise of "concrete operations" leads to the curbing and ordering of the previous stage's imaginative composing of the world. The episodic quality of intuitive-projective faith gives way to a more linear, narrative construction of coherence and meaning. Story becomes the major way of giving unity and value to experience. This is the faith stage of the school child (though we sometimes find its structures dominant in adolescents and in adults). Marked by increased accuracy in taking the perspective of other persons, stage 2 composes a world based on reciprocal fairness and an immanent justice based on reciprocity. The actors in its cosmic stories are full-fledged anthropomorphic "personalities." Those in this stage can be affected deeply and powerfully by symbolic and dramatic materials, and can describe in endlessly detailed narrative what has occurred. Stage 2 does not, however, step back from the flow of its stories to formulate reflective, conceptual meanings. For this stage the meaning is both carried and "trapped" in the narrative.

The implicit clash or contradictions of stories leads to reflection on meanings. The transition to "formal operational" thought makes such reflection possible and necessary. Previous literalism breaks down; new "cognitive conceit" (Elkind) leads to disillusionment with previous teachers and teachings. Conflicts between authoritative stories (i.e., Genesis on creation vs. evolutionary theory) must be faced. The emergence of mutual interpersonal perspective-taking ("I see you seeing me; I see me as you see me; I see you seeing me seeing you") creates the need for a more personal relationship with the unifying power of the ultimate environment.

Stage 3. Synthetic-Conventional Faith

The person's experience of the world now extends beyond the family. A number of spheres demand attention: family, school or work, peers, street society and media, and perhaps religion. Faith must provide a coherent orientation in the midst of that more complex and diverse range of involvements. Faith must synthesize values and information; it must provide a basis for identity and outlook.

> Stage 3 typically has its rise and ascendancy in adolescence, but for many adults it becomes a permanent equilibration. It structures the ultimate environment in interpersonal terms. Its images of unifying value and power derive from the extension of qualities experienced in personal relationships. It is a "conformist" stage in the sense that it is acutely tuned to the expectations and judgments of significant others, and as yet does not have a sure enough grasp on its own identity and autonomous judgment to construct and maintain an independent perspective. While beliefs and values are deeply felt, they typically are tacitly held—the person "dwells" in them and the meaning world they mediate. But there has not been occasion to reflectively step outside them so as to examine them explicitly or systematically. At stage 3 a person has an "ideology," a more or less consistent clustering of values and beliefs, but he or she has not objectified it for examination, and in a sense is unaware of having it. Differences of outlook with others are experienced as differences in "kind" of person. Authority is located in the incumbents of traditional authority-roles (if perceived as personally worthy) or in the consensus of a valued, face-to-face group.

Factors contributing to the breakdown of stage 3 and to readiness for transition may include any one or more of the following: serious clashes or contradictions between valued authority sources; marked changes, by officially sanctioned leaders, of policies or practices previously deemed sacred and unbreachable (e.g., in the Catholic church, changing the mass from Latin to the vernacular, or no longer requiring abstinence from meat on Friday); the encounter with experiences or perspectives that lead to critical reflection on how one's beliefs and values have formed and changed, and on how "relative" they are to one's particular group or background.

Stage 4. Individuative-Reflective Faith

The movement from stage 3 to stage 4 is particularly critical, for it is in this transition that the late adolescent or adult must begin to take seriously the burden of responsibility for his or her own commitments, lifestyle, beliefs, and attitudes. Where genuine movement toward stage 4 is underway, the person must face certain unavoidable tensions: individuality vs. being defined by a group or group membership; subjectivity and the power of one's strongly felt but unexamined feelings vs. objectivity and the requirement of critical reflection; self-fulfillment or self-actualization as a primary concern vs. service to and being for others; the question of being committed to the relative vs. struggle with the possibility of an absolute.

This stage most appropriately takes form in young adulthood (but let us remember that many adults do *not* construct it and that for a significant group it emerges only in the mid-thirties or forties). This stage is marked by a double development. The self, previously sustained in its identity and faith compositions by an interpersonal circle of significant others, now claims an identity no longer defined by the composite of one's roles or meanings to others. To sustain that new identity it composes a meaning frame conscious of its own boundaries and inner connections, and aware of itself as a "worldview." Self (identity) and outlook (worldview) are differentiated from those of others, and become acknowledged factors in the reactions, interpretations, and judgments one makes on the actions of the self and others. The self expresses its intuitions of coherence in an ultimate environment in terms of an explicit system of meanings. Stage 4 typically translates symbols into conceptual meanings. This is a "demythologizing" stage. The self is likely to attend minimally to unconscious factors influencing its judgments and behaviors.

Restless with the self-images and outlook maintained by stage 4, the person ready for transition finds him/herself attending to what may feel like anarchic and disturbing inner voices. Elements from a childish past, images and energies from a deeper self, a gnawing sense of the sterility and flatness of the meanings one serves—any or all of these may signal readiness for something new. Stories, symbols, myths paradoxes from one's own or other traditions may insist on breaking in upon the neatness of the previous faith. Disillusionment with one's compromises, and recognition that life is more complex than stage 4's logic of clear distinctions and abstract concepts can comprehend, press one toward a more dialectical and multileveled approach to life-truth.

Stage 5. Paradoxical-Consolidative Faith

This stage involves the integration into self and outlook of much that was suppressed or evaded in the interest of stage 4's self-certainty and conscious cognitive and affective adaptation to reality. This stage develops a "second naivete" (Ricoeur) in which symbolic power is reunited with conceptual meanings. Here there must also be a new reclaiming and reworking of one's past. There must be an opening to the voices of one's "deeper self." Importantly, this involves a critical recognition of one's *social* unconscious—the myths, ideal images, and prejudices built deeply into the self-system by virtue of one's being nurtured within a particular social class, religious tradition, ethnic group, or the like.

Unusual before midlife, stage 5 knows the sacrament of defeat and the reality of irrevocable commitments and acts. What the previous stage struggled to clarify, in terms of the boundaries of self and outlook, this stage now makes porous and permeable. Alive to paradox and the truth in apparent contradictions, this stage strives to unify opposites in mind and experience. It generates and maintains vulnerability to the strange truths of those who are "other."

178

Ready for closeness to that which is different and threatening to self and outlook (including new depths of experience in spirituality and religious revelation), this stage's commitment to justice is freed from the confines of tribe, class, religious community, or nation. And with the seriousness that can arise when life is more than half over, this stage is ready to spend and be spent for the cause of conserving and cultivating the possibility of others' generating identity and meaning.

Stage 5 can appreciate symbols, myths and rituals (its own and others') because it has been grasped, in some measure, by the depth of reality to which they refer. It also sees the divisions of the human family vividly because it has been apprehended by the possibility (and imperative) of an inclusive community of being. But this stage remains divided. It lives and acts between an untransformed world and a transforming vision and loyalties. In some few cases this division yields to the call of the radical actualization that we call stage 6.

Stage 6. Universalizing Faith

This stage is exceedingly rare. The persons best described by this stage have generated faith compositions in which their felt sense of an ultimate environment is inclusive of all being. They become incarnators and actualizers of the spirit of a fulfilled human community.

They are "contagious" in the sense that they create zones of liberation from the social, political, economic, and ideological shackles we place and endure on human futurity. Living with felt participation in a power that unifies and transforms the world, universalizers are often experienced as subversive of the structures (including religious structures) by which we sustain our individual and corporate survival, security, and significance. Many persons in this stage die at the hands of those whom they hope to change. Universalizers are often more honored and revered after death than during their lives. The rare persons who may be described by this stage have a special grace that makes them seem more lucid, more simple, and yet somehow more fully human than the rest of us. Their community is universal in extent. Particularities are cherished because they are vessels of the universal, and are thereby valuable apart from any utilitarian considerations. Life is both loved and held to loosely. Such persons are ready for fellowship with persons at any of the other stages and from any other faith tradition.

179

MORAL STAGES AND THE DEVELOPMENT OF FAITH

As I conceive them, the faith stages are more comprehensive constructs than are the Kohlberg stages of moral reasoning. A faith stage is meant to integrate operations of knowing and valuing which underlie and give form to the contents of a person's system of meaning. As such, faith stages represent modes of knowing, commitment, and action, in which thought and emotion, rationality and passionality, are held together. This does not mean, as some critics have suggested, that faith is an irrational or a'rational matter.[21] It does mean, however, that the logic of faith is more comprehensive than the logic of rational certainty characterizing Piaget's and Kohlberg's cognitive theories. Faith employs images and ontological intuitions. It relies on historical and present experiences of disclosure and "revelation." Faith works with elements of religious, philosophical, and ideological traditions. The culture of myths, symbols, and ritual are part of its media. These elements faith interrogates by means of rational operations testing for sense and consistency. The resulting "logic of conviction" (as I have called it elsewhere)[22] is open to ongoing tests for existential validity, generalizable truth, and reflective equilibrium. To recognize that the logic of conviction has this dialectical character in no way renders it a'rational or irrational. This recognition simply reminds us that a logic of rational certainty alone cannot resolve ontological and axiological questions.

Kohlberg's only published response to the stage theory of faith development in "Education, Moral Development and Faith" seems uncertain as to how to regard the relation of faith stages to stages of moral reasoning. In some passages he writes as though faith and moral judgment stages are two comparable strands of a larger developmental process, such as ego. In other passages he seems to recognize the kind of claim I make here, that faith stages are broader constructs aiming to comprehend and contextualize stages of moral judgment. Finally the choice between these options is less important for him than the issues of whether moral judgment stages precede faith stages (both logically and chronologically) in development, and whether faith stage development is *caused* by moral stage change rather than vice versa. Kohlberg—because of his deep concern for the foundations of a nonsectarian approach to moral education in the public schools of the United States—wants to demonstrate that moral reason requires faith rather than that morality derives from faith. In his words,

We may then expect a parallel development of faith stages and moral stages. The critical question, both psychologically and philosophically, is whether moral development precedes (and causes) faith development or vice versa. The data on this question is not yet available. We hypothesize, however, that development to a given moral stage precedes development to the parallel faith stage. Psychologically I believe that it takes a long time to work out a moral stage in terms of its elaboration as an organized pattern of belief and feeling about the cosmos which Fowler calls a faith stage. Philosophically I incline to Kant's solution that faith is grounded on moral reason because moral reason "requires" faith rather than that moral reason is grounded on faith.... Universal moral principles cannot be derived from faith because not all men's faith is, or can be, the same.

Moral principles, then, do not require faith for their formulation or for their justification. In some sense, however, to ultimately live up to moral principles requires faith.[23]

Consistant with my understanding of faith stages as the more comprehensive constructs, inclusive of moral judgment making, and drawing on our interview data, my associates and I have distinguished seven structural "aspects" of each faith stage. I have tried to suggest in my longer writings how these aspects undergo transformations from stage to stage.[24] Among these aspects I have included the patterns of cognitive development as identified by Piaget. I have included the stagelike levels of social-perspective taking as researched by Robert Selman.[25] Kohlberg's stages of moral reasoning have been included, showing the broad parallels he predicted, and which we have found, between moral and faith stages. In addition to these three aspects, we have distinguished four others in the integrated operations of a faith stage. They are: (1) the locus of authority, (2) the bounds of social awareness, (3) the form of world coherence, and (4) the role of symbols.[26] In Table 1 we suggest the correspondences we find between these aspects in the faith stages.

Notice that our data supports Kohlberg's prediction that there

TABLE 1: FAITH STAGES BY ASPECTS
(FROM "FAITH AND STRUCTURING OF MEANING")

Aspect Stage	Form of Logic (Piaget)	Role-Taking (Selman)	Form of Moral Judgment (Kohlberg)	Bounds of Social Awareness	Locus of Authority	Form of World Coherence	Role of Symbols
0	Undifferentiated combination of basic trust, organismic courage, premonitory hope with admixtures of their opposites—preconceptual, prelinguistic mutuality.						
1	Preoperational.	Rudimentary empathy (egocentric).	Punishment—reward.	Family, primal others.	Attachment/dependence relationships. Size, power, visible symbols of authority.	Episodic.	Magical-numinous.
2	Concrete operational.	Simple Perspective taking.	Instrumental hedonism (reciprocal fairness).	"Those like us" (in familial, ethnic, racial, class and religious terms).	Incumbents of authority roles, salience increased by personal relatedness.	Narrative-dramatic.	One-dimensional; literal.
3	Early formal operations.	Mutual Interpersonal.	Interpersonal expectations and concordance.	Composite of groups in which one has interpersonal relationships.	Consensus of valued groups and in personally worthy representatives of belief-value tradi-	Tacit system, felt meanings symbolically mediated, globally held.	Symbols multi-dimensional; evocative power inheres in symbol.

4	Formal Operation. (Dichotomizing)	Mutual, with self-selected group or class (societal).	Societal perspective; Reflective Relativism or class-biased universalism.	Ideologically compatible communities with congruence to self. Authorities and norms must be congruent with this.	One's own judgment as informed by a self-ratified ideological perspective. Authorities and inner connections of norms must be consistent with this system.	Explicit system, conceptually mediated, clarity about boundaries and inner connections of meaning.	Symbols separated from symbolized. Translated (reduced) to ideations. Evocative power inheres in meaning conveyed by symbols.
5	Formal operations. (Dialectical)	Mutual with groups, classes and traditions "other" than one's own. (Dialectical)	Prior to society, principled higher law (universal).	Extends beyond class norms and interests. Disciplined ideological vulnerability to "truths" and "claims" of out-groups and other traditions.	Dialectical joining of judgment-experience processes with reflective claims of others and of various expressions of cumulative human wisdom.	Multisystemic symbolic and conceptual mediation.	Postcritical rejoining of irreducible symbolic power and ideational meaning. Evocative power inherent in the reality in and beyond symbol *and* in the power of unconscious processes in the self.
6	Formal operations. (Synthetic)	Mutual, with the commonwealth of being.	Loyalty to being.	Identification with the species. Trans-narcissistic love of being.	In a personal judgment informed by the experiences and truths of previous stages, purified of egoic striving, and linked by disciplined intuition to the principle of being.	Unitive actuality felt and participated unity of "One beyond the many."	Evocative power of symbols actualized through unification of reality mediated by symbols and the self.

will be a close parallel between moral and faith stages. Variations come around stages 3 and 4, however. Up to and through faith stage 3, the parallels are exact. Some faith stage 3s, however (usually men), are best described by moral stage 4. Most faith stage 4s are best described by a position which Kohlberg, for a time, would have called moral "stage 4½," a transitional position exhibiting a relativistic outlook.[27] These persons take account of the need for occasional departures from law or the rules governing systemically defined roles in the service of the "greater good." However, they lack a consistently principled basis for shaping and justifying actions on these occasions. We call this position "reflective relativism" or "class-biased universalism." The latter reference is to persons who recognize higher law principles and claims, but in applying them fall into a pattern of distorting the interests and well-being of other persons and groups by assimilating them to their own, resulting in a kind of moral pseudo-stage 5.

This latter point indicates that moral stage 5, as an intellectual or cognitive construct, is possible at faith stage 4. But a moral stage 5 which integrates and forms a person's consistent moral action appears to be unlikely apart from a faith stage 5. Faith stage 5, we believe, can exhibit either moral stages 5 or 6 with authentic comprehension. Our data on faith stage 5 is far more limited than our studies of faith stages 3, 3(4), 4(3), and 4; therefore, our claims about the relations between faith and moral stages 5 and 6 are more speculative than our claims about the middle stages.

Considerably more detailed data, testing the issue of precedence and cause of development between moral judgment and faith stages, are found in the doctoral dissertation completed by Eugene J. Mischey at the University of Toronto, in 1976.[28] "Faith Development and Its Relationship to Moral Reasoning and Identity Status in Young Adults" is the title of this study. Mischey used the Fowler faith development interview and scoring procedures. He tested for identity status with Marcia's (1966) interview format. In addition he administered Kohlberg's moral dilemmas in a written form, Faulkner and Dejong's Religiosity Scale, and Rotter's Internal-External Locus of Control Scale. His subjects were 30 young adults between the ages of 20 and 35. While we must observe some caution about the adequacy of relying upon pencil and paper measurement of response to Kohlberg's moral dilemmas, Mischey's findings about the relations between faith and moral stages of his respondents are quite interesting. Of the 30 subjects, only 4 showed a level of moral judgment more developed than their faith stage. Interestingly, these 4 were not randomly distributed throughout the sample, but were clustered together in the group Mischey scored as faith stage 3(2). Each of the four scored this way showed a somewhat more fully developed moral judgment stage than faith stage. Nine of his respondents, this time representing faith stages 3, 4(3), 4, and 4(5), showed directly parallel development in faith and moral stages. Surprisingly, 17 of his subjects reflected faith stages more developed than their moral stages.

Most striking in this study are Mischey's findings about the relations between the faith and moral stages and the identity status of his respondents. The 4 subjects whose moral stages exceeded their faith stages in development were the lowest of the sample on both stage scales. In addition, all 4 reflected a *diffuse* pattern of identity. Of those who showed either direct stage parallels (9) or more developed faith stages (17), 4 were described as "mixed" in identity status and 7 showed characteristics of identity "foreclosure." The remaining 15, the most developed by both faith and moral measures, all reflected Marcia's "identity achieved" status. This represents an important independent corroboration of the faith theory's findings about faith stage 4 and individuating identity. It also provides significant light on the question of precedence in faith and moral growth, and concerning the "causes" of the development. Mischey summarizes these implications:

If the present sample of young adults can be considered "random" to the extent that it is not "deviant" in any form or fashion, then it seems that Kohlberg's contention that development to a given moral stage precedes development to the parallel faith stage is open to question. It seems ironical that not *one* individual, who has achieved an identity for himself, tends to score higher on morality than on faith. Consequently it is imperative to ask whether it is truly possible that this sample of individuals fails to provide at least *one* example of where an identity-achieved person is found to be in the process of "working out a moral stage in terms of its elaboration as an organized pattern of belief and feeling about the cosmos which Fowler calls a faith stage." In terms of Kohlberg's perspective it would stand to reason that the present sample should exemplify individuals scoring higher in moral reasoning and in the midst of formulating a parallel faith stage since, as he notes, the faith element is a wider, more comprehensive system of constructs requiring more time and experience; this latter situation would then predicate a lower faith score. The results of the present study, however, show no evidence to validate such an assumption.[29]

Mischey himself acknowledges that while his data provide a basis for questioning Kohlberg's theoretical prediction that moral stages will precede faith stages, and in some sense "cause" them, much more research on these issues is needed. Of most significance is his relation of moral and faith stage to identity formation. Mischey's work supports my claim, made earlier, that forms of moral judgment at each stage are anchored in and supported by the larger frames of meaning and value we call faith. Mischey's work suggests that in young adults who have exercised some choice about the kind of persons they intend to be—and have formed ways of seeing the world and leaning into life that express those intentions—forms of moral judgment which are congruent with these value and belief choices then emerge. He writes:

... (T)he present results indicate that ontological issues and perspectives are an integral part of the "developing personality" and that these perspectives significantly contribute to the structuring of one's moral reasoning and behavior. . . . (I)t seems that an individual initially seeks out answers to questions surrounding his existence as a human being and the general purpose of his life before he realizes the *need* to be ethically responsible in society. It seems that if individuals do not find answers or, at the very least, do not come to some general understanding of ontologically based questions, then the incentive or motivation to be morally inclined may be placed in a precarious position. . . . [30]

Clark Power, a research associate of both Kohlberg and Fowler, undertood a careful study of 21 protocols which included both faith and moral dilemma interviews.[31] Power's careful paper delineates the separable but integrally related domains of morality and faith as they appear in these interviews. His sample included Jews,

Catholics, Protestants, and Orthodox (Eastern) representatives, as well as agnostics and atheists. Ten females and 11 males were included, and the interviews were distributed from stages 1–5. Power was only incidentally interested in the question of precedence. He found "a hundred percent agreement between the major faith stage and the major moral stage through stage three. At stage four I found moral stage four only with faith stage four, but moral five with both [faith] stages four and five."[32] Power's paper represents an original clarification of the interrelatedness of moral and faith stages, but is too substantive and nuanced for brief summary. For our purposes his conclusions about the moral and faith domains can be presented and placed alongside those of Mischey.

Referring to faith as a kind of relatedness of human beings to the ultimate conditions of our existence, Power speaks of six functions faith plays in supporting and informing moral judgment. First, faith constitutes an "onlook"—a way of seeing, a mode of interpreting a moral situation. "An onlook can provide an interpretation of a situation which can motivate action."[33] Second, faith represents a sense of commitment. The experience of one's contingency or finitude gives rise, Power argues, to a renewed sense of purpose: "I must be here to do something." Third, faith impacts ethical sensitivity. As Power puts it, "If the order of the universe is sensed as being lawful or loving then we feel that we should conform our spirit so as to be at one with all that is." (I might point out that conversely, and in a less benign sense, a faith vision that sees the universe as ultimately indifferent or hostile would also have powerful determinative impact on moral judgment.) Fourth, faith can offer "the reassurance that ethical actions in an unjust world are not fruitless, that they (may) have some eternal or eschatological significance."[34] Faith requires a complementarity with being, which relativizes the tendency of persons to center their meanings in themselves. Finally, Power suggests, faith functions "to support human action especially in the ambiguities of life when one cannot control or predict the outcomes of one's actions."[35] As a summary of his claims Power writes,

The role of faith in relation to moral judgment would seem to be that of providing the very condition for the possibility of making any moral judgment. That is, in every moral judgment there is an implicit future judgment that the activity of moral judging is in fact necessary. . . . It is the very ground to our ethical judgment which I hold to be the province of faith.[36]

CONCLUSION

Kohlberg has so far opted not to develop a theory of the moral self or of the development of virtue.[37] He has aimed instead to restore that dimension of the natural law tradition which affirms that there is a rational core to moral decision making and action, and that this rational core is universal. Further, he has had a passionate commitment to the development of an approach to moral education which avoids dependence upon specific religious or ideological traditions which could not meet the constitutional requirements regarding separation of church and state. While Kohlberg has been clear that his developmental stages focus upon and are limited to the structures of moral reasoning, he has frequently—especially in connection with his educational writings—propounded a commitment to justice as the unitary virtue (or comprehensive value) in a faith-like moral ideology. His writing about "stage 7" is, in a sense, his owning of a faith vision which sustains and is the culmination of the moral stage sequence.

The faith development theory conceptually and empirically offers a way of broadening Kohlberg's account of moral development. I have suggested here that each moral judgment stage implies and requires anchorage in a more extensive framework of belief and value. We have examined the research of Mischey and Power which corroborates and extends this claim. Our stage theory attempts to describe this sequence of structural approaches to the forming and maintenance of faith visions in formal, non-content-specific terms. I hope Kohlberg and his followers will consider whether the faith theory opens a way to expand the focus of moral development research without jettisoning its heuristic power. I hope those Kohlberg critics who find his research and educational approaches too narrowly cognitive[38] may see in the faith stages a more adequate, though still formally descriptive and normative, model for investigating and sponsoring moral development.

NOTES

1. In *Journal of Moral Education*, Vol. 4, No. 1, pp. 5–16. Cited hereafter as Kohlberg, 1974.

2. See also Kohlberg, "Education for Justice: A Modern Statement of the Platonic View," in Nancy F. and Theodore R. Sizer, Eds., *Moral Education*. Cambridge, Mass.: Harvard University Press, 1970, pp. 57–83.

3. See Kohlberg, "From Is to Ought: How to Commit the Naturalistic Fallacy and Get Away with It in the Study of Moral Development," in T. Mischel, Ed., *Cognitive Development and Epistemology*. New York: Academic Press, 1971, pp. 151–284.

4. Kohlberg, 1974, p. 5.

5. Ibid., p. 10.

6. Ibid., p. 11.

7. For other, more detailed discussions of our understanding of faith, see Fowler, "Stages in Faith: The Structural-Developmental Perspective," in Thomas Hennessy, Ed., *Values and Moral Development*. New York: Paulist Press, 1976, pp. 173–179, and Fowler and Keen, *Life Maps: Conversations on the Journey of Faith*, Waco, Texas: Word Books, 1978, pp. 14–25.

8. See Fowler, "Faith and the Structuring of Meaning," to be published by Silver Burdett as part of a Symposium on Moral and Faith Development in 1980, James W. Fowler, Ed.

9. Kohlberg, 1974, p. 14.

10. In Thomas Lickona, Ed., *Moral Development and Behavior*. New York: Holt, Rinehart and Winston, 1976, pp. 34–35.

11. Ibid.

12. Kohlberg, 1974, pp. 14–15.

13. Ibid. p. 15.

14. See Fowler, "Stages in Faith: The Structural Developmental Perspective," in Hennessy, op.cit., pp. 207–211.

15. Kohlberg in Lickona, op.cit., pp. 34–35.

16. Fowler in *Life Maps* and "Faith and the Structuring of Meaning."

17. See Fowler, *To See the Kingdom: The Theological Vision of H. Richard Niebuhr*. Nashville, Tenn.: Abingdon Press, 1974, especially Ch. 5.

18. Fowler, "Stages in Faith: The Structural Developmental Perspective," in Hennessey, op.cit., pp. 179–183.

19. Erik H. Erikson, *Childhood and Society* (Second Ed.). New York: WW Norton, 1963, Ch. 7.

20. For more detailed accounts of the structural features of the stages and for examples from interviews, see *Life Maps,* pp. 39–95.

21. See the critical perspective of Ernest Wallwork in this volume.

22. See"Faith and the Structuring of Meaning."

23. Kohlberg, 1974, p. 14.

24. *Life Maps;* "Stages in Faith . . . "

25. Robert L. Selman, "The Developmental Conceptions of Interpersonal Relations." Publication of the Harvard-Judge Baker Social Reasoning Project, December, 1974, Vols. I and II. See also Selman, "Social-Cognitive Understanding," in T. Lickona, Ed., *Moral Development and Behavior.* New York: Holt, Rinehart and Winston, 1976, pp. 299–316.

26. For explications of these categories see *Life Maps* and "Faith and the Structuring of Meaning."

27. Kohlberg, "Continuities in Childhood and Adult Moral Development Revisited," in P. B. Baltes and K. W. Schaie, Eds., *Life-Span Developmental Psychology: Personality and Socialization.* New York: Academic Press, 1973, pp. 179–204.

28. Eugene J. Mischey, *Faith Development and Its Relationship to Moral Reasoning and Identity Status in Young Adults.* Unpublished doctoral dissertation, Department of Educational Theory, University of Toronto, 1976.

29. Ibid., pp. 227–28.

30. Ibid., p. 235.

31. Clark Power, Unpublished and untitled paper prepared for presentation at the American Psychological Association Convention, Section 36, San Francisco, August 26, 1977.

32. Power, p. 4.

33. Ibid., p. 47.

34. Ibid.

35. Ibid.

36. Ibid., pp. 47–48.

37. See indications of the promising ways in which he could move in these directions in "Stage and Sequence: The Cognitive-Developmental Approach to Socialization," in David A. Goslin, Ed., *Handbook of Socialization Theory and Research,* Chicago: Rand-McNally, 1969, pp. 347–480. See especially parts 5–10, pp. 397–433.

38. The most helpful of these constructive critiques are those by Paul J. Philibert, "Kohlberg's Use of Virtue," in *International Philosophical Quarterly,* Vol. 15, No. 4, 1975, pp. 455–479; and Andre Guindon, "Moral Development: Form, Content and Self. A Critique of Kohlberg's Sequence." Unpublished paper, 1978.

Identity in Context

A Minority Identity Development Model

One of the most promising approaches to the field of cross-cultural counseling has been the renewed interest in racial/cultural identity development (Parham & Helms, 1981; Helms, 1985; D. W. Sue & D. Sue, in press). While it is undeniable that each minority group has a unique cultural heritage that makes it distinct from other groups, this fact has erroneously been interpreted as evidence of cultural conformity—a monolithic approach which views all Asians, Blacks, Hispanics, American Indians, and other minorities as possessing the same group attitudes and behaviors.

Clearly, uniformity of attitudes and behaviors is no more true for minority individuals than it is for members of the dominant culture. With regard to the very issue of cultural distinction, minority attitudes may vary from desire for total assimilation into the dominant culture to total rejection of the dominant culture and immersion in the minority culture (Parham & Helms, 1981).

D. Sue and S. Sue (1972) provide evidence of the disparate ways in which Chinese Americans respond to cultural conflict. Some reject their Chinese background entirely and try to assimilate into the dominant society. Others adhere to traditional cultural values and attempt to resist assimilation. Still others stress pride in their racial identity while refraining from the conformity inherent in both the traditional Chinese practices and assimilation into the mainstream culture. Ruiz and Padilla (1977) suggest there is a danger inherent in trying to isolate the "true nature" of the Hispanic character since each person's attitudes and behaviors are a function of his/her degree of acculturation. Furthermore, these writings suggest that not only do intragroup differences exist, but attitudes and behaviors within individuals can fluctuate greatly as their identification with one culture or another changes.

The purpose of this chapter is to explicate a model of identity development that acknowledges coincidental identity transformational processes involving minority groups and utilize these processes to help explain individual differences within minority groups.

A number of earlier authors have also attempted to explain individual differences within racial/ethnic groups. Some of these early attempts took the form of simple typologies in which a particular minority group was divided into smaller subcategories or types based on their degree of ethnic identification. As Hall, Cross, and Freedle (1972) point out, these subgroups generally included both "conservative" and "militant" types and one or two categories in between. Vontress (1971), for instance, theorized that Afro-Americans conformed to three distinct subgroups: (1) Colored, (2) Negro, and (3) Black. Briefly, these subcategories represented decreasing levels of dependence upon White society and culture as the source of self-definition and worth, and an increasing degree of identification with Black society and culture. As another example, Mayovich (1973) typed Japanese Americans according to four separate categories: (1) Conformists, (2) Anomic, (3) Liberal, and (4) Militant. Mayovich (1973) hypothesized that as a result of their acceptance or rejection of traditional values and their involvement or detachment from social issues, all Japanese Americans (at least those of the Sansei generation) fell into one of these four types.

This method of "typing" minority individuals has come under heavy criticism in recent years, however (Parham & Helms, 1981; Helms, 1985; Atkinson & Schein, 1986; Ponterotto & Wise, 1987). Banks (1972), for instance, contends that these theorists have mistakenly proposed labels that attribute certain fixed personality traits to people, when in fact their behavior is a function of a specific situation. Others (Cross, 1970; Hall, Cross & Freedle, 1972; Jackson, 1975) have suggested that any attempt to define minority "types" must acknowledge movement of individuals across categories. Helms (1985) goes further and states that these models may (a) unintentionally "blame the victim" by placing too much emphasis on individual rather than system change; (b) become obsolete since they are so dependent on societal forces which may have changed; (c) erroneously assume that identity development follows a linear and continuous course; and (d) make us view the "stages" as static, discrete entities rather than a dynamic and evolving process. In spite of such criticisms, it is important to recognize the early topologies as pioneering attempts that paved the way for more sophisticated models of identity development.

A second major approach has viewed minority attitudes and behavior as a product of an identity development continuum. This approach differs from earlier topologies in that minority attitudes and behaviors are viewed as flexible and a function of the individual's stage of identity development. Rather than type the individual, stages of development through which any minority person may pass are described. Attitudinal and behavioral attributes, therefore, are not viewed as fixed characteristics but as related to identity development.

These early attempts to define a process of minority identity development were almost exclusively the work of Black intellectuals who were obviously influenced in their thinking by the impact of social, psychological, and cultural events in the sixties. Hall, Cross, and Freedle (1972) describe how these events highlighted the process of Black identity transformation:

> We have seen a change in the nature of black-white relations in America. To be sure, this change has produced many consequences, one of which has been an identity transformation among American blacks. The transformation has been from an older orientation whereby most blacks viewed themselves as inadequate, inferior, incapable of self-determination, and unable to cope with the intricacies of life in a complex society, to one of feeling adequate, self-reliant, assertive, and self-determinative (p. 156).

The most highly developed models of Black identity transformation have been offered by Cross (1970, 1971) and Jackson (1975). Each of these men, independent of the other, developed a multistage identity development process, although each acknowledges the influence of earlier writers (Crawford & Naditch, 1970; Sherif & Sherif, 1970; Thomas, 1971; Wallace, 1964).

Cross (1971) described his model as "Negro-to-Black Conversion Experience," consisting of preencounter, encounter, immersion, and internalization stages. According to the model, Blacks at the preencounter stage are "programmed to view and think of the world as being nonblack, anti-black, or the opposite of Black" (Hall, Cross, & Freedle, 1972, p. 159). At the next stage, the Encounter stage, the Black individual becomes aware of what being Black means and begins to validate him/herself as a Black person. During the Immersion stage, the Black person rejects all nonblack values and totally immerses him/herself in Black culture. Finally, in the Internalization stage, the Black person gains a sense of inner security and begins to focus on ". . . things other than himself and his own ethnic or racial group" (Hall, Cross, & Freedle, 1972, p. 160). Although there is considerable debate about the validity of the model and the existence of several stages, tentative exploratory studies provide support, if somewhat mixed (Hall, Cross, & Freedle, 1972).

Jackson (1975) identifies a similar four-stage process as the Black Identity Development Model. In stage one, Passive Acceptance, the Black person accepts and conforms to White social, cultural, and institutional standards (p. 21). In stage two, Active Resistance, the Black person rejects all that is White and attempts to remove all White influences upon his/her life (p. 22). In stage three, Redirection, the Black individual no longer admires or despises what is White but rather considers it irrelevant to Black Culture (p. 23). Finally, in stage four, Internalization, the Black person acknowledges and appreciates the uniqueness of the Black culture and comes to accept and reject various aspects of American culture based on their own merits.

Although these identity development models pertain specifically to the Black experience, the editors of the present text believe that some of the basic tenets of these theories can be generalized and applied to other minority groups, due to their shared experience of oppression. Several earlier writers (Stonequist, 1937; Berry, 1965) have also observed that minority groups share the same patterns of adjustment to cultural oppression. Parallels are most easily drawn between Blacks and other racial/ethnic groups. The fact that other minority groups such as Asian Americans (S. Sue & D. W. Sue, 1971; Mayovich, 1973), Hispanics (Szapocznik & Associates, 1980), and women (Downing & Roush, 1985) have proposed similar models may indicate experiential validity. During the past two decades, the social and political activity of Hispanics, Asian Americans, and American Indians has resulted in an identity transformation for persons within these groups similar to that experienced by Black Americans. A Third World consciousness has emerged, with the common experience of oppression clearly serving as the unifying force.

Parallels between the Black experience and those of other minority groups have also been suggested. Women, gays, the aged, the handicapped, and other oppressed groups have become increasingly conscious of themselves as objects of oppression, and this has resulted in changed attitudes toward themselves, their own minority groups, other minority groups, and members of the dominant culture. Based on views expressed by earlier writers and our own clinical observation that these changes in attitudes and subsequent behavior follow a predictable sequence, we propose a five-stage Minority Identity Development (MID) model.

The MID model we propose is not presented as a comprehensive theory of personality development, but rather as a schema to help counselors understand minority client attitudes and behaviors within existing personality theories. The model defines five stages of development that oppressed people may experience as they struggle to understand themselves in terms of their own minority culture, the dominant culture, and the oppressive relationship between the two cultures. Although five distinct stages are presented in the model, the MID is more accurately conceptualized as a continuous process in which one stage blends with another and boundaries between stages are not clear.

It is our observation that not all minority individuals experience the entire range of these stages in their lifetimes. Prior to the turbulent 1960s— a decade in which the transition of many individuals through this process was accelerated and, therefore, made more evident—many people were raised and lived out their lives in the first stage. Nor is the developmental process to be interpreted as irreversible. It is our opinion that many minority individuals are raised by parents functioning at level five, but in coming to grips with their own identity, offsprings often move from level five to one of the lower levels. On the other hand, it does not appear that functioning at lower levels of development is prerequisite to functioning at higher levels. Some people born and raised in a family functioning at level five appear never to experience a level-one sense of identity.

At each level we provide examples of four corresponding attitudes that may assist the counselor to understand behaviors displayed by individuals operating at or near these levels. (It is our contention that minority behavior, like all human behavior, can only be fully understood within the context of the attitudes that motivated it.) Each attitude is believed to be an integral part of any minority person's identity or of how he/she views (a) self, (b) others of the same minority, (c) others of another minority, and (d) majority individuals. It was not our intention to define a hierarchy with more valued attitudes at higher levels of development. Rather, the model is intended to reflect a process that we have observed in our work with minority clients over the past three decades.

Minority Identity Development Model

Stage One—Conformity Stage

Minority individuals in this stage of development are distinguished by their unequivocal preference for dominant cultural values over those of their own culture. Their choices of role models, life-styles, value system, etc., all follow the lead of the dominant group. Those physical and/or cultural characteristics that single them out as minority persons are a source of pain and are either viewed with disdain or are repressed from consciousness. Their views of self, fellow group members, and other minorities in general are clouded by their identification with the dominant culture. Minorities may perceive the ways of the dominant group as being much more positive, and there is a high desire to "assimilate and acculturate." The attitudes which minorities may have about themselves in this stage are ones of devaluation and depreciation on both a conscious and subconscious level. For example, Asians may perceive their own physical features as less desirable and their cultural values and Asian ways as a handicap to successful adaptation in White society. Their attitudes towards members of their own group tend to be highly negative in that they share the dominant culture's belief that Asians are less desirable. For example, stereotypes portraying Asians as inarticulate, good with numbers, poor managers, and aloof in their personal relationship are believed. Other minority groups are also viewed according to the dominant group's system of minority stratification (i.e., those minority groups that most closely resemble the dominant group in physical and cultural characteristics are viewed more favorably than those less similar). Attitudes toward members of the dominant group, however, tend to be highly appreciative in that the members are admired, respected, and often viewed as ideal models.

It is quite obvious that in the Conformity stage of development Asian Americans and other minorities view themselves as deficient in the "desirable" characteristics held up by the dominant society. Feelings of racial self-hatred caused by cultural racism may accompany this type of adjustment (S. Sue & D. W. Sue, 1972).

A. *Attitude toward self: Self-depreciating attitude.* Individuals who acknowledge their distinguishing physical and/or cultural characteristics consciously view them as a source of shame. Individuals who repress awareness of their distinguishing physical and/or cultural characteristics depreciate themselves at a subconscious level.
B. *Attitude toward members of same minority: Group-depreciating attitude.* Fellow minority group members are viewed according to dominant-held beliefs of minority strengths and weaknesses.
C. *Attitude toward members of different minority: Discriminatory attitude.* Other minorities are viewed according to the dominant group's system of minority stratification (i.e., those minority groups that most closely resemble the dominant group in physical and cultural characteristics are viewed more favorably than those less similar).
D. *Attitude toward members of dominant group: Group-appreciating attitude.* Members of the dominant group are admired, respected, and often viewed as ideal models. Cultural values of the dominant society are accepted without question.

Stage Two—Dissonance Stage

The movement into the Dissonance stage is most often a gradual process, but as Cross (1971) points out a monumental event such as the assassination of Martin Luther King may propel the Black person into the next stage. In this case, since denial seems to be a major tool used by Conformity-stage persons, minorities in the Dissonance stage begin to experience a breakdown in their denial system. A Latino who may feel ashamed of his/her cultural upbringing may encounter a Latino who seems proud of his/her cultural heritage. A Black who may have deceived himself/herself into believing that race problems are due to laziness, untrustworthiness, or personal inadequacies of his/her group, suddenly encounters racism on a personal level.

A. *Attitude toward self: Conflict between self-depreciating and self-appreciating attitudes.* With a growing awareness of minority cultural strengths comes a faltering sense of pride in self. The individual's attitude toward distinguishing physical and/or cultural characteristics is typified by alternating feelings of shame and pride in self.
B. *Attitude toward members of same minority: Conflict between group-depreciating and group-appreciating attitudes.* Dominant-held views of minority strengths and weaknesses begin to be questioned, as new, contradictory information is received. Cultural values of the minority group begin to have appeal.

C. *Attitude toward members of different minority: Conflict between dominant-held views of minority hierarchy and feelings of shared experience.* The individual begins to question the dominant-held system of minority stratification and experiences a growing sense of comradeship with other oppressed people. Most of the individual's psychic energy at this level, however, is devoted to resolving conflicting attitudes toward self, the same minority, and the dominant group.

D. *Attitude toward members of dominant group: Conflict between group-appreciating and group-depreciating attitude.* The individual experiences a growing awareness that not all cultural values of the dominant group are beneficial to him/her. Members of the dominant group are viewed with growing suspicion.

Stage Three—Resistance and Immersion Stage

In this stage of development, the minority individual completely endorses minority-held views and rejects the dominant society and culture. Desire to eliminate oppression of the individual's minority group becomes an important motivation of the individual's behavior.

D. W. Sue and D. Sue (in press) believe that movement into this stage seems to occur for two reasons. First, the person begins to resolve many of the conflicts and confusions in the previous stage. As a result, a greater understanding of societal forces (racism, oppression, and discrimination) emerges, along with a realization that he/she has been victimized by it. Second, the individual begins to ask him/herself the following question: "Why should I feel ashamed of who and what I am?" The answers to that question will evoke both guilt and anger (bordering on rage): guilt that he/she has "sold out" in the past and contributed to his/her own group's oppression, and anger at having been oppressed and "brainwashed" by the forces in the dominant society.

A. *Attitude toward self: Self-appreciating attitude.* The minority individual at this stage acts as an explorer and discoverer of his/her history and culture, seeking out information and artifacts that enhance his/her sense of identity and worth. Cultural and physical characteristics which once elicited feelings of shame and disgust at this stage become symbols of pride and honor.

B. *Attitude toward members of same minority: Group-appreciating attitude.* The individual experiences a strong sense of identification with, and commitment to, his/her minority group, as enhancing information about the group is acquired. Members of the group are admired, respected, and often viewed as ideal models. Cultural values of the minority group are accepted without question.

C. *Attitude toward members of different minority: Conflict between feelings of empathy for other minority experiences and feelings of culturocentrism.* The individual experiences a growing sense of

199

camaraderie with persons from other minority groups, to the degree that they are viewed as sharing similar forms of oppression. Alliances with other groups tend to be short-lived, however, when their values come in conflict with those of the individual's minority group. The dominant group's system of minority stratification is replaced by a system which values most those minority groups that are culturally similar to the individual's own group.

D. *Attitude toward members of dominant group: Group-depreciating attitude.* The individual totally rejects the dominant society and culture and experiences a sense of distrust and dislike for all members of the dominant group.

Stage Four—Introspection Stage

In this stage of development, the minority individual experiences feelings of discontent and discomfort with group views rigidly held in the Resistance and Immersion stage, and diverts attention to notions of greater individual autonomy.

What occurs at this stage is very interesting. First, the minority individual may begin to feel progressively more comfortable with his or her own sense of identity. This security allows the person to begin to question some of the rigidly held beliefs of the Resistance stage that all "Whites are bad." There is also a feeling that too much negativism and hatred directed at White society tends to divert energies from more positive exploration of identity questions. This stage is characterized by greater individual autonomy. During this stage the person may begin to experience conflict between notions of responsibility and allegiance to his/her own minority group, and notions of personal autonomy. There is now a belief that perhaps not everything in the dominant culture is bad and that there are many positive as well as negative elements within it.

A. *Attitude toward self: Concern with basis of self-appreciating attitude.* The individual experiences conflict between notions of responsibility and allegiance to minority group and notions of personal autonomy.

B. *Attitude toward members of same minority: Concern with unequivocal nature of group appreciation.* While attitudes of identification are continued from the preceding Resistance and Immersion stages, concern begins to build up regarding the issue of group usurpation of individuality.

C. *Attitude toward members of different minority: Concern with ethnocentric basis for judging others.* The individual experiences a growing uneasiness with minority stratification that results from culturocentrism and placing a greater value on groups experiencing the same oppression than on those experiencing a different oppression.

D. *Attitude toward members of dominant group: Concern with the basis of group depreciation.* The individual experiences conflict between an attitude of complete distrust for the dominant society and culture, and an attitude of selective trust and distrust according to dominant individuals' demonstrated behaviors and attitudes. The individual also recognizes the utility of many dominant cultural elements yet is uncertain whether or not to incorporate such elements into his/her minority culture.

Stage Five—Synergetic Articulation and Awareness Stage

Minority individuals in this stage experience a sense of self-fulfillment with regard to cultural identity. Conflicts and discomforts experienced in the Introspection stage have been resolved, allowing greater individual control and flexibility. Cultural values of other minorities as well as those of the dominant group are objectively examined and accepted or rejected on the basis of experience gained in earlier stages of identity development. Desire to eliminate *all* forms of oppression becomes an important motivation for the individual's behavior.

A. *Attitude toward self: Self-appreciating attitude.* The individual experiences a strong sense of self-worth, self-confidence, and autonomy as the result of having established his/her identity as an individual, a member of a minority group, and/or a member of the dominant culture.

B. *Attitude toward members of same minority: Group-appreciating attitude.* The individual experiences a strong sense of pride in the group without having to accept group values unequivocally. Strong feelings of empathy with the group experience are coupled with an awareness that each member of the group is an individual.

C. *Attitude toward members of different minority: Group-appreciating attitude.* The individual experiences a strong sense of respect for the group's cultural values coupled with awareness that each member of the group is an individual. The individual also experiences a greater understanding and support for all oppressed people, regardless of their similarity or dissimilarity to the individual's minority group.

D. *Attitude toward members of dominant group: Attitude of selective appreciation.* The individual experiences selective trust and liking for members of the dominant group who seek to eliminate repressive activities of the group. The individual also experiences an openness to the constructive elements of the dominant culture.

Table 3.1
Summary of Minority Identity Development Model

Stages of Minority Development Model	Attitude toward self	Attitude toward others of the same minority	Attitude toward others of different minority	Attitude toward dominant group
Stage 1— Conformity	self-depreciating	group-depreciating	discriminatory	group-appreciating
Stage 2— Dissonance	conflict between self-depreciating and appreciating	conflict between group-depreciating and group-appreciating	conflict between dominant-held views of minority hierarchy and feelings of shared experience	conflict between group-appreciating and group-depreciating
Stage 3— Resistance and Immersion	self-appreciating	group-appreciating	conflict between feelings of empathy for other minority experiences and feelings of culturo-centrism	group-depreciating
Stage 4— Introspection	concern with basis of self-appreciation	concern with nature of unequivocal appreciation	concern with ethnocentric basis for judging others	concern with the basis of group depreciation
Stage 5— Synergetic Articulation and Awareness	self-appreciating	group-appreciating	group-appreciating	selective appreciation

Implications of the MID Model for Counseling

As suggested earlier, the MID model is not intended as a comprehensive theory of personality, but rather as a paradigm to help counselors understand minority client attitudes and behaviors. In this respect, the model is intended to sensitize counselors to (1) the role oppression plays in a minority individual's identity development, (2) the differences that can exist between members of the same minority group with respect to their cultural identity, and (3) the potential which each individual minority person has for changing his/her sense of identity. Beyond helping to understand minority client behavior, the model has implications for the counseling process itself.

The general attitudes and behaviors that describe minority individuals at the Conformity stage (e.g., denial of minority problems, strong dependence on and identification with dominant group, etc.) suggest that clients from this stage are unlikely to seek counseling related to their cultural identity. It is more likely that they will perceive problems of cultural identity as problems related to their personal identity. Clients at this stage are more inclined to visit and be influenced by counselors of the dominant group than those of the same minority. Indeed, clients may actively request a White counselor and react negatively toward a minority counselor. Because of the client's strong identification with dominant group members, counselors from the dominant group may find the conformist client's need to please and appease a powerful force in the counseling relationship. Attempts to explore cultural identity or to focus in on feelings may be threatening to the client. This is because exploration of identity may eventually touch upon feelings of racial self-hatred and challenge the client's self-deception ("I'm not like other minorities"). Clients at the Conformity stage are likely to present problems that are most amenable to problem solving and goal-oriented counseling approaches.

Minority individuals at the Dissonance stage of development are preoccupied by questions concerning their concept of self, identity, and self-esteem; they are likely to perceive personal problems as related to their cultural identity. Emotional problems develop when these individuals are unable to resolve conflicts which occur between dominant-held views and those of their minority group. Clients in the Dissonance stage are more culturally aware than Conformity clients and are likely to prefer to work with counselors who possess a good knowledge of the client's cultural group. Counseling approaches that involve considerable self-exploration appear to be best suited for clients at this stage of development.

Minority individuals at the Resistance and Immersion stage are inclined to view all psychological problems (whether personal or social in nature) as a product of their oppression. The likelihood that these clients will seek formal counseling regarding their cultural identity is very slim. In those cases when counseling is sought, it will tend to be only between members of the same minority group, and generally in response to a crisis situation. Therapy for Stage Three clients often takes the form of exposure to, and practice of, the ways and artifacts of their cultures. An example of this might be a woman who experiences a release of tension and anxiety because of her involvement in a class concerning women's liberation. Clients at this stage who do seek counseling are likely to prefer group process and/or alloplastic approaches to counseling. In addition, approaches that are more action-oriented and aimed at external change (challenging racism) are well received. D. W. Sue and D. Sue (in press) believe that most counselors find minorities at this stage difficult to work with. A counselor (even if a member of the client's own race) is often viewed by the culturally different client as a symbol of the oppressive establishment. A great amount of direct anger and distrust may be expressed toward the counselor. The counselor will be frequently tested and challenged as to his/her own racism and role in society.

Clients at the Introspection stage are torn between their preponderant identification with their minority group and their need to exercise greater personal freedom. When these individuals are unable to resolve mounting conflict between these two forces, they often seek counseling. While Introspective clients still prefer to see a counselor from their own cultural group, counselors from other cultures may be viewed as credible sources of help if they share world views similar to those of their clientele and appreciate their cultural dilemmas. Counselors who use a self-exploration and decision-making approach can be most effective with these clients.

Clients at the fifth stage of identity development have acquired the internal skills and knowledge necessary to exercise a desired level of personal freedom. Their sense of minority identity is well balanced by an appreciation of other cultures. And, while discrimination and oppression remain a painful part of their lives, greater psychological resources are at their disposal in actively engaging the problem. Attitudinal similarity between counselor and client becomes a more important determinant of counseling success than membership-group similarity.

Discussion of the MID model's implications for counseling is admittedly highly speculative at this point, and the model itself requires empirical verification before more definitive inferences are drawn. We hope the model will stimulate much-needed research with regard to minority identity development and that it will help the reader distinguish and comprehend intragroup differences that are evident in the readings to follow.

References

Atkinson, D. R., & Schein, S. (1986). Similarity in counseling. *The Counseling Psychology, 14,* 319–354.

Banks, W. (1972). The Black client and the helping professional. In R. I. Jones (Ed.), *Black psychology.* New York: Harper & Row.

Berry, B. (1965). *Ethnic and race relations.* Boston: Houghton Mifflin.

Crawford, T. J., & Naditch, M. (1970). Relative deprivation, powerlessness, and militancy: The psychology of social protest. *Psychiatry, 33,* 208–223.

Cross, W. E. (1970). The black experience viewed as a process: A crude model for black self-actualization. Paper presented at the Thirty-fourth Annual Meeting of the Association of Social and Behavioral Scientists, April 23–24, Tallahassee, Fla.

Cross, W. E. (1972). The Negro-to-Black conversion experience. *Black World, 20,* 13–27.

Downing, N. E., & Roush, K. L. (1985). From passive acceptance to active commitment: A model of feminist identity development for women. *The Counseling Psychologist, 13,* 695–709.

Hall, W. S., Cross, W. E., & Freedle, R. (1972). Stages in the development of Black awareness: An exploratory investigation. In R. I. Jones (Ed.), *Black psychology* (pp. 156–165). New York: Harper & Row.

Helms, J. E. (1985). Cultural identity in the treatment process. In P. Pedersen (Ed.), *Handbook of cross-cultural counseling and therapy.* Westport, Conn.: Greenwood Press.

Jackson, B. (1975). Black identity development. *MEFORM: Journal of Educational Diversity & Innovation, 2,* 19–25.

Maykovich, M. H. (1973). Political activation of Japanese American youth. *Journal of Social Issues, 29,* 167–185.

Parham, T. A., & Helms, J. E. (1981). The influence of black students' racial identity attitudes on preference for counselor's race. *Journal of Counseling Psychology, 28,* 250–257.

Parks, R. E. (1950). *Race and culture.* Glencoe, Ill.: The Free Press.

Ponterotto, J. G., & Wise, S. L. (1987). Construct validity study of the racial identity attitude scale. *Journal of Counseling Psychology, 34,* 123–131.

Ruiz, R. A., & Padilla, A. M. (1977). Counseling Latinos. *Personnel and Guidance Journal, 55,* 401–408.

Sherif, M., & Sherif, C. (1970). Black unrest at a social movement toward an emerging self-identity. *Journal of Social and Behavioral Sciences, 15,* 41–52.

Stonequist, E. V. (1937). *The marginal man.* New York: Charles Scribner's Sons.

Sue, D. W., & Sue, D. (in press). *Counseling the culturally different: Theory and practice.* New York: John Wiley & Sons.

Sue, S., & Sue, D. W. (1971). Chinese-American personality and mental health. *Amerasia Journal, 1,* 36–49.

Szapocznik, J., Kurtines, W. M., & Fernandez, T. (1980). Bicultural involvement and adjustment in Hispanic-American youths. *International Journal of Intercultural Relations, 4,* 353–365.

Thomas, C. W. (1971). *Boys no more.* Beverly Hills, Calif.: Glencoe Press.

Vontress, C. E. (1971). Racial differences: Impediments to rapport. *Journal of Counseling Psychology, 18,* 7–13.

Wallace, A. F. C. (1964). *Culture and personality.* New York: Random House.

Toward a Model of White Racial Identity Development

JANET E. HELMS

The development of White identity in the United States is closely inter-twined with the development and progress of racism in this country. The greater the extent that racism exists and is denied, the less possible it is to develop a positive White identity. J. M. Jones (1972, 1981) has identified three types of racism: (a) individual, that is, personal attitudes, beliefs, and behaviors designed to convince oneself of the superiority of Whites and the inferiority of non-White racial groups; (b) institutional, meaning social policies, laws, and regulations whose purpose is to main-tain the economic and social advantages of Whites over non-Whites; and (c) cultural, that is, societal beliefs and customs that promote the as-sumption that the products of White culture (e.g., language, traditions, appearance) are superior to those of non-White cultures.

Because each of these three types of racism is so much a part of the cultural milieu, each can become a part of the White person's racial identity or consciousness ipso facto. In order to develop a healthy White identity, defined in part as a nonracist identity, virtually every White person in the United States must overcome one or more of these aspects of racism. Additionally, he or she must accept his or her own Whiteness, the cultural implications of being White, and define a view of Self as a racial being that does not depend on the perceived superiority of one racial group over another.

Thus, the evolution of a positive White racial identity consists of two processes, the abandonment of racism and the development of a non-racist White identity. Because White racism in the United States seems

207

to have developed as a means of justifying the enslavement of Black Americans during the slavery eras of the 1700s and 1800s (cf. Comer, 1980; Cross et al., in press; Giddings, 1984), Blacks and/or Black culture have been the primary "outgroup" or reference group around which White racial identity development issues revolve. Thus, as is the case with Black racial identity, White racial identity contains parallel beliefs and attitudes about Whites as well as Blacks.

For the most part, theories or models of White racial identity development have focused on defining racism. Some of these perspectives are summarized in Table 4.1. As shown in Table 4.1, most of these models are typologies, that is, they assume that racists can be classified according to various categories. Moreover, most of these early perspectives were fueled by the implicit assumption that racism was only damaging to the victims of the resulting oppression but did not consider their effects on the beneficiaries or perpetrators of racism.

Only recently have theorists begun to speculate about the harmful consequences of racism on the perpetuators of racism, which include the absence of a positive White racial identity. In presenting the case for the need to help Whites develop a positive White identity, various authors have discussed the defense mechanisms by which Whites pretend that they are not White. For instance, J. Katz and Ivey (1977) noted that when faced with the question of their racial identification, Whites merely deny that they are White. They observed: "Ask a White person what he or she is racially and you may get the answer "Italian," "English," "Catholic," or "Jewish." *White people do not see themselves as White*" (p. 486). Relatedly, Terry (1981) commented, "To be white in America is not to have to think about it. Except for hard-core racial supremacists, the meaning of being White is having the choice of attending to or ignoring one's own Whiteness" (p. 120). If these authors' surmises are accurate, then it appears that most Whites may have no consistent conception of a positive White identity or consciousness. As a consequence, Whites may feel threatened by the actual or presupposed presence of racial consciousness in non-White racial groups.

In exploring the emotional consequences of racism to Whites, Karp (1981) indicated that major concomitants of racism and Whites' distorted views of racial identity are negative feelings such as "self-deception," "self-hate," and "guilt and shame," along with feeling bad about being white (sometimes expressed as a flip side—rigid pride in 'superiority')" (p. 89). She further suggests that these feelings can contribute to distorted behaviors as well as distorted views of the world. Dennis (1981) discussed the many "selves" into which a White person must compartmentalize her or his feelings and thoughts in order to be accepted by other Whites. In passing, it should be noted that theorists and researchers have viewed similar symptoms (e.g., racial denial, self-hate, feelings of

Table 4.1
Summary of White Racial Identity Models

Author	Model Type	Components Name	Description
Carney & Kahn (1984)	Stage	1. Stage 1	1. Knowledge of ethnically dissimilar people is based on stereotypes.
		2. Stage 2	2. Recognizes own cultural embeddedness, but deals with other groups in detached scholarly manner.
		3. Stage 3	3. Either denies the importance of race or expresses anger toward her/his own cultural group.
		4. Stage 4	4. Begins blending aspects of her/his cultural reference group with those of other groups to form a new self-identity.
		5. Stage 5	5. Attempts to act to promote social equality and cultural pluralism.
Ganter (1977)	Stage	1. Phase 1	1. Protest and denial that Whites are patrons and pawns of racism.
		2. Phase 2	2. Guilt and despair as racism is acknowledged.
		3. Phase 3	3. Integrates awareness of Whites' collective loss of human integrity and attempts to free oneself from racism.
Hardiman (1979)	Stage	1. Acceptance	1. Active or passive acceptance of White superiority.
		2. Resistance	2. Person becomes aware of own racial identity for the first time.
		3. Redefinition	3. Attempts to redefine Whiteness from a non-racist perspective.
		4. Internali-zation	4. Internalizes non-racist White identity.
Helms (1984)	Stage	1. Contact	1. Obliviousness to own racial identity.
		2. Disinte-gration	2. First acknowledgment of White identity.

Table 4.1 (continued)

Author	Model Type	Components Name	Description
		3. Reinte-gration	3. Idealizes Whites/ denigrates Blacks.
		4. Pseudo-In-dependence	4. Intellectualized acceptance of own and others' race.
		5. Immersion/ Emersion	5. Honest appraisal of racism and significance of Whiteness.
		6. Autonomy	6. Internalizes a multi-cultural identity with non-racist Whiteness as its core.
Kovel (1970) Gaertner (1976) Jones (1972)	Type	1. Dominative racist	1. Openly seeks to keep Black people in inferior positions and will use force to do so.
		2. Aversive Dominative Racist	2. Believes in White superiority, but tries to ignore the existence of Black people to avoid intrapsychic conflict.
		3. Aversive Liberal racist	3. Despite aversion to Blacks, uses impersonal social reforms to improve Blacks' conditions.
		4. Ambivalent	4. Expresses exaggeratedly positive or negative responses toward Blacks depending on the consequences to the White person.
		5. Non-racist	5. Does not reveal any racist tendencies.
Terry (1977)	Type	1. Color blind	1. Attempts to ignore race; feels one can exonerate self from being White by asserting one's humanness; equates acknowledgment of color with racism.
		2. White Blacks	2. Abandons Whiteness in favor of overidentifying with Blacks; denies own Whiteness; tries to gain personal recognition from Blacks for being "almost Black".
		3. New Whites	3. Holds a pluralistic racial view of the world; recognizes that racism is a White problem and attempts to eliminate it.

Note: Gaerther (1976) and J. M. Jones (1972) elaborated the typology originally proposed by Kovel (1970).

inferiority, etc.) as cause for alarm and serious psychological intervention in Black communities. However, it does not seem that similar enthusiasm has been expended in promoting healthy White racial identity development.

Implicit in much of the contemporary writings on White racial identity development is the awareness that, in spite of the pervasive socialization toward racism, some White people do appear not only to have developed a White consciousness, but one that is not predominated by racial distortions. Some authors have even loosely described an orderly process by which a White person can move from a racist identity to a positive White consciousness. In describing the process by which some Whites have overcome racism, Dennis observed: "one sees them moving from 'knowing' Blacks to knowing Blacks, from deracialization to reracialization, toward a more 'objective' approach to race with a clearer understanding of the role of race and culture in society" (p. 74). Karp (1981) described the process as follows: "Whites [must address] their feelings of oppression [must seek out] accurate information, [must discharge] feelings related to racism, and [consequently change] their attitudes and behaviors" (p. 88). Thus, Dennis essentially proposes a cognitive process of White identity development, whereas Karp emphasizes the interrelatedness of emotions, attitudes, and behaviors.

At least two of the White identity typologists (Pettigrew, 1981; Terry, 1981) have speculated more systematically about the relationship of White racial identity to Whites' psychological health. Applying Jahoda's (1958) trichotomy of "sick," "not healthy," and "well" to describe the psychological consequences to Whites of racism, Pettigrew (1981) concluded that roughly 15 to 75% of Whites were in the categories of sick or not healthy as a consequence of internalizing some form of personal racial bigotry. Terry's (1977) categorical system recognized that there were different ways that one could acknowledge and, consequently, be White (see Table 4.1), just as there were different ways that one could be racist. However, from none of the typological perspectives is it clear how or whether a person can shift from one type of identity or category to another.

Working independently, in separate places and at different times, Hardiman (1979) and Helms (1984b) proposed developmental models of White racial identity development. Both models are similar in that they propose a linear process of attitudinal development in which the White person potentially progresses through a series of stages differing in the extent to which they involve acknowledgment of racism and consciousness of Whiteness. They differ in the particulars of some of the stages, though both agree that the highest stage involves an awareness of personal responsibility for racism, consistent acknowledgment of one's Whiteness, and abandonment of racism in any of its forms as a defining aspect of one's personality. Hardiman's theoretical model is summarized

211

in Table 4.1. However, since Helms's model has been subjected to empirical investigation and (to the author's knowledge) Hardiman's has not, Helms's model is the primary theoretical basis for the subsequent presentation of White racial identity development. Consequently, it will be presented in some detail.

STAGES OF WHITE RACIAL IDENTITY DEVELOPMENT

One of the concomitants of being a White person in the United States is that one is a member of a numerical majority as well as the socioeconomically and politically dominant group. One result of this racial status is that, as Dennis (1981) points out, even if one has few resources oneself, as long as one has White skin in America, one is entitled to feel superior to Blacks. This sense of entitlement seems to be a basic norm of White society.

Perhaps more importantly, as previously noted, if one is a White person in the United States, it is still possible to exist without ever having to acknowledge that reality. In fact, it is only when Whites come in contact with the idea of Blacks (or other visible racial/ethnic groups) that Whiteness becomes a potential issue. Whether or not this initial contact has any implications for racial identity development depends upon the extent to which it is unavoidable. Thus, if the Black (in this instance) presence "intrudes" into the White person's environment, and the intrusion cannot be ignored or controlled, then the White person is likely to be forced to deal with White racial identity issues somewhat. However, to the extent that such intrusions can be avoided, which may still be the case in much of White America, one can avoid resolving White racial identity issues. That is, one can choose to be oblivious to race and the differential effects of race on how one is perceived and treated by society at large; or one can decide to remain fixated at one of the identity stages to be described subsequently.

There are two primary ways by which one can become aware of the presence of Blacks as an outgroup: vicariously or directly. Vicarious awareness occurs when significant persons in one's life (e.g., media, parents, peers) inform one of the existence of Blacks as well as how one ought to think about them. Dennis (1981) does an excellent job of describing how Whites are socialized directly and indirectly to fear and devalue Blacks. Direct awareness occurs when the White person interacts with Blacks himself or herself. These two means of awareness are not necessarily exclusive, as Dennis points out. Nevertheless, though one's own initial experiences with Blacks may be pleasant and non-individually racist, significant White persons in one's environment may use the socialization pressures available to them to ensure that the White person learns the rules of being a socially accepted White person. A number of autobiographical accounts (e.g., McLaurin, 1987; L. Smith, 1961), usually written from a Southern perspective, describe how Whites are taught to develop individual racism.

Recall that institutional and cultural racism are so much a part of the White (or Black) individual's world that he or she is often blind to their presence. Thus, the White person's developmental tasks with regard to development of a healthy White identity, according to both Hardiman's (1979) and Helms's (1984b) perspectives, require the abandonment of individual racism as well as the recognition of and active opposition to institutional and cultural racism. Concurrently, the person must become aware of her or his Whiteness, learn to accept Whiteness as an important part of herself or himself, and to internalize a realistically positive view of what it means to be White.

Helms (1984) originally proposed that White racial identity development occurred via a five-stage process, each involving attitudes, emotions, and behaviors in which Whites as well as Blacks are referents. More recently, she has included a sixth stage, Immersion/Emersion, to reflect Hardiman's (1979) contention that it is possible for Whites to seek out accurate information about their historical, political, and cultural contributions to the world, and that the process of self-examination within this context is an important component of the process of defining a positive White identity.

Thus, presently, Helms conceptualizes a two-phase process of White identity development. As illustrated in Figure 4.1, Phase 1, the abandonment of racism, begins with the Contact stage and ends with the Reintegration stage. Phase 2, defining a positive White identity, begins with the Pseudo-Independent stage and ends with the Autonomy stage.

Contact

As soon as one encounters the idea or the actuality of Black people, one has entered the Contact stage of identity. Depending somewhat upon one's racial (particularly) familial environment, one will enter Contact with either naive curiosity or timidity and trepedation about Blacks and a superficial and inconsistent awareness of being White. When one is in Contact, if one exhibits individual racism, it is probably exhibited in a weak and unsophisticated form since the person is just beginning to try her or his racial wings. Nevertheless, the person in Contact automatically benefits from institutional and cultural racism without necessarily being aware that he or she is doing so.

Oddly enough, the person in Contact may enjoy being a racist more than persons at the other stages simply because he or she has not had to confront the moral dilemmas resulting from such an identification. The Contact person's White racial identification is equally subtle. Thus,

Figure 4.1
Stages and Phases of White Racial Identity Development

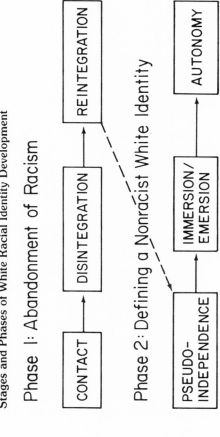

Phase I: Abandonment of Racism

CONTACT → DISINTEGRATION → REINTEGRATION

Phase 2: Defining a Nonracist White Identity

PSEUDO-INDEPENDENCE → IMMERSION/EMERSION → AUTONOMY

although such a person evaluates Blacks according to White criteria (e.g., White physical appearance, standardized tests, etc.), he or she does so automatically without awareness that other criteria are possible, and that he or she might be as legitimately evaluated according to other racial/cultural groups' criteria.

Behaviors thought to characterize Contact people are limited inter-racial social or occupational interaction with Blacks, unless the interaction is initiated by Blacks who "seem" White except for skin color or other "Black" physical characteristics. In such interactions, the White person uses the Black person to teach him or her about what Black people in general are like and often uses societal stereotypes of Blacks as the standard against which the Black person is evaluated. Comments such as "You don't act like a Black person," or "I don't notice what race a person is," are likely to be made by Contact persons.

Affectively, Contact persons can be expected to have positive self-esteem because they have not yet learned to compartmentalize and dif-ferentially value their different selves (cf. Dennis, 1981). They should generally have positive feelings about the "idea" of Blacks and fair treat-ment of Blacks; though trait anxiety should be low, state anxiety or arousal may be present when actual interactions with Blacks are expe-rienced or anticipated.

One's longevity in the Contact stage depends upon the kinds of ex-periences one has with Blacks and Whites with respect to racial issues. For instance, as the White person becomes aware of Blacks, if this aware-ness is based on vicarious information rather than actual experiences, then he or she is likely to remain in the Contact stage, particularly the aspect of the stage associated with fearfulness and caution. This sup-position is based on the common observation (e.g., Karp, 1981; Reid, 1979) that the bulk of information available to Whites (and Blacks) about Blacks is negative. In such cases, the person is likely to continue to engage in minimal cross-racial interaction, is unlikely to be forced to rethink her or his racial perspective, is tolerated by her or his racial peers if he or she makes known her or his Contact perspective, and, of course, is warmly accepted if he or she remains silent about it.

On the other hand, if the Contact person continues to interact with Blacks, sooner or later significant others in the person's environment will make it known that such behavior is unacceptable if one wishes to remain a member in good standing of the "White" group (cf. Boyle, 1962; L. Smith, 1961). Where Blacks are concerned, if Whites in the Contact stage continue to interact with them, sooner or later the Contact person will have to acknowledge that there are differences in how Blacks and Whites in the United States are treated regardless of economic status. Sometimes this awareness may occur because the Black person points out the differences; sometimes it occurs because of obvious acts of discrimination (e.g., cab drivers who pass by Blacks regardless of how they are dressed, but stop for their White associates). Moreover, many Blacks will not join the Contact person in pretending that he or she is also Black (see Terry, 1980). When enough of these "socialization" experiences penetrate the White person's identity system, then he or she can enter the Disintegration stage.

Disintegration

Entry into the Disintegration stage implies conscious, though conflicted, acknowledgment of one's Whiteness. Moreover, it triggers the recognition of moral dilemmas associated with being White as described by Dennis (1981). If some of his dilemmas are reworded to refer to Whites regardless of religion or geographic origin, then they can be summarized as follows:

(a)   the desire to be a religious or moral person versus the recognition that to be accepted by Whites one must treat Blacks immorally;

"[b]   the belief in freedom and democracy versus the belief in racial inequality";

"[c]   the desire to show love and compassion versus the desire to keep Blacks in their place at all costs";

(d)   the belief in treating others with dignity and respect versus the belief that Blacks are not worthy of dignity or respect;

"[e]   the belief that each person should be treated according to his or her individual merits versus the belief that Blacks should be evaluated as a group without regard to individual merits and talents" (p. 78).

Accompanying the conflicted White identification is a questioning of the racial realities the person has been taught to believe. It is probably during this stage, for instance, that the person first comes to realize that in spite of mouthings to the contrary, Blacks and Whites are not considered equals and negative social consequences can besiege the White person who does not respect the inequalities. Moreover, the Disintegration stage may be the time in which the person comes to realize that the social skills and mores he or she has been taught to use in interacting with Blacks rarely work. Thus, the person in Disintegration may not only perceive for the first time that he or she is caught between two racial groups, but may also come to realize that his or her position amongst Whites depends upon his or her ability to successfully "split" her or his personality.

Self-actualization personality theorists such as Rogers (1951) suggest that emotional discomfort, which Rogers calls "incongruence," results when one must markedly alter one's real self in order to be accepted by

216

significant others in one's environment. The feelings of guilt, depression, helplessness, and anxiety described by various authors (e.g., J. Baldwin, 1963; Karp, 1981; J. Katz, 1976) as correlates of Whiteness probably have their origins in the Disintegration stage:

Festinger (1957) theorized that when two or more of a person's cognitions (e.g., beliefs or feelings about oneself) are in conflict, an uncomfortable psychological state that he calls "dissonance" likely results. He suggests that when dissonance is present, a person will not only attempt to reduce it, but will also take steps to avoid situations and information that are likely to increase it. Thus, if one thinks of the uncomfortable feelings resulting from White moral ambivalence as previously described as dissonance, then it seems plausible that the same sorts of strategies used to reduce dissonance in general may also be used to reduce race-related dissonance.

Festinger proposed three ways of reducing dissonance: (a) changing a behavior, (b) changing an environmental belief, and (c) developing new beliefs. Accordingly, the person in the Disintegration stage might reduce discomfort by (a) avoiding further contact with Blacks (changing a behavior), (b) attempting to convince significant others in her or his environment that Blacks are not so inferior (changing an environmental belief), or (c) seeking information from Blacks or Whites to the effect that either racism is not the White person's fault or does not really exist (adding new beliefs). Additionally, as a means of avoiding an increase in dissonance, the person may selectively attend only to information that gives him or her greater confidence in the new beliefs and/or he or she will interact only with those who can be counted on to support the new belief.

Which alternative the White person chooses probably depends on the extent to which her or his cross-racial interactions are voluntary. It seems likely that the person who can remove herself or himself from interracial environments or can remove Blacks from White environments will do so. Given the racial differences in social and economic power, most Whites can choose this option. If they do so, they will receive much support in an exclusively White environment for the development of individual racism as well as the maintenance of cultural and institutional racism.

Attempts to change others' attitudes probably occur initially amongst Whites who were raised and/or socialized in an environment in which White "liberal" attitudes (though not necessarily behaviors) were expressed. However, due to the racial naiveté with which this approach may be undertaken and the person's ambivalent racial identification, this dissonance-reducing strategy is likely to be met with rejection by Whites as well as Blacks.

To the extent that cross-racial interaction is unavoidable, the White person will attempt to develop new beliefs. However, the desire to be accepted by one's own racial group and the prevalence in the White group of the covert and overt belief in White superiority and Black inferiority virtually dictates that the content of the person's belief system will also change in a similar direction. As this reshaping of the person's cognitions or beliefs occurs, he or she enters the Reintegration stage.

Reintegration

In the Reintegration stage, the person consciously acknowledges a White identity. In the absence of contradictory experiences, to be White in America is to believe that one is superior to people of color. Consequently, the Reintegration person accepts the belief in White racial superiority and Black inferiority. He or she comes to believe that institutional and cultural racism are the White person's due because he or she has earned such privileges and preferences. Race-related negative conditions are assumed to result from Black people's inferior social, moral, and intellectual qualities, and thus, it is not unusual to find persons in the Reintegration stage selectively attending to and/or reinterpreting information to conform to societal stereotypes of Black people. Cross-racial similarities are minimized and/or denied.

Any residual feelings of guilt and anxiety are transformed into fear and anger toward Black people. Much of the person's cross-racial behavior is motivated by these feelings. Though the feelings may not be overtly expressed, they lie just below the surface of the person's awareness, and it only takes an event(s) that can be characterized (whether or not it actually is) by the White person as personally threatening for these feelings to be unleashed.

Behaviorally, people in the Reintegration stage may express their beliefs and feelings either passively or actively. Passive expression involves deliberate removal of oneself and/or avoidance of environments in which one might encounter Black people. In this instance, honest discussion of racial matters is most likely to occur among same-race peers who share or are believed to share a similar view of the world. Active expression may include treating Blacks as inferior and involve acts of violence or exclusion designed to protect White privilege.

In this society, it is fairly easy to remain or fixate at the Reintegration stage, particularly if one is relatively passive in one's expression of it. A personally jarring event is probably necessary for the person to begin to abandon this essentially racist identity. Again, the event can be direct or vicarious; it can be caused by painful or insightful encounters with Black or White persons. Changes in the environmental racial climate may also trigger transition from the Reintegration stage. For instance, the Civil Rights Movement of the 1960s and the Vietnam War caused some Whites to question their racial identity, though hopefully the catalyst for such self-examination does not have to be so major. Be that as it may, once the person begins to question her or his previous definition of Whiteness and the justifiability of racism in any of its forms, then he or she has begun the movement into the Pseudo-Independent or Liberal stage.

Pseudo-Independent

Pseudo-Independent is the first stage of redefining a positive White identity. In this stage, the person begins actively to question the proposition that Blacks are innately inferior to Whites. Instead, in this stage, the person begins to acknowledge the responsibility of Whites for racism and to see how he or she wittingly and unwittingly perpetuates racism. Consequently, he or she is no longer comfortable with a racist identity and begins to search for ways to redefine her or his White identity. Usually the redefining process takes the form of intellectual acceptance and curiosity about Blacks.

The Pseudo-Independent stage is primarily a stage of intellectualization in which the person attempts to submerge the tumultuous feelings about Whiteness that were aroused in previous stages. To the extent that feelings concerning racial identity issues are allowed to emerge, they are apt to be feelings of commiseration with Blacks and perhaps disquietude concerning racial issues in White peer groups.

Nevertheless, though the person in the Pseudo-Independent stage is abandoning the belief in White superiority/Black inferiority, he or she may still behave in ways that unwittingly perpetuate this belief system. That is, though the person may seek greater interaction with Blacks, much of this interaction involves helping Blacks to change themselves so that they function more like Whites on White criteria for success and acceptability rather than recognizing that such criteria might be inappropriate and/or too narrowly defined. Furthermore, cultural or racial differences are likely to be interpreted by using White life experiences as the standards. Moreover, the Pseudo-Independent person still looks to Black rather than White people to explain racism and seeks solutions for it in hypothetical Black cultural dysfunctionalities.

Although the person in the Pseudo-Independent stage no longer has a negative White identity or consciousness, neither does he or she have a positive one. The paucity of White models of positive Whiteness means that the person usually has no visible standards against which to compare and/or modify himself or herself. Additionally, such a person is likely to be met with considerable suspicion from other Whites as well as Blacks.

Many Whites will treat the Pseudo-Independent person, who actively expresses this identity, as though he or she has violated White racial norms. Many Black people will be suspicious of the motives of a person who devotes so much attention to helping Blacks rather than changing Whites. Consequently, the Pseudo-Independent person may not feel entirely comfortable with her or his White identity, but overidentification with Blacks is also not likely to be very comfortable. Thus, the person may come to feel rather marginal where race and racial issues are concerned. However, if the personal rewards (e.g., self-esteem, monetary, etc.) are great enough to encourage continued strengthening of a positive White identity, then the person may begin the quest for those positive aspects of Whiteness that are unrelated to racism. The quest for a better definition of Whiteness signals the person's entry into the Immersion/Emersion stage.

Immersion/Emersion

Redefining a positive White identity requires that the person replace White and Black myths and stereotypes with accurate information about what it means and has meant to be White in the United States as well as in the world in general. The person in this stage is searching for the answers to the questions: "Who am I racially?" and "Who do I want to be?" and "Who are you really?"

Often such a person will immerse herself or himself in biographies and autobiographies of Whites who have made similar identity journeys. He or she may participate in White consciousness-raising groups whose purpose is to help the person discover her or his individual self-interest in abandoning racism and acknowledging a White racial identity. Changing Black people is no longer the focus of her or his activities, but rather the goal of changing White people becomes salient.

Emotional as well as cognitive restructuring can happen during this stage. Successful resolution of this stage apparently requires emotional catharsis in which the person reexperiences previous emotions that were denied or distorted (cf. Lipsky, 1978). Once these negative feelings are expressed, the person may begin to feel a euphoria perhaps akin to a religious rebirth. These positive feelings not only help to buttress the newly developing White identity, but provide the fuel by which the person can truly begin to tackle racism and oppression in its various forms.

Autonomy

Internalizing, nurturing, and applying the new definition of Whiteness evolved in the earlier stages are major goals of the Autonomy stage. In this stage, the person no longer feels a need to oppress, idealize, or denigrate people on the basis of group membership characteristics such

Figure 4.2
A Workshop Activity on Self-Assessing White Racial Identity

For each of the subsequent items, use the following scale to indicate the extent to which the item is true of you.

> 4 - Strongly Agree
> 3 - Agree
> 2 - Disagree
> 1 - Strongly Disagree

Write the numbers of your responses on the line next to the item. Add together your responses to the item preceded by the same combination of letters and plot your scores on the graph. Draw a line to connect your C total, R total, D total, P total, E total, and A total. Draw another line to connect the totals preceded by double letters (e.g., CB). This will give you a racial identity profile.

C1. _____ There is no race problem in the United States.

C2. _____ Racism only exists in the minds of a few Black people.

C3. _____ I personally do not notice what race a person is.

_____ C TOTAL

CB1. _____ I have asked or would ask a Black person to help me understand how I might be prejudiced.

CB2. _____ I contribute or would contribute money or time to social programs to help Blacks.

CB3. _____ I participate or would participate in an activity to help Blacks overcome their poor environment.

_____ CB TOTAL

R1. _____ I believe that White culture or Western civilization is the most highly developed, sophisticated culture ever to have existed on earth.

R2. _____ Africans and Blacks are more sexually promiscuous than Europeans and Whites.

R3. _____ The White race will be polluted by intermarriage with Blacks.

_____ R TOTAL

RB1. _____ When a Black male stranger sits or stands next to me in a public place, I move away from him.

RB2. _____ I live or would live in a segregated (White) neighborhood.

RB3. _____ The people I do my non-business related socializing with either are Whites or Blacks who "act White."

_____ RB TOTAL

D1. _____ American society is sick, evil, and racist.

D2. _____ There is nothing I can do to prevent racism.

D3. _____ I avoid thinking about racial issues.

_____ D TOTAL

221

Figure 4.2 (continued)

P1. _____ It is White people's responsibility to eliminate racism in the United States.

P2. _____ Eliminating racism would help Whites feel better about themselves.

P3. _____ White people should help Black people become equal to Whites.

_____ P TOTAL

PB1. _____ I have boycotted a company or its products because of its racist programs.

PB2. _____ For Martin Luther King's Birthday, I attend or would attend a commemorative event.

PB3. _____ I have tried to help Whites understand Blacks.

_____ LB TOTAL

E1. _____ White culture and society must be restructured to eliminate racism and opposition.

E2. _____ Whites and White culture are not superior to Blacks and Black culture.

E3. _____ A multi-cultural society cannot exist unless Whites give up their racism.

_____ E TOTAL

EB1. _____ I have studied the history of White and Western European people.

EB2. _____ I meet with Whites to discuss our feelings and attitudes about being White and White racism.

EB3. _____ I have conducted activities to help Whites overcome their racism.

_____ EB TOTAL

A1. _____ I accept that being White does not make me superior to any other racial group.

A2. _____ Being a member of a multi-racial environment is a must for me.

A3. _____ My Whiteness is an important part of who I am.

_____ A TOTAL

AB1. _____ I speak up in a White group situation when I feel that a White person is being racist.

AB2. _____ I express my honest opinion when a Black person is present without worrying about whether I appear racist.

AB3. _____ I attempt to explain to White friends and relatives the relationship of racism to other forms of oppression.

_____ AB TOTAL

64

Figure 4.2 (continued)

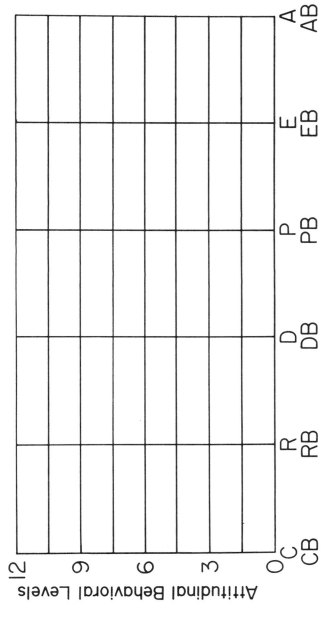

This workshop activity is adapted from Hardiman (1979) and Helms (1984). These items are not from a validated scale and are presented here for the reader's possible self-exploration. Abbreviations are: C = Contact attitudes, CB = Contact behavior, R = Reintegration attitudes, RB = Reintegration behavior, D = Disintegration attitudes, DB = Disintegration behavior, P = Pseudo-Independent attitudes, PB = Pseudo-Independent behavior, E = Emersion attitudes, EB = Emersion behavior, A = Autonomy attitudes, AB = Autonomy behavior. Higher scores indicate higher levels of the attitudes/behaviors.

65

as race because race no longer symbolizes threat to him or her. Since he or she no longer reacts out of rigid world views, it is possible for him or her to abandon cultural and institutional racism as well as personal racism. Thus, one finds the Autonomous person actively seeking opportunities to learn from other cultural groups. One also finds him or her actively becoming increasingly aware of how other forms of oppression (e.g., sexism, ageism) are related to racism and acting to eliminate them as well. Terry's (1977) description of the characteristics of the New White (see Table 4.1) seems to describe the Autonomous person.

Although Autonomy represents the highest level of White racial identity and might be thought of as racial self-actualization or transcendence, perhaps it is best to think of it as an ongoing process. It is a process wherein the person is continually open to new information and new ways of thinking about racial and cultural variables. Nevertheless, reaching the Autonomy stage does not necessarily mean that the person is perfect with respect to all aspects of her or his identity. Chances are if the person had a grouchy personality (i.e., personal identity) before he or she began movement through the racial identity development process, then he or she will still be a grouch once the process is completed. It is just that his or her grouchiness will no longer be governed by cultural or racial determinants. In other words, one might find a variety of personality characteristics and styles among people who have reached the Autonomy stage.

CONCLUSIONS

As might be apparent, each of the White racial identity stages is hypothesized to have its own unique effect on attitudes, behaviors, and emotions. Nevertheless, it is probably not the case that each of these develops at the same rate. In fact, studies of symbolic racism (e.g., McConaghy & Hough, 1976) suggest that attitudes (at least racist attitudes as opposed to White identity attitudes) may change faster than behaviors. As an example of how this is possible, the reader might wish to try out the workshop exercise in Figure 4.2. It seems reasonable to speculate that the greatest discomfort occurs for those individuals whose attitudes, emotions, and behaviors are not in harmony.

The Journal of Sex Research   Vol. 20, No. 2, pp. 143-167   May, 1984

Homosexual Identity Formation: Testing a Theoretical Model

VIVIENNE C. CASS

Abstract

Of late, researchers in the area of homosexuality have emphasized the study of homosexual identity formation. Several models have been put forward depicting the process of identity acquisition, but little attempt has been made to test either their accuracy or generality. The study outlined in this paper assesses the validity of several important aspects of my six-stage model of homosexual identity acquisition. To this end, a questionnaire was constructed to measure a number of factors believed to be critical to homosexual identity development. Responses of subjects at each stage were examined to ascertain the degree to which they corresponded with ideal stage descriptions predicted from the model. Results provided some support for the validity of these descriptions and for the order of the stages. The data describe a four-stage, rather than a six-stage model. To check that these findings were not the result of researcher bias, a discriminant analysis was carried out. This indicated that the postulated six-stage groups could be distinguished. Ways of revising the scoring keys so as to maximize group differences are discussed. Both similarities and differences were apparent between male and female subjects, but the small sample limited the degree to which conclusions could be drawn about these. Implications of these findings for other models of homosexual identity formation are discussed.

In the last decade, research into homosexuality has taken on new directions, moving increasingly away from the earlier emphasis on etiology, treatment programs, and psychological adjustment, to focus instead on the homosexual situation as experienced and perceived by homosexuals themselves. This change of emphasis has given impetus to the study of areas hitherto ignored in the scientific literature.

Of these, the question of *how* people come to adopt a homosexual identity has consistently attracted the interest of modern researchers.

Vivienne C. Cass, PhD, is a Clinical Psychologist in the Department of Social Inquiry at Murdoch University in Western Australia. The author wishes to thank K. Gibbons of the Department of Psychology, Murdoch University, for his continued support and guidance, and T. Speed and R. Owens of the Department of Mathematics, University of Western Australia, for their invaluable assistance with the statistical analyses.

Requests for reprints should be sent to Vivienne C. Cass, PhD, Psychology Section, Department of Social Inquiry, Murdoch University, Murdoch 6153, Western Australia.

mental process marked by a series of changes, growth points, or stages along which certain experiences can be ordered. Progress through the stages is characterized by, firstly, increasing acceptance of the label *homosexual* as descriptive of self; secondly, development of a positive attitude towards this self-identity; thirdly, a growing desire to disclose the existence of this identity to both homosexuals and nonhomosexuals; and fourthly, increasingly more personalized and frequent social contacts with homosexuals.

Although all models attach importance in varying degrees to these behavioral, cognitive, and affective aspects of the developmental process, comparison between the models in this regard is extremely difficult. In most models there has been little attempt to detail the changes that occur at each stage of identity development. The result is an often vague and poorly conceptualized picture of the developmental process. Particularly obvious is the seeming confusion among many theorists as to what identity actually means and how this meaning can be translated into the developmental process. Typically, some stages are outlined in terms of their cognitive content, and behavioral and affective aspects are neglected, yet other stages within the same model may be described in behavioral terms only. This lack of clarity and consistency limits both the degree to which the validity of a model can be adequately tested and also the extent to which the models can be compared. Therefore, it is not surprising that, to date, neither the accuracy nor the generalizability of the various models of homosexual identity formation have been submitted to rigorous testing.

Three of the 10 models (those of McLellan [1977], Troiden [1977], and Weinberg [1977]), were empirically tested using the interview technique, with authors claiming some support for their theories from the results. However, methods for analyzing the interview material were notably lacking in the necessary safeguards against subjectivity (i.e., blind judges, multiple raters, inter-judge reliability measures), rendering the conclusions open to claims of bias and casting doubt on attempts to generalize these findings to other samples. Thus, despite the enthusiasm of these theorists in putting forward their conceptualizations of homosexual identity formation, little is known at this point about the validity of their models.

In an attempt to change this situation, I am currently carrying out a research program to test the validity of my model. In brief, I have outlined (Cass, 1979, 1984) in some detail the changes that occur over stages on a number of significant factors, and the way in which incongruency or dissonance, created when individuals assign homosexual meaning to their behavior, and the need to enhance self-esteem act as motivating forces in the identity formation. Identity is perceived as a cognitive construct, the components of which are accompanied by unique affect. Identity is invariably translated into psychological activity (behavior) which in turn may result in changes occurring in identity. This model differs from most others in its rejection of the commonly held assumption that people perceive the acquisition of a homosexual identity in a negative light. Within each stage, several different paths of development are proposed. Where the other models were applied to either male or female homosexuals, this model is intended to explain the identity formation process for both groups. I hypothesize that the process of homosexual identity formation can be usefully conceptualized as compromising six stages of development, or points of growth along the developmental continuum.

This developmental process may be described according to a number of cognitive, behavioral, and affective dimensions (see Table 1). It is on the basis of these dimensions that the stages can be distinguished. The stages can be distinguished by which dimensions are present in individuals at each stage and by the degree of importance given to these dimensions. For example, the factors of *Disclosure* and *Acculturation* have little relevance to Stage 1 and 2, where focus is on cognitive restructuring rather than on behavior occurring in *response* to self-concept changes. Similarly, *Professional Contact* is not an important aspect of Stages 5 and 6, where any confusion or doubts about identity have been well and truly sorted out. The following summary of the ideal stage descriptions indicates the broad developmental changes that I believe occur across stages and the variables that assume central importance in this process.

Stage 1: Identity Confusion

Individuals perceive that their behavior (actions, feelings, thoughts) may be defined as homosexual. This brings about considerable confusion and bewilderment, since previously held identities relating to sexual orientation are now questioned.

One of three possible paths of development will be chosen, depending on whether this homosexual definition is perceived as correct or not and as desirable or not. Each path incorporates different cognitive and behavioral strategies in order to cope with the incongruency and/or lowered self-esteem that has been created. The individual will either

Table 1

Dimensions Used to Describe Stages of Homosexual Identity Formation

Factors	Cognitive	Behavioral	Affective
1. Commitment	Degree that individual accepts a homosexual and/or heterosexual self-image.		Feelings about accepting a homosexual self-image.
	Degree of confusion about own self-image regarding sexual orientation.		
	Degree of acceptance of others' view of self as a homosexual and a heterosexual.		
	Clarity of perception of homosexual meaning of behavior and self-image.		
2. Disclosure	Degree of wanting to disclose homosexual behavior/self-image to homosexual/heterosexual others.	Degree of disclosure of homosexual behavior/self-image to homosexual/heterosexual others.	Feelings about disclosing homosexual behavior/self-image to homosexual/heterosexual others.
	Types of homosexual/heterosexual others that individual would like to disclose to.	Types of homosexual/heterosexual others that individual discloses to.	
	Perceived elements of relationship between self and others that lead to desire to disclose.	Elements of relationship between self and others leading to disclosure.	
3. Generality	Degree that a homosexual/heterosexual self-image is seen as being a part of self.	Degree that homosexual and/or heterosexual behavior occurs when possible situation arises.	
	The way that individual imagines others perceive the generality of their homosexual self-image.		
4. Identity evaluation	Degree of acceptance for self of negative stereotypes of homosexuals.		Evaluation of homosexual and/or heterosexual self-image/behavior.
			Evaluation of others' view of homosexual/heterosexual self-image/behavior.

Table 1—continued
Dimensions Used to Describe Stages of Homosexual Identity Formation

Factors	Cognitive	Behavioral	Affective
5. Group identification	Sense of belonging felt with homosexuals and/or heterosexual groups. Degree that individual perceives self as similar to homosexuals/heterosexuals. Degree that homosexual/heterosexual groups are seen to meet own needs.		Degree of pride felt towards homosexuals as a whole.
6. Social interaction	Perceived quality of interaction with homosexuals and/or heterosexuals.	Frequency of social contacts with homosexuals/heterosexuals. Types of settings in which social contacts with homosexuals/heterosexuals take place.	Degree of satisfaction with interactions with homosexuals and/or heterosexuals.
7. Alienation	Degree that individual feels different from others, a stranger to self.		Degree that individual likes feeling different from others.
8. Inconsistency	Degree that individual's perception of self, behavior, and others' view of self are inconsistent with regard to sexual orientation.		Degree of discomfort felt about inconsistency between self, behavior, and others' view of self as pertains to homosexuality.
9. Sexual orientation activity	Degree that individual desires increased/ decreased frequency of homosexual erotic, emotional, and sexual activity.	Frequency with which homosexual erotic, emotional, and sexual activity are engaged in.	Degree of enjoyment felt from homosexual erotic, emotional, and sexual activity.
10. Acculturation		Forms of homosexual subcultural activities engaged in.	Degree of comfort felt in participating in homosexual subcultural activities.
11. Deference to others	Degree of importance attached to opinions of homosexuals/ heterosexuals. Types of homosexuals/heterosexuals perceived as important.		

Table 1—continued
Dimensions Used to Describe Stages of Homosexual Identity Formation

Factors	Cognitive	Behavioral	Affective
12. Dichoto-mization	Degree that homosexuals and heterosexuals perceived as two separate and distinct groups.		
13. Personal control	Amount of influence that a homosexual identity is seen to have on day-to-day living and on future prospects. Degree that a homosexual identity is seen to interfere with running of life.		
14. Strategies	Degree that individual wants to continue using strategies outlined in model.	Degree that strategies outlined in model are adopted. Ease with which strategies are carried out. Types of strategies used.	
15. Personal satisfaction	Degree that individual is satisfied with current life. Degree that individual wants to change current life. Degree that life is perceived as settled and stable.		
16. Professional contact	Degree that individual wants to see professional for help regarding homosexual behavior/self-image. Reasons for seeing/wanting to see professional.	Whether is seeing or has seen professional for help regarding homosexual behavior/self-image.	

consider the possibility of a homosexual identity (accepting this as positive or negative), or reject this possibility entirely, foreclosing further development. (In each stage, identity foreclosure in which individuals may choose not to proceed any further in the development of a homosexual identity is possible.)

Stage 2: Identity Comparison .

Having accepted the *potentiality* of a homosexual identity, the individual is then faced with feelings of alienation as the difference between self and nonhomosexual others becomes clearer. Development proceeds along one of four possible paths, selection of which is dependent upon whether the individual perceives his/her self-perception (which is "maybe homosexual") or homosexual behavior, or both these factors, as undesirable or not. As in Stage 1, each path requires different cognitive and behavioral strategies to arrive at either the point of saying, "I probably am a homosexual" or a position of completely denying such a possibility. Where identity foreclosure does not occur, the individual may contemplate making contacts with homosexuals as a means of lessening the alienation felt at this stage.

Stage 3: Identity Tolerance

With increasing commitment to a homosexual self-image, the individual seeks out the company of homosexuals in order to fulfill social, sexual, and emotional needs. There is a selectiveness about such contacts which are frequently seen as "necessary" rather than desirable. That is, there is a tolerance of the homosexual self-image rather than an acceptance of it.

Two paths of development are postulated: one taken by those who perceive a homosexual self-identity as desirable and the other by those who do not. Within each of these streams, the quality of the contact with other homosexuals becomes an important factor that leads to different forms of behavior, depending on whether the contact is perceived as positive or negative. Disclosure to heterosexuals at this point is extremely limited, with the emphasis placed on the maintenance of two separate images: a public or presenting one (heterosexual) and a private one (homosexual) exhibited when only in the company of homosexuals. The presentation of a heterosexual image calls upon the individual to play out a heterosexual role.

Stage 4: Identity Acceptance

Increased contact with the homosexual subculture encourages a more positive view of homosexuality and the gradual development of a network of homosexual friends. A philosophy of fitting into society, while also retaining a homosexual lifestyle, is adopted and entails the continued maintenance of a passing strategy (pretending heterosexuality) at pertinent times. This strategy effectively prevents one from being faced with the (possibly negative) reactions of others towards one's homosexuality.

Selective disclosure is made to others, particularly friends and relatives. Generally speaking, this stage represents a relatively peaceful and stable time for the homosexual since the questions of "Who am I?" and "Where do I belong?" have been resolved.

Developmental paths are chosen according to the degree to which the individual accepts the idea of homosexuals as a negatively valued group and can maintain strategies to avoid confrontation with antagonistic others. Where this is possible, identity foreclosure occurs; otherwise the individual moves into the next stage.

Stage 5: Identity Pride

This stage is characterized by feelings of pride towards one's homosexual identity and fierce loyalty to homosexuals as a group, who are seen as important and creditable while heterosexuals have become discredited and devalued. Anger about society's stigmatization of homosexuals leads to disclosure and purposeful confrontation with nonhomosexuals in order to promote the validity and equality of homosexuals.

With this, the path of identity development becomes dichotomized, with direction being steered by the degree of incongruency generated when confrontation brings forth reactions. Where such reactions are seen as consistently negative, identity foreclosure takes place. When they are not, this is inconsistent with expectations, and dissonance is created. Attempts to resolve this dissonance lead to movement into the final stage.

Stage 6: Identity Synthesis

Positive contacts with nonhomosexuals help create an awareness of the rigidity and inaccuracy of dividing the world into good homosexuals and bad heterosexuals. Anger and pride associated with the previous stage are retained but in less emotional terms. A homosexual identity is no longer seen as overwhelmingly *the* identity by which an individual can be characterized. Individuals come to see themselves as people having many sides to their character, only one part of which is related to homosexuality. A lifestyle is developed in which the homosexual identity is no longer hidden, so that disclosure becomes a nonissue. Own view of self and views of self believed to be held by others are therefore synthesized into one integrated identity that unites both private and public aspects of self. This gives rise to feelings of peace and stability. With this, the process of identity formation is completed.

A longitudinal study is clearly the most rigorous form of testing that could be given to this developmental model. However, the ambitiousness of such a project prompted me to plan a cross-sectional research program first. It was expected that this would provide data indicating the degree to which the model validly depicts the homosexual identity formation process.

The first main study of this program, detailed in this paper, tests the validity of the proposed stage descriptions. If these profiles are accurate, then individuals expressing the belief that homosexuality was a personal issue in their lives would be able to describe their attitudes, feelings, and actions in terms of the dimensions proposed, and in a way that corresponded to one of the six stage descriptions.

It was hypothesized that where individuals were allocated into stages, on some external measure, those at a particular stage would acknowledge the profile of *that* stage (rather than those of other stages) as being the most accurate account of their current functioning.

Since the six stages were hypothesized to follow a certain order, it was also expected that the degree of similarity or correspondence between an individual's current functioning and the various stage profiles would decrease progressively as a function of the distance of all other stages (as proposed by the model) from that to which the individual belonged.

A questionnaire was developed to test these hypotheses. Items were constructed to measure the affective, cognitive, and behavioral factors previously mentioned as relevant to the identity development process. The model was then used to predict how people at each stage would respond to each of the items, and ideal stage descriptions or profiles were formulated.

The hypotheses were tested by comparing these predicted response patterns with actual response patterns provided by individuals who had been allocated a priori into stages on a separate measure. In these terms, the hypotheses tested in this study can be specified as follows:

Across-Profiles Hypothesis

For all stage profiles, the actual response patterns of subjects nominated a priori to a particular stage would show greatest similarity (highest score) with the predicted profile of that stage, compared with the predicted profiles of all other stages. Moreover, the degree of similarity between actual response patterns at a particular stage and the predicted response patterns (or stage profiles) of all other stages (size of score) will decrease progressively as a function of the hypothesized distance of these stages from the nominated one. For example, Stage 1 subjects would be expected to obtain highest scores on the Stage 1 predicted profile, with scores on Stage 2 to 6 profiles decreasing progressively (scores on the Stage 6 profile being the lowest).

Across-Groups Hypothesis

For any of the predicted stage profiles, the actual response patterns of the subjects nominated a priori to that stage would show greatest similarity (highest score) with the predicted profile when compared with those of subjects at other stages. The degree of similarity (size of score) between any predicted profile and actual response patterns obtained by subjects at all stages would decrease as a function of the distance of those stages from the one measured by the predicted profile. For example, on the Stage 1 profile, Stage 1 subjects would be expected to obtain highest scores, with Stage 2 to 6 subjects showing progressively decreasing scores (Stage 6 subjects having lowest scores).

Method

Subjects

I obtained subjects by contacting individuals and asking them to participate in a research project investigating ways people adjust to homosexuality. Contact sources included private social functions, a homosexual rights march, a homosexual counseling service, personal acquaintances, newspaper advertisements, and clients referred to the researcher from various agencies for counseling regarding homosexuality. (The design did not require that subjects be randomly selected.) Of those contacted, 227 individuals agreed to participate and were sent questionnaires. Of the 227 sent out, 178 (78.4%) were completed and returned, resulting in 109 male and 69 female candidate subjects. Of these, 103 and 63 respectively were able to define themselves into one of the stages (see *Procedure*, below). Frequencies obtained for each stage are presented in Table 2.

The remaining 12 subjects indicated that they fit into more than one of the stages. Their responses were excluded from the final analysis.

Table 2

Number of Subjects Self-Defined in Each Stage

Stage	Female	Male	Total
1	5	6	11
2	3	10	13
3	4	7	11
4	30	41	71
5	6	10	16
6	15	29	44
Total	63	103	166

An analysis of the biographical data revealed no significant differences between subjects in any of the six stages by gender, occupation, religious upbringing, birth order, birthplace, age of first awareness of homosexual feelings, and age of first labeling of self as a homosexual.[1]

Instruments

Stage Allocation Measure. A measure was developed by which subjects could be allocated into one of the six stages. From the 16 dimensions hypothesized to be relevant to the identity acquisition process, those considered central to the process at each stage were selected. Drawing upon these, one-paragraph descriptions were constructed for each stage which outlined the ways that individuals might ideally be characterized at that phase of development. A description of a *pre-Stage 1* person was also added. These ideal profiles are presented in Table 3. Subjects were told that these profiles were descriptions of seven types of people and that they must select the one that best fit the way they saw themselves at the time of responding. Allocation was, therefore, made by self-definition.

Homosexual Identity Questionnaire. Items were constructed that appeared to measure the various aspects of the 16 dimensions presented in Table 1. The structure was primarily that of the multiple-response type, with some checklists. Examples of these are presented in Table 4. The questionnaire was tested for clarity of wording and meaning by administering it individually to six subjects (three female, three male) representing a variety of educational, intellectual, and socioeconomic levels. After revision, the questionnaire contained 210 items. Subjects were instructed to complete them according to the way they felt, thought, and/or acted at the time of responding to the questionnaire.

[1]Details of these may be obtained from the author.

Table 3

Ideal Stage Descriptions from the Stage Allocation Measure

Pre-Stage 1   You believe you are a heterosexual and never question this. You rarely, if ever, wonder "Am I a homosexual?" You do not believe that homosexuality has anything to do with you personally.

Stage 1   You are not sure who you are. You are confused about what sort of person you are and where your life is going. You ask yourself the questions "Who am I?," "Am I a homosexual?," "Am I really a heterosexual?" You sometimes feel, think, or act in a homosexual way, but would rarely, if ever, tell anyone about this. You're fairly sure that homosexuality has something to do with you personally.

Stage 2   You feel that you *probably* are a homosexual, although you're not definitely sure. You realize that this makes you different from other people and you feel distant or cut off from them. You may like being different or you may dislike it and feel very alone. You feel you would like to talk to someone about "feeling different." You are beginning to think that it might help to meet other homosexuals but you're not sure whether you really want to or not. You don't want to tell anyone about the fact that you might be a homosexual, and prefer to put on a front of being completely heterosexual.

Stage 3   You feel sure you're a homosexual and you put up with, or tolerate this. You see yourself as a homosexual for *now* but are not sure about how you will be in the future. You are not happy about other people knowing about your homosexuality and usually take care to put across a heterosexual image. You worry about other people's reactions to you. You sometimes mix socially with homosexuals, or would like to do this. You feel a need to meet others like yourself.

Stage 4   You are quite sure you are a homosexual and you accept this fairly happily. You are prepared to tell a few people about being a homosexual (such as friends, family members etc.) but you carefully select whom you will tell. You feel that other people can be influential in making trouble for homosexuals and so you try to adopt an attitude of getting on with your life like anyone else, and fitting in where you live and work. You can't see any point in confronting people with your homosexuality if it's going to embarrass all concerned. A lot of the time you mix socially with homosexuals.

Stage 5   You feel proud to be a homosexual and enjoy living as one. You like reading books and magazines about homosexuals, particularly if they portray them in a good light. You are prepared to tell many people about being a homosexual and make no attempt to hide this fact. You prefer not to mix socially with heterosexuals because they usually hold anti-homosexual attitudes. You get angry at the way heterosexuals talk about and treat homosexuals and often openly stand up for homosexuals. You are happy to wear badges that bear slogans such as "How dare you presume I'm heterosexual?" You believe it is more important to listen to the opinions of homosexuals than heterosexuals.

Stage 6   You are prepared to tell *anyone* that you are a homosexual. You are happy about the way you are but feel that being a homosexual is not the most important part of you. You mix socially with fairly equal numbers of homosexuals and heterosexuals and with all of these you are open about your homosexuality. You still get angry at the way homosexuals are treated, but not as much as you once did. You believe there are many heterosexuals who happily accept homosexuals and whose opinions are worth listening to. There are some things about a heterosexual way of life that seem worthwhile.

Table 4

Examples of Questionnaire Items in the Homosexual Identity Questionnaire

Example 1: Commitment
    I am quite certain I am not a homosexual.
    I am fairly certain I am not a homosexual.
    I believe I may be a homosexual.
    I am fairly certain I am a homosexual.

Example 2: Group Identification
    How much do you feel you fit into homosexual groups?
    Not at all.
    A little.
    Some.
    A fair amount.
    Totally.

Example 3: Social Interaction
    At what type of social function do you mix with homosexuals?
    Private parties.
    Visiting friends at private homes.
    Organized political meeting.
    Organized social function (e.g. dance).
    Bars.
    Discoteques.
    Beats, public toilets etc.
    Other _____
    None.

To develop a means for scoring the questionnaire, I predicted how subjects at each stage of identity development might respond on each item. To illustrate, using Example 1 of Table 4, it was predicted that Stage 1 individuals would typically choose the first response; Stage 2 the first or second response; Stage 3 the third or fourth response; and Stages 4, 5, and 6 the fifth response. Predictions were based upon the model—that is, upon the notion of how an individual at a particular stage would respond if the model was a valid conception of the identity formation experience. Predicted responses were then considered to be correct responses for each of the six stages. Predicted responses were made for all items, regardless of the degree of significance they were allotted in the identity development process, to test all dimensions of the model and not just a few.

For the checklist items each possible answer was considered separately. Using Example 3 of Table 4 to illustrate, each of the nine possible responses was considered a separate item, to be endorsed or not. Predictions were made as to whether subjects at each stage would select a particular response. For example, on response 3, "Do you mix with homosexuals at organized political meetings?" it was expected that Stages 5 and 6 individuals would select this while the remainder would not. A selection of this item for Stages 5 and 6 was therefore deemed a correct score for these groups, whereas the reverse was considered a correct score for the other stages. By following this procedure with all checklist items, the total number of items included in the scoring procedure was 364.

Correct (predicted) scores for each stage on each of these items were grouped together to form a scoring key. In this way, six separate scoring keys were generated, one for each stage.

Questionnaire responses of subjects in each stage group (self-defined according to the Stage Allocation Measure) were scored against the scoring key of their particular stage. Where the *given* response tallied with the *predicted* (correct) response, one point was recorded. Summation of all points gave the total score. All scoring procedures were done by computer. In addition to being scored on their matching scoring key, each subject was also scored on each of the remaining keys. Six total scores were thus obtained for each subject.

Procedure

Subjects were sent the Homosexual Identity Questionnaire, Stage Allocation Measure, and a biographical sheet. A cover letter informed participants of the purpose of the study, assured them of anonymity, and asked them to return the questionnaire as soon as possible. A pre-addressed, stamped, return envelope was included with the questionnaire package. After 2 weeks, reminder letters were sent to those who had not yet responded.

Results

Mean scores of subjects at each stage for all scoring keys are plotted in Figure 1. To provide a test of the across-profiles hypothesis (that subjects at each stage would obtain highest scores on the profile of their particular stage compared with other stage profiles, and that scores on these latter profiles would decrease progressively as predicted) an analysis for comparison of means under order restrictions was carried out over profile scores for each subject (stage) group. This was done using a single degree of freedom special contrast test (Abelson & Tukey, 1963; Barlow, Bartholomew, Bremner, & Brunk, 1978) with 1 and 4 degrees of freedom. Results are presented in Table 5. The hypothesis was given strong support ($p < .001$) from Stage 1, 5, and 6 subjects. Results from Stage 2 and 4 groups were very nearly signifi-

cant at the .05 level, but those for Stage 3 subjects were clearly unsup-
portive of the hypothesis. From Figure 1 it would appear that results
were likely to have been affected by the similarity (and sometimes

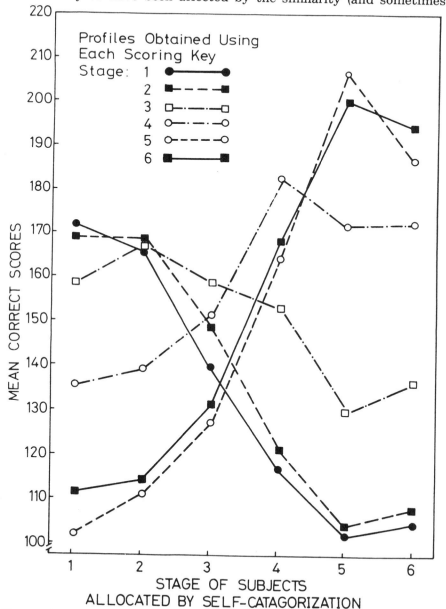

Figure 1. Stage profiles derived from self-allocation (abscissa) plotted against mean correct scores on key (ordinate). Maximum correct score possible: 364.

239

Table 5

Tested[a] Order of Mean Profile Scores for Each Subject Group

Group												F
Stage 1	μ_1	$\geq$	μ_2	$\geq$	μ_3	$\geq$	μ_4	$\geq$	μ_5	$\geq$	μ_6	13.7*
Stage 2	μ_1	$\leq$	μ_2	$\geq$	μ_3	$\geq$	μ_4	$\geq$	μ_5	$\geq$	μ_6	3.3[b]
Stage 3	μ_1	$\leq$	μ_2	$\leq$	μ_3	$\geq$	μ_4	$\geq$	μ_5	$\geq$	μ_6	0.5
Stage 4	μ_1	$\leq$	μ_2	$\leq$	μ_3	$\leq$	μ_4	$\geq$	μ_5	$\geq$	μ_6	3.4[b]
Stage 5	μ_1	$\leq$	μ_2	$\leq$	μ_3	$\leq$	μ_4	$\leq$	μ_5	$\geq$	μ_6	6.9*
Stage 6	μ_1	$\leq$	μ_2	$\leq$	μ_3	$\leq$	μ_4	$\leq$	μ_5	$\leq$	μ_6	18.3*

[a] A single degree of freedom contrast test for comparison of means under order restrictions with 1 and 4 degrees of freedom.
[b] These results almost reach significance at the .05 level.
*$p < .001$.

reversal) of scores on profiles 1 and 2, and profiles 5 and 6. The Stage 3 group indicated the predicted ordering of means on five of the six occasions, but differences between means were too small to be significant.

The across-groups hypothesis (that subjects at each stage would obtain highest scores on the profile of their particular stage compared with subjects at other stages whose scores would be expected to decrease progressively as predicted) was assessed similarly to the first hypothesis. Results are presented in Table 6. This hypothesis received strong support from all profiles. From Figure 1 it is apparent that although the general direction of results was as postulated, two order reversals occurred, one of which was between Stage 2 and Stage 3 subject groups. Also notable was the similarity between scores on almost

Table 6

Tested[a] Order of Mean Group Scores for Each Profile

Profile												F
Stage 1	μ_1	$\geq$	μ_2	$\geq$	μ_3	$\geq$	μ_4	$\geq$	μ_5	$\geq$	μ_6	200.0**
Stage 2	μ_1	$\leq$	μ_2	$\geq$	μ_3	$\geq$	μ_4	$\geq$	μ_5	$\geq$	μ_6	66.0**
Stage 3	μ_1	$\leq$	μ_2	$\leq$	μ_3	$\geq$	μ_4	$\geq$	μ_5	$\geq$	μ_6	5.0*
Stage 4	μ_1	$\leq$	μ_2	$\leq$	μ_3	$\leq$	μ_4	$\geq$	μ_5	$\geq$	μ_6	82.3**
Stage 5	μ_1	$\leq$	μ_2	$\leq$	μ_3	$\leq$	μ_4	$\leq$	μ_5	$\geq$	μ_6	68.5**
Stage 6	μ_1	$\leq$	μ_2	$\leq$	μ_3	$\leq$	μ_4	$\leq$	μ_5	$\leq$	μ_6	194.2**

[a] A single degree of freedom contrast test for comparison of means under order restrictions with 1 and 4 degrees of freedom.
*$p < .05$. **$p < .001$.

all profiles of Stage 5 and Stage 6 subject groups. To a lesser extent, this was also evident for Stage 1 and Stage 2 subjects.

Mean scores for male and female subjects were calculated to check for sex differences. These are reported in Table 7. Small cell frequencies prevented statistical analyses being carried out; these findings are therefore seen as exploratory only. Support for the hypotheses was given by both groups, although more so by male subjects than female on the Stage 2 and 3 profiles (across groups), and by Stage 2 and 3 groups (across profiles). Female subjects tended to provide somewhat more support for the across-groups hypothesis on the Stage 5 and 6 profiles.

To ascertain that the differences found between subject groups were not an artifact of the researcher's bias in constructing the questionnaire and scoring keys, a discriminant analysis was carried out. As shown in Table 8, five significant functions were obtained, the first two of which accounted for a large proportion (76.6%) of the variance. The position of group centroids along the first two discriminant function continua (Figure 2) indicates that the six groups were distinguishable. The percentage of cases correctly classified by the discriminant analysis was 97.0%. These results suggest that it is possible to distin-

Table 7

Mean Total Scores for Male and Female Subjects in Each Stage Group

Stage group	Stage 1	Stage 2	Scoring Key—Males Stage 3	Stage 4	Stage 5	Stage 6
Stage 1	177.0	173.0	159.7	133.0	105.3	114.8
Stage 2	173.4	175.3	167.7	138.7	107.0	113.5
Stage 3	140.7	149.4	162.6	149.3	121.0	125.9
Stage 4	117.7	124.0	158.3	184.2	160.2	165.2
Stage 5	102.0	104.9	132.8	172.5	202.0	199.4
Stage 6	103.7	108.8	139.0	173.3	181.8	189.6

Stage group	Stage 1	Stage 2	Scoring Key—Females Stage 3	Stage 4	Stage 5	Stage 6
Stage 1	166.4	164.6	157.4	139.4	99.0	108.0
Stage 2	139.3	147.7	166.3	140.7	124.7	119.3
Stage 3	138.3	146.3	151.5	155.3	138.5	141.8
Stage 4	115.8	118.7	145.7	179.8	170.0	173.9
Stage 5	100.8	102.5	124.7	170.3	213.8	201.5
Stage 6	105.5	105.5	130.9	169.7	196.5	203.9

Table 8

Canonical Discriminant Functions

Function	Eigenvalue	% of Variance	Cumulative %	Canonical correlation
1	10.90	57.6	57.6	.957
2	3.59	19.0	76.6	.884
3	1.63	8.6	85.2	.787
4	1.56	8.2	93.5	.780
5	1.23	6.5	100.0	.743

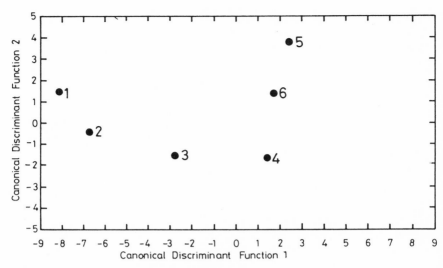

Figure 2. Group centroids plotted for each stage.

guish among the six groups and that the scoring keys were unable to maximize group differences as much as the discriminant analysis.

Discussion

The results from the analysis using the scoring keys provide general support for the hypotheses: There is an overall trend for subjects self-allocated into each stage to acknowledge the hypothesized profile or ideal description of their particular stage (rather than profiles of other stages) as corresponding more closely to their current mode of functioning. There is also a tendency for subjects at a particular stage to show greater similarity with the hypothesized profile of that particular stage when compared with subjects at all other stages.

Overall, this suggests that individuals who acknowledge homosexuality to be an aspect of their lives can, to some degree, be distinguished on those characteristics I proposed in my model of homosexual identity formation. The findings also support the hypothesis that any grouping of individuals according to such characteristics will follow the order predicted by the model. Where results are not clearcut, this is almost always due to a blurring of adjacent stages rather than a more dramatic repatterning of stages. This finding is not inconsistent with a process model of identity development, although it in no way provides evidence for the concept of process.

Indistinction between stages is most obvious between Stages 1 and 2 and between Stages 5 and 6, suggesting that identity formation may involve four stages instead of the proposed six. However, the discriminant analysis indicated that six stage groups could be adequately distinguished, suggesting that the scoring keys were unable to measure fully the differences between groups. This could be partly due to item sensitivity: It is possible that the range of responses available on some items was too narrow to allow for clear predictions. Bias may have also resulted from making predictions about those items hypothesized as having less importance to a specific stage. I may not have clearly conceptualized the part these items play in stage differentiation.

To find out whether these and other factors influenced the results, I am currently completing item analyses to refine the questionnaire, define its factors, and reduce its size. Reliability measures will then be conducted on the refined version. The development of an adequate questionnaire is essential for future research on homosexual identity formation. In contrast to the lengthy and subjective interviewing techniques used by other theorists in the area (e.g., McLellan, 1977; Troiden, 1977; Weinberg, 1977), a standardized, reliable questionnaire will provide a more efficient data collecting method for use by any researcher studying homosexual identity formation. This, in turn, should encourage a more intensive, varied, and critical examination of the model, as well as provide the opportunity for comparison of diverse subject groups.

Another factor that may have affected the results obtained with the scoring keys is the method of stage allocation used. The study included individuals who, if permitted to do so, might have categorized themselves between the stages. The instructions, however, called for a choice to be made from among the given stages. Although some subjects did place themselves between stages, there is no way of assessing how many more would have done so if given the opportunity. This forced choice would have blurred any distinctions between groups.

Some unevenness appeared in the degree to which subject groups acknowledge similarity with the ideal stage descriptions. For example, responses for Stage 3 subjects averaged 157 out of a possible 364 correct on the Stage 3 scoring key, whereas Stage 5 subjects obtained an average of 208 correct responses on their scoring key. This suggests the need to check for poor item construction and unclear predictions, as well as incorrect theorizing. While the present findings suggest that the model provides a valid picture of homosexual identity formation, some stages may be depicted more accurately than others.

It is important to consider what implications these findings have for other models of homosexual identity formation. Since none of these other models incorporate all of the dimensions described in this model, comparisons must necessarily be broad. In general, each of the stages described in the present study has been alluded to by other theoreticians, although never all together in one model. Further, the sequence of stages proffered in other models is in all cases identical to that defined in this model. Plummer (1975) and Weinberg (1977) describe elements of the Identity Confusion, Identity Tolerance, and Identity Acceptance stages, in that order. Several authors (Hencken & O'Dowd, 1977; Lee, 1977; B. Miller, 1978; Schultz, 1976) propose, in addition to these three stages, elements of Stage 5 (Identity Pride). Schafer (1976) makes reference to stages that are most like Stages 1, 2, and 3, whereas Coleman (1981-1982) prefers a sequence similar to that of Stages 1, 3, and 6. The model that most nearly approximates the basic stage content and sequence of my model is that of McLellan (1977) who postulates all except Stage 5 as characteristic of homosexual identity formation. The results from the present study, therefore, provide some initial validation of the elements put forward by these theoreticians. On the other hand, finding that six stage groups could be distinguished suggests that some of these alternative models may offer a too narrow conception of the developmental process.

Although small numbers make it impossible to draw firm conclusions regarding the responses of male and female subjects, the data indicate both similarities and differences between the two groups. Further work in this area is indicated since the existence of such differences would require either the modification of the model or the development of separate ones for men and women.

A recent study by Allen (1980), which tested for differences (comparable to those which I have hypothesized) between political and nonpolitical homosexuals, suggests that the question of gender differentiation is likely to be complex. On most variables tested (locus of control, own attitudes toward homosexuality, self-esteem, and perceived societal attitudes toward homosexuality), the predicted differences were found between her two subject groups. At the same time, significant sex differences were also evident. Allen noted that the differences between political and nonpolitical lesbians were consistently far greater than those between male homosexuals, and she offers a feminist analysis to explain this finding.

As a comment on the spatial arrangment of the profile scores obtained by each group, the distance found between scores could indicate the psychological distance experienced by individuals at each stage as they compare themselves with those at other stages. As an example, Stages 1 to 3 subjects might be said to perceive Stage 5 (with its call to radical confrontation and divisiveness) as the most extreme position from themselves, whereas for Stages 4 to 6 subjects, the confusion of Stage 1 represents the furthermost point of development. If confirmed, such a hypothesis would not only clarify the perceptions of those involved in identity formation, but may also offer ways to order the stages quantitatively, thereby expanding the scope for statistical analysis. This avenue should be explored in future research.

Although I have not yet addressed the important concept of *process*, or stage sequence, some support is provided by Allen's (1980) study in which this hypothesis was examined using retrospective methods. Results indicated that subjects acknowledged experiencing the relevant stages in the chronological order I have predicted.

Moreover, in the study of Troiden and Goode (1980) subjects reported certain experiences in a specific sequence: suspecting they might be homosexual, labeling self as homosexual and first interactions with the homosexual subculture, and entering into a homosexual love relationship. The authors concluded that the acquisition of a homosexual identity occurs step-by-step over a period of time.

Although a great deal of work must be done in the area of homosexual identity formation, the present results, together with those of other studies in the area, provide some evidence that the concept of homosexual identity is important to understanding the homosexual perspective. DuBay (1979) strongly argues against accepting such a concept, believing that homosexual behavior is the only reality in homosexual experience. He perceives homosexual identity as a construct expressly created by professionals in the field. Yet such a stance ignores the finding that individuals *do* have some sense of "persistent sameness within oneself" (Erickson, 1959, p. 102) that can take different forms for different people and which they term *homosexual*, and that this identity is experienced as a psychological reality in their personal worlds.

References

ABELSON, R. P., & TUKEY, J. W. (1963). Efficient utilization of non-numerical information in quantitative analysis: General theory and the case of simple order. *Annals of Mathematical Statistics, 34,* 1347-1369.

ALLEN, S. (1980). *Relationship of selected personality variables and attitudinal measures to two homosexual groups: Politically active and nonpolitically active.* Unpublished manuscript, Murdoch University, Murdoch, Western Australia.

ALTMAN, D. (1972). *Homosexual: Oppression and liberation.* Sydney: Angus & Robertson.

BARLOW, R. E., BARTHOLEMEW, D. J., BREMNER, J. M., & BRUNK, H. D. (1978). *Statistical inference under order restrictions.* New York: John Wiley & Sons.

BERZON, B. (1979). Developing a positive gay identity. In B. Berzon & R. Leighton (Eds.), *Positively gay* (pp. 1-14). Millbrae, CA: Celestial Arts.

CASS, V. C. (1979). Homosexual identity formation: A theoretical model. *Journal of Homosexuality, 4,* 219-235.

CASS, V. C. (1984). *Homosexual identity formation: The presentation and testing of a socio-cognitive model.* Unpublished manuscript, Murdoch University, Murdoch, Western Australia.

CASS, V. C. (in press). Homosexual identity: A concept in need of definition. *Journal of Homosexuality, 7*(2/3), 31-43.

CLARK, D. (1977). *Loving someone gay.* Millbrae, CA: Celestial Arts.

COLEMAN, E. (1981-1982). Developmental stages of the coming out process. *Journal of Homosexuality.*

DUBAY, W. H. (1979). *Gay identity: Concept problems and alternatives.* Unpublished manuscript.

ERIKSON, E. (1959). The problems of ego identity. *Psychological Issues, 1,* 101-164.

FISHER, R. (1972). *The gay mystique: The myth and reality of male homosexuality.* New York: Stein & Day.

HENCKEN, J. D., & O'DOWD, W. T. (1977). Coming out as an aspect of identity formation. *Gay Academic Union Journal: Gay Saber, 1,* 18-26.

JAY, K., & YOUNG, A. (Eds.). (1975). *After you're out: Personal experiences of gay men and lesbian women.* New York: Link Books.

LEE, J. A. (1977). Going public: A study in the sociology of homosexual liberation. *Journal of Homosexuality, 3,* 49-78.

LEWIS, S. G. (1979). *Sunday's women.* Boston: Beacon Press.

MACDONALD, A. P. (1981). Bisexuality: Some comments on research and theory. *Journal of Homosexuality, 6*(3), 21-35.

MARTIN, D., & LYON, P. (1972). *Lesbian women.* New York: Bantam Books.

MCLELLAN, E. A. (1977). *Lesbian identity: A theological and psychological inquiry into the developmental stages of identity in a lesbian.* Unpublished manuscript, School of Theology at Claremont, Ann Arbor, MI.

MILLER, B. (1978). Adult sexual resocialization: Adjustments towards a stigmatized identity. *Alternative Lifestyles, 1,* 207-234.

MILLER, D. R. (1963). The study of social relationships: Situation, identity, and social interaction. In S. Koch (Ed.), *Psychology: A study of a science. Vol. 5: The process areas, the person, and some applied fields* (pp. 639-737). New York: McGraw Hill.

MILLER, M. (1971). *On being different: What it means to be homosexual.* New York: Random House.

MORIN, S. F., & MILLER, J. S. (1974, March). *On fostering positive identity in gay men: Some developmental issues.* Paper presented at the meeting of the American Orthopsychiatric Association, San Francisco.

OMARK, R. C. (1978). A comment on the homosexual role. *The Journal of Sex Research, 14,* 273-274.

PLUMMER, K. (1975). *Sexual stigma: An interactionist account.* New York: Routledge & Kegan Paul.

RICHARDSON, D. (1981). Theoretical perspectives on homosexuality. In J. Hart & D. Richardson (Eds.), *The theory and practice of homosexuality* (pp. 5-37). London: Routledge & Kegan Paul.

SCHAFER, S. (1976). Sexual and social problems of lesbians. *The Journal of Sex Research, 12,* 50-69.

SCHLENKER, B. R. (1982). Translating actions into attitudes: An identity-analytic approach to the exploration of social conduct. *Advances in Experimental Social Psychology, 15,* 193-247.

SCHULTZ, S. (1976). *Coming out and the growth of gay people and society.* Unpublished manuscript, University of California, Berkeley.

TROIDEN, R. R. (1977). *Becoming a homosexual: Research on acquiring a homosexual identity.* Unpublished manuscript, State University of New York at Stony Brook, Stony Brook.

TROIDEN, R. R., & GOODE, E. (1980). Variables related to the acquisition of a gay identity. *Journal of Homosexuality, 5,* 383-392.

WEINBERG, T. (1977). *Becoming homosexual: Self-discrepancy, self-identity, and self-maintenance.* Unpublished manuscript, University of Connecticut. Storrs, CT.

WEINBERG, T. (1978). On "doing" and "being" gay: Sexual behavior and homosexual male self-identity. *Journal of Homosexuality, 4,* 143-156.

Accepted for publication February 28, 1983

Person in Context

Student Involvement: A Developmental Theory for Higher Education

Alexander W. Astin   Graduate School of Education, University of California, Los Angeles

A student development theory based on student involvement is presented and described, and the implications for practice and research are discussed.

Even a casual reading of the extensive literature on student development in higher education can create confusion and perplexity. One finds not only that the problems being studied are highly diverse but also that investigators who claim to be studying the same problem frequently do not look at the same variables or employ the same methodologies. And even when they are investigating the same variables, different investigators may use completely different terms to describe and discuss these variables.

My own interest in articulating a theory of student development is partly practical—I would like to bring some order into the chaos of the literature—and partly self-protective. I am increasingly bewildered by the muddle of findings that have emerged from my own research in student development, research that I have been engaged in for more than 20 years.

The theory of student involvement that I describe in this article appeals to me for several reasons. First, it is simple: I have not needed to draw a maze consisting of dozens of boxes

interconnected by two-headed arrows to explain the basic elements of the theory to others. Second, the theory can explain most of the empirical knowledge about environmental influences on student development that researchers have gained over the years. Third, it is capable of embracing principles from such widely divergent sources as psychoanalysis and classical learning theory. Finally, this theory of student involvement can be used both by researchers—to guide their investigation of student development—and by college administrators and faculty—to help them design more effective learning environments.

BASIC ELEMENTS OF THE THEORY

Let me first explain what I mean by *involvement*, a construct that should not be either mysterious or esoteric. Quite simply, student involvement refers to the amount of physical and psychological energy that the student devotes to the academic experience. Thus, a highly involved student is one who, for example, devotes considerable energy to studying, spends much time on campus, participates actively in student organizations, and interacts frequently with faculty members and other students. Conversely, a typical uninvolved student neglects studies, spends little time on campus, abstains

The preparation of this article was supported in part by a grant from the Ford Foundation.

from extracurricular activities, and has infrequent contact with faculty members or other students. These hypothetical examples are only intended to be illustrative; there are many other possible forms of involvement, which are discussed in detail below.

In certain respects the concept of involvement closely resembles the Freudian concept of *cathexis*, which I learned about in my former career as a clinical psychologist. Freud believed that people invest psychological energy in objects and persons outside of themselves. In other words, people can *cathect* on their friends, families, schoolwork, and jobs. The involvement concept also resembles closely what the learning theorists have traditionally referred to as *vigilance* or *time-on-task*. The concept of *effort*, although much narrower, has much in common with the concept of involvement.

To give a better sense of what I mean by the term *involvement*, I have listed below the results of several hours that I spent recently looking in dictionaries and a thesaurus for words or phrases that capture some of the intended meaning. Because involvement is, to me, an active term, the list uses verb forms.

attach oneself to
commit oneself to
devote oneself to
engage in
go in for
incline toward
join in
partake of
participate in
plunge into
show enthusiasm for
tackle
take a fancy to
take an interest in
take on
take part in
take to
take up
undertake

Most of these terms are behavioral in meaning. I could have also included words and phrases that are more "interior" in nature, such as *value*, *care for*, *stress*, *accentuate*, and *emphasize*. But in the sense that I am using the term, involvement implies a behavioral component. I am not denying that motivation is an important aspect

of involvement, but rather I am emphasizing that the behavioral aspects, in my judgment, are critical: It is not so much what the individual thinks or feels, but what the individual does, how he or she behaves, that defines and identifies involvement.

At this stage in its development, the involvement theory has five basic postulates:

1. Involvement refers to the investment of physical and psychological energy in various objects. The objects may be highly generalized (the student experience) or highly specific (preparing for a chemistry examination).
2. Regardless of its object, involvement occurs along a continuum; that is, different students manifest different degrees of involvement in a given object, and the same student manifests different degrees of involvement in different objects at different times.
3. Involvement has both quantitative and qualitative features. The extent of a student's involvement in academic work, for instance, can be measured quantitatively (how many hours the student spends studying) and qualitatively (whether the student reviews and comprehends reading assignments or simply stares at the textbook and daydreams).
4. The amount of student learning and personal development associated with any educational program is directly proportional to the quality and quantity of student involvement in that program.
5. The effectiveness of any educational policy or practice is directly related to the capacity of that policy or practice to increase student involvement.

These last two propositions are, of course, the key educational postulates, because they provide clues for designing more effective educational programs for students. Strictly speaking, they do not really qualify as postulates, because they are subject to empirical proof. Indeed, much of the recommended research on involvement (discussed below) would be designed to test these two propositions.

TRADITIONAL PEDAGOGICAL THEORIES

A major impetus for the development of the student involvement theory was my exasperation at the tendency of many academicians to treat the student as a kind of "black box." On the input end of this black box are the various policies and programs of a college or university; on the output end are various types of achievement measures such as the GPA or scores on standardized tests. It seemed that something was missing: some mediating mechanism that would explain how these educational programs and policies are translated into student achievement and development.

I am not implying that the actions and policies of most faculty members and administrators are not guided by some kind of educational theory. But usually any such theory is only implicit in their actions; it is seldom stated formally or examined critically. Even when college personnel are aware of the theories that guide their actions, they seem to accept them as gospel rather than as testable propositions. In any event, it may be useful to examine these implicit pedagogical theories and to show how the theory of student involvement can help tie them more directly to student developmental outcomes. I have identified three implicit pedagogical theories, labeled for simplicity the *subject-matter*, the *resource*, and the *individualized* (or eclectic) theories.

The Subject-Matter Theory

The subject-matter theory of pedagogy, which could also be labeled the *content theory*, is popular among college professors. According to this theory, student learning and development depend primarily on exposure to the right subject matter. Thus, a "liberal education" consists of an assortment of "worthwhile" courses. Individual courses, in turn, are evaluated in terms of the content reflected, for example, in course syllabi. Indeed, in most colleges and universities teaching performance is evaluated by inspecting the professor's course syllabi. Given this strong emphasis on course content, it is not surprising that proponents of this theory tend to believe that students learn by attending lectures, doing the reading assignments, and working in the library. To the extent that written and oral presentations by the student are used as learning tools, they generally focus on the content of the reading or the lecture.

In the subject-matter approach to learning, those professors with the greatest knowledge of a particular subject matter have the highest pres-

tige. Indeed, because of this emphasis on specialized knowledge, this approach seems to encourage the fragmentation and specialization of faculty interests and to equate scholarly expertise with pedagogical ability.

But perhaps the most serious limitation of the subject-matter theory is that it assigns students a passive role in the learning process: The "knowledgeable" professor lectures to the "ignorant" student so that the student can acquire the same knowledge. Such an approach clearly favors highly motivated students and those who tend to be avid readers and good listeners. Students who are slow readers or who have no intrinsic interest in the subject matter of a particular course are not well served by this approach. In fact, recent attempts to expand educational opportunities for underprepared students have probably been hindered by the continued adherence of most faculty members to the subject-matter theory of learning (Astin, 1982).

The Resource Theory

The resource theory of pedagogy is a favorite among administrators and policymakers. Used here, the term *resources* includes a wide range of ingredients believed to enhance student learning: physical facilities (laboratories, libraries, and audiovisual aids), human resources (well-trained faculty members, counselors, and support personnel), and fiscal resources (financial aid, endowments, and extramural research funds). In effect, the resource theory maintains that if adequate resources are brought together in one place, student learning and development will occur. Many college administrators believe that the acquisition of resources is their most important duty.

One resource measure that is particularly popular is the student-faculty ratio. Many administrators believe that the lower the ratio, the greater the learning and personal development that will occur. But the resource theory has qualitative as well as quantitative aspects, such as the belief that increasing the proportion of "high-quality" professors on the faculty (*quality* in this instance is defined primarily in terms of scholarly productivity and national visibility) will strengthen the educational environment. Actually, many research-oriented institutions could probably afford to hire more faculty members if they were less committed to recruiting and retaining faculty members who are highly visible in their disciplines. In short, such policies involve a trade-off between quantity and quality.

The resource theory of pedagogy also tends to include the belief that high-achieving students are a resource, that large numbers of such students on the campus enhance the quality of the learning environment for all students. Acting on this belief, many institutions invest substantial financial resources in the recruitment of high-achieving students.

The resource theory has two principal limitations. First, certain resources, such as bright students and prestigious faculty, are finite. As a result, the institutional energies expended in recruiting high-achieving students and prestigious faculty serve merely to redistribute these finite resources rather than to add to the total pool of such resources. In other words, a successful faculty or student recruitment program may benefit a particular institution, but the benefit comes at the expense of other institutions. As a consequence, widespread acceptance of the resource theory as it applies to faculty and students tends, paradoxically, to reduce the total resources available to the entire higher education community.

The second problem with this approach is its focus on the mere accumulation of resources with little attention given to the use or deployment of such resources. For instance, having established a multimillion-volume library, the administration may neglect to find out whether students are making effective use of that library. Similarly, having successfully recruited a faculty "star," the college may pay little attention to whether the new faculty member works effectively with students.

The Individualized (Eclectic) Theory

The individualized theory—a favorite of many developmental and learning psychologists (Chickering & Associates, 1981)—assumes that no single approach to subject matter, teaching, or resource allocation is adequate for all students. Rather, it attempts to identify the curricular content and instructional methods that best meet the needs of the individual student. With its emphasis on borrowing what is most useful from other pedagogical approaches, this flexible approach could also be termed *eclectic*.

In contrast to the subject-matter approach, which generally results in a fixed set of curric-

ular requirements (i.e., courses that all students must take), the individualized approach emphasizes electives. Most college curricula represent a mixture of the subject-matter and individualized theories; that is, students must take certain required courses or satisfy certain distributional requirements but also have the option of taking a certain number of elective courses.

But the individualized theory goes far beyond curriculum. It emphasizes, for instance, the importance to the student of advising and counseling and of independent study. The philosophy underlying most student personnel work (guidance, counseling, selective placement, and student support services) implicitly incorporates the individualized or eclectic theory of student development.

The individualized approach is also associated with particular instructional techniques such as self-paced instruction. This theory has led some educators to espouse the "competency-based" learning model (Grant et al., 1979), whereby common learning objectives (competencies) are formulated for all students, but the time allowed to reach these objectives is highly variable and the instructional techniques used are highly individualized.

The most obvious limitation of the individualized theory is that it can be extremely expensive to implement, because each student normally requires considerable individualized attention. In addition, because there are virtually no limitations to the possible variations in subject matter and pedagogical approach, the individualized theory is difficult to define with precision. Furthermore, given the state of research on learning, it is currently impossible to specify which types of educational programs or teaching techniques are most effective with which types of learners. In other words, although the theory is appealing in the abstract, it is extremely difficult to put into practice.

THE PLACE OF THE THEORY OF STUDENT INVOLVEMENT

In what way does the theory of student involvement relate to these traditional pedagogical theories? I believe that it can provide a link between the variables emphasized in these theories (subject matter, resources, and individualization of approach) and the learning outcomes desired by the student and the professor. In other words, the theory of student involvement argues that a particular curriculum, to achieve the effects intended, must elicit sufficient student effort and investment of energy to bring about the desired learning and development. Simply exposing the student to a particular set of courses may or may not work. The theory of involvement, in other words, provides a conceptual substitute for the black box that is implicit in the three traditional pedagogical theories.

The content theory, in particular, tends to place students in a passive role as recipients of information. The theory of involvement, on the other hand, emphasizes active participation of the student in the learning process. Recent research at the precollegiate level (Rosenshine, 1982) has suggested that learning will be greatest when the learning environment is structured to encourage active participation by the student.

On a more subtle level, the theory of student involvement encourages educators to focus less on what they do and more on what the student does: how motivated the student is and how much time and energy the student devotes to the learning process. The theory assumes that student learning and development will not be impressive if educators focus most of their attention on course content, teaching techniques, laboratories, books, and other resources. With this approach, student involvement—rather than the resources or techniques typically used by educators—becomes the focus of concern.

Thus, the construct of student involvement in certain respects resembles a more common construct in psychology: *motivation*. I personally prefer the term involvement, however, because it implies more than just a psychological state; it connotes the behavioral manifestation of that state. Involvement, in other words, is more susceptible to direct observation and measurement than is the more abstract psychological construct of motivation. Moreover, involvement seems to be a more useful construct for educational practitioners. "How do you motivate students?" is probably a more difficult question to answer than "How do you get students involved?"

The theory of student involvement is qualitatively different from the developmental theories that have received so much attention in the literature of higher education during the past few years. These theories are of at least two types: those that postulate a series of hierarchically arranged developmental stages (e.g., Heath, 1968; Kohlberg, 1971; Loevinger, 1966; Perry,

1970) and those that view student development in multidimensional terms (e.g., Brown & DeCoster, 1982; Chickering, 1969). (For recent, comprehensive summaries of these theories see Chickering & Associates, 1981; Hanson, 1982.)

Whereas these theories focus primarily on developmental outcomes (the *what* of student development), the theory of student involvement is more concerned with the behavioral mechanisms or processes that facilitate student development (the *how* of student development). These two types of theories can be studied simultaneously (see "Research Possibilities" section below).

Student Time as a Resource

College administrators are constantly preoccupied with the accumulation and allocation of fiscal resources; the theory of student involvement, however, suggests that the most precious institutional resource may be student time. According to the theory, the extent to which students can achieve particular developmental goals is a direct function of the time and effort they devote to activities designed to produce these gains. For example, if increased knowledge and understanding of history is an important goal for history majors, the extent to which students reach this goal is a direct function of the time they spend at such activities as listening to professors talk about history, reading books about history, and discussing history with other students. Generally, the more time students spend in these activities, the more history they learn.

The theory of student involvement explicitly acknowledges that the psychic and physical time and energy of students are finite. Thus, educators are competing with other forces in the student's life for a share of that finite time and energy. Here are the basic ingredients of a so-called "zero-sum" game, in which the time and energy that the student invests in family, friends, job, and other outside activities represent a reduction in the time and energy the student has to devote to educational development.

Administrators and faculty members must recognize that virtually every institutional policy and practice (e.g., class schedules; regulations on class attendance, academic probation, and participation in honors courses; policies on office hours for faculty, student orientation, and advising) can affect the way students spend their time and the amount of effort they devote to academic pursuits. Moreover, administrative decisions about many nonacademic issues (e.g., the location of new buildings such as dormitories and student unions; rules governing residency; the design of recreational and living facilities; on-campus employment opportunities; number and type of extracurricular activities and regulations regarding participation; the frequency, type, and cost of cultural events; roommate assignments; financial aid policies; the relative attractiveness of eating facilities on and off campus; parking regulations) can significantly affect how students spend their time and energy.

RELEVANT RESEARCH

The theory of student involvement has its roots in a longitudinal study of college dropouts (Astin, 1975) that endeavored to identify factors in the college environment that significantly affect the student's persistence in college. It turned out that virtually every significant effect could be rationalized in terms of the involvement concept; that is, every positive factor was likely to increase student involvement in the undergraduate experience, whereas every negative factor was likely to reduce involvement. In other words, the factors that contributed to the student's remaining in college suggested involvement, whereas those that contributed to the student's dropping out implied a lack of involvement.

What were these significant environmental factors? Probably the most important and pervasive was the student's residence. Living in a campus residence was positively related to retention, and this positive effect occurred in all types of institutions and among all types of students regardless of sex, race, ability, or family background. Similar results had been obtained in earlier studies (Astin, 1973; Chickering, 1974) and have been subsequently replicated (Astin, 1977, 1982). It is obvious that students who live in residence halls have more time and opportunity to get involved in all aspects of campus life. Indeed, simply by eating, sleeping, and spending their waking hours on the college campus, residential students have a better chance than do commuter students of developing a strong identification and attachment to undergraduate life.

The longitudinal study also showed that students who join social fraternities or sororities or participate in extracurricular activities of almost any type are less likely to drop out. Participation in sports, particularly intercollegiate sports, has an especially pronounced, positive effect on persistence. Other activities that enhance retention include enrollment in honors programs, involvement in ROTC, and participation in professors' undergraduate research projects.

One of the most interesting environmental factors that affected retention was holding a part-time job on campus. Although it might seem that working while attending college takes time and energy away from academic pursuits, part-time employment in an on-campus job actually facilitates retention. Apparently such work, which also includes work-study combinations, operates in much the same way as residential living: The student is spending time on the campus, thus increasing the likelihood that he or she will come into contact with other students, professors, and college staff. On a more subtle psychological level, relying on the college as a source of income can result in a greater sense of attachment to the college.

Retention suffers, however, if the student works off campus at a full-time job. Because the student is spending considerable time and energy on nonacademic activities that are usually unrelated to student life, full-time work off campus decreases the time and energy that the student can devote to studies and other campus activities.

Findings concerning the effects of different types of colleges are also relevant to the theory of involvement. Thus, the most consistent finding—reported in almost every longitudinal study of student development—is that the student's chances of dropping out are substantially greater at a 2-year college than at a 4-year college. The negative effects of attending a community college are observed even after the variables of entering student characteristics and lack of residence and work are considered (Astin, 1975, 1977). Community colleges are places where the involvement of both faculty and students seems to be minimal. Most (if not all) students are commuters, and a large proportion attend college on a part-time basis (thus, they presumably manifest less involvement simply because of their part-time status). Similarly, a large proportion of faculty members are employed on a part-time basis.

The 1975 study of dropouts also produced some interesting findings regarding the "fit" between student and college: Students are more likely to persist at religious colleges if their own religious backgrounds are similar; Blacks are more likely to persist at Black colleges than at White colleges; and students from small towns are more likely to persist in small than in large colleges. The origin of such effects probably lies in the student's ability to identify with the institution. It is easier to become involved when one can identify with the college environment.

Further support for the involvement theory can be found by examining the reasons that students give for dropping out of college. For men the most common reason is boredom with courses, clearly implying a lack of involvement. The most common reason for women is marriage, pregnancy, or other responsibilities, a set of competing objects that drain away the time and energy that women could otherwise devote to being students.

The persister-dropout phenomenon provides an ideal paradigm for studying student involvement. Thus, if we conceive of involvement as occurring along a continuum, the act of dropping out can be viewed as the ultimate form of noninvolvement, and dropping out anchors the involvement continuum at the lowest end.

Because of the apparent usefulness of the involvement theory as it applied to the earlier research on dropping out, I decided to investigate the involvement phenomenon more intensively by studying the impact of college on a wide range of other outcomes (Astin, 1977). This study, which used longitudinal data on several samples totaling more than 200,000 students and examined more than 80 different student outcomes, focused on the effects of several different types of involvement: place of residence, honors programs, undergraduate research participation, social fraternities and sororities, academic involvement, student-faculty interaction, athletic involvement, and involvement in student government. In understanding the effects of these various forms of involvement it is important to keep in mind the overall results of this study: College attendance in general seems to strengthen students' competency, self-esteem, artistic interests, liberalism, hedonism, and religious apostasy and to weaken their business interests.

Perhaps the most important general conclusion I reached from this elaborate analysis was

that nearly all forms of student involvement are associated with greater than average changes in entering freshman characteristics. And for certain student outcomes involvement is more strongly associated with change than either entering freshman characteristics or institutional characteristics. The following is a summary of the results for specific forms of involvement.

Place of Residence

Leaving home to attend college has significant effects on most college outcomes. Students who live in campus residences are much more likely than commuter students to become less religious and more hedonistic. Residents also show greater gains than commuters in artistic interests, liberalism, and interpersonal self-esteem. Living in a dormitory is positively associated with several other forms of involvement: interaction with faculty, involvment in student government, and participation in social fraternities or sororities.

Living on campus substantially increases the student's chances of persisting and of aspiring to a graduate or professional degree. Residents are more likely than commuters to achieve in such extracurricular areas as leadership and athletics and to express satisfaction with their undergraduate experience, particularly in the areas of student friendships, faculty-student relations, institutional reputation, and social life.

Honors Programs

Students who participate in honors programs gain substantially in interpersonal self-esteem, intellectual self-esteem, and artistic interests. They are more likely than other students to persist in college and to aspire to graduate and professional degrees. Honors participation is positively related to student satisfaction in three areas—quality of the science program, closeness to faculty, and quality of instruction—and negatively related to satisfaction with friendships and with the institution's academic reputation. These findings suggest that honors participation enhances faculty-student relationships but may isolate students from their peers.

Academic Involvement

Defined as a complex of self-reported traits and behaviors (e.g., the extent to which students work hard at their studies, the number of hours they spend studying, the degree of interest in their courses, good study habits), academic involvement produces an unusual pattern of effects. Intense academic involvement tends to retard those changes in personality and behavior that normally result from college attendance. Thus, students who are deeply involved academically are less likely than average students to show increases in liberalism, hedonism, artistic interests, and religious apostasy or decreases in business interests. The only personality change accentuated by academic involvement is need for status, which is strengthened. Being academically involved is strongly related to satisfaction with all aspects of college life except friendships with other students.

This pattern reinforces the hypothesis that students who become intensely involved in their college studies tend to become isolated from their peers and, consequently, are less susceptible to the peer group influences that seem critical to the development of political liberalism, hedonism, and religious apostasy. On the other hand, they experience considerable satisfaction, perhaps because of the many institutional rewards for good academic performance.

Student-Faculty Interaction

Frequent interaction with faculty is more strongly related to satisfaction with college than any other type of involvement or, indeed, any other student or institutional characteristic. Students who interact frequently with faculty members are more likely than other students to express satisfaction with all aspects of their institutional experience, including student friendships, variety of courses, intellectual environment, and even the administration of the institution. Thus, finding ways to encourage greater student involvement with faculty (and vice versa) could be a highly productive activity on most college campuses.

Athletic Involvement

The pattern of effects associated with involvement in athletic activities closely parallels the pattern associated with academic involvement; that is, students who become intensely involved in athletic activities show smaller than average increases in political liberalism, religious apostasy, and artistic interests and a smaller than average decrease in business interests. Athletic involvement is also associated with satisfaction in four areas: the institution's academic reputation, the intellectual environment, student

friendships, and institutional administration. These results suggest that athletic involvement, like academic involvement, tends to isolate students from the peer group effects that normally accompany college attendance. For the studious person, this isolation results from the time and effort devoted to studying. For the athlete, the isolation probably results from long practice hours, travel to athletic competitions, and special living quarters.

Involvement in Student Government

Involvement in student government is associated with greater than average increases in political liberalism, hedonism, artistic interests, and status needs as well as greater than average satisfaction with student friendships. This pattern of relationships supports the hypothesis that the changes in attitudes and behavior that usually accompany college attendance are attributable to peer-group effects. That is, students who become actively involved in student government interact frequently with their peers, and this interaction seems to accentuate the changes normally resulting from the college experience.

Research on Cognitive Development

Although most research on classroom learning has been carried out at the precollegiate level, most of the evidence from this research strongly supports the concept of involvement as a critical element in the learning process. The concepts of time-on-task and effort, for example, appear frequently in the literature as key determinants of a wide range of cognitive learning outcomes (Bloom, 1974; Fisher et al., 1980; Gagne, 1977).

PRACTICAL APPLICATIONS

There are several implications of the theory of involvement for practitioners in higher education. Some of the possible uses that could be made of the theory by faculty, administrators, and student personnel workers are briefly described below.

Faculty and Administrators

As already suggested, the content and resource approaches to pedagogy tend to favor the well-prepared, assertive student. In contrast, the concept of student involvement emphasizes giving greater attention to the passive, reticent, or unprepared student. Of course, not all passive students are uninvolved in their academic work, nor are they necessarily experiencing academic difficulties. But passivity is an important warning sign that may reflect a lack of involvement.

Perhaps the most important application of the student involvement theory to teaching is that it encourages the instructor to focus less on content and teaching techniques and more on what students are actually doing—how motivated they are and how much time and energy they are devoting to the learning process. Teaching is a complex art. And, like other art forms, it may suffer if the artist focuses exclusively on technique. Instructors can be more effective if they focus on the intended outcomes of their pedagogical efforts: achieving maximum student involvement and learning. (Final examinations monitor learning, but they come too late in the learning process to have much value for the individual student.)

The art-form analogy can perhaps be better illustrated with an example from sports. Any professional baseball player will confirm that the best way to develop skill in pitching is to focus not on the mechanics but on the intended results: getting the ball over the plate. If the player overemphasizes such techniques as the grip, the stance, the windup, and the kick without attending to where the ball goes, he will probably never learn to pitch well. In fact, the technique involved in pitching a baseball, shooting a basketball, or hitting a golf ball is really unimportant as long as the ball goes where the player wants it to. If the ball fails to behave as intended, then the player begins to worry about adjusting his or her technique.

In education, teachers and administrators often concentrate on their own techniques or processes and thus ignore or overlook what is going on with the student. I believe that the involvement approach has the advantage of encouraging educators to focus more on what the student is actually doing.

Counselors and Student Personnel Workers

If an institution commits itself to achieving maximum student involvement, counselors and other student personnel workers will probably occupy a more important role in institutional operations. Because student personnel workers frequently operate on a one-to-one basis with students, they are in a unique position to monitor the involvement of their clients in the academic process and to work with individual clients in an attempt to increase that involvement. One of the challenges confronting student personnel workers these days is to find a "hook" that will stimulate students to get more involved in the college experience: taking a different array of courses, changing residential situations, joining student organizations, participating in various kinds of extracurricular activities, or finding new peer groups.

The theory of involvement also provides a useful frame of reference for working with students who are having academic difficulties. Perhaps the first task in working with such students is to understand the principal objects on which their energies are focused. It might be helpful, for example, to ask the student to keep a detailed diary, showing the time spent in various activities such as studying, sleeping, socializing, daydreaming, working, and commuting. From such a diary the counselor can identify the principal activities in which the student is currently involved and the objects of cathexis and can then determine if the academic difficulties stem from competing involvements, poor study habits, lack of motivation, or some combination of these factors.

In short, the theory of student involvement provides a unifying construct that can help to focus the energies of all institutional personnel on a common objective.

RESEARCH POSSIBILITIES

My research over the past several years, applying the theory of student involvement, has generated many ideas for further research. There are possibilities not only for testing the theory itself but also for exploring educational ideas that grow out of the theory. The following are just a few examples of the kinds of research that could be undertaken.

Assessing Different Forms of Involvement

Clearly, one of the most important next steps in developing and testing the involvement theory is to explore ways of assessing different forms of involvement. As already suggested, a time diary could be valuable in determining the relative importance of various objects and activities to the student. Judging from my first attempt to develop time diaries (Astin, 1968), students vary considerably in the amount of time they spend on such diverse activities as studying, socializing, sleeping, daydreaming, and traveling. It would also be useful to assess how frequently students interact with each other, with faculty members and other institutional personnel, and with people outside the institution. In addition, it is important not only to identify the extracurricular activities in which the student participates but also to assess the time and energy that the student devotes to each activity.

Quality Versus Quantity

My colleague, C. Robert Pace, has developed an extensive battery of devices to assess the quality of effort that students devote to various activities (Pace, 1982). A number of research questions arise in connection with the quality versus quantity issue: To what extent can high-quality involvement compensate for lack of quantity? Can students be encouraged to use time more wisely? To what extent does low-quality involvement reflect such obstacles as lack of motivation and personal problems?

Involvement and Developmental Outcomes

The research reviewed earlier (Astin, 1977) suggests that different forms of involvement lead to different developmental outcomes. The connection between particular forms of involvement and particular outcomes is an important question that should be addressed in future research. For example, do particular forms of involvement facilitate student development along the various dimensions postulated by theorists such as Chickering (1969), Loevinger (1966), Heath (1968), Perry (1970), and Kohlberg (1971)? It would also be useful to determine whether particular student characteristics (e.g., socioeconomic status, academic preparation, sex) are significantly related to different forms of involvement and whether a given form of involvement produces different outcomes for different types of students.

The Role of Peer Groups

Considerable research at the precollegiate level suggests that the student's commitment of time and energy to academic work can be strongly influenced by student peers (Coleman, 1961; McDill & Rigsby, 1973). It would be useful to determine whether similar relationships exist at the postsecondary level and, in particular, whether different types of student peer groups can be consciously used to enhance student involvement in the learning process.

Attribution and Locus of Control

In recent years learning and developmental theorists have shown an increasing interest in the concepts of *locus of control* (Rotter, 1966) and *attribution* (Weiner, 1979). Considerable research, for example, suggests that students' degree of involvement in learning tasks can be influenced by whether they believe that their behavior is controlled by internal or by external factors. Weiner (1979) argued that even if students tend to view their locus of control as internal, involvement may be further contingent on whether the internal factors are controllable (e.g., dependent on effort) or uncontrollable (e.g., dependent on ability). It seems clear that the effectiveness of any attempt to increase student involvement is highly contingent on the student's perceived locus of control and attributional inclinations.

Other Questions

Other questions that could be explored in future research on the involvement theory include the following:

Exceptions to the rule. What are the characteristics of highly involved students who drop out? What are the characteristics of uninvolved students who nonetheless manage to persist in college? Are there particular developmental outcomes for which a high degree of involvement is contraindicated?

Temporal patterns of involvement. Two students may devote the same total amount of time and energy to a task but may distribute their time in very different ways. For example, one student preparing a term paper may work for 1 hour each night over a period of 2 weeks; another may stay up all night to do the paper. What are the developmental consequences of these different patterns?

Combining different forms of involvement. How do different forms of involvement interact? Does one form of involvement (e.g., in extracurricular activities) enhance or diminish the effects of another form (e.g., in academic work)? What are the ideal combinations that facilitate maximum learning and personal development?

Desirable limits to involvement. Although the theory of involvement generally holds that "more is better," there are probably limits beyond which increasing involvement ceases to produce desirable results and can even become counterproductive. Examples of excessive involvement are the "workaholic," the academic "grind," and others who manifest obsessive-compulsive behavior. What are the ideal upper limits for various forms of involvement? Are problems more likely to develop if the student is excessively involved in a single object (e.g., academic work) rather than in a variety of objects (e.g., academic work, part-time job, extracurricular activities, social activities, and political activities)?

Epidemiology of involvement. Can student involvement be increased if professors interact more with students? Can administrators bring about greater faculty-student interaction by setting an example themselves? Does focusing on student involvement as a common institutional goal tend to break down traditional status barriers between faculty and student personnel workers?

SUMMARY

I have presented a theory of student development, labeled the *student involvement theory*, which I believe is both simple and comprehensive. This theory not only elucidates the considerable findings that have emerged from decades of research on student development; it also offers educators a tool for designing more effective learning environments.

Student involvement refers to the quantity and quality of the physical and psychological energy that students invest in the college experience. Such involvement takes many forms, such as absorption in academic work, participation in extracurricular activities, and interaction with faculty and other institutional personnel. According to the theory, the greater the student's involvement in college, the greater will be the amount of student learning and personal development. From the standpoint of the educator, the most important hypothesis in the theory is that the effectiveness of any educational policy or practice is directly related to the capacity of

that policy or practice to increase student involvement.

The principal advantage of the student involvement theory over traditional pedagogical approaches (including the subject-matter, the resource, and the individualized or eclectic theories) is that it directs attention away from subject matter and technique and toward the motivation and behavior of the student. It views student time and energy as institutional resources, albeit finite resources. Thus, all institutional policies and practices—those relating to nonacademic as well as academic matters—can be evaluated in terms of the degree to which they increase or reduce student involvement. Similarly, all college personnel—counselors and student personnel workers as well as faculty and administrators—can assess their own activities in terms of their success in encouraging students to become more involved in the college experience.

REFERENCES

Astin, A. W. (1968). *The college environment.* Washington, DC: American Council on Education.
Astin, A. W. (1973). The impact of dormitory living on students. *Educational Record, 54*, 204–210.
Astin, A. W. (1975). *Preventing students from dropping out.* San Francisco: Jossey-Bass.
Astin, A. W. (1977). *Four critical years.* San Francisco: Jossey-Bass.
Astin, A. W. (1982). *Minorities in American higher education.* San Francisco: Jossey-Bass.
Bloom, B. (1974). Time and learning. *American Psychologist, 29*, 682–688.
Brown, R. D., & DeCoster, D. A. (Eds.). (1982). *Mentoring-transcript systems for promoting student growth: New directons for student services no. 19.* San Francisco: Jossey-Bass.
Chickering, A. W. (1969). *Education and identity.* San Francisco: Jossey-Bass.
Chickering, A. W. (1974). *Commuters versus residents.* San Francisco: Jossey-Bass.
Chickering, A. W., & Associates. (1981). *The modern American college.* San Francisco: Jossey-Bass.
Coleman, J. S. (1961). *The adolescent society.* New York: Free Press.
Fisher, C. W., Berliner, D., Filby, N., Marliave, R. Cahen, L., & Dishaw, M. (1980). Teaching behaviors, academic learning time and student achievement. In C. Denham & A. Lieberman (Eds.), *Time to learn.* Washington, DC: National Institute of Education.
Gagne, R. M. (1977). *The conditions of learning.* (3rd ed.). New York: Holt, Rinehart and Winston.
Grant, G., Elbow, P., Ewens, T., Gamson, Z., Kohli, W., Neumann, W., Olesen, V., & Riesman, D. (1979). *On competence.* San Francisco: Jossey-Bass.

Hanson, G. R. (Ed.). (1982). *Measuring student development: New directions for student services no. 20*. San Francisco: Jossey-Bass.

Heath, D. (1968). *Growing up in college*. San Francisco: Jossey-Bass.

Kohlberg, L. (1971). Stages of moral development. In C. M. Beck, B. S. Crittenden, & E. V. Sullivan (Eds.), *Moral education*. Toronto: University of Toronto Press.

Loevinger, J. (1966). The meaning and measure of ego development. *American Psychologist, 21*, 195–206.

McDill, E. L., & Rigsby, L. C. (1973). *Structure and process in secondary schools: The academic impact of educational climates*. Baltimore: Johns Hopkins University Press.

Pace, C. R. (1982). *Achievement and the quality of student effort: Report prepared for the National Commission on Excellence in Education*. Los Angeles: Higher Education Research Institute, University of California at Los Angeles.

Perry, W. G. (1970). *Forms of intellectual and ethical development in the college years*. New York: Holt, Rinehart and Winston.

Rosenshine, B. (1982). *Teaching functions in instructional programs*. Paper presented at the National Institute of Education's National Invitational Conference on Research on Teaching: Implications for Practice, Washington, DC.

Rotter, J. (1966). Generalized expectations for internal versus external control of reinforcement. *Psychological Monographs, 1*(Whole No. 609).

Weiner, B. A. (1979). Theory of motivation for some classroom experiences. *Journal of Educational Psychology, 71*, 3–25.

Psychological Review
1991, Vol. 98, No. 2, 224–253

Culture and the Self: Implications for Cognition, Emotion, and Motivation

Hazel Rose Markus
University of Michigan

Shinobu Kitayama
University of Oregon

People in different cultures have strikingly different construals of the self, of others, and of the interdependence of the 2. These construals can influence, and in many cases determine, the very nature of individual experience, including cognition, emotion, and motivation. Many Asian cultures have distinct conceptions of individuality that insist on the fundamental relatedness of individuals to each other. The emphasis is on attending to others, fitting in, and harmonious interdependence with them. American culture neither assumes nor values such an overt connectedness among individuals. In contrast, individuals seek to maintain their independence from others by attending to the self and by discovering and expressing their unique inner attributes. As proposed herein, these construals are even more powerful than previously imagined. Theories of the self from both psychology and anthropology are integrated to define in detail the difference between a construal of the self as independent and a construal of the self as interdependent. Each of these divergent construals should have a set of specific consequences for cognition, emotion, and motivation; these consequences are proposed and relevant empirical literature is reviewed. Focusing on differences in self-construals enables apparently inconsistent empirical findings to be reconciled, and raises questions about what have been thought to be culture-free aspects of cognition, emotion, and motivation.

In America, "the squeaky wheel gets the grease." In Japan, "the nail that stands out gets pounded down." American parents who are trying to induce their children to eat their suppers are fond of saying "think of the starving kids in Ethiopia, and appreciate how lucky you are to be different from them." Japanese parents are likely to say "Think about the farmer who worked so hard to produce this rice for you; if you don't eat it, he will feel bad, for his efforts will have been in vain" (H. Yamada, February 16, 1989). A small Texas corporation seeking to elevate productivity told its employees to look in the mirror and say "I am beautiful" 100 times before coming to work each day. Employees of a Japanese supermarket that was recently opened in New Jersey were instructed to begin the day by holding hands and telling each other that "he" or "she is beautiful" ("A Japanese Supermarket," 1989).

Such anecdotes suggest that people in Japan and America may hold strikingly divergent construals of the self, others, and the interdependence of the two. The American examples stress attending to the self, the appreciation of one's difference from others, and the importance of asserting the self. The Japanese examples emphasize attending to and fitting in with others and

Many thanks to Hiroko Akiyama, Nancy Cantor, Steve Cousins, Susan Cross, Alan Fiske, Carol Gilligan, Tom Givon, Lawrence Hirschfeld, Chie Kanagawa, John Kihlstrom, Joan Miller, Richard Nisbett, Jeanne Oggins, Richard Shweder, Mark Snyder, Harry Triandis, Hiroko Yamada, and Robert Zajonc for their extremely helpful comments on earlier versions of this article, and thanks to Debbie Apsley for preparing the manuscript.

Correspondence concerning this article should be addressed to Hazel Rose Markus, Research Center for Group Dynamics—ISR, University of Michigan, Ann Arbor, Michigan 48106-1248, or to Shinobu Kitayama, Department of Psychology, University of Oregon, Eugene, Oregon 97403-1227.

the importance of harmonious interdependence with them. These construals of the self and others are tied to the implicit, normative tasks that various cultures hold for what people should be doing in their lives (cf. Cantor & Kihlstrom, 1987; Erikson, 1950; Veroff, 1983). Anthropologists and psychologists assume that such construals can influence, and in many cases determine, the very nature of individual experience (Chodorow, 1978; Dumont, 1970; Geertz, 1975; Gergen, 1968; Gilligan, 1982; Holland & Quinn, 1987; Lykes, 1985; Marsella, De Vos, & Hsu, 1985; Sampson, 1985, 1988, 1989; Shweder & LeVine, 1984; Smith, 1985; Triandis, 1989; Weisz, Rothbaum, & Blackburn, 1984; White & Kirkpatrick, 1985).

Despite the growing body of psychological and anthropological evidence that people hold divergent views about the self, most of what psychologists currently know about human nature is based on one particular view—the so-called Western view of the individual as an independent, self-contained, autonomous entity who (a) comprises a unique configuration of internal attributes (e.g., traits, abilities, motives, and values) and (b) behaves primarily as a consequence of these internal attributes (Geertz, 1975; Sampson, 1988, 1989; Shweder & LeVine, 1984). As a result of this monocultural approach to the self (see Kennedy, Scheier, & Rogers, 1984), psychologists' understanding of those phenomena that are linked in one way or another to the self may be unnecessarily restricted (for some important exceptions, see Bond, 1986, 1988; Cousins, 1989; Fiske, in press; Maehr & Nicholls, 1980; Stevenson, Azuma, & Hakuta, 1986; Triandis, 1989; Triandis, Bontempo, Villareal, Asai, & Lucca, 1988). In this article, we suggest that construals of the self, of others, and of the relationship between the self and others may be even more powerful than previously suggested and that their influence is clearly reflected in differences among cultures. In particular, we compare an *independent* view of the self with one other, very different view, an *interdependent* view. The independent view is most clearly exemplified in some sizable segment of American culture, as well as in many Western European cultures. The interdependent view is exemplified in Japanese culture as well as in other Asian cultures. But it is also characteristic of African cultures, Latin-American cultures, and many southern European cultures. We delineate how these divergent views of the self—the independent and the interdependent—can have a systematic influence on various aspects of cognition, emotion, and motivation.

We suggest that for many cultures of the world, the Western notion of the self as an entity containing significant dispositional attributes, and as detached from context, is simply not an adequate description of selfhood. Rather, in many construals, the self is viewed as *inter*dependent with the surrounding context, and it is the "other" or the "self-in-relation-to-other" that is focal in individual experience. One general consequence of this divergence in self-construal is that when psychological processes (e.g., cognition, emotion, and motivation) explicitly, or even quite implicitly, implicate the self as a target or as a referent, the nature of these processes will vary according to the exact form or organization of self inherent in a given construal. With respect to cognition, for example, for those with interdependent selves, in contrast to those with independent selves, some aspects of knowledge representation and some of the processes involved in social and nonsocial thinking alike are influenced by a pervasive attentiveness to the relevant *others* in the social context. Thus, one's actions are more likely to be seen as situationally bound, and characterizations of the individual will include this context. Furthermore, for those with interdependent construals of the self, both the expression and the experience of emotions and motives may be significantly shaped and governed by a consideration of the reactions of others. Specifically, for example, some emotions, like anger, that derive from and promote an independent view of the self may be less prevalent among those with interdependent selves, and self-serving motives may be replaced by what appear as other-serving motives. An examination of cultural variation in some aspects of cognition, emotion, and motivation will allow psychologists to ask exactly what is universal in these processes, and it has the potential to provide some new insights for theories of these psychological processes.

In this analysis, we draw on recent research efforts devoted to characterizing the general differences between American or Western views of personhood and Eastern or Asian perspectives (e.g., Heelas & Lock, 1981; Hofstede, 1980; Marsella et al., 1985; Roland, 1988; Schwartz & Bilsky, 1990; Shweder, 1990; Shweder & LeVine, 1984; Stigler, Shweder, & Herdt, 1990; Triandis, 1989; Triandis & Brislin, 1980; Weisz et al., 1984). We extract from these descriptions many important differences that may exist in the specific content, structure, and functioning of the self-systems of people of different cultural backgrounds. The distinctions that we make between independent and interdependent construals must be regarded as general tendencies that may emerge when the members of the culture are considered as a whole. The prototypical American view of the self, for example, may prove to be most characteristic of White, middle-class men with a Western European ethnic background. It may be somewhat less descriptive of women in general, or of men and women from other ethnic groups or social classes.[1] Moreover, we realize that there may well be important distinctions among those views we discuss as similar and that there may be views of the self and others that cannot easily be classified as either independent or interdependent.

Our intention is not to catalog all types of self-construals, but rather to highlight a view of the self that is often assumed to be universal but that may be quite specific to some segments of Western culture. We argue that self-construals play a major role in regulating various psychological processes. Understanding the nature of divergent self-construals has two important consequences. On the one hand, it allows us to organize several apparently inconsistent empirical findings and to pose questions about the universality assumed for many aspects of cognition, emotion, and motivation (see Shweder, 1990). On the other hand, it permits us to better specify the precise role of the self in mediating and regulating behavior.

The Self: A Delicate Category

Universal Aspects of the Self

In exploring the possibility of different types of self-construals, we begin with Hallowell's (1955) notion that people everywhere are likely to develop an understanding of themselves as physically distinct and separable from others. Head (1920), for example, claimed the existence of a universal schema of the body that provided one with an anchor in time and space. Similarly, Allport (1937) suggested that there must exist an aspect of personality that allows one, when awakening each morning, to be sure that he or she is the same person who went to sleep the night before. Most recently, Neisser (1988) referred to this aspect of self as the *ecological self*, which he defined as "the self as perceived with respect to the physical environment: 'I' am the person here in this place, engaged in this particular activity" (p. 3). Beyond a physical or ecological sense of self, each person probably has some awareness of internal activity, such as dreams, and of the continuous flow of thoughts and feelings, which are private to the extent that they cannot be directly known by others. The awareness of this unshared experience will lead the person to some sense of an inner, private self.

Divergent Aspects of the Self

Some understanding and some representation of the private, inner aspects of the self may well be universal, but many other aspects of the self may be quite specific to particular cultures. People are capable of believing an astonishing variety of things about themselves (cf. Heelas & Lock, 1981; Marsella et al., 1985; Shweder & LeVine, 1984; Triandis, 1989). The self can be construed, framed, or conceptually represented in multiple ways. A cross-cultural survey of the self lends support to Durkheim's (1912/1968) early notion that the category of the self is primar-

[1] The prototypical American view may also be further restricted to a particular point in history. It may be primarily a product of late, industrial capitalism (see Baumeister, 1987). For an analysis of the origins of the independent view, see Bellah, Madsen, Sullivan, Swidler, & Tipton (1985) and Weber (1958).

ily the product of social factors, and to Mauss's (1938/1985) claim that as a social category, the self is a "delicate" one, subject to quite substantial, if not infinite, variation.

The exact content and structure of the inner self may differ considerably by culture. Furthermore, the nature of the outer or public self that derives from one's relations with other people and social institutions may also vary markedly by culture. And, as suggested by Triandis (1989), the significance assigned to the private, inner aspects versus the public, relational aspects in regulating behavior will vary accordingly. In fact, it may not be unreasonable to suppose, as did numerous earlier anthropologists (see Allen, 1985), that in some cultures, on certain occasions, the *individual*, in the sense of a set of significant inner attributes of the person, may cease to be the primary unit of consciousness. Instead, the sense of belongingness to a social relation may become so strong that it makes better sense to think of the *relationship* as the functional unit of conscious reflection.

The current analysis focuses on just one variation in what people in different cultures can come to believe about themselves. This one variation concerns what they believe about the relationship between the self and *others* and, especially, the degree to which they see themselves as *separate* from others or as *connected* with others. We suggest that the significance and the exact functional role that the person assigns to the other when defining the self depend on the culturally shared assumptions about the separation or connectedness between the self and others.

Two Construals of the Self: Independent and Interdependent

The Independent Construal

In many Western cultures, there is a faith in the inherent separateness of distinct persons. The normative imperative of this culture is to become independent from others and to discover and express one's unique attributes (Johnson, 1985; Marsella et al., 1985; J. G. Miller, 1988; Shweder & Bourne, 1984). Achieving the cultural goal of independence requires construing oneself as an individual whose behavior is organized and made meaningful primarily by reference to one's own internal repertoire of thoughts, feelings, and action, rather than by reference to the thoughts, feelings, and actions of others. According to this construal of self, to borrow Geertz's (1975) often quoted phrase, the person is viewed as "a bounded, unique, more or less integrated motivational and cognitive universe, a dynamic center of awareness, emotion, judgment, and action organized into a distinctive whole and set contrastively both against other such wholes and against a social and natural background" (p. 48).

This view of the self derives from a belief in the wholeness and uniqueness of each person's configuration of internal attributes (Johnson, 1985; Sampson, 1985, 1988, 1989; Waterman, 1981). It gives rise to processes like "self-actualization," "realizing oneself," "expressing one's unique configuration of needs, rights, and capacities," or "developing one's distinct potential." The essential aspect of this view involves a conception of the self as an autonomous, independent person; we thus refer to it as the

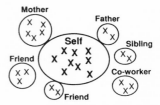

A. Independent View of Self

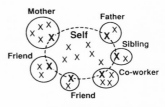

B. Interdependent View of Self

Figure 1. Conceptual representations of the self. (A: Independent construal. B: Interdependent construal.)

independent construal of the self. Other similar labels include *individualist, egocentric, separate, autonomous, idiocentric,* and *self-contained.* We assume that, on average, relatively more individuals in Western cultures will hold this view than will individuals in non-Western cultures. Within a given culture, however, individuals will vary in the extent to which they are good cultural representatives and construe the self in the mandated way.

The independent self must, of course, be responsive to the social environment (Fiske, in press). This responsiveness, however, is fostered not so much for the sake of the responsiveness itself. Rather, social responsiveness often, if not always, derives from the need to strategically determine the best way to express or assert the internal attributes of the self. Others, or the social situation in general, are important, but primarily as standards of reflected appraisal, or as sources that can verify and affirm the inner core of the self.

The Western, independent view of the self is illustrated in Figure 1A. The large circle represents the self, and the smaller circles represent specific others. The *X*s are representations of the various aspects of the self or the others. In some cases, the larger circle and the small circle intersect, and there is an X in the intersection. This refers to a representation of the self-in-relation-to-others or to a particular social relation (e.g., "I am very polite in front of my professor"). An X within the self circle but outside of the intersection represents an aspect of the self perceived to be relatively independent of specific others and, thus, invariant over time and context. These self-representations usually have as their referent some individual desire, preference, attribute, or ability (e.g., "I am creative"). For those with independent construals of the self, it is these inner attributes that are most significant in regulating behavior and that are assumed, both by the actor and by the observer alike, to be diagnostic of the actor. Such representations of the inner self are thus the most elaborated in memory and the most accessible when thinking of the self (as indicated by Xs in Figure 1A). They can be called *core conceptions, salient identities,* or *self-schemata* (e.g., Gergen, 1968; Markus, 1977; Stryker, 1986).

The Interdependent Construal

In contrast, many non-Western cultures insist, in Kondo's (1982) terms, on the fundamental *connectedness* of human beings to each other. A normative imperative of these cultures is to maintain this interdependence among individuals (De Vos, 1985; Hsu, 1985; Miller, 1988; Shweder & Bourne, 1984). Experiencing interdependence entails seeing oneself as part of an encompassing social relationship and recognizing that one's behavior is determined, contingent on, and, to a large extent organized by what the actor perceives to be the thoughts, feelings, and actions of *others* in the relationship. The Japanese experience of the self, therefore, includes a sense of interdependence and of one's status as a participant in a larger social unit (Sampson, 1988). Within such a construal, the self becomes most meaningful and complete when it is cast in the appropriate social relationship. According to Lebra (1976) the Japanese are most fully human in the context of others.

This view of the self and the relationship between the self and others features the person not as separate from the social context but as more connected and less differentiated from others. People are motivated to find a way to fit in with relevant others, to fulfill and create obligation, and in general to become part of various interpersonal relationships. Unlike the independent self, the significant features of the self according to this construal are to be found in the interdependent and thus, in the more public components of the self. We therefore call this view the *interdependent construal of the self.* The same notion has been variously referred to, with somewhat different connotations, as *sociocentric, holistic, collective, allocentric, ensembled, constitutive, contextualist, connected,* and *relational.* As with the independent self, others are critical for social comparison and self-validation, yet in an interdependent formulation of the self, these others become an integral part of the setting, situation, or context to which the self is connected, fitted, and assimilated. The exact manner in which one achieves the task of connection, therefore, depends crucially on the nature of the context, particularly the others present in the context. Others thus participate actively and continuously in the definition of the interdependent self.

The interdependent self also possesses and expresses a set of internal attributes, such as abilities, opinions, judgments, and personality characteristics. However, these internal attributes are understood as situation specific, and thus as sometimes elusive and unreliable. And, as such, they are unlikely to assume a powerful role in regulating overt behavior, especially if this behavior implicates significant others. In many domains of social life, one's opinions, abilities, and characteristics are assigned only secondary roles—they must instead be constantly controlled and regulated to come to terms with the primary task of interdependence. Such voluntary control of the inner attributes constitutes the core of the cultural ideal of becoming mature. The understanding of one's autonomy as secondary to, and constrained by, the primary task of interdependence distinguishes interdependent selves from independent selves, for whom autonomy and its expression is often afforded primary significance. An independent behavior (e.g., asserting an opinion) exhibited by a person in an interdependent culture is likely to be based on the premise of underlying interdependence and thus may have a somewhat different significance than it has for a person from an independent culture.

The interdependent self is illustrated in Figure 1B. For those with interdependent selves, the significant self-representations (the Xs) are those in relationship to specific others. Interdependent selves certainly include representations of invariant personal attributes and abilities, and these representations can become phenomenologically quite salient, but in many circumstances they are less important in regulating observable behavior and are not assumed to be particularly diagnostic of the self.[2] Instead, the self-knowledge that guides behavior is of the self-in-relation to specific others in particular contexts. The fundamental units of the self-system, the core conceptions, or self-schemata are thus predicated on significant interpersonal relationships.

An interdependent self cannot be properly characterized as a bounded whole, for it changes structure with the nature of the particular social context. Within each particular social situation, the self can be differently instantiated. The uniqueness of such a self derives from the specific configuration of relationships that each person has developed. What is focal and objectified in an interdependent self, then, is not the inner self, but the *relationships* of the person to other actors (Hamaguchi, 1985).

The notion of an interdependent self is linked with a monistic philosophical tradition in which the person is thought to be of the same substance as the rest of nature (see Bond, 1986; Phillips, 1976; Roland, 1988; Sass, 1988). As a consequence, the relationship between the self and other, or between subject and object, is assumed to be much closer. Thus, many non-Western cultures insist on the inseparability of basic elements (Galtung, 1981), including self and other, and person and situation. In Chinese culture, for instance, there is an emphasis on synthesizing the constituent parts of any problem or situation into an integrated or harmonious whole (Moore, 1967; Northrop, 1946). Thus, persons are only parts that when separated from the larger social whole cannot be fully understood (Phillips, 1976; Shweder, 1984). Such a holistic view is in opposition to the Cartesian, dualistic tradition that characterizes Western thinking and in which the self is separated from the object and from the natural world.

Examples of the interdependent self. An interdependent view of the self is common to many of the otherwise highly diverse cultures of the world. Studies of the mainland Chinese, for example, summarized in a recent book by Bond (1986), show that even among the most rapidly modernizing segments of the Chinese population, there is a tendency for people to act

---

[2] For a discussion of how interdependent selves strive to maintain a balance between internal (private) and extensive (public) representations, see T. Doi (1986).

primarily in accordance with the anticipated expectations of others and social norms rather than with internal wishes or personal attributes (Yang, 1981b). A premium is placed on emphasizing collective welfare and on showing a sympathetic concern for others. Throughout the studies of the Chinese reported by Bond, one can see the clear imprint of the Confucian emphasis on interrelatedness and kindness. According to Hsu (1985), the supreme Chinese virtue, *jen*, implies the person's capability to interact with fellow human beings in a sincere, polite, and decent fashion (see also Elvin, 1985).

Numerous other examples of cultures in which people are likely to have some version of an interdependent self can also be identified. For example, Triandis, Marin, Lisansky, and Betancourt (1984) have described the importance of simpatico among Hispanics. This quality refers to the ability to both respect and share others' feelings. In characterizing the psychology of Filipinos, Church (1987) described the importance that people attribute to smooth interpersonal relations and to being "agreeable even under difficult circumstances, sensitive to what others are feeling and willing to adjust one's behavior accordingly." Similarly, Weisz (in press) reported that Thais place a premium on self-effacement, humility, deference, and on trying to avoid disturbing others. Among the Japanese, it is similarly crucial not to disturb the *wa*, or the harmonious ebb and flow of interpersonal relations (see also Geertz, 1974, for characterizations of similar imperatives among the Balinese and Moroccans).

Beattie (1980) claimed that Africans are also extremely sensitive to the interdependencies among people and view the world and others in it as extensions of one another. The self is viewed not as a hedged closure but as an open field. Similarly, Marriott (1976) argued that Hindu conceptions assume that the self is an open entity that is given shape by the social context. In his insightful book, Kakar (1978) described the Hindu's ideal of interpersonal fusion and how it is accompanied by a personal, cultural sense of hell, which is separation from others. In fact, Miller, Bersoff, and Harwood (1990), in a recent, carefully controlled study on moral reasoning, found that Indians regard responsiveness to the needs of others as an objective moral obligation to a far greater extent than do Americans. Although the self-systems of people from these cultures are markedly different in many other important respects, they appear to be alike in the greater value (when compared with Americans) that is attached to proper relations with others, and in the requirement to flexibly change one's own behavior in accordance with the nature of the relationship.

Even in American culture, there is a strong theme of interdependence that is reflected in the values and activities of many of its subcultures. Religious groups, such as the Quakers, explicitly value and promote interdependence, as do many small towns and rural communities (e.g., Bellah, Madsen, Sullivan, Swidler, & Tipton, 1985). Some notion of a more connected, ensembled, interdependent self, as opposed to a self-contained, independent self, is also being developed by several of what Sampson (1989) calls "postmodern" theorists. These theorists are questioning the sovereignty of the American view of the mature person as autonomous, self-determined, and unencumbered. They argue that psychology is currently dominated by a view of the person that does not adequately reflect the extent to which

people everywhere are created by, constrained by, and responsive to their various interpersonal contexts (see Gergen & Gergen, 1988; Gilligan, 1982; Miller, 1986; Tajfel, 1984).

Further definition of the interdependent self. Theorists of Japanese culture are beginning to characterize the interdependent self much more specifically than was previously attempted. These descriptions offer some more refined ideas of how an interdependent view of self can depart markedly from an independent view of self (see Nakane, 1970; Plath, 1980; R. J. Smith, 1983). For example, building on a study of L. T. Doi (1973), Bachnik (1986) wrote

> (in Japanese society) rather than there being a single social reality, a number of possible perspectives of both self and social life are acknowledged. Interaction in Japanese society then focuses on the definition of the appropriate choice, out of all the various possibilities. This means that what one says and does will be different in different situations, depending on how one defines one's particular perspective versus the social other. (p. 69)

In Japan, the word for self, *jibun*, refers to "one's share of the shared life space" (Hamaguchi, 1985). The self, Kimura (cited in Hamaguchi, 1985) claimed, is "neither a substance nor an attribute having a constant oneness" (p. 302). According to Hamaguchi (1985), for the Japanese, "a sense of identification with others (sometimes including conflict) pre-exists and selfness is confirmed only through interpersonal relationships. . . . Selfness is not a constant like the ego but denotes a fluid concept which changes through time and situations according to interpersonal relationships" (p. 302).

The Japanese anthropologist Lebra (1976) defined the essence of Japanese culture as an "ethos of social relativism." This translates into a constant concern for belongingness, reliance, dependency, empathy, occupying one's proper place, and reciprocity. She claimed the Japanese nightmare is exclusion, meaning that one is failing at the normative goal of connecting to others. This is in sharp contrast to the American nightmare, which is to fail at separating from others, as can occur when one is unduly influenced by others, or does not stand up for what one believes, or when one goes unnoticed or undistinguished.

An interdependent view of self does not result in a merging of self and other, nor does it imply that one must always be in the company of others to function effectively, or that people do not have a sense of themselves as agents who are the origins of their own actions. On the contrary, it takes a high degree of self-control and agency to effectively adjust oneself to various interpersonal contingencies. Agentic exercise of control, however, is directed primarily to the inside and to those inner attributes, such as desires, personal goals, and private emotions, that can disturb the harmonious equilibrium of interpersonal transaction. This can be contrasted with the Western notion of control, which primarily implies an assertion of the inner attributes and a consequent attempt to change the outer aspects, such as one's public behaviors and the social situation (see also Weisz et al., 1984).

Given the Japanese notion of control that is inwardly directed, the ability to effectively adjust in the interpersonal domain may form an important basis of self-esteem, and individualized styles of such adjustment to social contingencies may contribute to the sense of self-uniqueness. Thus, Hamaguchi

(1985), for example, reported that for the Japanese, "the straightforward claim of the naked ego" (p. 303) is experienced as childish. Self-assertion is not viewed as being authentic, but instead as being immature. This point is echoed in M. White and LeVine's (1986) description of the meaning of *sunao*, a term used by Japanese parents to characterize what they value in their children:

A child that is *sunao* has not yielded his or her personal autonomy for the sake of cooperation; cooperation does not suggest giving up the self, as it may in the West; it implies that working with others is the appropriate way of expressing and enhancing the self. Engagement and harmony with others is, then, a positively valued goal and the bridge—to open-hearted cooperation, as in *sunao*— is through sensitivity, reiterated by the mother's example and encouragement. (p. 58)

Kumagai (1981) said *sunao* "assumes cooperation to be an act of affirmation of the self" (p. 261). Giving in is not a sign of weakness; rather, it reflects tolerance, self-control, flexibility, and maturity.

The role of the other in the interdependent self. In an interdependent view, in contrast to an independent view, others will be assigned much more importance, will carry more weight, and will be relatively focal in one's own behavior. There are several direct consequences of an interdependent construal of the self. First, relationships, rather than being means for realizing various individual goals, will often be ends in and of themselves. Although people everywhere must maintain some relatedness with others, an appreciation and a need for people will be more important for those with an interdependent self than for those with an independent self. Second, maintaining a connection to others will mean being constantly aware of others and focusing on their needs, desires, and goals. In some cases, the goals of others may become so focal in consciousness that the goals of others may be experienced as personal goals. In other cases, fulfilling one's own goals may be quite distinct from those of others, but meeting another's goals, needs, and desires will be a necessary requirement for satisfying one's own goals, needs, and desires. The assumption is that while promoting the goals of others, one's own goals will be attended to by the person with whom one is interdependent. Hence, people may actively work to fulfill the others' goals while passively monitoring the reciprocal contributions from these others for one's own goal-fulfillment. Yamagishi (1988), in fact, suggested that the Japanese feel extremely uncomfortable, much more so than Americans, when the opportunity for such passive monitoring of others' actions is denied.

From the standpoint of an independent, "self-ish" self, one might be led to romanticize the interdependent self, who is ever attuned to the concerns of others. Yet in many cases, responsive and cooperative actions are exercised only when there is a reasonable assurance of the "good-intentions" of others, namely their commitment to continue to engage in reciprocal interaction and mutual support. Clearly, interdependent selves do not attend to the needs, desires, and goals of *all* others. Attention to others is not indiscriminate; it is highly selective and will be most characteristic of relationships with "in-group" members. These are others with whom one shares a common fate, such as family members or members of the same lasting social group, such as the work group. Out-group members are typically treated quite differently and are unlikely to experience either the advantages or disadvantages of interdependence. Independent selves are also selective in their association with others but not to the extent of interdependent selves because much less of their behavior is directly contingent on the actions of others. Given the importance of others in constructing reality and regulating behavior, the in-group–out-group distinction is a vital one for interdependent selves, and the subjective boundary of one's "in-group" may tend to be narrower for the interdependent selves than for the independent selves (Triandis, 1989).

To illustrate the reciprocal nature of interaction among those with interdependent views, imagine that one has a friend over for lunch and has decided to make a sandwich for him. The conversation might be: "Hey, Tom, what do you want in your sandwich? I have turkey, salami, and cheese." Tom responds, "Oh, I like turkey." Note that the friend is given a choice because the host assumes that friend has a right, if not a duty, to make a choice reflecting his inner attributes, such as preferences or desires. And the friend makes his choice exactly because of the belief in the same assumption. This script is "natural," however, only within the independent view of self. What would happen if the friend were a visitor from Japan? A likely response to the question "Hey, Tomio, what do you want?" would be a little moment of bewilderment and then a noncommital utterance like "I don't know." This happens because under the assumptions of an interdependent self, it is the responsibility of the host to be able to "read" the mind of the friend and offer what the host perceives to be the best for the friend. And the duty of the guest, on the other hand, is to receive the favor with grace and to be prepared to return the favor in the near future, if not right at the next moment. A likely, interdependent script for the same situation would be: "Hey, Tomio, I made you a turkey sandwich because I remember that last week you said you like turkey more than beef." And Tomio will respond, "Oh, thank you, I really like turkey."

The reciprocal interdependence with others that is the sign of the interdependent self seems to require constant engagement of what Mead (1934) meant by taking the role of the other. It involves the willingness and ability to feel and think what others are feeling and thinking, to absorb this information without being told, and then to help others satisfy their wishes and realize their goals. Maintaining connection requires inhibiting the "I" perspective and processing instead from the "thou" perspective (Hsu, 1981). The requirement is to "read" the other's mind and thus to know what the other is thinking or feeling. In contrast, with an independent self, it is the individual's responsibility to "say what's on one's mind" if one expects to be attended to or understood.

Consequences of an Independent or an Interdependent View of the Self

Table 1 presents a brief, highly simplified summary of some of the hypothesized differences between independent and interdependent construals of the self. These construals of self and other are conceptualized as part of a repertoire of self-relevant schemata used to evaluate, organize, and regulate one's experience and action. As schemata, they are patterns of one's past behaviors as well as patterns for one's current and future behav-

Table 1
*Summary of Key Differences Between an Independent and an
Interdependent Construal of Self*

Feature compared	Independent	Interdependent
Definition	Separate from social context	Connected with social context
Structure	Bounded, unitary, stable	Flexible, variable
Important features	Internal, private (abilities, thoughts, feelings)	External, public (statuses, roles, relationships)
Tasks	Be unique	Belong, fit-in
	Express self	Occupy one's proper place
	Realize internal attributes	Engage in appropriate action
	Promote own goals	Promote others' goals
	Be direct; "say what's on your mind"	Be indirect; "read other's mind"
Role of others	*Self-evaluation:* others important for social comparison, reflected appraisal	*Self-definition:* relationships with others in specific contexts define the self
Basis of self-esteem[a]	Ability to express self, validate internal attributes	Ability to adjust, restrain self, maintain harmony with social context

[a] Esteeming the self may be primarily a Western phenomenon, and the concept of self-esteem should perhaps be replaced by self-satisfaction, or by a term that reflects the realization that one is fulfilling the culturally mandated task.

iors (Neisser, 1976). Markus and Wurf (1987) called this assortment of self-regulatory schemata the *self-system.* Whenever a task, an event, or a situation is self-relevant, the ensuing processes and consequences are likely to be influenced by the nature of the self-system. The self-system has been shown to be instrumental in the regulation of intrapersonal processes such as self-relevant information processing, affect regulation, and motivation and in the regulation of interpersonal processes such as person perception, social comparison, and the seeking and shaping of social interaction (see Cantor & Kihlstrom, 1987; Greenwald & Pratkanis, 1984; Markus & Wurf, 1987, for reviews). The goal of this article is to further specify the role of the self-system in behavior by examining how these divergent cultural self-schemata influence individual experience.

In the current analysis, we hypothesize that the independent versus interdependent construals of self are among the most general and overarching schemata of the individual's self-system. These construals recruit and organize the more specific self-regulatory schemata.[3] We are suggesting here, therefore, that the exact organization of many self-relevant processes and their outcomes depends crucially on whether these processes are rooted in an independent construal of the self or whether they are based primarily on an interdependent construal of the self. For example, in the process of lending meaning and coherence to the social world, we know that people will show a heightened sensitivity to self-relevant stimuli. For those with an independent view of self, this includes information relevant to one's self-defining attributes. For one with an interdependent view of self, such stimuli would include information about significant others with whom the person has a relationship or information about the self in relation to another person.

Affect regulation involves seeking positive states and avoiding negative ones. Positive states are those that enhance or promote one's view of the self, and negative states are those that challenge this view. For a person with an independent view of self, this involves seeking information that confirms or en-

hances one's internal, private attributes. The most desirable situations are those that allow one to verify and express those important internal attributes and that convey the sense that one is appropriately autonomous. In contrast, for a person with an interdependent view of self, one might expect the most desirable states to be those that allow one to be responsive to one's immediate context or that convey the sense that one is succeeding in his or her interdependent relationships or statuses.

A third important function of the self-concept suggested by Markus and Wurf (1987) is that of motivating persons, of moving them to action. The person with an independent view of self should be motivated to those actions that allow expression of one's important self-defining, inner attributes (e.g., hardworking, caring, independent, and powerful), whereas the person with an interdependent view of self should be motivated to

---

[3] What these very general cultural self-schemata of independence or interdependence mean for a given individual's articulated view of self cannot be specified, however. The self-concept derives not only from the cultural self-schema that is the focus herein but from the complete configuration of self-schemata, including those that are a product of gender, race, religion, social class, and one's particular social and developmental history. Not all people who are part of an independent culture will thus characterize themselves as independent, nor will all those who live as part of an interdependent culture claim to be interdependent. Within independent and interdependent cultures, there is great diversity in individual self-definition, and there can also be strong similarities across cultures. For example, many artists, whether Japanese or American, may describe themselves as nonconformist, innovative, and breaking with tradition. And many aspects of their behavior are indeed very similar. Yet, nonconformity Japanese-style and nonconformity American-style, although similar in some respects, will not, because of the differences in their supporting cultural contexts, be identical. For Japanese, nonconformity is a privilege afforded only to selected, talented individuals whose deviance from the norm of interdependence is implicitly sanctioned by the rest of society. For Americans, nonconformity is regarded as every individual's birthright.

those actions that enhance or foster one's relatedness or connection to others. On the surface, such actions could look remarkably similar (e.g., working incredibly hard to gain admission to a desirable college), but the exact source, or etiology, of the energizing motivation may be powerfully different (De Vos, 1973; Maehr & Nicholls, 1980).

In the following sections, we discuss these ideas in further detail and review the empirical literature, which suggests that there are significant cognitive, emotional, and motivational consequences of holding an independent or an interdependent view of the self.

Consequences for Cognition

If a cognitive activity implicates the self, the outcome of this activity will depend on the nature of the self-system. Specifically, there are three important consequences of these divergent self-systems for cognition. First, we may expect those with interdependent selves to be more attentive and sensitive to others than those with independent selves. The attentiveness and sensitivity to others, characterizing the interdependent selves, will result in a relatively greater cognitive elaboration of the other or of the self-in-relation-to-other. Second, among those with interdependent selves, the unit of representation of both the self and the other will include a relatively specific social context in which the self and the other are embedded. This means that knowledge about persons, either the self or others, will not be abstract and generalized across contexts, but instead will remain specific to the focal context. Third, a consideration of the social context and the reactions of others may also shape some basic, nonsocial cognitive activities such as categorizing and counterfactual thinking.

In exploring the impact of divergent cultural construals on thinking, we assume that how people think (the process) in a social situation cannot be easily separated from what they think about (the content; Shweder, 1990; Shweder & Bourne, 1984). Extensive research on social cognition in the past decade has suggested the power of content in social inference (e.g., see Fiske & Taylor, 1984; Markus & Zajonc, 1985, for reviews). It is the nature of the representation (e.g., self, another person, a weed, or clam chowder) that guides attention, and that determines what other relevant information will be retrieved to fill in the gap of available sense data. For example, investigations by D'Andrade (1981) and Johnson-Laird (1983) indicate that the greater the familiarity with the stimulus materials, the more elaborate the schemata for framing the problem, and the better the problem solving. In general, then, how a given object is culturally construed and represented in memory should importantly influence and even determine how one thinks about the object. Accordingly, the divergent representations of the self we describe should be expected to have various consequences for all cognition relevant to self, others, or social relationships.

More interpersonal knowledge. If the most significant elements of the interdependent self are the self-in-relation-to-others elements, there will be a need, as well as a strong normative demand, for knowing and understanding the social surrounding, particularly others in direct interaction with the self. That is, if people conceive of themselves as interdependent parts of larger social wholes, it is important for them to be

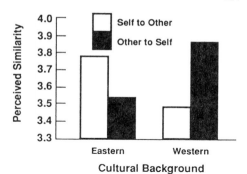

Figure 2. Mean perceived similarity of self to other and other to self by subjects with Eastern and Western cultural backgrounds.

sensitive to and knowledgeable about the others who are the coparticipants in various relationships, and about the social situations that enable these relationships. Maintaining one's relationships and ensuring a harmonious social interaction requires a full understanding of these others, that is, knowing how they are feeling, thinking, and likely to act in the context of one's relationships to them. It follows that those with interdependent selves may develop a dense and richly elaborated store of information about others or of the self in relation.

Kitayama, Markus, Tummala, Kurokawa, and Kato (1990) examined this idea in a study requiring similarity judgments between self and other. A typical American finding is that the self is judged to be more dissimilar to other than other is to the self (Holyoak & Gordon, 1983; Srull & Gaelick, 1983). This finding has been interpreted to indicate that for the typical American subject, the representation of the self is more elaborated and distinctive in memory than the representation of another person. As a result, the similarity between self and other is judged to be less when the question is posed about a more distinctive object (Is *self* similar to other?) than when the question is posed about a less distinctive object (Is *other* similar to self?). If, however, those with interdependent selves have at least as much knowledge about some others as they have about themselves, this American pattern of findings may not be found.

To test these predictions, Kitayama et al. (1990) compared students from Eastern cultural backgrounds (students from India) with those from Western cultural backgrounds (American students). As shown in Figure 2, for the Western subjects, Kitayama et al. replicated the prior findings in which the self is perceived as significantly more dissimilar to the other than is the other to the self. Such a finding is consistent with a broad range of studies showing that for individuals with a Western background, supposedly those with independent selves, self-knowledge is more distinctive and densely elaborated than knowledge about other people (e.g., Greenwald & Pratkanis, 1984). This pattern, however, was nonsignificantly reversed for the Indian subjects, who judged the self to be somewhat more similar to the other than is the other to the self. It appears, then, that for the latter, more interdependent subjects, knowledge about others is relatively more elaborated and distinctive than knowledge about the self. Asymmetry in similarity judgments is an indirect way to evaluate knowledge accessibility, but a more direct measure of cross-cultural differences in knowledge of the other should reveal that those with interdependent selves have more readily accessible knowledge of the other.

Context-specific knowledge of self and other. A second consequence of having an interdependent self as opposed to an independent self concerns the ways in which knowledge about self and other is processed, organized, and retrieved from memory. For example, given an interdependent self, knowledge about the self may not be organized into a hierarchical structure with the person's characteristic attributes (e.g., intelligent, competent, and athletic) as the superordinate nodes, as is often assumed in characterizations of the independent self. In other words, those with interdependent selves are less likely to organize knowledge about the "self in general" or about the "other in general." Specific social situations are more likely to serve as the unit of representation than are attributes of separate persons. One learns about the self with respect to a specific other in a particular context and, conversely, about the other with respect to the self in a particular context.

In exploring variations in the nature of person knowledge, Shweder and Bourne (1984) asked respondents in India and America to describe several close acquaintances. The descriptions provided by the Indians were more situationally specific and more relational than those of Americans. Indian descriptions focused on behavior; they described what was done, where it was done, and to whom and with whom it was done. The Indian respondents said, "He has no land to cultivate but likes . to cultivate the land of others," or "When a quarrel arises, he cannot resist the temptation of saying a word," or "He behaves properly with guests but feels sorry if money is spent on them." It is the behavior itself that is focal and significant rather than the inner attribute that supposedly underlies it. Notably this tendency to provide the specific situational or interpersonal context when providing a description was reported to characterize the free descriptions of Indians regardless of social class, education, or literacy level. It appears, then, that the concreteness in person description is not due to a lack of skill in abstracting concrete instances to form a general proposition, but rather a consequence of the fact that global inferences about persons are typically regarded as not meaningful or informative.

Americans also describe other people in terms of the specifics of their behavior, but typically this occurs only at the beginning of relationships when the other is relatively unknown, or if the behavior is somehow distinctive and does not readily lend itself to a trait characterization. Rather than saying "He does not disclose secrets," Americans are more likely to say "He is discreet or principled." Rather than "He is hesitant to give his money away," Americans say "He is tight or selfish." Shweder and Bourne (1984) found that 46% of American descriptions were of the context-free variety, whereas this was true of only 20% from the Indian sample.

A study by J. G. Miller (1984) on patterns of explanation among Indian Hindus and Americans revealed the same tendency for contextual and relational descriptions of behavior

among Indian respondents. In the first phase of her study, respondents generated two prosocial behaviors and two deviant behaviors and then explained why each behavior was undertaken. For example, in the prosocial case, respondents were asked to "describe something a person you know well did recently that you considered good for someone else." Miller coded the explanations for reference to dispositional explanations; for reference to social, spatial, temporal location; and for reference to specific acts or occurrences. Like Shweder and Bourne (1984), she found that on average, 40% of the reasons given by American respondents referred to the general dispositions of the actor. For the Hindu respondents, dispositional explanations constituted less than 20% of their responses.

In a second phase of the study, Miller (1984) asked both American and Indian respondents to explain several accounts of the deviant behaviors generated by the Indian respondents. For example, a Hindu subject narrated the following incident:

> This concerns a motorcycle accident. The back wheel burst on the motorcycle. The passenger sitting in the rear jumped. The moment the passenger fell, he struck his head on the pavement. The driver of the motorcycle—who is an attorney—as he was on his way to court for some work, just took the passenger to a local hospital and went on and attended to his court work. I personally feel the motorcycle driver did a wrong thing. The driver left the passenger there without consulting the doctor concerning the seriousness of the injury—the gravity of the situation—whether the passenger should be shifted immediately—and he went on to the court. So ultimately the passenger died. (p. 972)

Respondents were asked why the driver left the passenger at the hospital without staying to consult about the seriousness of the passenger's injury. On average, Americans made 36% of their attributions to dispositions of the actors (e.g., irresponsible, pursuing success) and 17% of their attributions to contextual factors (driver's duty to be in court). In comparison, only 15% of the attributions of the Indians referred to dispositions, whereas 32% referred to contextual reasons. Both the American and the Indian subjects focused on the state of the driver at the time of the accident, but in the Indian accounts, the social role of the driver appears to be very important to understanding the events. He is obligated to his role, he has a job to perform. Actions are viewed as arising from relations or interactions with others; they are a product of obligations, responsibilities, or commitments to others and are thus best understood with respect to these interpersonal relations. This preference for contextual explanations has also been documented by Dalal, Sharma, and Bisht (1983).

These results call into question the exact nature of the fundamental attribution error (Ross, 1977). In this error, people, in their efforts to understand the causes of behavior, suffer from an inescapable tendency to perceive behavior as a consequence of the internal, personal attributes of the person. Miller's (1984) Indian respondents also explained events in terms of properties or features of the person, yet these properties were their role relationships—their socially determined relations to specific others or groups. Because role relationships necessarily implicate the social situation that embeds the actor, it is unclear whether the explanations of the Indian respondents can be viewed as instances of the fundamental attribution error. It may be that the fundamental attribution error is only characteristic of those with an independent view of the self.

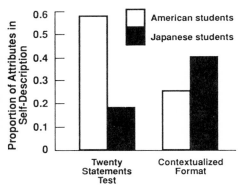

Figure 3. Mean proportion of psychological attributes endorsed by American and Japanese students in two self-description tasks.

The tendency to describe a person in terms of his or her specific behavior and to specify the context for a given behavior is also evidenced when those with interdependent selves provide self-descriptions. Cousins (1989) compared the self-descriptions of American high school and college students with the self-descriptions of Japanese high school and college students. He used two types of free-response formats, the original Twenty Statements Test (TST; Kuhn & McPartland, 1954), which simply asks "Who Am I?" 20 consecutive times, and a modified TST, which asks subjects to describe themselves in several specific situations (me at home, me with friends, and me at school). When responding to the original TST, the Japanese self-descriptions were like those of the Indians in the Shweder and Bourne (1984) study. They were more concrete and role specific ("I play tennis on the weekend"). In contrast, the American descriptions included more psychological trait or attribute characterizations ("I am optimistic," and "I am friendly"). However, in the modified TST, where a specific interpersonal context was provided so that respondents could envision the situation (e.g., me at home) and presumably who was there and what was being done to whom or by whom, this pattern of results was reversed. As shown in Figure 3, the Japanese showed a stronger tendency to characterize themselves in psychological trait or attribute terms than did Americans. In contrast, Americans tended to qualify their self-descriptions, claiming, for example, "I am sometimes lazy at home."

Cousins (1989) argued that the original TST essentially isolates or disembeds the "I" from the relational or situational context, and thus self-description becomes artificial for the Japanese respondents, who are more accustomed to thinking about themselves within specific social situations. For these respondents, the contextualized format "Describe yourself as you are with your family" was more "natural" because it locates the self in a habitual unit of representation, namely in a particular interpersonal situation. Once a defining context was specified, the Japanese respondents were decidedly more willing to make generalizations about their behavior and to describe themselves abstractly using trait or attribute characterizations.

American students, in contrast to their Japanese counterparts, were more at home with the original TST because this test elicits the type of abstract, situation-free self-descriptions that form the core of the American, independent self-concept. Such abstract or global characterizations, according to Cousins (1989), reflect a claim of being a separate individual whose nature is not bound by a specific situation. When responding to the contextualized self-description questions, the American students qualified their descriptions as if to say "This is how I am at home, but don't assume this is the way I am everywhere." For American respondents, selfness, pure and simple, seems to transcend any particular interpersonal relationships.

Basic cognition in an interpersonal context. One's view of self can have an impact even on some evidently nonsocial cognitive activities. I. Liu (1986) described the emphasis that the Chinese place on being loyal and pious to their superiors and obedience to them, whether they are parents, employers, or government officials. He claimed that most Chinese adhere to a specific rule that states "If your superiors are present, or indirectly involved, in any situation, then you are to respect and obey them" (I. Liu, 1986, p. 78). The power and the influence of this rule appear to go considerably beyond that provided by the American admonition to "respect one's elders." I. Liu (1986) argued that the standard of self-regulation that involves the attention and consideration of others is so pervasive that it may actually constrain verbal and ideational fluency. He reasoned that taking account of others in every situation is often at odds with individual assertion or with attempts at innovation or unique expression. This means, for example, that in an unstructured creativity task in which the goal is to generate as many ideas as possible, Chinese subjects may be at a relative disadvantage. In a similar vein, T. Y. Liu and Hsu (1974) suggested that consideration of the rule "respect and obey others" uses up cognitive capacity that might otherwise be devoted to a task, and this may be the reason that Chinese norms for some creativity tasks fall below American norms.

Charting the differences between an independent self and interdependent self may also illuminate the controversy surrounding the debate between Bloom (1981, 1984) and Au (1983, 1984) over whether the Chinese can reason counterfactually (for a thorough review of this debate, see Moser, 1989). Bloom's studies (1981) on the counterfactual began when he asked Chinese-speaking subjects questions like "If the Hong Kong government were to pass a law requiring that all citizens born outside of Hong Kong make weekly reports of their activities to the police, how would you react?" Bloom noted that his respondents consistently answered "But the government hasn't," "It can't," or "It won't." Pressed to think about it anyway, the respondents became frustrated, claiming that it was unnatural or un-Chinese to think in this way. American and French respondents answered similar questions readily and without complaint. From this and subsequent studies, Bloom (1981, 1984) concluded that Chinese speakers "might be expected typically to encounter difficulty in maintaining a counterfactual perspective as an active point of orientation for guiding their cognitive activities" (1984, p. 21).

Au (1983) challenged Bloom's conclusions. Using different

stimulus materials and also different translations of the same stimulus materials, she reported that Chinese subjects performed no differently from their Western counterparts. The controversy continues, however, and many investigators remain unconvinced that the differences Bloom and others have observed in a large number of studies on counterfactual reasoning are solely a function of awkward or improper translations of stimulus materials.

Moser (1989), for example, discussed several of Bloom's (1981, 1984) findings that are not easily explained away. He described the following question that Bloom (1981, pp. 53–54) gave to Taiwanese, Hong Kong, and American subjects in their native language.

> Everyone has his or her own method for teaching children to respect morality. Some people punish the child for immoral behavior, thereby leading him to fear the consequences of such behavior. Others reward the child for moral behavior, thereby leading him to want to behave morally. Even though both of these methods lead the child to respect morality, the first method can lead to some negative psychological consequences—it may lower the child's self-esteem.
>
> According to the above paragraph, what do the two methods have in common? Please select only one answer.
>
> A. Both methods are useless.
> B. They have nothing in common, because the first leads to negative psychological consequences.
> C. Both can reach the goal of leading the child to respect morality.
> D. It is better to use the second.
> E. None of the above answers makes sense. (If you choose this answer, please explain.)

Bloom (1984) reported that 97% of American subjects responded C, but that only 55% of the Taiwanese and 65% of the Hong Kong respondents answered C. In explaining his results, he wrote:

> Most of the remaining Chinese-speaking subjects chose D or E and then went on to explain, based on their own experience and often at great length and evidently after much reflection, why, for instance, the second method might be better, or why neither method works, or why both methods have to be used in conjunction with each other, or perhaps, why some other specified means is preferable. For the majority of these subjects, as was evident from later interviewing, it was not that they did not see the paragraph as stating that both methods lead the child to respect morality, but they felt that choosing that alternative and leaving it at that would be misleading since in their experience that response was untrue. As they saw it, what was expected, desired, must be at a minimum an answer reflecting their personal considered opinion, if not a more elaborated explanation of their own experiences relevant to the matter at hand. Why else would anyone ask the question? American subjects, by contrast, readily accepted the question as a purely "theoretical" exercise to be responded to according to the assumptions of the world it creates rather than in terms of their own experiences with the actual world. (Bloom, 1981, p. 54)

It is our view that the differences in response between the Americans and the Chinese may be related to whether the respondent has an independent or interdependent construal of the self. If one's actions are contingent on, determined by, or made meaningful by one's relationships and social situations, it is reasonable to expect that respondents with interdependent selves might focus on the motivation of the person administer-

ing the question and on the nature of their current relationship with this person. Consequently, in the process of responding, they might ask themselves, "What is being asked of me here? What does this question expect of me or require from me? What are potential ramifications of answering in one way or another in respect to my relationship with this person?" In Lebra's (1976) terms, what is "my proper place?" in this social interaction [i.e., me and the interviewer], and what are the "obligations attached to [it?]" (p. 67). To immediately respond to the question as a purely abstract or theoretical exercise would require ignoring the currently constituted social situation and the nature of one's relationship with the other. This, of course, can be done, but it does not mean that it will be easily, effortlessly, or automatically done. And this is especially true when the pragmatics of a given context appears to require just the opposite. It requires ignoring the other's perspective and a lack of attention to what the other must be thinking or feeling to ask such a question. One's actions are made meaningful by reference to a particular set of contextual factors. If these are ignored or changed, then the self that is determined by them changes also. Those with relatively unencumbered, self-contained, independent selves can readily, and without hesitation, entertain any of a thousand fanciful possible worlds because there are fewer personal consequences—the bounded, autonomous self remains essentially inviolate.

One important implication of this analysis is that people with interdependent selves should have no disadvantage in counterfactual reasoning if the intent of the questioner and the demand of the situation is simply to test the theoretical reasoning capacities of the person. One such situation would involve an aptitude test such as the Scholastic Aptitude Test (SAT). Indeed, on the quantitative portion of the SAT that requires substantial hypothetical and counterfactual reasoning (e.g., "If Tom walked 2 miles per hour, then how far will he have walked in 4 hours?"), both Taiwanese and Japanese children perform considerably better than their American peers (Stevenson et al., 1986).

It would appear important, therefore, to distinguish between competence and performance or between the presence of particular inference skills and the application of these skills in a particular pragmatic context (see also Laboratory of Comparative Human Cognition, 1982). The discussion thus far implies that regardless of the nature of the self-system, most people with an adequate level of education possess the skills of hypothetical reasoning and the ability to think in a counterfactual fashion. Yet, the application of these skills in a particular situation varies considerably with the nature of the self-system. Some people may invoke these skills much more selectively. For those with interdependent selves, in contrast to those with independent selves, a relatively greater proportion of all inferences will be contingent on the pragmatic implications of a given situation, such as the perceived demands of the interviewer, the convention of the situation, and the rules of conversation.

Do styles of thinking and inference vary above and beyond those that derive from the pragmatic considerations of particular social situations? This question has yet to be more carefully addressed. However, given the tendency to see people, events, and objects as embedded within particular situations and relationships, the possibility seems genuine. Chiu (1972), for example, claimed that the reasoning of American children is characterized by an inferential–categorical style, whereas the reasoning of Taiwanese Chinese subjects displays a relational–contextual style. When American children described why two objects of a set of three objects went together, they were likely to say "because they both live on a farm." In contrast, Chinese children were more likely to display a relational–contextual style, putting two human figures together and claiming the two go together "because the mother takes care of the baby." In the latter case, the emphasis is on synthesizing features into an organized whole. Bruner (1986) referred to such differences as arising from a paradigmatic versus a narrative mode of thought. In the former, the goal is abstraction and analyzing common features, in the latter, establishing a connection or an interdependence among the elements.

Consequences for Emotion

In psychology, emotion is often viewed as a universal set of largely prewired internal processes of self-maintenance and self-regulation (Buck, 1988; Darwin, 1896; Ekman, 1972; LeDoux, 1987). This does not mean, though, that emotional experience is also universal. On the contrary, as suggested by anthropologists Rosaldo (1984), Lutz (1988), and Solomon (1984), culture can play a central role in shaping emotional experience. As with cognition, if an emotional activity or reaction implicates the self, the outcome of this activity will depend on the nature of the self-system. And apart from the fear induced by bright lights and loud sounds, or the pleasure produced by a sweet taste, there are likely to be few emotions that do not directly implicate one's view of the self. Thus, Rosaldo (1984) contended "feelings are not substances to be discovered in our blood but social practices organized by stories that we both enact and tell. They are structured by our forms of understanding" (p. 143), and we would add, specifically, by one's construal of the self. In an extension of these ideas, Lutz (1988) argued that although most emotions are viewed as universally experienced "natural" human phenomena, emotions are anything but natural. Emotion, she contended, "can be viewed as cultural and interpersonal products of naming, justifying, and persuading by people in relationship to each other. Emotional meaning is then a social rather than an individual achievement—an emergent product of social life" (Lutz, 1988, p. 5).

Among psychologists, several cognitively oriented theorists of emotion have suggested that emotion is importantly implicated and embedded in an actual social situation as construed by the person (e.g., De Riviera, 1984; Roseman, 1984; Scherer, 1984). Accordingly, not only does the experience of an emotion depend on the current construal of the social situation (e.g., Frijda, Kuipers, & ter Schure, 1989; Shaver, Schwartz, Kirson, & O'Connor, 1987; C. Smith & Ellsworth, 1987), but the experienced emotion in turn plays a pivotal role in changing and transforming the very nature of the social situation by allowing a new construal of the situation to emerge and, furthermore, by instigating the person to engage in certain actions. From the current perspective, construals of the social situation are constrained by, and largely derived from, construals of the self, others, and the relationship between the two. Thus, emotional experience should vary systematically with the construal of the self.

The present analysis suggests several ways in which emotional processes may differ with the nature of the self-system. First, the predominant eliciting conditions of many emotions may differ markedly according to one's construal of the self. Second, and more important, which emotions will be expressed or experienced, and with what intensity and frequency, may also vary dramatically.

Ego-focused versus other-focused emotions. The emotions systematically vary according to the extent to which they follow from, and also foster and reinforce, an independent or an interdependent construal of the self. This is a dimension that has largely been ignored in the literature. Some emotions, such as anger, frustration, and pride, have the individual's internal attributes (his or her own needs, goals, desires, or abilities) as the primary referent. Such emotions may be called *ego focused.* They result most typically from the blocking (e.g., "I was treated unfairly"), the satisfaction, or the confirmation (e.g., "I performed better than others") of one's internal attributes. Experiencing and expressing these emotions further highlights these self-defining, internal attributes and leads to additional attempts to assert them in public and confirm them in private. As a consequence, for those with independent selves to operate effectively, they have to be "experts" in the expression and experience of these emotions. They will manage the expression, and even the experience, of these emotions so that they maintain, affirm, and bolster the construal of the self as an autonomous entity. The public display of one's own internal attributes can be at odds with the maintenance of interdependent, cooperative social interaction, and when unchecked can result in interpersonal confrontation, conflict, and possibly even overt aggression. These negative consequences, however, are not as severe as they might be for interdependent selves because the expression of one's internal attributes is the culturally sanctioned task of the independent self. In short, the current analysis suggests that, in contrast to those with more interdependent selves, the ego-focused emotions will be more frequently expressed, and perhaps experienced, by those with independent selves.

In contrast to the ego-focused emotions, some other emotions, such as sympathy, feelings of interpersonal communion, and shame, have another person, rather than one's internal attributes, as the primary referent. Such emotions may be called *other focused.* They typically result from being sensitive to the other, taking the perspective of the other, and attempting to promote interdependence. Experiencing these emotions highlights one's interdependence, facilitates the reciprocal exchanges of well-intended actions, leads to further cooperative social behavior, and thus provides a significant form of self-validation for interdependent selves. As a consequence, for those with interdependent selves to operate effectively, they will have to be "experts" in the expression and experience of these emotions. They will manage the expression, and even the experience, of these emotions so that they maintain, affirm, and reinforce the construal of the self as an interdependent entity. The other-focused emotions often discourage the autonomous expression of one's internal attributes and may lead to inhibition and ambivalence. Although among independent selves these consequences are experienced negatively (e.g., as timidity) and can, in fact, have a negative impact, they are tolerated, among interdependent selves, as the "business of living" (Kakar, 1978,

p. 34). Creating and maintaining a connection to others is the primary task of the interdependent self. In short, this analysis suggests that, in contrast to those with more independent selves, these other-focused emotions will be more frequently expressed and perhaps even experienced among those with interdependent selves.

Ego-focused emotions—emotions that foster and create independence. In a comparison of American and Japanese undergraduates, Matsumoto, Kudoh, Scherer, and Wallbott (1988) found that American subjects reported experiencing their emotions *longer* than did Japanese subjects, even though the two groups agreed in their ordering of which emotions were experienced longest (i.e., joy = sad > anger = guilt > fear = shame = disgust). Americans also reported feeling these emotions more intensely than the Japanese and reported more bodily symptoms (e.g., lump in throat, change in breathing, more expressive reactions, and more verbal reactions) than did the Japanese. Finally, when asked what they would do to cope with the consequences of various emotional events, significantly more of the Japanese students reported that no action was necessary.

One interpretation of this pattern of findings may assume that most of the emotions examined, with the exception of shame and possibly guilt, are what we have called ego-focused emotions. Thus, people with independent selves will attend more to these feelings and act on the basis of them, because these feelings are regarded as diagnostic of the independent self. Not to attend to one's inner feelings is often viewed as being inauthentic or even as denying the "real" self. In contrast, among those with more interdependent selves, one's inner feelings may be less important in determining one's consequent actions. Ego-focused feelings may be regarded as by-products of interpersonal relationships, but they may not be accorded privileged status as regulators of behavior. For those with interdependent selves, it is the interpersonal context that assumes priority over the inner attributes, such as private feelings. The latter may need to be controlled or de-emphasized so as to effectively fit into the interpersonal context.

Given these differences in emotional processes, people with divergent selves may develop very different assumptions about the etiology of emotional expressions for ego-focused emotions. For those with independent selves, emotional expressions may literally "express" or reveal the inner feelings such as anger, sadness, and fear. For those with interdependent selves, however, an emotional expression may be more often regarded as a public instrumental action that may or may not be related directly to the inner feelings. Consistent with this analysis, Matsumoto (1989), using data from 15 cultures, reported that individuals from hierarchical cultures (that we would classify as being generally interdependent; see Hofstede, 1980), when asked to rate the intensity of an angry, sad, or fearful emotion displayed by an individual in a photograph, gave lower intensity ratings than those from less hierarchical cultures. Notably, although the degree of hierarchy inherent in one's cultures was strongly related to the intensity ratings given to those emotions, it was not related to the correct identification of these emotions. The one exception to this finding was that people from more hierarchical cultures (those with more interdependent selves) were less likely to correctly identify emotional expressions of happiness. Among those with interdependent selves (often those from hier-

archical cultures), positive emotional expressions are most frequently used as public actions in the service of maintaining interpersonal harmony and, thus, are not regarded as particularly diagnostic of the actor's inner feelings or happiness.

For those with interdependent selves (composed primarily of relationships with others instead of inner attributes), it may be very important not to have intense experiences of ego-focused emotions, and this may be particularly true for negative emotions like anger. Anger may seriously threaten an interdependent self and thus may be highly dysfunctional. In fact, some anthropologists explicitly challenge the universalist view that all people experience the same negative emotions. Thus, in Tahiti, anger is highly feared, and various anthropological accounts claim that there is no expression of anger in this culture (see Levy, 1973; Solomon, 1984). It is not that these people have learned to inhibit or suppress their "real" anger but that they have learned the importance of attending to others, considering others, and being gentle in all situations, and as a consequence very little anger is elicited. In other words, the social reality is construed and actually constructed in such a way that it does not lend itself to the strong experience, let alone the outburst, of negative ego-focused emotions such as anger. The same is claimed for Ukta Eskimos (Briggs, 1970). They are said not to feel anger, not to express anger, and not even to talk about anger. The claim is that they do not show anger even in those circumstances that would certainly produce complete outrage in Americans. These Eskimos use a word that means "childish" to label angry behavior when it is observed in foreigners.

Among the Japanese, there is a similar concern with averting anger and avoiding a disruption of the harmony of the social situation. As a consequence, experiencing anger or receiving anger signals may be relatively rare events. A study by Miyake, Campos, Kagan, and Bradshaw (1986), which compared Japanese and American infants of 11 months of age, provides suggestive evidence for this claim. These investigators showed each infant an interesting toy and paired it with a mother's vocal expression of joy, anger, or fear. Then they measured the child's latency to resume locomotion toward the toy after the mother's utterance. The two groups of infants did not differ in their reactions to expressions of joy or fear. But, after an angry vocal expression of the mother, there was a striking difference between the two groups. The Japanese children resumed locomotion toward the toy after 48 s, American children after only 18 s. It may be that the Japanese children are relatively more traumatized by their mother's anger expressions because these are such rare events.

Notably, in the West, a controversy exists about the need, the desirability, and the importance of expressing one's anger. Assuming a hydraulic model of anger, some argue that it is necessary to express anger so as to avoid boiling over or blowing up at a later point (Pennebaker, 1982). Others argue for the importance of controlling one's anger so as not to risk losing control. No such controversy appears to exist among those in predominantly interdependent cultures, where a seemingly unchallenged norm directs individuals to restrain their inner feelings and particularly the overt expression of these feelings. Indeed, many interdependent cultures have well-developed strategies that render them expert at avoiding the expression of negative emotions. For example, Bond (1986) reported that in China discussions have a clear structure that is explicitly designed to prevent conflict from erupting. To begin with, discussants present their common problems and identify all the constraints that all the participants must meet. Only then do they state their own views. To Westerners, such a pattern appears as vague, beating around the bush, and not getting to the heart of the matter, but it is part of a carefully executed strategy of avoiding conflict, and thus perhaps the experience of negative emotions. Bond, in fact, noted that among school children in Hong Kong and Taiwan, there is a tendency to cooperate with opponents even in a competitive reward structure and to rate future opponents more positively than others who will not be opponents (Li, Cheung, & Kau, 1979, 1982).

In a recent cross-cultural comparison of the eliciting conditions of several emotions, Matsumoto et al. (1988) also found that Japanese respondents appear to be avoiding anger in close relations. Specifically, for the Japanese, closely related others were rarely implicated in the experience of anger. The Japanese reported feeling anger primarily in the presence of strangers. It thus appears that not only the expression but also the experience of such an ego-focused emotion as anger is effectively averted within an interdependent structure of relation. When anger arises, it happens outside of the existing interdependence, as in confrontation with out-groups (e.g., Samurai warfare in feudal Japan). In contrast, Americans and Western Europeans report experiencing anger primarily in the presence of closely related others. This is not surprising, given that expressing and experiencing ego-focused, even negative emotions, is one viable way to assert and affirm the status of the self as an independent entity. Consistent with this analysis, Stipek, Weiner, and Li (1989) found that when describing situations that produce anger, Chinese subjects were much more likely than American subjects to describe a situation that happened to someone else ("a guy on a bus did not give up a seat to an old woman"). For Americans, the major stimulus to anger was the situation where the individual was the victim ("a friend broke a promise to me").

Other emotions, such as pride or guilt, may also differ according to the nature of the mediating self-system. As with anger, these expressions may be avoided, or they will assume a somewhat different form. For example, if defined as being proud of one's *own* individual attributes, *pride* may mean hubris, and its expression may need to be avoided for those with interdependent selves.[4] Consistent with the idea that pride in one's own performance may be inhibited among those with interdependent selves, Stipek et al. (1989) found that the Chinese were decidedly less likely to claim their own successful efforts as a source of pride than were Americans. These investigators also reported that the emotion of guilt takes on somewhat different connotations as well. Among those with independent selves, who are more likely to hold stable, cross-situational beliefs and to consider them self-definitional, "violating a law or a moral principle" was the most frequently mentioned cause of guilt. Among Chinese, however, the most commonly reported source of guilt was "hurting others psychologically."

Other-focused emotions—emotions that create and foster interdependence. Those with interdependent selves may inhibit the experience, or at least the expression, of some ego-focused emotions, but they may have a heightened capacity for the expe-

rience and expression of those emotions that derive primarily from focusing on the other. In Japan and China, for example, there is a much greater incidence of cosleeping, cobathing, and physical contact between mother and child than is typically true in most Western countries. The traditional Japanese mother carries the child on her back for a large part of the first 2 years. Lebra (1976) claimed that Japanese mothers teach their children to fear the pain of loneliness, whereas Westerners teach children how to be alone. Japanese and Chinese socialization practices may help the child develop an interdependent self in the first place, and at the same time, the capacity for the experience of a relatively greater variety of other-focused emotions.

The greater interdependence that results between mothers and their children is reflected in the finding that the classification of infants according to the nature of their attachments to their mothers (i.e., secure, ambivalent, and avoidant) departs markedly from the pattern typically observed in Western data. Specifically, many more Japanese infants are classified as "ambivalently attached" because they seem to experience decidedly more stress following a brief separation from the mother than do American infants (Ainsworth, Bell, & Stayton, 1974; Miyake, Chen, & Campos, in press). This finding also indicates that a paradigm like the typical stranger situation is inherently linked to an independent view of self and, thus, may not be appropriate for gauging attachment in non-Western cultures.

In Japan, socialization practices that foster an intense closeness between mother and child give rise to the feeling of *amae.* *Amae* is typically defined as the sense of, or the accompanying hope for, being lovingly cared for and involves depending on and presuming another's indulgence. Although, as detailed by Kumagai and Kumagai (1985), the exact meaning of *amae* is open to some debate, it is clear that "the other" is essential. When a person experiences *amae,* she or he "feels the freedom to do whatever he or she wills" while being accepted and cared for by others with few strings attached. Some say *amae* is a type of complete acceptance, a phenomenal replication of the ideal mother–infant bond (L. T. Doi, 1973). From our point of view, experiencing *amae* with respect to another person may be inherent in the formation and maintenance of a mutually reciprocal,

---

[4] In interdependent cultures, if pride is overtly expressed, it may often be directed to a collective, of which the self is a part. For example, the Chinese anthropologist Hsu (1975) described an event in which a Japanese company official showed a "gesture of devotion to his office superior which I had never experienced in the Western world" (p. 215). After talking to Hsu in his own small, plain office, the employee said, "Let me show you the office of my section chief." He then took Hsu to a large, elaborately furnished office, pointed to a large desk, and said proudly, "This is the desk of my section chief." Hsu's account makes clear that this was not veiled cynicism from the employee, just complete, unabashed pride in the accomplishments of his boss. Americans with independent self-systems can perhaps understand this type of pride in another's accomplishment if the other involved is one's relative, but it is typically unfathomable in the case of one's immediate supervisor. Without an understanding of the close alignment and interdependence that occurs between employees and supervisors, the emotion experienced by the employee that prompted him to show off his supervisor's office would be incomprehensible.

interdependent relationship with another person. If the other person accepts one's *amae,* the reciprocal relationship is symbolically completed, leading to a significant form of self-validation. If, however, the other person rejects one's *amae,* the relationship will be in jeopardy.

For the purpose of comparing indigenous feelings, such as *amae,* with the more universal ones, such as anger and happiness, Kitayama and Markus (1990) used a multidimensional scaling technique, which allows the identification of the dimensions that individuals habitually or spontaneously use when they make judgments about similarities among various emotions. Recent studies have demonstrated that people are capable of distinguishing among various emotions on as many as seven or eight cognitive dimensions (Mauro, Sato, & Tucker, 1989; C. Smith & Ellsworth, 1987). In these studies, however, the dimensions have been specified a priori by the experimenter and given explicitly to the respondents to use in describing the emotions. When the dimensions are not provided but allowed to emerge in multidimensional scaling studies, only two dimensions are typically identified: activation (or excitement) and pleasantness (e.g., Russell, 1980). And it appears that most Western emotions can be readily located on a circumplex plane defined by these two dimensions. Thus, although people are capable of discriminating among emotions on a substantial number of dimensions, they habitually categorize the emotions only on the dimensions of activation and pleasantness.

More recently, Russell (1983; Russell, Lewicka, & Niit, 1989) applied the same technique to several non-Western cultural groups and replicated the American findings. He thus argued that the lay understanding of emotional experience may indeed be universal. Russell used, however, only those terms that have clear counterparts in the non-Western groups he studied. He did not include any emotion terms indigenous to the non-Western groups such as *amae.* It is possible that once terms for such indigenous feeling states are included in the analysis, a new dimension, or dimensions, may emerge. To explore this possibility, Kitayama and Markus (1990) sampled 20 emotions from the Japanese language. Half of these terms were also found in English and were sampled so that they evenly covered the circumplex space identified by Russell. The remaining terms were those indigenous to Japanese culture and those that presuppose the presence of others. Some (e.g., *fureai* [feeling a close connection with someone else]) refer primarily to a positive association with others (rather than events that happen within the individual, such as success), whereas others refer to interpersonal isolation and conflict (e.g., *oime* [the feeling of indebtedness]). Japanese college students rated the similarity between 2 emotions for each of the 190 pairs that could be made from the 20 emotions. The mean perceived similarity ratings for these pairs were then submitted to a multidimensional scaling.

Replicating past research, Kitayama and Markus (1990) identified two dimensions that closely correspond to the activation and the pleasantness dimensions. In addition, however, a new dimension emerged. This third dimension represented the extent to which the person is engaged in or disengaged from an interpersonal relationship. At the interpersonal engagement end were what we have called other-focused emotions, such as shame, *fureai* [feeling a close connection with somebody else], and shitashimi [feeling familiar], whereas at the disengagement

end were found some ego-centered emotions, such as pride and *tukeagari* [feeling puffed up with the sense of self-importance], along with sleepiness and boredom. This interpersonal engagement–disengagement dimension also differentiated between otherwise very similar emotions. Thus, pride and elation were equally positive and high in activation, yet pride was perceived as considerably less interpersonally engaged than elation. Furthermore, anger and shame were very similar in terms of activation and pleasantness, but shame was much higher than anger in the extent of interpersonal engagement.

More important, this study located the indigenous emotions within the three-dimensional structure, permitting us to understand the nature of these emotions in reference to more universal emotions. For instance, *amae* was low in activation, and neither positive nor negative, fairly akin to sleepiness, except that the former was much more interpersonally engaged than the latter. This may indicate the passive nature of *amae,* involving the hopeful expectation of another person's favor and indulgence without any active, agentic solicitation of them. Completion of *amae* depends entirely on the other person, and, therefore, *amae* is uniquely ambivalent in its connotation on the pleasantness dimension. Another indigenous emotion, *oime,* involves the feeling of being psychologically indebted to somebody else. *Oime* was located at the very negative end of the pleasantness dimension, perceived even more negatively than such universal negative emotions as anger and sadness. The extreme unpleasantness of *oime* suggests the aversive nature of unmet obligations and the press of the need to fulfill one's obligations to others and to return favors. It also underscores the significance of balanced and harmonious relationships in the emotional life of those with interdependent selves.

The finding that the Japanese respondents clearly and reliably discriminated between ego-focused emotions and other-focused emotions on the dimension of interpersonal engagement versus disengagement strongly suggests the validity of this distinction as an essential component of emotional experience at least among Japanese and, perhaps, among people from other cultures as well. In a more recent study, Kitayama and Markus (1990) further tested whether this theoretical dimension of emotion also underlies and even determines how frequently people may experience various emotions and whether the frequency of emotional experience varies with their dominant construal of self as independent or interdependent.

Kitayama and Markus (1990) first sampled three emotions common in Japanese culture that were expected to fall under one of the five types theoretically derived from the current analysis. These types are listed in Table 2. Ego-focused positive emotions (*yuetukan* [feeling superior], pride, and *tukeagari* [feeling puffed up]) are those that are most typically associated with the confirmation or fulfillment of one's internal attributes, such as abilities, desires, and needs. Ego-focused, negative emotions (anger, *futekusare* [sulky feeling], and *yokyufuman* [frustration]) occur primarily when such internal attributes are blocked or threatened. Also included were those correspondingly positive or negative emotions associated with the maintenance or enhancement of interdependence. Thus, three emotions are commonly associated with the affirmation or the completion of interdependent relationships (*fureai* [feeling of connection with someone], *shitashimi* [feeling of familiarity to someone], *sonkei* [feeling of respect for someone]) and thus were designated as positive and other focused. In contrast, some negative emotions are typically derived from one's failure to offer or reciprocate favors to relevant others and thus to fully participate in the relationship. They are thus closely linked to disturbance to interdependence and a consequent desire to repair the disturbance. They include *oime* [feeling of indebtedness], shame, and guilt. Finally, as noted before, interdependent selves are likely to tolerate ambivalence regarding one's interdependent status with some relevant others. Interestingly, some emotions are uniquely linked to this interpersonal ambivalence. Three such emotions (*amae* [hopeful expectation of others' indulgence or favor], *tanomi* [feeling like relying on someone], and *sugari* [feeling like leaning on someone]) were examined.

Japanese respondents reported how frequently they experienced each of the 15 emotions listed in Table 2. The five-factor structure implied by the theoretical designation of the 15 emotions to one of the five types was verified in a confirmatory factor analysis (Jöreskog, 1969). A correlation matrix for the five types is given in Table 3. There was a strong correlation between positive and negative ego-focused emotions, as may be expected if both of them are derived from and also foster and reinforce an independent construal of self. Furthermore, these ego-focused emotions are clearly distinct from the other-focused emotions. Thus, neither positive nor negative ego-focused emotions had any significant relationship with other-focused, positive emotions. Interestingly, however, these ego-focused emotions were significantly associated with the ambivalent and, to a larger extent, with the negative other-focused emotions, suggesting that the experience of ego-focused emotions, either positive or negative, is readily accompanied, at least in Japanese culture, by the felt disturbance of a relationship and, thus, by a strong need to restore harmony. Alternatively, being embedded

Table 2
The 15 Emotions and Their Meaning

Emotion type (factor)	Emotion	Meaning
Ego focused		
Positive	*Yuetukan*	Feeling superior
	Tukeagari	Feeling puffed up with the
	Pride	sense of self-importance
Negative	*Futekusare*	Sulky feeling
	Yokyufuman	Frustration
	Anger	
Other focused		
Positive	*Fureai*	Feeling of connection with someone
	Shitashimi	Feeling of familiarity to someone
	Sonkei	Feeling of respect for someone
Ambivalent	*Amae*	Hopeful expectation of someone's indulgence and favor
	Tanomi	Feeling like relying on someone
	Sugari	Feeling like leaning on someone
Negative	*Oime*	Feeling of indebtedness
	Shame	
	Guilt	

Table 3
Correlations Among the Five Types of Emotions

Emotion	1	2	3	4	5
Ego focused					
1. Positive	—				
2. Negative	.70	—			
Other focused					
3. Positive	−.05	−.18	—		
4. Ambivalent	.35	.63	.40	—	
5. Negative	.49	.69	.18	.43	—

in a highly reciprocal relation and feeling obliged to contribute to the relationship may sometimes be perceived as a burden or pressure, hence rendering salient some of the ego-focused emotions.[5] Finally, the three types of other-focused emotions (positive, ambivalent, and negative) are all positively correlated (see Table 3).

Can the frequency of experiencing the five types of emotions be predicted by one's predominant construal of self as independent or interdependent? To address this issue, Kitayama and Markus (1990) also asked the same respondents eight questions designed to measure the extent to which they endorse an independent construal of self (e.g., "Are you a kind of person who holds on to one's own view?"; "How important is it to hold on to one's own view?") and eight corresponding questions designed to measure the extent to which they endorse an interdependent construal of self (e.g., "Are you the kind of person who never forgets a favor provided by others?"; "How important is it to never forget a favor provided by others?"). Consistent with the current analysis, the frequency of experiencing both positive and negative ego-focused emotions significantly increased with the independent construal of self. They were, however, either negatively related (for positive emotions) or unrelated (for negative emotions) to the interdependent construal of self. In marked contrast to this pattern for the ego-focused emotions, all three types of other-focused emotions were significantly more frequently experienced by those with more interdependent construals of self. These emotions, however, were either unrelated (for positive and negative other-focused emotions) or negatively related (for the ambivalent emotions) to the independent construal of self.

Consequences for Motivation

The study of motivation centers on the question of why people initiate, terminate, and persist in specific actions in particular circumstances (e.g., Atkinson, 1958; Mook, 1986). The answer given to this question in the West usually involves some type of internal, individually rooted need or motive—the motive to enhance one's self-esteem, the motive to achieve, the motive to affiliate, the motive to avoid cognitive conflict, or the motive to self-actualize. These motives are assumed to be part

[5] On these occasions, perhaps interdependent selves are most clearly aware of their internal attributes. Such awareness (the *honne* in Japanese) may be typically accompanied by a situational demand (the *tatemae* in Japanese).

of the unique, internal core of a person's self-system. But what is the nature of motivation for those with interdependent self-systems? What form does it take? How does the ever-present need to attend to others and to gain their acceptance influence the form of these internal, individual motives? Are the motives identified in Western psychology the universal instigators of behavior?

As with cognition and emotion, those motivational processes that implicate the self depend on the nature of the self-system. If we assume that *others* will be relatively more focal in the motivation of those with interdependent selves, various implications follow. First, those with interdependent selves should express, and perhaps experience, more of those motives that are social or that have the other as referent. Second, as we have noted previously, for those with independent selves, agency will be experienced as an effort to express one's internal needs, rights, and capacities and to withstand undue social pressure, whereas among those with interdependent selves, agency will be experienced as an effort to be receptive to others, to adjust to their needs and demands, and to restrain one's own inner needs or desires. Motives related to the need to express one's agency or competency (e.g., the achievement motive) are typically assumed to be common to all individuals. Yet among those with interdependent selves, striving to excel or accomplish challenging tasks may not be in the service of achieving separateness and autonomy, as is usually assumed for those with independent selves, but instead in the service of more fully realizing one's connectedness or interdependence. Third, motives that are linked to the self, such as self-enhancement, self-consistency, self-verification, self-affirmation, and self-actualization, may assume a very different form depending on the nature of the self that is being enhanced, verified, or actualized.

More interdependent motives? Murray (1938) assembled what he believed to be a comprehensive list of human motivations (see also Hilgard, 1953, 1987). Many of these motives seem most relevant for those with independent selves, but the list also includes some motives that should have particular salience for those with interdependent selves. These include *deference,* the need to admire and willingly follow a superior, to serve gladly; *similarity,* the need to imitate or emulate others, to agree and believe; *affiliation,* the need to form friendships and associations; *nurturance,* the need to nourish, aid, or protect another; *succorance,* the need to seek aid, projection, or sympathy and to be dependent; *avoidance of blame,* the need to avoid blame, ostracism, or punishment by inhibiting unconventional impulses and to be well behaved and obey the law; and *abasement,* the need to comply and accept punishment or self-deprecation. Many of the social motives suggested by Murray seem to capture the types of strivings that should characterize those with interdependent selves. When the cultural imperative is to seek connectedness, social integration, and interpersonal harmony, most of these motives should be typically experienced by the individual as positive and desirable. In contrast, when the cultural task centers on maintaining independence and separateness, holding any of these motives too strongly (e.g., similance and succorance) often indicates a weak or troubled personality. Thus, Murray, for example, gave the need to comply the pejorative label of *need for abasement.*

The limited evidence for the idea that those with interdependent selves will experience more of the social or interdependent motives comes from Bond (1986), who summarized several studies exploring the motive patterns of the Chinese (see also McClelland, 1961). He found that the level of various motives are a fairly direct reflection of the collectivist or group-oriented tradition of the Chinese. Thus, Chinese respondents show relatively high levels of need for abasement, socially oriented achievement, change, endurance, intraception, nurturance, and order; moderate levels of autonomy, deference, and dominance, and succorance; and low levels of individually oriented achievement, affiliation, aggression, exhibition, heterosexuality, and power. The socially oriented achievement motive has, as its ultimate goal, a desire to meet expectations of significant others, whereas the individually oriented achievement motive implies a striving for achievement for its own sake (discussed later). Hwang (1976) found, however, that with continuing rapid social change in China, there is an increase in levels of exhibition, autonomy, intraception, and heterosexuality and a decrease in levels of deference, order, nurturance, and endurance. Interestingly, it appears that those with interdependent selves do not show a greater need for affiliation, as might at first be thought, but instead they exhibit higher levels of those motives that reflect a concern with adjusting oneself so as to occupy a proper place with respect to others.

The motive for cognitive consistency. Another powerful motive assumed to fuel the behavior of Westerners is the need to avoid or reduce cognitive conflict or dissonance. Classic dissonance occurs when one says one thing publicly and feels another, quite contrasting thing privately (Festinger & Carlsmith, 1959). And such a configuration produces particular difficulty when the private attitude is a self-defining one (Greenwald, 1980). One might argue, however, that the state of cognitive dissonance arising from counterattitudinal behavior is not likely to be experienced by those with interdependent selves. First it is the individuals' roles, statuses, or positions, and the commitments, obligations, and responsibilities they confer, that are the constituents of the self, and in that sense they are self-defining. As outlined in Figure 1, one's internal attributes (e.g., private attitudes or opinions) are not regarded as the significant attributes of the self. Furthermore, one's private feelings are to be regulated in accordance with the requirements of the situation. Restraint over the inner self is assigned a much higher value than is expression of the inner self. Thus, Kiefer (1976) wrote:

> Although Japanese are often acutely aware of discrepancies between inner feelings and outward role demands, they think of the latter . . . as the really important center of the self. Regarding feelings as highly idiosyncratic and hard to control, and therefore less reliable as sources of self-respect than statuses and roles, the Japanese tends to include within the boundaries of the concept of self much of the quality of the intimate social group of which he is a member. (R. J. Smith, 1985, p. 28)

More recently, T. Doi (1986) has argued that Americans are decidedly more concerned with consistency between feelings and actions than are the Japanese. In Japan there is a virtue in controlling the expression of one's innermost feelings; no virtue accrues from expressing them. Triandis (1989), for example, reported a study by Iwao (1988), who gave respondents a series of scenarios and asked them to judge which responses would be appropriate for the person described in the scenario. In one scenario, the daughter brings home a person from another race. One of the possible responses given was "thought that he would never allow them to marry but told them he was in favor of their marriage." This answer was rated as best by only 2% of Americans. In sharp contrast, however, it was rated as best by 44% of the Japanese. Among the Americans, 48% thought it was the worst response, whereas only 7% of the Japanese rated it as the worst.

Common motives in an interdependent context. Of those motives assumed by Murray (1938) and Hilgard (1987) to be universally significant, the achievement motive is the most well-documented example. Variously defined as the desire to overcome obstacles, to exert power, to do something as well as possible, or to master, manipulate, or organize physical objects, human beings, or ideas (Hall & Lindzey, 1957; Hilgard, 1987), the achievement motive is thought to be a fundamental human characteristic. However, the drive for achievement in an interdependent context may have some very different aspects from the motive for achievement in an independent cultural context. In a recent analysis of the content and structure of values in seven cultures (i.e., Australia, United States, Spain, Finland, Germany, Israel, and Hong Kong), S. H. Schwartz and Bilsky (1990) found a conflict between values that emphasize independent thought and action and those that emphasize restraining of one's own impulses in all samples except Hong Kong. In the Hong Kong sample, self-restraint appeared to be quite compatible with independent thought and action.

Although all individuals may have some desire for agency or control over their own actions, this agency can be accomplished in various ways (Maehr, 1974). Pushing oneself ahead of others and actively seeking success does not appear to be universally valued. An illuminating analysis of control motivation by Weisz et al. (1984) suggests that acting on the world and altering the world may not be the control strategy of choice for all people. Instead, people in many Asian cultures appear to use what is termed *secondary control.* This involves accommodating to existing realities "sometimes via acts that limit individualism and personal autonomy but that enhance perceived alignment or goodness of fit with people, objects, or circumstances" (Weisz et al., 1984, p. 956).

The American notion of achievement involves breaking away, pushing ahead, and gaining control over surroundings. How do selves concerned with fitting in and accommodating to existing realities achieve? The question of achievement motive in an interdependent context is all the more compelling because many of the most collective societies of the world currently appear extremely preoccupied with achievement. In an analysis of Chinese children's stories, for example, Blumenthal (1977) found that the most common behavior was achievement-oriented in nature, the second most frequent was altruism, and the third was social and personal responsibility. Among junior high school students in Japan, the motto "pass with four, fail with five" is now common. This refers to the fact that if one is sleeping 5 hr a night, he or she is probably not studying hard enough to pass exams. It appears, however, that this strong emphasis on achievement motivation is, in part, other motivated. It is motivated by a desire to fit into the group and to meet the expectations of the group. In the child's case,

the group is the family, and the child's mission is to enhance the social standing of the family by gaining admission to one of the top universities. The motive to achieve need not necessarily reflect a motive to achieve for "me" personally (Maehr & Nicholls, 1980). It can have social or collective origins. Children are striving to achieve the goals of others, such as family and teachers, with whom they are reciprocally interdependent. Consistent with this notion, Yu (1974) reported that the strength of achievement motivation was correlated positively with familism and filial piety. Striving for excellence necessarily involves some distancing or separating from some others, but the separation allows the child to properly accomplish the task of the student and thus to fulfill his or her role within the family.

Several studies by Yang (Yang, 1982/1985; Yang & Liang, 1973) have sought to distinguish between two types of achievement motivation: individually oriented and socially oriented. Individually oriented achievement motivation is viewed as a functionally autonomous desire in which the individual strives to achieve some internalized standards of excellence. In contrast, socially oriented achievement motivation is not functionally autonomous; rather, individuals persevere to fulfill the expectations of significant others, typically the family (Bond, 1986). With socially oriented achievement, when the specific achievement goal is met, the intense achievement motivation formerly evident may appear to vanish. This analysis indeed fits many anecdotal reports indicating that once admitted into the college of their choice, or hired by their preferred company, Japanese high school and college students are no longer particularly interested in achievement.

Once a new goal is established, of course, the socially oriented achievement motive may be easily reengaged by any figure who can serve as a symbolic substitute for family members. A longitudinal survey conducted in Japan over the last 30 years (Hayashi, 1988) has repeatedly shown that approximately 80% of the Japanese, regardless of sex, age, education, and social class, prefer a manager with a fatherlike character (who demands a lot more than officially required in the work, yet extends his care for the person's personal matters even outside of work) over a more Western-type, task-oriented manager (who separates personal matters from work and demands as much as, yet no more than, officially required). In a large number of surveys and experiments, Misumi and his colleagues (summarized in Misumi, 1985) have demonstrated that in Japan a leader who is both demanding and personally caring is most effective regardless of the task or the population examined (e.g., college students, white-collar workers, and blue-collar workers). This is in marked contrast to the major conclusion reached in the leadership literature in the United States, which suggests that leadership effectiveness depends on a complex interaction between characteristics of leaders, characteristics of followers, and, most important, on the nature of the task (Fiedler, 1978; Hollander, 1985). According to our analysis, in Japan as well as in other interdependent cultures, it is the personal attachment to the leader and the ensuing obligation to him or her that most strongly motivate people to do their work. Motivation mediated by a strong personal relationship, then, is unlikely to be contingent on factors associated with the specific task or environment.

The self-related motives. The motive to maintain a positive view of the self is one motive that psychologists since James (1890) through Greenwald (1980), Harter (1983), Steele (1988), and Tesser (1986) have assumed to be universally true. What constitutes a positive view of self depends, however, on one's construal of the self.[6] For those with independent selves, feeling good about oneself typically requires fulfilling the tasks associated with being an independent self; that is, being unique, expressing one's inner attributes, and asserting oneself (see Table 1). Although not uncontested, a reasonable empirical generalization from the research on self-related motives is that Westerners, particularly those with high self-esteem, try to enhance themselves whenever possible, and this tendency results in a pervasive self-serving bias. Studies with American subjects demonstrate that they take credit for their successes, explain away their failures, and in various ways try to aggrandize themselves (e.g., Gilovich, 1983; Lau, 1984; J. B. Miller, 1986; Whitley & Frieze, 1985; Zuckerman, 1979). Maintaining self-esteem requires separating oneself from others and seeing oneself as different from and better than others. At 4 years old, children already show a clear self-favorability bias (Harter, 1989). When asked to compare themselves with others with respect to intelligence, friendliness, or any skill, most children think they are better than most others. Wylie (1979) reported that American adults also consider themselves to be more intelligent and more attractive than average, and Myers (1987), in a national survey of American students, found that 70% of students believe they are above average in leadership ability, and with respect to the "ability to get along with others," 0% thought they were below average, 60% thought they were in the top 10%, and 25% thought they were in the top 1%. Moreover, as documented by Taylor and Brown (1988), among Americans, most people feel that they are more in control and have more positive expectations for themselves and their future than they have for other people. This tendency toward false uniqueness presumably derives from efforts of those with independent selves to maintain a positive view of themselves.

The motive to maintain a positive view of the self may assume a somewhat different form, however, for those with interdependent selves. Feeling good about one's interdependent self may not be achieved through enhancement of the value attached to one's internal attributes and the attendant self-serving bias. Instead, positive feelings about the self should derive from fulfilling the tasks associated with being interdependent with relevant others: belonging, fitting in, occupying one's proper place, engaging in appropriate action, promoting others' goals, and maintaining harmony (see Table 1). This follows for at least two reasons. First, people with interdependent selves are likely to be motivated by other-focused emotions, such as empathy and *oime* (i.e., the feeling of psychological indebtedness) and to act in accordance with the perceived needs and desires of their partners in social relations, and this may produce a social dynamic where individuals strive to enhance each other's self-esteem. In such reciprocal relationships, *other* enhancement could be more instrumental to self-enhancement because the latter are likely to isolate the individual from the network of reciprocal relationships. Second, self-esteem among those with interdependent selves may be based in some large measure on their capacity to

exert control over their own desires and needs so that they can indeed belong and fit in. As noted earlier (see also Weisz et al., 1984), such self-control and self-restraint are instrumental to the ability to flexibly adjust to social contingencies and thus are highly valued in interdependent cultures. Indeed, self-restraint together with flexible adjustment is often regarded as an important sign of the moral maturity of the person.

A developmental study by Yoshida, Kojo, and Kaku (1982, Study 1) has documented that self-enhancement or self-promotion are perceived quite negatively in Japanese culture. Second (7–8 years old), third (8–9 years old), and fifth graders (10–11 years old) at a Japanese elementary school were asked how their classmates (including themselves) would evaluate a hypothetical peer who commented on his own superb athletic performance either in a modest, self-restrained way or in a self-enhancing way. The evaluation was solicited on the dimension of personality ("Is he a good person?") and on the dimension of ability ("Is he good at [the relevant athletic domain]?"). As shown in Figure 4A, the personality of the modest peer was perceived much more positively than was that of the self-enhancing peer. Furthermore, this difference became more pronounced as the age (grade) of the respondents increased. A similar finding also has been reported for Chinese college students in Hong Kong by Bond, Leung, and Wan (1982), who found that individuals giving humble or self-effacing attributions following success were liked better than those giving self-enhancing attribution. The most intriguing aspect of the Yoshida et al. (1982) study, however, is their finding for the ability evaluation, which showed a complete crossover interaction (see Figure 4B). Whereas the second graders took the comment of the peer at face value, perceiving the self-enhancing peer to be more competent than the modest peer, this trend disappeared for the third graders, and then completely reversed for the fifth graders. Thus, the fifth graders perceived that the modest peer was more competent than the self-enhancing peer. These findings indicate that as children are socialized in an interdependent cultural context, they begin to appreciate the cultural value of self-restraint and, furthermore, to believe in a positive association between self-restraint and other favorable attributes of the person not only in the social, emotional domains but also in the domains of ability and competence. Although it is certainly possible for those with independent selves to overdo their self-enhancement (see Schlenker & Leary, 1982), for the most part, the American prescription is to confidently display and express one's strengths, and those who do so are evaluated positively (e.g., Greenwald, 1980; Mullen & Riordan, 1988).

Self- or other-serving bias. Given the appreciation that those with interdependent selves have for self-restraint and self-control, the various self-enhancing biases that are common in Western culture may not be prevalent in many Asian cultures. In an initial examination of potential cultural variation in the tendency to see oneself as different from others, Markus and Kitayama (in press) administered questionnaires containing a series of false-uniqueness items to large classes of Japanese college students in Japan and to large classes of American college

---

[6] For a compelling analysis of how self-esteem is related to culture, see Solomon, Greenberg, and Pyszczynski (in press).

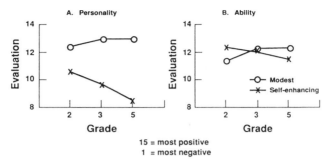

Figure 4. Mean evaluations by second, third, and fifth graders. (A: Personality of target person. B: Ability of target person. Drawn from results reported by Yoshida, Kojo, and Kaku, 1982.)

students in the United States. In both cases, the classes were chosen to be representative of university students as a whole. They asked a series of questions of the form "What proportion of students in this university have higher intellectual abilities than yourself?" There were marked differences between the Japanese and the American students in their estimations of their own uniqueness; the Americans displayed significantly more false uniqueness than the Japanese. American students assumed that only 30% of people on average would be better than themselves on various traits and abilities (e.g., memory, athletic ability, independence, and sympathy), whereas the Japanese students showed almost no evidence of this false uniqueness. In most cases, the Japanese estimated that about 50% of students would be better than they were or have more of a given trait or ability. This is, of course, the expected finding if a representative sample of college students were evaluating themselves in a relatively nonbiased manner.

In a recent series of studies conducted in Japan with Japanese college students, Takata (1987) showed that there is no self-enhancing bias in social comparison. In fact, he found just the opposite—a strong bias in the self-effacing direction. Participants performed several anagram problems that were alleged to measure memory ability. After completion of the task, the participants were presented with their actual performance on some of the trials and also the performance of another person picked at random from the pool of subjects who had allegedly completed the study. The direction of the self–other difference was manipulated to be either favorable or unfavorable to the subject. The dependent measures were collected in a private situation to minimize self-presentational concerns. Furthermore, because it was considered possible that the subjects might still believe they had a chance of seeing the other person afterward, in a followup study the "other person" was replaced with a computer program that allegedly simulated the task performance of the average college student.

Several studies (e.g., Goethals, 1989; Marks, 1984; Wylie, 1979) reveal that with respect to abilities, Americans typically give themselves higher ratings than they give to others. Thus, when a comparison with another is unfavorable to the self, the self-enhancement hypothesis predicts that Americans should

show little confidence in this estimate of their ability and seek further information. This, in fact, was the case in an American study by J. M. Schwartz and Smith (1976), which used a procedure very similar to Takata's (1987). When subjects performed poorly relative to another person, they had very little confidence in their own score. These American data contrast sharply with the Japanese data. Takata's study shows a tendency exactly the opposite of self-enhancement. Furthermore, the pattern did not depend on whether the comparison was made with another person or with the computer program. The Japanese subjects felt greater confidence in their self-evaluation and were less interested in seeking further information when they had unfavorable self-evaluations than when they had favorable ones. Similarly, Wada (1988) also reported that Japanese college students were convinced of their level of ability on a novel, information-integration task after failure feedback, but not after success feedback. These data suggest what might be called a modesty bias or an other-enhancement bias in social comparison.

A similar modesty bias among those with interdependent selves has also been suggested by Shikanai (1978), who studied the causal attribution for one's own success or failure in an ability task. Typically, American subjects believe that their internal attributes such as ability or competence are extremely important to their performance, and this is particularly the case when they have succeeded (e.g., Davis & Stephan, 1980; Gilmor & Reid, 1979; Greenberg, Pyszczynski, & Solomon, 1982; Weiner, 1986). In the Shikanai study, Japanese college students performed an anagram task. Half of them were subsequently led to believe that they scored better than the average and thus "succeeded," whereas the other half were led to believe that they scored worse than the average and thus "failed." Subjects were then asked to choose the most important factor in explaining the success or the failure for each of 10 pairs made from the 5 possible causes for performance (i.e., ability, effort, task difficulty [or ease], luck, and mental–physical "shape" of the day). Shikanai analyzed the average number of times each cause was picked as most important (possible minimum of 0 and maximum of 4). As shown in Figure 5, a modesty bias was again obtained, especially after success. Whereas failure was attributed mainly to the lack of effort, success was attributed primar-

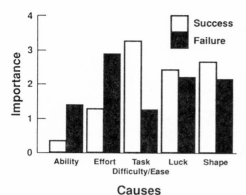

Causes

Figure 5. Mean importance rating given to each of five causes following success and failure. (Drawn from results reported by Shikanai, 1978.)

ily to the ease of the task. Furthermore, the potential role of ability in explaining success was very much downplayed. Indeed, ability was perceived to be more important after a failure than after a success, whereas task difficulty (or its ease) was regarded to be more important after a success than after a failure. Subsequent studies by Shikanai that examined attribution of success and failure of others did not find this pattern (Shikanai, 1983, 1984). Thus, the pattern of "modest" appraisal seems to be specific to the perception and the presentation of the self and does not derive from a more general causal schema applicable to both self and others. For others, ability is important in explaining success. Yoshida et al. (1982, Studies 2 and 3), who studied explanations of performance in a Japanese elementary school, found the tendency to de-emphasize the role of ability in explaining success as early as the second grade.

Observations of a tendency to self-efface, and not to reveal the typical American pattern of blaming others or the situation when explaining failure, have been made outside of the experimental laboratory as well. In a study by Hess et al. (1986), Japanese mothers explained poor performance among their fifth graders by claiming a lack of effort. In marked contrast, American mothers implicated effort in their explanations but viewed ability and the quality of the training in the school as equally important. This study also required the children to explain their own poor performance by assigning 10 points to each of five alternatives (ability, effort, training at school, bad luck, and difficulty of math). Japanese children gave 5.6 points to lack of effort, but American children gave 1.98 points. H. Stevenson (personal communication, September 19, 1989) noted that in observations of elementary school classrooms, Japanese teachers, in contrast to American teachers, rarely refer to differences in ability among their students as an explanation for performance differences, even though the range of ability as assessed by standardized tests is approximately the same. Those with interdependent selves thus seem more likely to view intellectual achievement not as a fixed attribute that one has a cer-

tain amount of, but instead as a product that can be produced by individual effort in a given social context.[7]

The nature of modesty. The exact nature of these modesty, self-effacing, or other-enhancing biases has yet to be specified. Perhaps those from interdependent cultures have simply learned that humility is the desired response, or the culturally appropriate response, and that it is wise not to gloat over their performance or to express confidence in their ability. This interpretation implies that the modesty biases observed in the studies described herein are primarily the result of impression management and that the subjects involved actually could have held different, perhaps opposite, beliefs about themselves and their ability. However, it is also possible that these other-enhancement biases reflect, or are accompanied by, psychologically authentic self-perceptions. There are two related possibilities consistent with this suggestion.

First, given the press not to stand out and to fit in, people in interdependent cultures may acquire through socialization a habitual modest-response tendency. In large part, it may be a function of the need to pay more attention to the other than to the self, just as the self-serving bias is believed to result from a predominant focus on the self (see Ross & Fletcher, 1985). Consequently, for those with interdependent selves, whenever certain aspects of self need to be appraised in public, a modest, self-effacing pattern of responses may occur spontaneously. Furthermore, this modesty can be motivated by many other-focused emotions that are central to the construal of self as an interdependent entity. From an independent viewpoint, such modesty seems false and the result of suppressing a "natural" pride in one's attributes. Yet, such pride is only natural within a view of the self as an independent entity. From an interdependent view, modest responses may be experienced quite positively and engender the pleasant, other-focused feelings that are associated with connecting and maintaining interdependence.

Such positive, other-focused feelings also may be responsible for the finding that Japanese students are more convinced of and more confident in their ability after failure than success. The satisfaction of doing well that can accompany good performance on a novel, decontextualized task may be mitigated by the threat of potential uniqueness and uncertainty about how to respond to it. Moreover, if a predominant basis of self-esteem is how well one fits in and preserves relationships and interpersonal harmony, then failing to distinguish oneself with a highly successful performance may not be particularly devastating.[8]

---

[7] Of course, because those in Asian cultures believe high ability to be a result of effort does not mean that they do not differentiate between ability and effort. In all likelihood, they believe that effort and ability are related in a multiplicative fashion to determine performance. Thus, for instance, in a recent study by Stipek, Weiner, and Li (1989), Chinese respondents reasoned, just as their American counterparts did, that if a person shows the same level of performance with much less effort expended on the task, the person must have a high level of the relevant ability. Our point is simply that those in Asian cultures believe that abilities are relatively more changeable over a long span of time through the effort the person expends.

[8] As noted, achievement may sometimes be construed as a means to complete one's interdependence, as may well be the case for a Japanese high school student who studies hard to gain admission to a prestigious college. In this case, failure may well be extremely troubling for those with interdependent selves.

Certainly it will not be as devastating as it is to the person whose self-esteem rests primarily on doing well individually and on separating oneself from others.

Second, among those with interdependent selves, there may not be an awareness of one's own ability in general or in the abstract. Instead, one's own ability in a given task under a given condition may be inferred from whatever cues are available in the specific situation in which the task is performed. And whatever is inferred in this way may be experienced as authentic and genuine. For example, upon receipt of feedback about their ability, interdependent selves may first attend and think not so much about their ability as about the approval or disapproval of the person who gives the feedback. If approval or disapproval can be strongly and unambiguously inferred, then the perception of approval or disapproval may provide a strong heuristic clue about ability; if one receives approval, one must have high ability in this situation, whereas if one receives disapproval, then one must have low ability in this situation. In the absence of a strong, enduring belief about one's ability in the abstract, such a heuristic may provide a subjectively genuine self-appraisal. This analysis also suggests why those with interdependent selves may be convinced of their low ability after a failure feedback to a much greater extent than they are convinced of their high ability after a success feedback. Because of the prevalent social norms for polite behavior in interdependent cultures, disapproval can be more unequivocally inferred from negative feedback than approval can be inferred from positive feedback.

These suggestions about the source of a modest self-appraisal have yet to be empirically tested, but they are worthy of careful inquiry because these forms of self-appraisal may be quite unique to interdependent cultures. On the basis of empirical evidence, however, this much seems clear: Those with interdependent selves will typically not claim that they are better than others, will not express pleasure in the state of feeling superior to others, and indeed may not enjoy it. A strong, pervasive motive for self-enhancement through taking personal credit for success, denying personal responsibility for failure, and believing oneself to be better than average may be primarily a Western phenomenon. It is akin to being the nail that stands out.

So far, the empirical evidence on cultural variation in self-related motives is limited largely to differences in self-enhancement versus other enhancement. However, other self-related motives, such as self-affirmation (Steele, 1988), self-verification (Swann & Read, 1981), and self-actualization (Maslow, 1954), may also differ across cultures in similar ways. A series of studies by Steele has shown that the negative psychological impact of one's own misdeed, blunder, or public embarrassment can be reduced once another, significant aspect of the self is activated and affirmed. Thus, one's threatened self-worth can be restored by a reminder of another, unthreatened aspect of the self (e.g., "I may not be athletic, but at least I'm creative"). To the extent that very different aspects of self are highly valued among those with interdependent selves, this process of self-affirmation may also differ. For those with independent selves it will be the internal attributes of self that may most effectively offset each other and reestablish threatened self-esteem, whereas for those with interdependent selves it may be the more public aspects of the self, like one's significant social roles, statuses, and important interpersonal relations, that must be focal in self-esteem mainte-

nance. Thus, self-affirmation for an interdependent self will require an opportunity to ensure that one is fitting in and engaging in proper action in a given situation.

In a similar vein, exactly what is verified in self-verification and what is actualized in self-actualization may also differ considerably across cultures. Currently, it is common to assume that individuals are motivated to verify and actualize an internally coherent set of attributes that they regard as significant. Our present analysis would imply, however, that people with interdependent selves may strive to verify and actualize the more public qualities of the self—the ones that allow them to conceive of themselves as respectable and decent participants in significant interpersonal relationships.

Furthermore, among those with interdependent selves, self-verification and self-actualization may even be achieved through the realization of some more general, abstract forms of relation, that is, one's relationship to or one's role in society or even in the natural or cosmic system. The self-description studies reviewed earlier suggest this possibility. In general, the self-descriptions of those with interdependent selves have been found to be quite concrete and situation specific (see Cousins, 1989). There is, however, one interesting, reliable exception to this. Subjects from Asian cultural backgrounds (presumably those with predominantly interdependent selves) often provide extremely global self-descriptions, such as "I am a unique creation," "I am a human being," "I am an organic form," and "I am a product of my environment." It could appear that these statements are too abstract to be informative in any pragmatic sense (Rosch, 1978). The lack of information contained in these descriptions, however, may be more apparent than real. Note that these global statements presuppose a view of the world as an encompassing whole in which these subjects perceive themselves to be a part or a participant. And for these subjects, it may be these relationships that must be verified and actualized.

We have suggested the different forms that some self-related motives might assume if they are based in an interdependent rather than an independent construal of self. Further empirical work is required to determine whether the types of self-related motives described herein are indeed as prevalent in Eastern interdependent cultures as they have been found to be in Western, particularly American, cultures. It could be that these self-relevant motives are not part of the set of universal individual strivings,[9] but instead an outgrowth of an independent self-system rooted in the press for separation and individuation.

Conclusions

We have described two divergent construals of the self—an *independent* view and an interdependent view. The most significant differences between these two construals is in the role that is assigned to the other in self-definition. Others and the surrounding social context are important in both construals, but for the interdependent self, others are included *within* the boundaries of the self because relations with others in specific

---

[9] It is intriguing that Murray's (1938) original study of motives, as well as Hilgard's (1953, 1987) update of it, did not include any of the self-focused motives that are so central to current research on the self.

contexts are the defining features of the self. In the words of Lebra (1976), the individual is in some respects "a fraction" and becomes whole when fitting into or occupying one's proper place in a social unit. The sense of individuality that accompanies an interdependent self includes an attentiveness and responsiveness to others that one either explicitly or implicitly assumes will be reciprocated by these others, as well as the willful management of one's other-focused feelings and desires so as to maintain and further the reciprocal interpersonal relationship. One is conscious of where one belongs with respect to others and assumes a receptive stance toward these others, continually adjusting and accommodating to these others in many aspects of behavior (Azuma, 1984; Weisz et al., 1984). Such acts of fitting in and accommodating are often intrinsically rewarding, because they give rise to pleasant, other-focused emotions (e.g., feeling of connection) while diminishing unpleasant ones (e.g., shame) and, furthermore, because the self-restraint required in doing so forms an important basis of self-esteem. Typically, then, it is others rather than the self that serve as the referent for organizing one's experiences.

With an independent construal of the self, others are less centrally implicated in one's current self-definition or identity. Certainly, others are important for social comparison, for reflected appraisal, and in their role as the targets of one's actions, yet at any given moment, the self is assumed to be a complete, whole, autonomous entity, without the others. The defining features of an independent self are attributes, abilities, traits, desires, and motives that may have been social products but that have become the "property" of the self-contained individual (see Sampson, 1989) and that are assumed to be the source of the individual's behavior. The sense of individuality that accompanies this construal of the self includes a sense of oneself as an agent, as a producer of one's actions. One is conscious of being in control over the surrounding situation, and of the need to express one's own thoughts, feelings, and actions to others, and is relatively less conscious of the need to receive the thoughts, feelings, and actions of others. Such acts of standing out are often intrinsically rewarding because they elicit pleasant, ego-focused emotions (e.g., pride) and also reduce unpleasant ones (e.g., frustration). Furthermore, the acts of standing out, themselves, form an important basis of self-esteem.

The Role of the Self

The relative importance that is accorded to others in these two construals has a wide range of psychological implications. In this article, we have outlined some of the cognitive, emotional, and motivational consequences of holding a view of the self that includes others and that requires others to define the self. Although a rapidly expanding volume of studies suggest that some aspects of cognitive functioning are relatively hardwired, many features of the way people perceive, categorize, or assign causality are probably not basic processes that derive in any straightforward way from the functioning of the human machinery or "hardware." Rather, these processes are to a large extent personal, reflecting the nature of the self that anchors them. Thus, they reflect all of those factors, including cultural aspects, that jointly determine the self. If one perceives oneself as embedded within a larger context of which one is an interde-

pendent part, it is likely that other objects or events will be perceived in a similar way. For example, a given event involving a particular actor will be perceived as arising from the situational context of which this actor is an interdependent part, rather than as stemming solely from the attributes of the actor. Or, in answering any question, one's first tendency may be to consider the particular social situation that is defined by the current interaction (e.g., teacher–student, worker–co-worker, and younger–elder) and then to gauge the range of responses that are most appropriate to this situation. These construals of self are probably abstracted through early patterns of direct interactions with parents and peers. The way people initially, and thus thereafter, most naturally or effortlessly perceive and understand the world is rooted in their self-perceptions and self-understandings, understandings that are themselves constrained by the patterns of social interactions characteristic of the given culture.

Consequences for Self-Processes

Our discussion of the cognitive, emotional, or motivational consequences has by no means exhausted the range of potential consequences of holding an independent or interdependent construal of the self. Consider first the set of processes connected by a hyphen to the self. It is reasonable to assume that all of these phenomena (e.g., self-affirmation [Steele, 1988], self-verification [Swann, 1983], self-consciousness [Fenigstein, Scheier, & Buss, 1975], self-control [Carver & Scheier, 1981], self-actualization [Maslow, 1954], or self-handicapping [Jones & Berglas, 1978]) could assume a somewhat different form depending on how interdependent the self is with others.

Self-esteem for those with an independent construal of the self depends on one's abilities, attributes, and achievements. The most widely used measure of self-esteem, the Rosenberg Self-Esteem Scale, requires the endorsement of items like "I am a person of worth" or "I am proud of my abilities." Self-esteem associated with an interdependent self could include endorsement of similar items, although what it means to be, for example, a person of worth could well have a different meaning. Or high self-esteem may be more strongly associated with an endorsement of items that gauge one's ability to read the situation and to respond as required. If this is the case, a threat or a challenge to the self may not come in the form of feedback that one is unlike a cherished conception of the inner or dispositional self (dumb instead of smart; submissive rather than dominant) but instead in terms of a threat of a disruption of, or a disconnection from, the relation or set of relations with which one forms an interdependent whole.

The focus on the distinction between independent versus interdependent selves has the potential to provide a means of integrating research on a large number of separate personality constructs. One of the significant distinctions that appears repeatedly throughout Western psychology reflects a variation among individuals in how tuned in, sensitive to, oriented toward, focused on, or concerned they are with others. The introversion–extraversion dimension reflects this difference, as does the inner-directed–outer-directed distinction (Reisman, Denney, & Glazer, 1950). Other related distinctions include high versus low self-monitoring (Snyder, 1979), personal identity versus social identity (Cheek, 1989; Hogan, 1975), public versus private self-consciousness (Fenigstein, 1984), social orientation versus individual orientation (Greenwald, 1980), collectivism–individualism (Hui, 1988; Triandis, 1989), and field independence–field dependence (Witkin & Goodenough, 1977). In fact, Witkin and his colleagues described a field-dependent person as one who includes others within the boundaries of the self and who does not make a sharp distinction between the self and others. Many of the empirical findings (described in Witkin & Goodenough, 1977; Witkin, Goodenough, & Oltman, 1979) about the interpersonal expertise and sensitivities of field-dependent people are similar to those described herein for people with interdependent selves.

Consequences for Social Psychological Phenomena

Other social behaviors may also depend on one's mediating model of the self (see Triandis, 1989, for a recent analysis of some of these effects). Thus, for one with an interdependent self, conformity may not reflect an inability to resist social pressure and to stick by one's own perceptions, attitudes, or beliefs (the defining features of the self). Instead, conformity to particular others with whom the other is interdependent can be a highly valued end state. It can signify a willingness to be responsive to others and to adjust one's own demands and desires so as to maintain the ever-important relation. The conformity observed for these subjects with interdependent selves when surrounded with others who form part of an important social unit, could well be much higher than typically observed. However, conformity to the desires and demands of those outside the important social unit or the self-defining in-group may not be required at all. Thus, for those with interdependent selves, a typical Asch-type conformity paradigm involving subjects and strangers as confederates may result in less conformity than typically observed in American studies.

Studies of other phenomena such as social facilitation or social loafing could also produce differential effects, depending on the self-systems of the subjects. Should those with interdependent construals of the self show pronounced social facilitation compared with those with individual selves? Or should those with interdependent selves be less susceptible to social loafing (decrements in performance when one's individual contribution to the group product cannot be identified; see Harkins, Latané, & Williams, 1980)? Our analysis is also relevant to two of the central problems in Western psychology—the inconsistency between attitudes and behavior and the inconsistency between personality and behavior. As we have noted, interdependent selves do not prescribe or require such a consistency between one's internal attributes and one's actions. Consequently, the press for consistency should be much less important and much less bemoaned when not observed. In fact, consistency from an interdependent perspective may reflect a lack of flexibility, insensitivity to the context, rigidity, or immaturity.

Further analysis of the consequences of different construals of the self may also prove fruitful in understanding some basic social psychological questions. Social psychologists report that people are enormously influenced by others, often to an extent that the investigators and certainly individuals themselves, find

unbelievable. People conform, obey, diffuse responsibility in a group, allow themselves to be easily persuaded about all manner of things, and become hopelessly committed to others on the basis of minimal action (e.g., see Myers, 1989). Even within highly individualist Western culture, most people are still much less self-reliant, self-contained, or self-sufficient than the prevailing cultural ideology suggests that they should be. Perhaps Western models of the self are quite at odds with actual individual social behavior and should be reformulated to reflect the substantial interdependence that characterizes even Western individualists. Sampson (1989) has recently argued that the reality of globalization and a shrinking world will force just such a rethinking of the nature of the individual.

Construals of the Self and Gender

Many important gender differences may also be linked to divergent construals of the self. Recent feminist theory on empathy suggests that relations have a power and a significance in women's lives that have gone largely unrecognized (e.g., Belenky, Clinchy, Goldberger, & Tarule, 1986; Jordan & Surrey, 1986; J. B. Miller, 1986; Stewart & Lykes, 1985). An awareness of and sensitivity to others is described as one of most significant features of the psychology of women. If this is the case, then self-esteem and self-validation should depend not only on being able to do a job well, but on fostering and sustaining relationships. As Gilligan (1986) claimed, a willingness and an ability to care are standards of self-evaluation for many women. This theoretical work is forging a new vision of dependence, one that is similar in many ways to some Eastern views. Being dependent does not invariably mean being helpless, powerless, or without control. It often means being interdependent. It thus signifies a conviction that one is able to have an effect on others and is willing to be responsive to others and to become engaged with them. In other words, there is an alternative to selfishness (which implies the exclusion of others) besides selflessness (which is to imply the exclusion of the self or self-sacrifice): There is a self defined in relationship to others (see Chodorow, 1978; Gilligan, 1982; Markus & Oyserman, 1988).

Difficult Questions

Carrying out the research necessary to systematically investigate the range of basic consequences of having one or another construal of the self raises several complex questions. Some of these we have only touched on. For example, a persistent issue is how deep or pervasive are these cultural differences? Are the observed differences primarily a reflection of differences in styles of behavioral expression, or do they also reflect differences in the phenomenology accompanying the behavior? If there are norms against the display or expression of anger, what happens to the nature of the felt anger? In other words, is it the case, as we suggest here, that these norms can sometimes be internalized to the extent that they determine the nature of one's experience? For example, a recent study by Bontempo, Lobel, and Triandis (1989) compared the public and private responses of individuals from a collectivist culture with those of individuals from an individualist culture. The researchers asked respondents to indicate how enjoyable it would be to engage in a time-consuming, individually costly behavior such as visiting a friend in the hospital. Only in the public condition did individualists claim that the behavior would be enjoyable. The collectivists, in contrast, claimed that the behavior would be enjoyable even when their responses were private.

The view that altruistic behaviors are only seemingly altruistic and that they are public actions without any subjective, private foundation can perhaps be traced to the insistence of Western psychologists on the internal attributes (feeling, thought, and traits) as the universal referents for behavior. They have thus understandably failed to attend to the possibility of the other as a referent for behavior, and thus to the possibility of other-focused emotions. There is, however, the possibility that such emotions can motivate genuine, other-oriented, altruistic behaviors, without any conscious, or even unconscious, calculation of individual payoff, and as such serve as the important glue of interdependent relationships.

Another thorny issue centers on the assessment of cultural differences. The use of introspective reports, for example, which are typically quite useful in the study of cognition, emotion, and motivation, may be problematic in cross-cultural research because within a given cultural context, people have little access to the absolute extent of their attention or responsiveness to others. This may explain, for example, why Triandis et al. (1988) found that those with collective selves do not report a greater than average awareness of or concern for the demands of others. Another persistent issue is that of translation and equating stimuli and questionnaires. Can psychologists readily assume that when an American and a Japanese use the word *embarrass* it indicates a similar emotional experience? Can they hypothesize, for example, that those with interdependent selves should show more high self-monitoring (i.e., attention to the behavior of others) than those with independent selves, and then assume that a translation of Snyder's (1979) scale into Japanese or Chinese will be sufficient to reflect these differences? One may even ask to what extent a construct such as self-monitoring can be unequivocally defined across different cultures with remarkably different construals of self.

In sum, we have argued that the view one holds of the self is critical in understanding individual behavior and also in understanding the full nature of those phenomena that implicate the self. A failure to replicate certain findings in different cultural contexts should not lead to immediate despair over the lack of generality of various psychological principles or to the conclusion of some anthropologists that culturally divergent individuals inhabit incomparably different worlds. Instead, it is necessary to identify the theoretical elements or processes that explain these differences. We suggest that how the self is construed may be one such powerful theoretical element.

References

Ainsworth, M. D. S., Bell, S. M., & Stayton, D. (1974). Infant–mother attachment and social development. In M. P. Richards (Eds.), *The introduction of the child into a social world* (pp. 95–135). London: Cambridge University Press.

Allen, N. J. (1985). The category of the person: A reading of Mauss's last essay. In M. Carrithers, S. Collins, & S. Lukes (Eds.), *The category of the person: Anthropology, philosophy, history* (pp. 26–35). Cambridge, England: Cambridge University Press.

Allport, G. W. (1937). *Personality: A psychological interpretation.* New York: Holt.

Atkinson, J. (Ed.). (1958). *Motives in fantasy, action and society.* New York: Van Nostrand.

Au, T. K. (1983). Chinese and English counterfactuals: The Sapir-Whorf hypothesis revisited. *Cognition, 15,* 162–163.

Au, T. K. (1984). Counterfactuals: In reply to Alfred Bloom. *Cognition, 17,* 289–302.

Azuma, H. (1984). Secondary control as a heterogeneous category. *American Psychologist, 39,* 970–971.

Bachnik, J. M. (1986). Time, space and person in Japanese relationships. In J. Hendry & J. Webber (Eds.), *Interpreting Japanese society: Anthropological approaches* (pp. 49–75). New York: Oxford University Press.

Baumeister, R. F. (1987). How the self became a problem: A psychological review of historical research. *Journal of Personality and Social Psychology, 52,* 163–176.

Beattie, J. (1980). Representations of the self in traditional Africa. *Africa, 50,* 313–320.

Belenky, M. F., Clinchy, B. M., Goldberger, N. R., & Tarule, J. M. (1986). *Women's ways of knowing: The development of self, voice, and mind.* New York: Basic Books.

Bellah, R. N., Madsen, R., Sullivan, W. M., Swidler, A., & Tipton, S. M. (1985). *Habits of the heart: Individualism and commitment in American life.* Berkeley, CA: University of California Press.

Bloom, A. (1981). *The linguistic shaping of thought.* Hillsdale, NJ: Erlbaum.

Bloom, A. (1984). Caution—the words you use may effect what you say: A response to Au. *Cognition, 17,* 281.

Blumenthal, E. P. (1977). Models in Chinese moral education: Perspectives from children's books. *Dissertation Abstracts International, 37*(10-A), 6357–6358.

Bond, M. H. (1986). *The psychology of the Chinese people.* New York: Oxford University Press.

Bond, M. H. (Ed.). (1988). *The cross-cultural challenge to social psychology.* Beverly Hills, CA: Sage.

Bond, M., Leung, K., & Wan, K.-C. (1982). The social impact of self-effacing attributions: The Chinese case. *Journal of Social Psychology, 118,* 157–166.

Bontempo, R., Lobel, S. A., & Triandis, H. C. (1989). *Compliance and value internalization among Brazilian and U.S. students.* Unpublished manuscript.

Briggs, J. (1970). *Never in anger.* Cambridge, MA: Harvard University Press.

Bruner, J. (1986). *Actual minds, possible worlds.* New York: Plenum Press.

Buck, R. (1988). *Human motivation and emotion* (2nd ed.). New York: Wiley.

Cantor, N., & Kihlstrom, J. (1987). *Personality and social intelligence.* Englewood Cliffs, NJ: Prentice-Hall.

Carver, C. S., & Scheier, M. F. (1981). *Attention and self-regulation: A control theory approach to human behavior.* New York: Springer-Verlag.

Cheek, J. M. (1989). Identity orientations and self-interpretation. In D. M. Buss & N. Cantor (Eds.), *Personality psychology: Recent trends and emerging directions* (pp. 275–285). New York: Springer-Verlag.

Chiu, L. H. (1972). A cross-cultural comparison of cognitive styles in Chinese and American children. *International Journal of Psychology, 7,* 235–242.

Chodorow, N. (1978). *The reproduction of mothering: Psychoanalysis and the sociology of gender.* Berkeley, CA: University of California Press.

Church, A. T. (1987). Personality research in a non-Western culture: The Philippines. *Psychological Bulletin, 102,* 272–292.

Cousins, S. (1989). Culture and selfhood in Japan and the U.S. *Journal of Personality and Social Psychology, 56,* 124–131.

Dalal, A. K., Sharma, R., & Bisht, S. (1983). Causal attributions of ex-criminal tribal and urban children in India. *Journal of Social Psychology, 119,* 163–171.

D'Andrade, R. (1981). The cultural part of cognition. *Cognitive Science, 5,* 179–185.

Darwin, C. R. (1896). *The expression of emotions in man and animals.* New York: Philosophical Library.

Davis, M. H., & Stephan, W. G. (1980). Attributions for exam performance. *Journal of Applied Social Psychology, 10,* 235–248.

De Riviera, J. (1984). The structure of emotional relationships. In P. Shaver (Ed.), *Review of personality and social psychology: Emotions, relationships, and health* (pp. 116–145). Beverly Hills, CA: Sage.

De Vos, G. A. (1973). *Socialization for achievement: Essays on the cultural psychology of the Japanese.* Berkeley: University of California Press.

De Vos, G. (1985). Dimensions of the self in Japanese culture. In A. Marsella, G. De Vos, & F. L. K. Hsu (Eds.), *Culture and self* (pp. 149–184). London: Tavistock.

Doi, L. T. (1973). *The anatomy of dependence.* Tokyo: Kodansha.

Doi, T. (1986). *The anatomy of self: The individual versus society.* Tokyo: Kodansha.

Dumont, L. (1970). *Homo hierarchicus.* Chicago: University of Chicago Press.

Durkheim, E. (1968). *Les formes elementaires de la vie religieuse* [Basic forms of religious belief] (6th ed.). Paris: Presses Universitarires de France. (Original work published 1912)

Ekman, P. (1972). Universals and cultural differences in facial expression of emotion. In J. K. Cole (Ed.), *Nebraska symposium on motivation* (pp. 207–283). Lincoln: University of Nebraska Press.

Elvin, M. (1985). Between the earth and heaven: Conceptions of the self in China. In M. Carrithers, S. Collins, & S. Lukes (Eds.), *The category of the person: Anthropology, philosophy, history* (pp. 156–189). New York: Cambridge University Press.

Erikson, E. (1950). Identification as the basis for a theory of motivation. *American Psychological Review, 26,* 14–21.

Fenigstein, A. (1984). Self-consciousness and the overperception of self as a target. *Journal of Personality and Social Psychology, 47,* 860–870.

Fenigstein, A., Scheier, M. F., & Buss, A. H. (1975). Public and private self-consciousness: Assessment and theory. *Journal of Consulting and Clinical Psychology, 43,* 522–527.

Festinger, L., & Carlsmith, J. M. (1959). Cognitive consequences of forced compliance. *Journal of Abnormal and Social Psychology, 58,* 203–210.

Fiedler, F. E. (1978). Recent development in research on the contingency model. In L. Berkowitz (Ed.), *Group processes* (pp. 209–225). New York: Academic Press.

Fiske, A. P. (in press). *Making up society: The four elementary relational structures.* New York: Free Press.

Fiske, S. T., & Taylor, S. E. (1984). *Social cognition.* Reading, MA: Addison-Wesley.

Frijda, N. H., Kuipers, P., & ter Schure, E. (1989). Relations among emotion appraisal and emotional action readiness. *Journal of Personality and Social Psychology, 57,* 212–228.

Galtung, J. (1981). Structure, culture, and intellectual style: An essay comparing Saxonic, Teutonic, Gallic and Nipponic approaches. *Social Science Information, 20,* 817–856.

Geertz, C. (1974). From the native's point of view: On the nature of anthropological understanding. In K. Basso & H. Selby (Eds.), *Meaning in anthropology* (pp. 221–237). Albuquerque: University of New Mexico Press.

Geertz, C. (1975). On the nature of anthropological understanding. *American Scientist, 63,* 47–53.

Gergen, K. J. (1968). Personal consistency and the presentation of self. In C. Gordon & K. J. Gergen (Eds.), *The self in social interaction: Classic and contemporary perspectives* (Vol. 1, pp. 299–308). New York: Wiley.

Gergen, K. J., & Gergen, M. M. (1988). Narrative and the self as relationship. In L. Berkowitz (Ed.), *Advances in experimental social psychology* (Vol. 21, pp. 17–56). New York: Academic Press.

Gilligan, C. (1982). *In a different voice: Psychological theory and women's development.* Cambridge, MA: Harvard University Press.

Gilligan, C. (1986). Remapping the moral domain: New images of the self in relationship. In T. C. Heller, M. Sosna, & D. E. Wellbery (Eds.), *Reconstructing individualism: Autonomy, individuality, and the self in Western thought* (pp. 237–252). Stanford, CA: Stanford University Press.

Gilmor, T. M., & Reid, D. W. (1979). Locus of control and causal attribution for positive and negative outcomes on university examinations. *Journal of Research in Personality, 13,* 154–160.

Gilovich, T. (1983). Biased evaluation and persistence in gambling. *Journal of Personality and Social Psychology, 40,* 797–808.

Goethals, A. (1989, April). *Studies of false uniqueness.* Paper presented at the Research Center for Group Dynamics Seminar, Institute for Social Research, University of Michigan, Ann Arbor, MI.

Greenberg, J., Pyszczynski, T., & Solomon, S. (1982). The self-serving attributional bias: Beyond self-presentation. *Journal of Experimental Social Psychology, 18,* 56–67.

Greenwald, A. G. (1980). The totalitarian ego: Fabrication and revision of personal history. *American Psychologist, 35,* 603–618.

Greenwald, A. G., & Pratkanis, A. R. (1984). The self. In R. S. Wyer & T. K. Srull (Eds.), *Handbook of social cognition* (Vol. 3, pp. 129–178). Hillsdale, NJ: Erlbaum.

Hall, C. S., & Lindzey, G. (1957). *Theories of personality.* New York: Wiley.

Hallowell, A. I. (1955). *Culture and experience.* Philadelphia: University of Pennsylvania Press.

Hamaguchi, E. (1985). A contextual model of the Japanese: Toward a methodological innovation in Japan studies. *Journal of Japanese Studies, 11,* 289–321.

Harkins, S. G., Latané, B., & Williams, K. (1980). Social loafing: Allocating effort or taking it easy? *Journal of Experimental Social Psychology, 16,* 457–465.

Harter, S. (1983). The development of the self-system. In E. M. Hetherington (Ed.), *Handbook of child psychology: Vol. 4. Socialization, personality, and social development* (4th ed.). New York: Wiley.

Harter, S. (1990). Causes, correlates and the functional role of global self-worth: A life span perspective. In R. J. Sternberg & J. Kolligian, Jr. (Eds.), *Competence considered* (pp. 67–97). New Haven, CT: Yale University Press.

Hayashi, C. (1988). *National character of the Japanese.* Tokyo: Statistical Bureau, Japan.

Head, H. (1920). *Studies in neurology.* London: Oxford University Press.

Heelas, P. L. F., & Lock, A. J. (Eds.). (1981). *Indigenous psychologies: The anthropology of the self.* London: Academic Press.

Hess, R., Azuma, H., Kashiwagi, K., Dickson, W. P., Nagano, S., Holloway, S., Miyake, K., Price, G., Hatano, G., & McDevitt, T. (1986). Family influences on school readiness and achievement in Japan and the United States: An overview of a longitudinal study. In H. Stevenson, H. Azuma, & K. Hakuta (Eds.), *Child development and education in Japan* (pp. 147–166). New York: Freeman.

Hilgard, E. R. (1953). *Introduction to psychology.* New York: Harcourt, Brace.

Hilgard, E. R. (1987). *Psychology in American: A historical survey.* New York: Harcourt Brace Jovanovich.

Hofstede, G. (1980). *Culture's consequences: International differences in work-related values.* Beverly Hills, CA: Sage.

Hogan, R. (1975). Theoretical egocentrism and the problem of compliance. *American Psychologist, 30,* 533–540.

Holland, D., & Quinn, N. (1987). *Cultural models in language and thought.* Cambridge, England: Cambridge University Press.

Hollander, E. P. (1985). Leadership and power. In G. Lindzey & E. Aronson (Eds.), *Handbook of social psychology* (Vol. 2, pp. 485–537). New York: Random House.

Holyoak, K. J., & Gordon, P. C. (1983). Social reference points. *Journal of Personality and Social Psychology, 44,* 881–887.

Hsu, F. L. K. (1975). *Iemoto: The heart of Japan.* New York: Wiley.

Hsu, F. L. K. (1981). *American and Chinese: Passage to differences.* Honolulu: University of Hawaii Press.

Hsu, F. L. K. (1985). The self in cross-cultural perspective. In A. J. Marsella, G. De Vos, & F. L. K. Hsu (Eds.), *Culture and self* (pp. 24–55). London: Tavistock.

Hui, C. H. (1988). Measurement of individualism–collectivism. *Journal of Research in Personality, 22,* 17–36.

Hwang, C. H. (1976). Change of psychological needs over thirteen years. *Bulletin of Educational Psychology* (Taipei), *9,* 85–94.

Iwao, S. (1988, August). *Social psychology's models of man: Isn't it time for East to meet West?* Invited address to the International Congress of Scientific Psychology, Sydney, Australia.

James, W. (1890). *Principles of psychology.* New York: Holt.

A Japanese supermarket in New Jersey. (1989, April 6). *New York Times,* p. 4.

Johnson, F. (1985). The Western concept of self. In A. Marsella, G. De Vos, & F. L. K. Hsu (Eds.), *Culture and self.* London: Tavistock.

Johnson-Laird, P. N. (1983). *Mental models: Towards a cognitive science of language, inference, and consciousness.* Cambridge, MA: Harvard University Press.

Jones, E. E., & Berglas, S. (1978). Control of attributions about the self through self-handicapping strategies: The appeal of alcohol and the role of underachievement. *Personality and Social Psychology Bulletin, 4,* 200–206.

Jordan, J. V., & Surrey, J. L. (1986). The self-in-relation: Empathy and the mother–daughter relationship. In T. Bernay & D. W. Cantor (Eds.), *The psychology of today's women* (pp. 81–104). Cambridge, MA: Harvard University Press.

Jöreskog, K. G. (1969). A general approach to confirmatory maximum likelihood factor analysis. *Psychometrika, 34,* 183–202.

Kakar, S. (1978). *The inner world: A psychoanalytic study of childhood and society in India.* Delhi, India: Oxford University Press.

Kennedy, S., Scheier, J., & Rogers, A. (1984). The price of success: Our monocultural science. *American Psychologist, 39,* 996–997.

Kiefer, C. W. (1976). The *danchi zoku* and the evolution of metropolitan mind. In L. Austin (Ed.), *The paradox of progress* (pp. 279–300). New Haven, CT: Yale University Press.

Kitayama, S., & Markus, H. (1990, August). *Culture and emotion: The role of other-focused emotions.* Paper presented at the 98th Annual Convention of the American Psychological Association, Boston.

Kitayama, S., Markus, H., Tummala, P., Kurokawa, M., & Kato, K. (1990). *Culture and self-cognition.* Unpublished manuscript.

Kondo, D. (1982). *Work, family and the self: A cultural analysis of Japanese family enterprise.* Unpublished doctoral dissertation, Harvard University.

Kuhn, M. H., & McPartland, T. S. (1954). An empirical investigation of self-attitudes. *American Sociological Review, 19,* 68–76.

Kumagai, H. A. (1981). A dissection of intimacy: A study of "bipolar posturing" in Japanese social interaction—*amaeru* and *amayakasu,*

indulgence and deference. *Culture, Medicine, and Psychiatry, 5,* 249–272.

Kumagai, H. A., & Kumagai, A. K. (1985). The hidden "I" in *amae:* "Passive love" and Japanese social perception. *Ethos, 14,* 305–321.

Laboratory of Comparative Human Cognition. (1982). Culture and intelligence. In R. J. Sternberg (Ed.), *Handbook of human intelligence* (pp. 642–719). London: Cambridge University Press.

Lau, R. R. (1984). Dynamics of the attribution process. *Journal of Personality and Social Psychology, 46,* 1017–1028.

Lebra, T. S. (1976). *Japanese patterns of behavior.* Honolulu: University of Hawaii Press.

LeDoux, J. E. (1987). Emotion. In V. Mount Castle (Ed.), *Handbook of physiology: Vol. 1. The nervous system* (pp. 419–459). Bethesda, MD: American Physiological Society.

Levy, R. (1973). *The Tahitians.* Chicago: University of Chicago Press.

Li, M.-C., Cheung, S.-F., & Kau, S.-M. (1979). Competitive and cooperative behavior of Chinese children in Taiwan and Hong Kong. *Acta Psychologica Taiwanica, 21,* 27–33. (From *Psychological Abstracts,* 1982, 67, Abstract No. 11922)

Liu, I. (1986). Chinese cognition. In M. H. Bond (Ed.), *The psychology of the Chinese people* (pp. 73–105). New York: Oxford University Press.

Liu, T. Y., & Hsu, M. (1974). Measuring creative thinking in Taiwan by the Torrance test. *Testing and Guidance, 2,* 108–109.

Lutz, C. (1988). *Unnatural emotions: Everyday sentiments on a Micronesian atoll and their challenge to Western theory.* Chicago: University of Chicago Press.

Lykes, M. B. (1985). Gender and individualistic vs. collectivist bases for notions about the self. In A. J. Stewart & M. B. Lykes (Eds.), *Gender and personality: Current perspectives on theory and research* (pp. 268–295). Durham, NC: Duke University Press.

Maehr, M. (1974). Culture and achievement motivation. *American Psychologist, 29,* 887–896.

Maehr, M., & Nicholls, J. (1980). Culture and achievement motivation: A second look. In N. Warren (Ed.), *Studies in cross-cultural psychology* (Vol. 2, pp. 221–267). New York: Academic Press.

Marks, G. (1984). Thinking one's abilities are unique and one's opinions are common. *Personality and Social Psychology Bulletin, 10,* 203–208.

Markus, H. (1977). Self-schemas and processing information about the self. *Journal of Personality and Social Psychology, 35,* 63–78.

Markus, H., & Kitayama, S. (in press). Cultural variation in the self-concept. In G. R. Goethals & J. Strauss (Eds.), *Multidisciplinary perspectives on the self.* New York: Springer-Verlag.

Markus, H., & Oyserman, D. (1988). Gender and thought: The role of the self-concept. In M. Crawford & M. Hamilton (Eds.), *Gender and thought* (pp. 100–127). New York: Springer-Verlag.

Markus, H., & Wurf, E. (1987). The dynamic self-concept: A social psychological perspective. *Annual Review of Psychology, 38,* 299–337.

Markus, H., & Zajonc, R. B. (1985). The cognitive perspective in social psychology. In G. Lindzey & E. Aronson (Eds.), *Handbook of social psychology* (3rd ed., pp. 137–230). New York: Random House.

Marriott, M. (1976). Hindu transactions: Diversity without dualism. In B. Kapferer (Ed.), *Transaction and meaning* (pp. 109–142). Philadelphia: Institute for Study of Human Issues.

Marsella, A., De Vos, G., & Hsu, F. L. K. (1985). *Culture and self.* London: Tavistock.

Maslow, A. H. (1954). *Motivation and personality.* New York: Harper.

Matsumoto, D. (1989). Cultural influences on the perception of emotion. *Journal of Cross-Cultural Psychology, 20,* 92–105.

Matsumoto, D., Kudoh, T., Scherer, K., & Wallbott, H. (1988). Antecedents of and reactions to emotions in the United States and Japan. *Journal of Cross-Cultural Psychology, 19,* 267–286.

Mauro, R., Sato, K., & Tucker, J. (1989). *A cross-cultural analysis of the cognitive dimensions of human emotion.* Unpublished manuscript, University of Oregon, Eugene, OR.

Mauss, M. (1985). A category of the human mind: The notion of person; the notion of self [W. D. Halls, Trans.]. In M. Carrithers, S. Collins, & S. Lukes (Eds.), *The category of the person: Anthropology, philosophy, history* (pp. 1–25). Cambridge, England: Cambridge University Press. (Original work published 1938)

McClelland, D. C. (1961). *The achieving society.* New York: Free Press.

Mead, G. H. (1934). *Mind, self and society.* Chicago: University of Chicago Press.

Miller, J. B. (1986). *Toward a new psychology of women* (2nd ed.). Boston: Beacon Press.

Miller, J. G. (1984). Culture and the development of everyday social explanation. *Journal of Personality and Social Psychology, 46,* 961–978.

Miller, J. G. (1988). Bridging the content–structure dichotomy: Culture and the self. In M. H. Bond (Ed.), *The cross-cultural challenge to social psychology* (pp. 266–281). Beverly Hills, CA: Sage.

Miller, J. G., Bersoff, D. M., & Harwood, R. L. (1990). Perceptions of social responsibilities in India and in the United States: Moral imperatives or personal decisions? *Journal of Personality and Social Psychology, 58,* 33–47.

Misumi, J. (1985). *The behavioral science of leadership: An interdisciplinary Japanese research program.* Ann Arbor, MI: University of Michigan Press.

Miyake, K., Campos, J., Kagan, J., & Bradshaw, D. L. (1986). Issues in socioemotional development. In H. Stevenson, H. Azuma, & K. Hakuta (Eds.), *Child development and education in Japan* (pp. 239–261). New York: Freeman.

Miyake, K., Chen, S., & Campos, J. J. (in press). Infant temperament, mother's mode of interaction, and attachment in Japan: An interim report. In I. Bretherton & E. Waters (Eds.), *Growing points of attachment theory and research. Monographs of the Society for Research in Child Development.* Chicago: University of Chicago Press.

Mook, D. G. (1986). *Motivation: The organization of action.* New York: Norton.

Moore, C. A. (Ed.). (1967). Introduction: The humanistic Chinese mind. In *The Chinese mind: Essentials of Chinese philosophy and culture* (pp. 1–10). Honolulu: University of Hawaii Press.

Moser, D. (1989). *If this paper were in Chinese, would Chinese people understand the title?* Unpublished manuscript, Indiana University.

Mullen, B., & Riordan, C. A. (1988). Self-serving attributions in naturalistic settings: A meta-analytic review. *Journal of Applied Social Psychology, 18,* 3–22.

Murray, H. A. (1938). *Explorations in personality.* New York: Oxford University Press.

Myers, D. (1987). *Social psychology* (2nd ed.). New York: McGraw-Hill.

Myers, D. (1989). *Social psychology* (3rd ed.). New York: McGraw-Hill.

Nakane, C. (1970). *Japanese society.* Berkeley: University of California Press.

Neisser, U. (1976). *Cognition and reality: Principles and implications of cognitive psychology.* San Francisco: Freeman.

Neisser, U. (1988). Five kinds of self-knowledge. *Philosophical Psychology, 1,* 35–59.

Northrop, F. S. C. (1946). *The meeting of East and West.* New York: Macmillan.

Pennebaker, J. W. (1982). *The psychology of physical symptoms.* New York: Springer-Verlag.

Phillips, D. C. (1976). *Holistic thought in social science.* Stanford, CA: Stanford University Press.

Plath, D. W. (1980). *Long engagements: Maturity in modern Japan.* Stanford, CA: Stanford University Press.

Reisman, D., Denney, R., & Glazer, N. (1950). *The lonely crowd: A study of the changing American culture.* New Haven, CT: Yale University Press.

Roland, A. (1988). *In search of self in India and Japan: Toward a cross-cultural psychology.* Princeton, NJ: Princeton University Press.

Rosaldo, M. Z. (1984). Toward an anthropology of self and feeling. In R. A. Shweder & R. A. LeVine (Eds.), *Culture theory: Essays on mind, self, and emotion* (pp. 137–157). Cambridge, England: Cambridge University Press.

Rosch, E. (1978). Principles of categorization. In E. Rosch & B. B. Lloyd (Eds.), *Cognition and categorization.* Hillsdale, NJ: Erlbaum.

Roseman, I. J. (1984). Cognitive determinants of emotion: A structural theory. In P. Shaver (Ed.), *Review of personality in social psychology* (Vol. 5, pp. 11–36). Beverly Hills, CA: Sage.

Ross, L. D. (1977). The intuitive psychologist and his shortcomings: Distortions in the attribution process. In L. Berkowitz (Ed.), *Advances in experimental social psychology* (Vol. 10, pp. 173–220). New York: Academic Press.

Ross, M., & Fletcher, G. J. O. (1985). Attribution and social perception. In G. Lindzey & E. Aronson (Eds.), *The handbook of social psychology* (3rd ed., Vol. 2, pp. 73–122). New York: Random House.

Russell, J. A. (1980). A circumplex model of affect. *Journal of Personality and Social Psychology, 39,* 1161–1178.

Russell, J. A. (1983). Pancultural aspects of the human conceptual organization of emotions. *Journal of Personality and Social Psychology, 36,* 1152–1168.

Russell, J. A., Lewicka, M., & Niit, T. (1989). A cross-cultural study of a circumplex model of affect. *Journal of Personality and Social Psychology, 57,* 848–856.

Sampson, E. E. (1985). The decentralization of identity: Toward a revised concept of personal and social order. *American Psychologist, 40,* 1203–1211.

Sampson, E. E. (1988). The debate on individualism: Indigenous psychologies of the individual and their role in personal and societal functioning. *American Psychologist, 43,* 15–22.

Sampson, E. E. (1989). The challenge of social change for psychology: Globalization and psychology's theory of the person. *American Psychologist, 44,* 914–921.

Sass, L. A. (1988). The self and its vicissitudes: An "archaeological" study of the psychoanalytic avant-garde. *Social Research, 55,* 551–607.

Scherer, K. R. (1984). Emotions as a multi-component process: A model and some cross-cultural data. In P. Shaver (Ed.), *Review of personality and social psychology: Emotions, relationships, and health* (pp. 37–63). Beverly Hills, CA: Sage.

Schlenker, B. R., & Leary, M. R. (1982). Social anxiety and self-presentation: A conceptualization and model. *Psychological Bulletin, 92,* 641–669.

Schwartz, J. M., & Smith, W. P. (1976). Social comparison and the inference of ability difference. *Journal of Personality and Social Psychology, 34,* 1268–1275.

Schwartz, S. H., & Bilsky, W. (1990). Toward a theory of the universal content and structure of values: Extensions and cross-cultural replications. *Journal of Personality and Social Psychology, 58,* 878–891.

Shaver, P., Schwartz, J., Kirson, D., & O'Connor, C. (1987). Emotion knowledge: Further exploration of a prototype approach. *Journal of Personality and Social Psychology, 52,* 1061–1086.

Shikanai, K. (1978). Effects of self-esteem on attribution of success–failure. *Japanese Journal of Experimental Social Psychology, 18,* 47–55.

Shikanai, K. (1983). Effects of self-esteem on attributions of others' success or failure. *Japanese Journal of Experimental Social Psychology, 23,* 27–37.

Shikanai, K. (1984). Effects of self-esteem and one's own performance on attribution of others' success and failure. *Japanese Journal of Experimental Social Psychology, 24,* 37–46.

Shweder, R. A. (1984). Preview: A colloquy of culture theorists. In R. A. Shweder & R. A. LeVine (Eds.), *Culture theory: Essays on mind, self, and emotion* (pp. 1–24). Cambridge, England: Cambridge University Press.

Shweder, R. A. (1990). Cultural psychology: What is it? In J. W. Stigler, R. A. Shweder, & G. Herdt (Eds.), *Cultural psychology: Essays on comparative human development* (pp. 1–46). Cambridge, England: Cambridge University Press.

Shweder, R. A., & Bourne, E. J. (1984). Does the concept of the person vary cross-culturally? In R. A. Shweder & R. A. LeVine (Eds.), *Culture theory: Essays on mind, self, and emotion* (pp. 158–199). Cambridge, England: Cambridge University Press.

Shweder, R. A., & LeVine, R. A. (Eds.). (1984). *Culture theory: Essays on mind, self, and emotion.* Cambridge, England: Cambridge University Press.

Smith, C., & Ellsworth, P. C. (1987). Patterns of appraisal and emotion related to taking an exam. *Journal of Personality and Social Psychology, 52,* 475–488.

Smith, R. J. (1983). *Japanese society: Tradition, self, and the social order.* Cambridge, England: Cambridge University Press.

Smith, R. J. (1985). A pattern of Japanese society: In society or knowledgement of interdependence? *Journal of Japanese Studies, 11,* 29–45.

Snyder, M. (1979). Self-monitoring process. *Advances in Experimental Social Psychology, 12,* 85–128.

Solomon, R. C. (1984). Getting angry: The Jamesian theory of emotion in anthropology. In R. A. Shweder & R. A. LeVine (Eds.), *Culture theory: Essays on mind, self, and emotion* (pp. 238–254). Cambridge, England: Cambridge University Press.

Solomon, S., Greenberg, J., & Pyszczynski, T. (in press). A terror management theory of social behavior: The psychological functions of self-esteem and cultural worldviews. *Advances in Experimental Social Psychology.*

Srull, T. K., & Gaelick, L. (1983). General principles and individual differences in the self as a habitual reference point: An examination of self–other judgments of similarity. *Social Cognition, 2,* 108–121.

Steele, C. (1988). The psychology of self-affirmation: Sustaining the integrity of the self. In L. Berkowitz (Ed.), *Advances in experimental social psychology* (Vol. 21, pp. 181–227). San Diego, CA: Academic Press.

Stevenson, H., Azuma, H., & Hakuta, K. (1986). *Child development and education in Japan.* New York: Freeman.

Stewart, A. J., & Lykes, M. B. (Eds.). (1985). Conceptualizing gender in personality theory and research. In *Gender and personality: Current perspectives on theory and research* (pp. 2–13). Durham, NC: Duke University Press.

Stigler, J. W., Shweder, R. A., & Herdt, G. (Eds.). (1990). *Cultural psychology: Essays on comparative human development.* Cambridge, England: Cambridge University Press.

Stipek, D., Weiner, B., & Li, K. (1989). Testing some attribution–emotion relations in the People's Republic of China. *Journal of Personality and Social Psychology, 56,* 109–116.

Stryker, S. (1986). Identity theory: Developments and extensions. In K. Yardley & T. Honess (Eds.), *Self and identity* (pp. 89–104). New York: Wiley.

Swann, W. B., Jr. (1983). Self-verification: Bringing social reality into

harmony with the self. In J. Suls & A. G. Greenwald (Eds.), *Psychological perspectives on the self* (Vol. 2, pp. 33–66). Hillsdale, NJ: Erlbaum.

Swann, W. B., Jr., & Read, S. J. (1981). Self-verification processes: How we sustain our self-conceptions. *Journal of Experimental Social Psychology, 17,* 351–372.

Tajfel, H. (1984). *The social dimension: European developments in social psychology.* Cambridge, England: Cambridge University Press.

Takata, T. (1987). Self-deprecative tendencies in self-evaluation through social comparison. *Japanese Journal of Experimental Social Psychology, 27,* 27–36.

Taylor, S. E., & Brown, J. D. (1988). Illusion and well-being: A social psychological perspective on mental health. *Psychological Bulletin, 103,* 193–210.

Tesser, A. (1986). Some effects of self-evaluation maintenance on cognition and action. In R. M. Sorrentino & E. T. Higgins (Eds.), *Handbook of motivation and cognition: Foundations of social behavior* (pp. 435–464). New York: Guilford Press.

Triandis, H. C. (1989). The self and social behavior in differing cultural contexts. *Psychological Review, 96,* 506–520.

Triandis, H. C., Bontempo, R., Villareal, M. J., Asai, M., & Lucca, N. (1988). Individualism and collectivism: Cross-cultural perspectives on self–ingroup relationships. *Journal of Personality and Social Psychology, 54,* 323–338.

Triandis, H. C., & Brislin, R. W. (Eds.). (1980). *Handbook of cross-cultural social psychology* (Vol. 5). Boston: Allyn & Bacon.

Triandis, H. C., Marin, G., Lisansky, J., & Betancourt, H. (1984). *Simpatía* as a cultural script of Hispanics. *Journal of Personality and Social Psychology, 47,* 1363–1375.

Veroff, J. (1983). Contextual determinants of personality. *Personality and Social Psychology Bulletin, 9,* 331–344.

Wada, M. (1988). Information seeking in self-evaluation of ability [Abstract]. In *Proceedings of Japanese Psychological Association Meeting, 52,* 222.

Waterman, A. S. (1981). Individualism and interdependence. *American Psychologist, 36,* 762–773.

Weber, M. (1958). *The Protestant ethic and the spirit of capitalism* (T. Parsons, Trans.). New York: Scribner.

Weiner, B. (1986). *An attributional theory of emotion and motivation.* New York: Springer-Verlag.

Weisz, J. R. (in press). Culture and the development of child psychopathology: Lessons from Thailand. In D. Cicchetti (Ed.), *Rochester Symposium on Developmental Psychopathology* (Vol. 1). New York: Cambridge University Press.

Weisz, J. R., Rothbaum, F. M., & Blackburn, T. C. (1984). Standing out and standing in: The psychology of control in America and Japan. *American Psychologist, 39,* 955–969.

White, G. M., & Kirkpatrick, J. (Eds.). (1985). *Person, self, and experience: Exploring Pacific ethnopsychologies.* Los Angeles: University of California Press.

White, M., & LeVine, R. A. (1986). What is an *Ii ko* (good child)? In H. Stevenson, H. Azuma, & K. Hakuta (Eds.), *Child development and education in Japan* (pp. 55–62). New York: Freeman.

Whitley, B. E., Jr., & Frieze, I. H. (1985). Children's causal attributions for success and failure in achievement settings: A meta-analysis. *Journal of Educational Psychology, 77,* 608–616.

Witkin, H. A., & Goodenough, D. R. (1977). Field dependence and interpersonal behavior. *Psychological Bulletin, 84,* 661–689.

Witkin, H. A., Goodenough, D. R., & Oltman, P. K. (1979). Psychological differentiation: Current status. *Journal of Personality and Social Psychology, 37,* 1127–1145.

Wylie, R. C. (1979). *The self-concept: Vol. 2. Theory and research on selected topics.* Lincoln: University of Nebraska Press.

Yamagishi, T. (1988). Exit from the group as an individualistic solution to the free-rider problem in the United States and Japan. *Journal of Experimental Social Psychology, 24,* 530–542.

Yang, K. S. (1981a). The formation of change of Chinese personality: A cultural–ecological perspective [In Chinese]. *Acta Psychologica Taiwanica, 23,* 39–56.

Yang, K. S. (1981b). Social orientation and individual modernity among Chinese students in Taiwan. *Journal of Social Psychology, 113,* 159–170.

Yang, K. S. (1982). Causal attributions of academic success and failure and their affective consequences. *Acta Psychologica Taiwanica, 24,* 65–83. (From *Psychological Abstracts,* 1985, *72,* Abstract No. 13126)

Yang, K. S. (1986). Chinese personality and its change. In M. H. Bond (Ed.), *The psychology of the Chinese people* (pp. 106–170). New York: Oxford University Press.

Yang, K. S., & Liang, W. H. (1973). Some correlates of achievement motivation among Chinese high school boys [In Chinese]. *Acta Psychologica Taiwanica, 15,* 59–67.

Yoshida, T., Kojo, K., & Kaku, H. (1982). A study on the development of self-presentation in children. *Japanese Journal of Educational Psychology, 30,* 30–37.

Yu, E. S. H. (1974). Achievement motive, familism, and *hsiao:* A replication of McClelland-Winterbottom studies. *Dissertation Abstracts International, 35,* 593A. (University Microfilms No. 74-14, 942)

Zuckerman, M. (1979). Attribution of success and failure revisited, or: The motivational bias is alive and well in attribution theory. *Journal of Personality, 47,* 245–287.

Received February 1, 1990
Revision received June 28, 1990
Accepted July 11, 1990 ■

1 The Ecology of Cognitive Development: Research Models and Fugitive Findings

Urie Bronfenbrenner
Cornell University

There is a text for this chapter. It is taken from the works of arguably the most cognitive of English 19th-century poets—Robert Browning. The familiar lines are from the imagined soliloquy of the painter, Andrea del Sarto:

> Ah, but a man's reach should exceed his grasp,
> Or what's a heaven for?

I am about to make that reach. My immodest aim is to move us toward a unifying theory of cognitive development. Whether the effort brings us closer to heaven or to hell remains to be seen. Perhaps the best I can hope for is to be left in limbo; by which I mean that the reader will reserve judgment, pending further developments. And, as becomes apparent here, further developments are indeed required. What I present here is less a theory than a theoretical perspective.

I must also admit my inadequacy to the task. The scope of that inadequacy becomes apparent once I lay out the dimensions of the endeavor. Under these circumstances, one may well ask why I presume to try. There is an answer. It is one that I give from time to time whenever I accept what I regard as our professional obligation to communicate to policymakers and to the public what we have learned from our research. I begin by acknowledging that there is much we do not know. I then go on to say: "We may not be very good, but, unfortunately we are the best there is." I then explain that, although we don't know many of the right answers, we do know how to ask the right questions. It is finding the right questions that is my aim here, not for social policy, but for science.

To turn to the task at hand. If the goal is to move toward a unifying theory, what is it that needs to be brought together? The first desired conceptual convergence is already implied in the first word of my title. Central to the ecological paradigm that I have proposed is a view of development as an evolving process of organism–environment interaction. I offer some notions about the nature of these interactive processes.

But the same ecological paradigm posits interaction not only between but also within each of its two constituent domains. Thus, the first comprehensive exposition of the theory, now a decade ago (Bronfenbrenner, 1979), was devoted primarily to what I then viewed as the necessary first task of constructing a differentiated conceptual framework for analyzing the developmental environment as a system of nested, interdependent, dynamic structures ranging from the proximal, consisting of immediate face-to-face settings, to the most distal, comprising broader social contexts such as classes and cultures. These constituent nested systems were also conceived as interdependent. In due course, I return to further consideration of these interactive contexts, and what I view as their critical role in cognitive development.

The task of constructing an analogous conceptual framework for analyzing the developmentally relevant characteristics of the person posed a different kind of challenge. Whereas in relation to the environment no such taxonomy existed, with respect to personal qualities the problem was one of overabundance. As I wrote in the 1979 monograph, in this domain, "the researcher has at his disposal a rich array of cognitive constructs, personality typologies, developmental stages, and dispositional tendencies, each equipped with ready-made measurement techniques" (pp. 16–17). How does one choose among them?

Nor is it simply a matter of too many disconnected concepts and variables. Beginning in the period after World War II, the discipline of psychology experienced rapid expansion accompanied by progressive, centrifugal fragmentation of the field, with the social-personality researchers ending up in one corner, cognitivists in another, and the biopsychologists in yet a third. Only in infancy could one still find an integrated organism, but the infant soon grew out of it, and conformed by breaking up into separate segments. For someone who had been trained in a generation taught that faculty psychology was extinct, it was an eerie feeling to see it coming back from the dead, but now garbed in modern dress, each faculty after its own fashion. (The cognitivists insisted on the most formal attire, but that was only after the learning theorists had lost their tails.)

And when that same someone was also attempting to develop an ecological paradigm for human development, the eerie feeling became an awesome obstacle. For within that paradigm, the human organism is conceived as a functional whole, an integrated system in its own right in which various psychological processes — cognitive, affective, emotional, motivational, and social — operate not in isolation, but in coordinated interaction with each other. From this perspective, research that deals only with one of these processes not only underspecifies the model, but risks overgeneralization of findings and, what is even more fatal for developmental science, can result in oversimplification and distortion of psychological realities.

The fact that intrapsychic processes are interdependent does not mean, however, that we cannot take one set of them, in this instance those in the cognitive domain, as a primary focus, and examine the systems in which they operate from that perspective.

Thus far, I have identified three systems — domains in which I attempt to effect some conceptual convergence. But there are still two other, often separated arenas that need to be linked — theory and reality.

It was Kurt Lewin who made the provocative assertion that "there is nothing so practical as a good theory." He then proceeded to demonstrate the validity of his claim by successfully applying his highly abstract, quasi-mathematical field theory to the design of effective programs of what he called "action research" for dealing with a variety of challenging problems confronting U.S. society, ranging from changing national food habits in order to cope with shortages during World War II (Lewin, 1943) to reducing racial tensions in New York City (Lewin, 1946).

I cite these examples in order to illustrate two essential requirements of a good theory: first, that it can be translated into concrete research designs; second, that it can be applied to the phenomena that it presumes to explain as they are manifested in the actual contexts in which they usually occur. Need I add that, in the case of human development, these are the contexts of everyday life.

I mention these two, perhaps seemingly obvious requirements, because not all developmental theories acknowledge their validity. Some remain so abstract as to defy unambiguous translation into research operations. Others confine such operations to settings so specialized as to preclude generalizing with any confidence to the environments in which human beings live and grow.

Accordingly, the fourth and final integration that this chapter attempts is that between theory and reality. Specifically, the abstract propositions or hypotheses I propose are followed, in due course, by the specification of research models appropriate for their operationalization in real-life settings.

Before beginning the integrative effort, I feel some obligation to try to forestall what I regard to be an altogether reasonable reaction to some of the material I present. Many psychologists are engaged in elegant research on specific domains of cognitive functioning, such as short-term memory, selective attention, encoding specificity, retrieval strategies, working memory capacity, and the like. These fundamental psychological processes may seem far removed from some of the topics I discuss here; for example, single-parent families, the relation between home and workplace peer groups, social class, ethnic differences in childrearing patterns, chaotic lifestyles, and, last but not least, the impact of historical events on life course development. One may well ask, with Hamlet, "What's Hecuba to me, or I to Hecuba?"

Or, in plainer English, "that's all well and good, but I am interested in basic cognitive processes that undergird behavior in all situations and are common to all human beings, no matter where they are. Moreover, these processes are best studied under uniform conditions, in which other factors are controlled, so that cognitive functions can become the principal focus of observation and interpretation."

To speak for myself, I regard scientific investigations of this kind as of the highest importance. But their very importance depends on the simultaneous conduct of scientific studies of the same processes in a rather different context; namely, in everyday life. Thus, it is equally essential for basic science that we understand how encoding operates in learning to read, how memory functions in courtroom testimony, or how selective attention operates in the family and the workplace, and how such processes develop.

But once the researcher admits to this broader kind of interest, the cognitive cat is out of the bag, no longer in a controlled environment, and other conditions and psychological processes come into play. In the case of species *Homo sapiens,* these conditions and processes become extraordinarily complex. This for two reasons. First, human beings are not only the partial products, but also the partial producers of their environments. Second, because of this species' unusual capacities for language and thought, the created environments are also symbolic in nature, and these symbols are not only cognitive in structure and content, they are also emotionally, socially, and motivationally loaded.

This means that once we as researchers become interested in cognition and cognitive development in everyday life, we need to develop more complex theoretical paradigms and research designs that are commensurate with the complexities of human beings functioning in human situations. This chapter represents one investigator's effort to contribute toward meeting this dual need. Need I add, there's a long way to go, and it will take many more of us, working from diverse perspectives, to make significant progress.

To turn, then, to the task at hand, I begin at the abstract level by presenting a formal definition of the general paradigm to which I have been referring. By now, the reader will find it somewhat familiar. The main reason for placing it before us is to provide the basis for expanding the terms in the definition.

Definition 1

The ecology of human development is the scientific study of the progressive, mutual accommodation, throughout the life course, between an active, growing, highly complex biopsychological organism — characterized by a distinctive complex of evolving interrelated, dynamic capacities for thought, feeling, and action — and the changing properties of the immediate settings in which the developing person lives, as this process is affected by the relations between these settings, and by the larger contexts in which the settings are embedded.

THE TRANSFORMED LEWINIAN EQUATION

When stated in this full, somewhat convoluted form, the definition hardly invites still further expansion and elaboration. But that is what has to be done if we are to translate the paradigm into operational form, as I promised to do. Paradoxically, we are going to accomplish that expansion first by contraction — that is, by collapsing each of the principal domains of the definition into a single term, and then expressing their relationship in the form of a seemingly simple equation. Those who are familiar with Lewinian theory, from which the ecological paradigm is in fact derived (Bronfenbrenner, 1977), will recognize this equation as a transformed and extended version of Kurt Lewin's (1935) classical formula:

$B = f(PE)$ [Behavior is a joint function of person and environment]

The transformation begins with a provocative substitution:

$D = f(PE)$ [Development is a joint function of person and environment]

The substitution is provocative because it focuses attention on the conceptual difference between "behavior" and "development." The key distinction lies in the fact that development involves a parameter not present in Lewin's original equation — the dimension of time.[1] The additional time factor can be represented in the formula itself by means of subscripts:

---

[1]The issue here raised is one that Lewin himself never directly addressed, or — perhaps putting it more precisely — it is an issue that he finessed by defining *psychology* as an ahistorical science. Lewin's failure to include this factor in his formula was not accidental, but deliberate. In his view, science was by its very nature ahistorical. In psychology as in physics, he argued, present events can be influenced only by forces existing in the present situation. In psychology, however, the latter consisted of what Lewin called the "psychological field"; that is, the situation defined not objectively but as perceived by the person. Hence, historical events could become "field forces" only to the extent that they existed in the person's present awareness. It was perhaps Lewin's predilection for the paradigms of physics, and their ahistorical orientation, that led him, and many other psychologists as well, to be far more interested in the study of behavior than of development. (For further discussion of these issues see Lewin, 1931, 1935.)

$$D_t = f_{(t-p)} \, (PE)_{(t-p)}$$

where t refers to the time at which a developmental outcome is observed and $t-p$ to the prior period, or periods, during which the joint forces, emanating both from the person and the environment, were operating over time to produce the outcome existing at the time of observation. To indicate that it is development in the cognitive sphere that is our primary focus of interest, we can add a second subscript c to the D on the left-hand side of the equation. It would not be appropriate, however, to add that same subscript to the term P on the right-hand side, for our ecological paradigm posits that other characteristics of the person, besides those that are strictly cognitive, play a critical role in shaping the course and content of intellectual development.

If we now relate this quasi-mathematical formula to the original definition for which it stands, it becomes apparent that the D term refers not to the phenomenon of development, but to its outcome at a particular point in time. Because as researchers we are concerned mainly not with effects, but with the processes that produce them, it is the right-hand side of the equation that identifies the focus of primary interest. Translating symbols into text, it defines development as the systematic study of the processes through which properties of the person and the environment interact to produce continuity and change in the characteristics of the person over the life course.

In the transformed equation, these processes are symbolized by the inconspicuous lower-case f, which stands for "function." As used by Lewin, this concept carries a signal implication that has also been incorporated in the ecological paradigm. Specifically, while indicating that the left-hand term of the equation is the joint result of some combination of forces arising from both the person and the environment, Lewin explicitly ruled out the assumption that the combination was only one of simple addition. The point is important because, despite occasional theoretical assertions to the contrary, many developmental investigations, including those in the cognitive sphere, employ analytic models that assume only *additive* effects; that is, the influences emanating from the person and the environment, as well as within each of these domains, are treated as operating independently of each other, with the net result estimated from an algebraic sum of the various factors included in the model.

Lewin used the terms *class-theoretical* and *field-theoretical* to distinguish between models in which the process was missing versus those in which it was explicitly defined. Class-theoretical models can provide useful information about how levels and modes of cognition vary in contrasting environments (e.g., cultures, social classes, types of family structure) and among groups with contrasting personal characteristics (such as gender and age). But they are limited by the fact that the processes producing the cognitive differences are left entirely open to speculation. For that reason, in the exposition that follows, I focus primarily on research that does not omit the f term in the revised Lewinian formula.

The last statement illustrates yet another feature of the transformed equation, one that provides a bridge from theory to practice. For, taken as a whole, that equation contains within it the full spectrum of operational models used and usable in developmental research. These models are defined by various combinations of the principal elements in the formula. Rather than present the full taxonomy in abstract terms, I identify each model as we encounter it in the context of specific studies. A systematic exposition and analysis of this taxonomy is presented elsewhere (Bronfenbrenner, 1988, 1989a).

PROPERTIES OF THE PERSON FROM AN ECOLOGICAL PERSPECTIVE

We are now in a position to expand each of the terms in the transformed Lewinian equation. Given our primary interest in the development of the cognitive characteristics of the *person,* it seems appropriate to begin the elaboration in that domain. However, because personal characteristics other than intellectual are presumed to play a critical role in affecting mental development, the appropriate question for guiding our inquiry becomes the following: What characteristics of the person are most likely to influence the course and outcome of subsequent cognitive development?

The results of a systematic effort to answer this question appear in a published chapter summarizing recent advances in theory and research on the ecology of human development (Bronfenbrenner, 1989a), and further work on this same theme is reported in Bronfenbrenner (1989b). For my purposes here, I focus on selected ideas and findings from both sources that seem especially relevant to research on cognitive functioning and growth.

As a first step in search of an answer to the question posed earlier, I undertook a survey of the relevant research literature to discover what personal characteristics had in fact been examined as possible antecedents of cognitive growth. Several instructive findings emerged from that inquiry. Perhaps most striking from a theoretical perspective was the discovery that the overwhelming majority of such characteristics are based on constructs that are *context free;* that is, the developmental attributes of the person are defined, both conceptually and operationally, without any explicit reference to the environment in which they occur, and are presumed to have the same psychological meaning irrespective of the culture, class, or setting in which they are observed, or in which the person lives. Examples of such noncontextual measures include conventional tests of intelligence and achievement, most analyses of Piagetian-type stages and processes, indices of cognitive style, or assessments based on theories of information processing and artificial intelligence.[2]

The tacit assumption of environmental generalizability, and I might add historical generalizability as well, underlay not only most cognitive studies but also, to no lesser degree, investigations of emotional, motivational, and social characteristics of the person—those traditionally included under the rubrics of temperament and personality. At the same time, the available empirical evidence does not support the underlying assumption (Bronfenbrenner, 1989a).

I describe some of this evidence later, but first I forestall a possible misinterpretation of the line of argument that I propose to take. In calling attention to the unwarranted assumptions typically underlying noncontextual assessments of cognitive and socioemotional functioning, I do not mean to imply that such indices are not appropriate in research based on an ecological paradigm. On the contrary, I contend here that the inclusion of such measures, and the constructs that underlie them, is invaluable in ecological research models when they also incorporate assessments of personal qualities based on context-oriented concepts.

An extended description and discussion of such concepts and associated measures appear in Bronfenbrenner (1989a). In this chapter, I focus on a particular type of context-oriented personal characteristic that, on theoretical grounds, emerges as most likely to exert influence on the course and content of subsequent psychological development in all spheres, including cognitive growth. I begin by tracing the theoretical roots of the concept.

Developmental Processes in the Immediate Setting

It is a first axiom of the ecological paradigm that development is an evolving function of person–environment interaction. It is a second axiom that, ultimately, this interaction must take place in the immediate, face-to-face setting in which the person exists, what I have referred to as the *microsystem*. What is the nature of the interactive developmental processes occurring at this, most proximal level of the environment?

Upon reviewing the research literature on this subject, I was somewhat surprised to discover that such processes are relatively few in number, at least in terms of existing knowledge. Essentially, they are of two general kinds. First, there are processes of social interaction between the developing person and one or more others, usually older, occasionally of the same age,

---

[2]For a fuller discussion of contextual versus noncontextual concepts of the person see Bronfenbrenner (1989a).

and rarely younger. (This unequal distribution reflects some tacit assumptions that can be called into question, but this is an issue beyond the scope of the present discussion.)

A second family of developmental processes has a rich theoretical base, but, as yet, is less grounded in systematic empirical work. I refer to the thesis, originally set forth by Lev Vygotsky (1978, 1979; Vygotsky & Luria, 1956) and subsequently further developed both by Soviet, and, more recently, U.S. scholars, that the principal engine of psychological, and especially cognitive, development is engagement in progressively more complex activities and tasks. Among Soviet psychologists, the key figure is Alexei Leont'ev (1932, 1959/1982, 1975/1978). On the U.S. side, the principal protagonists of activity theory have been Michael Cole, Barbara Rogoff, and James Wertsch (Cole, Gay, Glick, & Sharp, 1971; Laboratory of Comparative Human Cognition, 1983; Rogoff, 1990; Wertsch, 1985).

Given these two broad classes of proximal developmental processes, it appears plausible that, among the personal characteristics likely to be most potent in affecting the course of subsequent psychological growth, including cognitive development, are those that set in motion, sustain, and encourage processes of interaction between the person and two aspects of the proximal environment: first, the people present in the setting; and second, the physical and symbolic features of the setting that invite, permit, or inhibit engagement in sustained, progressively more complex interaction with and activity in the immediate environment.

In short, I propose that the attributes of the person most likely to shape the course of development, for better or for worse, are those that induce or inhibit dynamic dispositions toward the immediate environment. For great want of a better term I refer to such qualities as *developmentally instigative characteristics*.

Developmentally Instigative Characteristics

Four types of such characteristics are usefully distinguished. The first, and the one most often found in the research literature, consists of personal qualities that invite or discourage reactions from the environment of a kind that can disrupt or foster processes of psychological growth; for example, a fussy versus a happy baby; attractive versus unattractive physical appearance; or hyperactivity versus passivity. Half a century ago, Gordon Allport (1937), borrowing a term originally introduced by Mark A. May (1932), spoke of such characteristics as constituting *personality* defined in terms of its "social stimulus value." Accordingly, I refer to personal features of this kind as *personal stimulus characteristics*.

The developmental importance of such characteristics lies in the fact that they can set in motion reciprocal processes of interpersonal interaction, often escalating over time, that, in turn, can influence the course of development. Although a number of studies of the developmental effects of such characteristics have been conducted (e.g., Block, Buss, Block, & Gjerde, 1981; Caspi, Elder, & Bem, 1987, 1988; Gjerde, Block, & Block, 1986), almost all of them restrict themselves to looking for evidence for constancy over the years, while neglecting to investigate the complex of environmental forces and personal characteristics that produces departures from earlier patterns; this despite the fact that the data from such studies, when systematically examined, reveal that it is *discontinuity,* rather than continuity that is the rule.

The remaining three forms of developmentally instigative characteristics are probably even more powerful in their developmental impact, but have seldom been examined from this point of view. Attributes of this kind differ from social stimulus characteristics in the following respect: Rather than merely evoking a reaction from others, they share in common a differential responsiveness to, and an active, selective orientation toward, the environment—both social and physical. The three are distinguished from each other primarily on developmental grounds because they tend to emerge sequentially during childhood, and reflect progressively more complex levels of psychological functioning.

The first and earliest form of such an active orientation I call *selective responsivity.* It involves individual differences in reaction to, attraction by, and exploration of particular aspects of the physical and social environment.

The next type of developmentally instigative characteristic goes beyond individual differences in selective responsiveness to include the tendency to engage and persist in progressively more complex activities; for example, to elaborate, restructure, and even to create new features in one's environment—not only physical and social, but also symbolic. I refer to dispositions of this kind as *structuring proclivities.*

The transition from one to the other of these dynamic forms of psychological orientation during early childhood is illustrated in successive publications from a longitudinal study of infants being carried out by Leila Beckwith, Sarale Cohen, Claire Kopp, and Arthur Parmelee at UCLA (Beckwith & Cohen, 1984; Beckwith, Cohen, Kopp, Parmelee, & Marcy, 1976; Cohen & Beckwith, 1979; Cohen, Beckwith, & Parmelee, 1978; Cohen & Parmelee, 1983; Cohen, Parmelee, Beckwith, & Sigman, 1986). Their imaginative and careful work reveals a progressive sequence of such environmentally oriented orientations from birth through now 7 years of age. Thus, immediately after birth, infants are especially responsive to vestibular stimulation (being picked up and held in a vertical position close to the body), which has the effect of soothing the baby so that it begins to engage in mutual gazing; by 3 months, visual exploration extends beyond proximal objects, and it is the mother's voice that is most likely to elicit responses especially in the form of reciprocal vocalizations.

From about 6 months on, the infant begins actively to manipulate objects spontaneously in a purposeful way and to rearrange the physical environment. By now, both vocalization and gesture are being used to attract the parents' attention and to influence their behavior. In addition, there is a growing readiness, across modalities, to initiate and sustain reciprocal interaction with a widening circle of persons in the child's immediate environment. Here we see the emergence of what I have called "structuring proclivities."

A number of other investigations have yielded comparable findings, and have extended them to still other activity domains; for example, individual differences in children's creativity in play and fantasy behavior (Connolly & Doyle, 1984; MacDonald & Parke, 1984); Jean and Jack Block's longitudinal studies of "ego resiliency" and "ego control" (Block & Block, 1980; Block, Block, & Keyes, 1988); and, especially, the as-yet largely speculative ideas emerging from the field of behavioral genetics. Here, for example, Sandra Scarr (1988; Scarr & McCartney, 1983) and Robert Plomin (Plomin & Daniels, in press; Plomin & Nesselrode, in press) have proposed models emphasizing the emergence of genetically based dispositions to select, explore, conceptualize, elaborate, reorganize, and to construct physical, social, and symbolic environments both for the self and for the other. The possibility of developing reliable and valid measures of such dispositions does not seem to lie beyond the scope of our present knowledge and know-how.

The nature of the fourth and final class of developmentally instigative characteristics reflects the growing capacity and active propensity of children as they grow older to conceptualize their experience. It deals with what I have called *directive belief systems about the relation of the self to the environment,* or, for short, *directive beliefs.* The principal distinction between this construct and the familiar concepts of "locus of control" and "goal orientation" lies in the fact that they are conceived and analyzed not as developmental outcomes but as dynamic developmental forces interacting synergistically with particular features of the environment to produce successive levels of developmental advance or, as can and does happen in today's ecology, developmental stagnation and disarray.

These, then, are the four types of developmentally instigative characteristics that I propose for priority entry as "person" terms in ecological models for the study of human development. A number of them clearly involve cognitive components—especially in the case of structuring activities. But they also appear in the other spheres of selective responsiveness, belief systems, and even stimulus characteristics (e.g., the appearance of being intelligent or "not very bright").

In the analysis and interpretation of research findings in all four of these domains, it should be kept in mind that developmentally instigative characteristics do not *determine* the course of development; rather, they may be thought of as "putting a spin" on a body in motion. The effect of that spin depends on the other forces, and resources, in the total ecological system.

I am now in a position to provide a concrete illustration of my earlier assertion regarding the scientific importance of incorporating into ecological research designs more traditional, noncontextual measures of mental ability, cognitive process, as well as assessments of temperament or personality. All such assessments can be thought of as indexing *existing psychological resources and socioemotional states.* By combining such more static concepts with the dynamic element inherent in what I have called developmentally instigative characteristics, and then employing a design that can assess their joint, synergistic effect, the investigator can obtain a more powerful indication of the contribution of the person to his or her own development. To assess the one without the other treats the developing person either as devoid of psychological substance or of psychological force.

I refer to designs that meet the dual requirement as *force–resource* matches, or mismatches. An example might be the joint combination of levels of IQ with a measure of activity level. Where, as in this instance, one element of the dual combination involves a cognitive component, we can be more specific and speak of *force–resource cognitive matches.*

I recognize that what I am now expected to do is to provide some examples of the use of such force–resource combinations in developmental studies. But, alas, to date, I have not been able to find any. To be sure, there a number of investigations that have incorporated both static and dynamic personal characteristics in their research designs.[3] Upon closer examination, however, it becomes apparent that the design employed allowed only for assessment of additive effects thus providing no opportunity to detect any synergistic influence (positive or negative) of developmentally instigative

---

[3]Some outstanding examples are the California studies I have already mentioned, Helen Bee et al.'s (1982) investigation of cognitive and language development from early infancy through the preschool years, Lea Pulkkinen's (1982, 1983a, 1983b) follow-up studies in Finland of psychological development from preadolescence through early adulthood; and the work of Glen Elder and his colleagues (Elder, 1974; Elder & Caspi, 1988; Elder, Van Nguyen, & Caspi, 1985) in tracing the developmental consequences of the Great Depression of the 1930s now across three successive generations. All of these studies merit the attention of developmental researchers. Because some of the original sources are widely scattered, I have provided summaries in several of my own publications of the principal findings, and the research models employed (Bronfenbrenner, 1979, 1986, 1988, 1989a; Bronfenbrenner & Crouter, 1983).

characteristics on the realization of the person's psychological potential.[4]

Here then is a rich opportunity for future research in cognitive development. I suggest that the scientific yield of developmental investigations could be enhanced by incorporating prior assessments of such force-resource matches into the research design.

I hasten to add, however, that the sole inclusion of this one additional element is not likely to advance our knowledge by very much. Recall that, thus far, our concern has been focused on, and limited to, expansion only of the person term in the transformed Lewinian equation. Although context-oriented in their definition, developmentally instigative characteristics are properties of the person rather than of the external world. Unless appropriate complementary characteristics appear on the environmental side, we can hardly expect developmental processes to be substantially affected, one way or the other. It is time, then, to shift our attention to the environmental domain.

PROPERTIES OF CONTEXT FROM A DEVELOPMENTAL PERSPECTIVE

Paradoxically, the effort to identify and to conceptualize developmentally relevant characteristics of the person led to a reformulation of my earlier conceptualizations of the environment. Specifically, and not surprisingly, it suggested the notion of conceptualizing analogous developmentally instigative elements at each environmental systems level from the proximal to the distal.

The Microsystem in Action

For example, the definition of the *microsystem,* the immediate setting in which development ultimately occurs, has been expanded. The definition now reads as follows (I identify the added portion by italics):

Definition 2

A *microsystem* is a pattern of activities, roles, and interpersonal relations experienced by the developing person in a given face-to-face setting with particular physical, *social, and symbolic features that invite, permit, or inhibit, engagement in sustained, progressively more complex interaction with, and activity in, the immediate environment.*

---

[4]Should any colleagues know of any studies in which this scientific potential is realized, I would be most grateful for the information.

What does the addendum mean in concrete terms? The answer to this question is best conveyed by a concrete example. The research I have selected is well-suited for this purpose but unusual in its primary focus on the influence of' the physical environment on cognitive development, although social factors are also brought into the picture in its later phases.

A decade ago, Theodore Wachs (1979) published a seminal paper in which he showed a consistent pattern of relationships between certain features in the physical environment of infants during the first 2 years of life and their cognitive development over this same period. Assessments in the latter sphere were based on the child's level of performance on the Uzgiris–Hunt Infant Development Scale, which was developed in an attempt to operationalize and standardize the concepts and techniques used by Piaget. The instrument is comprised of eight separate subscales corresponding to particular Piagetian processes, such as object permanence, perspective-taking, foresight, and the understanding of causality. Physical features of the home environment were assessed by means of an inventory covering a wide range of specific items such as the following: noise level, space for movement, sheltered areas, audio-visual responsive toys, ratio of rooms to people, and decorations in the child's room. To permit examining effects over time, data were grouped into successive 3-month blocks. The results are reported in the form of correlations between characteristics of the environment at an earlier time and developmental status at a later time.

The results of the study were quite complex. For purposes here, I focus on those physical features in the environment that were most frequently and strongly associated with various types of cognitive functioning. These included a physically responsive environment, presence of sheltered areas, "the degree to which the physical set-up of the home permits exploration", low level of noise and confusion, and "the degree of temporal regularity" (p. 30).

These, then, are some of the developmentally instigative characteristics now not of the person, but of the physical environment. In summary, it would appear that two general aspects of the physical environment can affect the course of cognitive development—one for better, the other for worse. On the constructive side are objects and areas that invite manipulation and exploration, whereas the instability, lack of clear structure, and unpredictability of events undermines the developmental process. As I have documented elsewhere (Bronfenbrenner 1986, 1989a), these same two vectors continue to exert their opposing effects at older ages as well.

In the light of an ecological paradigm, the existence of these countervailing forces in the physical environment highlights the unexploited opportunity to carry out an even more revealing analysis of the influence of the physical environment on cognitive functioning. The two principal analytic techniques employed by Wachs—correlations and canonical analyses—are both based on an additive model. Implicit in such a model, both method-ologically and substantively, is the assumption that, in this particular instance, the positive environmental factors inviting manipulation and exploration have the same effect in a chaotic, unpredictable environment as in one that is stable; conversely, stable spatial and temporal structures exert the same positive influence whether or not the environment contains developmentally instigative features.

Such assumptions are of course incompatible with the ecological para-digm. To the contrary, the paradigm leads to the synergistic hypothesis that not only would developmentally instigative features of the surroundings have greater impact in more stable settings, but that they would also function as a buffer against the disruptive influences of disorganizing environments. Moreover, this hypothesis could be tested with data already available in Wach's pioneering research.

The availability of such data highlights another distinctive feature of Wach's investigation; namely, his use as a measure of developmental outcome of not a single composite index, like a Developmental Quotient (DQ), but a differentiated assessment of a pattern of cognitive processes.[5] Such assessments are of special importance for the simple reason that cognitive processes are in fact complex. Hence, as scientists, our primary interest should be not in the outcomes of cognition but the processes that produce it. Or, to put it another way, our main focus should be the forces that undergird the observed products, not the products themselves.

To return to—do I dare say—the "Wachsworks," thus far the findings discussed have dealt only with variations in cognitive outcomes as a function of characteristics of the environment. What about the character-istics of the person? Are all infants affected by the physical features of the setting in the same way? In his research design, Wachs included only one dimension in this person sphere, but its influence on the results, almost alone, justifies an affirmative answer to the question posed. All of his analyses were carried out separately for males and females.

In general, significant effects of the physical environment on cognitive development appeared much more frequently, and across a wider range of mental processes, for boys than for girls. Moreover, the features of the environment that were most influential differed in the two sexes. To quote Wachs' own summary:

Female development is positively and significantly related to long-term stimulus variety; males do not show this relationship. Male development is

---

[5] The progress that has been made over the past decade in the conceptualization and assessment of complex cognitive processes provides a far richer array of possible choices, both theoretically and operationally, than was available to Wachs at the time he carried out his pioneering study.

positively and significantly related to a lack of overcrowding; female development appears insensitive to overcrowding effects. Male development shows a significant and negative relationship between presence of noise-confusion in the home and the child's level of cognitive-intellectual development. For females the data indicate either non-significant or positive and significant relationships. (p. 28)

Beyond the specifics, we see here the beginnings of a general trend that continues to be observed through the life course, except perhaps during adolescence, when females begin to approach males in psychological vulnerability.[6]

In examining developmental outcomes as a joint function of characteristics of person and environment, Wachs' study provides an example of what I have called a *person–context* model. Because the processes underlying the observed variations in outcome remain unspecified, the design is still, in Lewin's terminology, only class-theoretical. Nevertheless, such models can often be useful, particularly in the early, exploratory phases of investigation. For example, at a purely descriptive level, the person–context model can be employed to identify what I have referred to as *ecological niches*. These are specified regions in the environment that are especially favorable or unfavorable to the development of individuals with particular personal characteristics. In the present instance, however, in which the design employed included only a single attribute of the person, gender — the niche is more properly called "sociological" than "ecological."

Yet, data already available within Wachs' study would in fact permit employing a highly informative person–context design that would define an entire complex of ecological niches, each associated with a possibly distinctive pattern of cognitive outcomes. The design becomes possible because the Uzgiris–Hunt assessment was administered every 3 months throughout the second year of life. Hence, the latest outcomes for the various Piagetian processes can be analyzed as a joint function of the corresponding earlier cognitive characteristics of the infant and of particular features of the environment. In the latter sphere, a 2×2 cross-classification by developmentally instigative versus disruptive elements of the setting would, in all likelihood, be particularly revealing.

But, at the moment, we can learn much more from Wachs' subsequent work. In his more recent investigations, he has focused on a question that is aptly defined by the title of an article currently in press: "Must the Physical Environment be Mediated by the Social Environment in Order to Influence Development: A Further Test" (Wachs, in press-a). Wachs addressed this problem in the following way. In addition to obtaining

---

[6]For evidence bearing on this point see Bronfenbrenner (1979, 1986, 1989a).

measures of the physical environment of the type previously described, he also administered an inventory of parental behaviors, such as responsiveness to the infant's vocalizations, involvement in child activities, and the use of parental coercion. Using the latter set as measures of the social environment, he then entered them first in a multiple regression equation, followed by assessments of the physical environment. The objective was to determine whether the latter still had a significant effect in predicting, in the first instance, language competence (Wachs & Chan, 1986), and then infant mastery as assessed in a play situation (Wachs, 1987a, 1987b).

In both cases, the effects of the physical environment — in particular, such factors as background noise, crowding, the presence of stimulus shelter, and the number of responsive toys — were still strong and significant after control for mother–child interaction. In the study of infant mastery, Wachs also reversed the order of entry, with the result that, after control for physical factors, socialization processes no longer exerted a significant effect, leading the author to conclude: "Contrary to what is commonly assumed, the physical environment acts to mediate the impact of the social environment and not the converse" (Wachs, 1987a, p. 10).

Is this interpretation correct? Yes and no. It is certainly the only conclusion that can be drawn, given the conceptual model implicit in the research design. An ecological paradigm, however, envisions a third possibility; namely, a synergistic interaction between the physical and social factors. Again, such a possibility could in fact be tested with the available data by comparing the effectiveness of socialization processes separately in developmentally "favorable" and "unfavorable" physical environments.[7]

The type of design I have just described represents a example of what I have called a *process-context model*. The defining property of such a model is that it allows for the possibility that the same process, in this instance, maternal socialization, may operate differently in different environments, here distinguished by the physical characteristics of the immediate setting. In this instance, the context in question is at the level of the *microsystem*. As I illustrate shortly, the same kind of design can also be applied in relation to broader environmental contexts.

At the moment, however, I want to take the opportunity provided by Wachs' pioneering research to introduce into his present model the missing domain of person characteristics. This is most easily done by asking whether the differing effects of context on the socialization process themselves vary as a function of the human beings involved. A simple way

---

[7]Wachs in fact envisaged such a possibility. In a footnote to his most recent published report he pointed out that "there is also [another] model, namely one in which physical and social factors co-vary in such a way that it is impossible to disentangle physical from social influences" (Wachs, in press-b).

to introduce this missing domain is to ask whether the effects of physical characteristics on socialization processes are the same for the two sexes. This is readily accomplished by analyzing the data separately for boys and girls, as Wachs had done in his first study.

Had he done so in the present investigation as well, we would have before us an example of a research design that incorporates all of the elements stipulated in the transformed Lewinian formula, and thereby implements an ecological paradigm of human development. I have referred to this type of design as a *process–person–context model*. Its distinctive feature is that it envisions the possibility of variation in developmental processes as a joint, synergistic function of the characteristics of the person and the environment.[8]

In surveying the research literature (Bronfenbrenner, 1989a), I found several studies that met at least the minimal requirements of this triadic model. None of them, however, focused explicitly on cognitive development, so that the best we will be able to do in this, our domain of primary interest is to infer the cognitive whole from its segmented parts. I proceed with that objective in view.

Note that in the examples examined thus far, the environment is limited to the immediate setting; that is, to a microsystem. We now move on to more distal ecological domains.

THE MESOSYSTEM: COGNITION FROM TWO SETTINGS

The next higher nested structure of the environment is briefly, accurately, but not very informatively defined as a system of two or more microsystems. Implied in this definition are a number of criteria. To begin with the most obvious, a mesosystem involves two or more settings frequented by the same person; for example, home and day care; day care and school, family and peer group, or, to mention a linkage of growing importance for both socioemotional and cognitive development in modern times from adolescence onward — school and workplace. Of course, higher order

---

[8]It is a further indication of Wachs' scientific prescience that he foresaw the possibility of applying just such a model in the next phase of his own research, and is currently engaged in that task. Witness the following concluding statement from an as-yet-unpublished symposium paper (Wachs, 1987b) in which he proposed:

> what I have called the "hypothesis of age specificity" — different aspects of the environment are relevant for development at different ages. I hope in the near future to begin to test this hypothesis, through longitudinal follow up of the comparative salience of physical and social environments upon the infant's development across the first few years of life.

combinations are also possible, but have rarely been investigated, despite the fact that, from a purely methodological perspective, this is not much more difficult to accomplish because, by definition, the same persons are to be found in every setting of a mesosystem. The difficulty derives from the fact that the mere availability of data from or about more than one setting is a necessary but not sufficient criterion for defining a mesosystem.

Perhaps the best way to convey the nature of the additional requirements is again by means of a concrete example. For this purpose I have selected a recent study by Laurence Steinberg and Bradford Brown (1989) that had as an explicit aim defining and demonstrating the distinctive properties of a mesosystem model. Substantively, the investigation focused on the impact on school performance of parental and peer support of academic activities and goals among high school students. The measure of parental influence was based on students' responses to items dealing with such topics as parental monitoring of homework and school performance, the parents' involvement in school programs and activities, and the encouragement of scholastic effort by their children. Corresponding items on the peer side concerned the importance to their close friends of doing well in school, of completing high school, and of going on to college.

Note that we are dealing here with the corresponding *belief systems* that each group holds with respect to the desirability and importance of academic achievement. Here we see another instance in which a characteristic originally defined as an attribute of the developing person becomes a feature of that person's environment when it occurs as a quality present in others who play an important role in that person's life.

The outcome measures in this study included a self-reported grade point average, a scale of how much the student enjoyed and valued going to school, and assessments of educational aspirations and expectations.

The authors' description of the conceptual model guiding their analysis of the data merits our attention. It reads as follows:

> There has been little effort among educational researchers devoted toward understanding how parental and peer influences may operate simultaneously, perhaps because the working model has been for so long that peer and parental influences are inherently antagonistic, with peers constantly trying to undermine the best intentions of parents. To draw on the ecological model proposed by Bronfenbrenner, most studies have focused on the microsystem of the family or the microsystem of the peer group, and not at all on the mesosystem that connects them . . . The failure of researchers to look jointly at parent and peer influences has left open important questions about (1) how these influences may themselves be related (e.g., are they antagonistic, independent, or synergistic) and (2) how the manner in which these influences are related may affect the school performance and behavior of the individual adolescent? (p. 2)

In sum, in terms of our ecological taxonomy, what the authors have described is a process–context model at the level of the mesosystem—a model that allows for detecting both additive and interactive effects of influences emanating from different settings, in this instance, home and school.

Application of the model yielded an informative set of findings, particularly with respect to synergistic effects. Contrary to the conventional cross-pressure conception of parent–peer influences, the data revealed no evidence of opposing forces. Without exception, both influences operated in the same direction, but the relative power of parents versus peers varied depending on the outcome being assessed. Thus, parents exerted a more powerful effect on educational aspirations, but peers were more influential with regard to day-to-day attitudes and behaviors. Finally, with respect to academic achievement, parental support was particularly effective when peers were nonsupportive, but this pattern was not reciprocated; that is, peers did not exhibit a special compensatory power when parental support was not forthcoming.

In their conclusion, the authors argued for a reorientation in the way in which researchers have usually conceived of multiple environmental influences on development: "Our position is that we may oversimplify the picture by continuing to study one [source of] influence without taking account of the concurrent influence of the other." In their view, the failure to assess synergistic processes contributes to the typically low proportion of explained variance in developmental research.

In the light of these considerations, we are now in a position to formulate a more expanded definition of the mesosystem as follows:

Definition 3

A *mesosystem* comprises the linkages and processes taking place between two or more settings containing the developing person. *Special attention is focused on the synergistic effects created by the interaction of developmentally instigative or inhibitory features and processes present in each setting.*

In the light of this definition it should be noted that, strictly speaking, Steinberg and Brown's design does not meet full the requirements for a mesosystem model, since no direct evidence is provided regarding the nature of the synergistic process taking place. For example, is it a function of the degree of face-to-face interaction between parents and peers, the knowledge and perceptions that each group has about the other, or the extent to which parents, peers, or children themselves play a role in the choice of their children's companions?

The preceding series of questions illustrates one of the fringe benefits of ecological models; namely, their capacity to call attention to missing elements and ambiguities of interpretation characterizing a particular set of findings or plan of investigation.

But, to return to our principal concern, what are the implications of a mesosystem model for research on cognitive development. Although it would be an interesting possibility, the implications do not lie primarily in the fact that one could substitute for, or perhaps more informatively add to, the single outcome measure in the above design, assessments of theoretically more significant and complex cognitive outcomes. Rather, in my view, the richest scientific opportunity involves introducing measures of actual processes of cognitive development as the operators in the mesosystem equation. There are a number of theoretically enticing possibilities. My own first choice derives from Vygotsky's theory of *activities* as the principal agents of cognitive development. Thus, I would propose introducing as the process element in the research design indices of the extent to which parents and peers have engaged the young person in reciprocal activities that become progressively more complex versus those that do not involve this presumed developmentally instigative characteristic.

It would also be important to introduce another factor not included in Steinberg and Brown's design; namely, the gender of all parties involved. Particularly in adolescence, there is reason to expect that the same processes of cognitive socialization may operate differently for males and females and for same-sex versus cross-sex dyads. Note that, once sex of subject is included in the design, we again have met the minimal criteria for a process–person–context model. The model would of course becomes far more informative if the entries in the person domain went beyond gender to include psychological characteristics, in particular those that I have referred to as developmentally instigative. If the beliefs of others regarding the importance of intellectual activities influence cognitive growth, then surely researchers should not overlook the person's own beliefs in that domain.

Although the research of Steinberg and his colleagues provides an excellent illustration of a mesosystem model at work, the use of grade point average as an outcome measure hardly qualifies it as truly a study of cognitive development. That criterion is clearly met, however, in a recent report by Morrison (1988) on the "five to seven shift." In order to investigate the factors involved in this phenomenon, Morrison employed a mesosystem design with the following features. The sample of Canadian 5- to 7-year-olds was divided into those whose birthdays fell just short of the cutoff for school, and those who were just beyond it. The two groups, equated on IQ and a variety of other cognitive measures assessed at age 5, differed in mean age by about 1 month, but the older group started schooling 1 year sooner. Both samples were then followed up at 1-year intervals over a 3-year period in order to evaluate progress in a variety of cognitive acquisitions, between ages 5 and 7, in such areas as concept formation, clustering, and short-term memory. Morrison then applied a regression model to evaluate the relative contributions of age, baseline competence scores, and schooling to the outcome measures. The results revealed that, at each follow-up, it was mainly the specific processes associated with formal schooling, and not age or prior cognitive status, that accounted for the observed gains in specific mental processes.

We see here the effects of transition to a new setting on changes in cognitive growth that cannot be attributed solely to maturation. At the same time, however, the analytic model is restricted only to the detection of additive effects. By treating both age and prior mental status as moderator variables, it would have been possible to determine the extent to which the cognitive advance instigated by transition to a new cognitive environment was in fact a joint, synergistic function of the interaction between the developmentally instigative properties of the new setting and the developmentally instigative characteristics of the person.

DEVELOPMENT AND THE BROADER ENVIRONMENT: EXOSYSTEMS AND MACROSYSTEMS

Thus far, we have been concerned only with developmental influences occurring in environments in which the developing person is actually present, and can therefore directly interact with persons and objects in the immediate situation. We turn next to environmental contexts in which such direct interaction is not possible because the environments are, so to speak, "out of reach."

Such environments are of two kinds. Because the next research example illustrates both, I present and discuss their definitions one after the other.

Definition 4

The *exosystem* comprises the linkages and processes taking place between two or more settings, at least one of which does not contain the developing person, but in which events occur that indirectly influence processes within the immediate setting in which the developing person lives.

An example for the developing child is the link between the home and the parent's workplace. Examples for developing adults are the link between the home and their children's peer group, or, increasingly nowadays, between the home or workplace and government offices, whatever they may be.

The definition of the *macrosystem* is more complex, both in relation to other, lower order systems, and to the original conceptualization of this overarching sphere. As in the case of the microsystem, this expansion was a by-product of the effort to develop a more differentiated conceptualization of the characteristics of the developing person, and it was again a Vygotskian construct that paved the way.

In his theory of the "sociohistorical evolution of the mind," Vygotsky (1978; Vygotsky & Luria, 1956) had set forth the thesis that the potential options for individual development are defined and delimited by the possibilities available in a given culture at a given point in its history. This means, for example, that, in a particular microsystem setting — such as the home, day-care setting, the classroom, or the workplace — the structure and content of the setting, and the forms of developmental process that can, or cannot, take place within it, are to a large extent provided by the culture, subculture, or other macrosystem structure in which the microsystem is embedded. It follows that the definition of the macrosystem should include provision for recognizing the developmentally instigative properties that it incorporates. Accordingly, the original definition of the macrosystem has been expanded as follows:

Definition 5

The *macrosystem* consists of the overarching pattern of micro- meso- and exosystems characteristic of a given culture, subculture, or other extended social structure, *with particular reference to the developmentally instigative belief systems, resources, hazards, lifestyles, opportunity structures, life course options and patterns of social interchange that are embedded in such overarching systems.*

This expanded definition has powerful implications at two levels, first in the realm of developmental theory, second with respect to research design. On the former count, the reformulation implies that developmental processes are likely to differ significantly — not just statistically, but substantively — from one macrosystem to the next. With respect to study design, it argues for the representation of characteristics of the culture, or of any other macrosystem, as a critical feature of research models for investigating developmental processes and outcomes — particularly, I would add, in the cognitive sphere.

Evidence in support of both of these propositions appears in the remaining research examples that I now present. It is my hope that that evidence is both provocative and persuasive.

The "Children of the Great Depression" Grow Up

The first example is the most recent report (Elder & Caspi, 1990) from Glen Elder's classic, now three-generational study of children from families that were either smitten or spared by the Great Depression of the 1930s (Elder, 1974). The present report describes and analyzes the contrasting life trajectories of the two ·original cohorts born, respectively, in the early and late 1920s. Its key feature derives from the fact that the two groups encountered profound social changes at *different ages and stages* of their lives. The second and more traditional design element was the inclusion of two control groups, corresponding in age, but differing in the fact that the family breadwinner (in those days, of course, the father) did not lose his job during the Great Depression.

The developmental consequences by young adulthood of this historical accident can be summarized as follows. The impact of economic hardship differed substantially as a joint function of both the subjects' gender, and the age at which their families suffered a heavy financial blow, with the most severe effects on psychological development occurring for boys who were of preschool age when the Depression hit. The principal shortcoming of this investigation from the perspective of our particular interest is the absence of more specific information about cognitive functioning at adolescence. From the perspective of an ecological model, one would expect that differences in cognitive processes and outcomes would have paralleled those documented in other psychological domains.

What is available, however, is information about the sequential chain of events and processes that produced the paradoxical pattern of developmental outcomes during adolescence and youth. Any summary does injustice both to the richness of the findings and the theoretical and methodological sophistication of the authors. In the hope that justice will be blind in this instance, I proceed to commit the crime of condensation, relying heavily on the authors' own words.

The "changes in family relationship initiated by men's loss of earning and job" . . . increased the relative power of mothers, reduced the level and effectiveness of paternal control, and diminished the attractiveness of fathers as role models" (p. 223). These changes in turn resulted in greater family "tensions, conflicts, and violence" with particular disruption of psychological functioning of men as manifested in "heavy drinking, emotional depression and health disabilities," and – what proved to be especially critical for the development of their young sons – "inconsistent discipline of their children" (p. 224).

Why were older sons not affected? Again in the authors' words: "As the economy worsened, their family hardship meant adult-like responsibilities . . . These, in turn, "enhanced their social and family independence and reduced their exposure to conflict and turmoil in the home." As a net result, "boys were more apt to aspire to grown-up status and to enter adult roles" (pp. 224–225).

And what about the girls? Theirs is a different story. To the extent that they were affected at all, the pattern by age appears to have been reversed, with the older ones at greater risk than the younger. The authors remain strangely silent about this phenomenon and its possible origins — at least in this report.[9]

The story for boys, however, not only continues but has a surprise happy ending. Contrary to the expectation that "young boys in the Great Depression would become a blighted generation, . . . these dire predictions did not materialize . . . By mid-life, a surprising number of men from deprived backgrounds were successful by any standard of work achievement." Employing a series of what we have called process–person–context models, the investigators trace the developmental turnabout to what they refer to as three "institutionalized transitions that involve new responsibilities and privileges"; the three are military service (mainly in the Korean War), further education, and marriage.

What were the distinguishing characteristics of the three settings in this sequential mesosystem that set in motion and propelled a rising developmental trajectory? Necessarily skipping over details of both substance and method, I can point to a complex of interactive factors and processes common to each of the three sequential experiences of those males who, seemingly fated for failure by early deprivation, emerged successful as adults. These critical elements were: an opportunity for a fresh start, the presence of both challenge and support in a new, complex but stable environment; and recognition of accomplishment in the new setting. Engagement in challenging activities within such settings ultimately led to greater competence on the job, more rapid advancement, and higher levels of occupational attainment. Especially significant is the fact that, in each setting, the presence of these elements had a greater positive effect on those men who had experienced deprivation in childhood.

Where do the characteristics of the person appear in this equation? In this domain the results are not as explicit, but some evidence nevertheless exists for the influence of individuals on their own development. The evidence is most clearly detectable in the contrasting characteristics of the young men from deprived and nondeprived backgrounds who entered the armed

---

[9]In an earlier study, Elder, Downey, and Cross (1986) traced the psychological life course of the women in the younger cohort — those who were young children when their families experienced the brunt of the Great Depression. On the basis of their findings, the authors suggest the following explanation for the absence of disruptive developmental effects of economic hardship in this group: "Mothers' and daughters' reactions to financial stress and its consequences facilitate an affectionate relationship that may protect daughters from the harshness of their fathers" (p. 162).

No comparable analysis appears to have been carried out for the older female cohort nor has there been any systematic assessment of differences in developmental processes and trajectories occurring for women in the two cohorts.

services. To begin with, those from disadvantaged backgrounds were not only more likely to enlist, but also to do so at an earlier age — that is, in late adolescence. Moreover, compared with age-mates from nondeprived backgrounds, they had ranked "at the bottom on adolescent competence," having emerged as less "assertive, self-confident, and ambitious" on previously administered project measures. The authors interpret such findings as indicating a "link between an incompetent self (e.g., feelings of self-inadequacy, passivity, lack of self-direction) and the appeal of military options" (p. 35). The investigators go on to state:

> Moreover, the early joiners, most of whom came from deprived circumstances, represent the clearest case of personal choice in the self-selection process. Indeed, their early history of social and psychological disadvantage suggests a self-enhancing choice; the selection of a setting may act as a resocialization mechanism . . . In particular, we have some evidence that military service, and especially early entry into the service, was a "planned" decision among adolescents from deprived circumstances . . . Indeed, cognate research on the psychological risk associated with early adversity (e.g., Rutter & Quinton, 1984) suggests that the tendency to exercise foresight or planning in dealing with environmental challenges is a critical variable in the reduction of continued risk. (pp. 35–38)

The foregoing pattern constitutes an example of what I referred to earlier as a "force–resource" combination of personal characteristics, in which cognitive capacities are coupled with developmentally instigative dynamic dispositions. Moreover, here we observe the formation of this fusion as a developmental change instigated by exposure to stress. One recalls the words of the Banished Duke in the Forest of Arden:

> Even till I shrink with cold, I smile and say
> 'This is not flattery; these are counsellors
> That feelingly persuade me what I am.'
> Sweet are the uses of adversity;
> Which, like the toad, ugly and venomous,
> Wears yet a precious jewel in his head.

> *As You Like It* (Act ii, Scene i)

Note where the hard-won gains of adversity are stored, and where they shine.

Still, is there any evidence that the subsequent experience in young adulthood brought about advancement not only in the outer world, but also in the inner workings of the mind? The results of identical psychological tests administered in adolescence and at mid-life revealed that early enlistees from deprived backgrounds, when compared both to late entrants and nonveterans, had, over the intervening period, felt less inadequate, less submissive, and more socially competent.

The developmental effects of further education were even more pronounced. Deprived men who had gone on to college surpassed nondeprived graduates on a wide range of psychological characteristics, including "achievement via independence," "flexibility," "spontaneity," "intellectual efficiency," and "ability to influence others." Although no comparable measures for the same set of variables were available from a prior period, the sharp contrast with the psychological picture presented by the same group at adolescence constitutes powerful evidence for the occurrence of substantial developmental changes as a function of having experienced and surmounted difficulties earlier in life.

Not, however, without some cost. In their final analysis, the authors obtained self-reports from their subjects on health and psychosomatic problems experienced at mid-life, including, for example, chronic fatigue, energy decline, and heavy drinking. Not only were such difficulties more prevalent among men from deprived families, but problems were reported most often by those from disadvantaged circumstances who had gone on to college, thus opening the way to higher job status. The authors report these findings under a poignant heading: "The Hidden Stresses of Surmounting Early Deprivation."

In the work of Elder and Caspi, we have followed development through space and time, and observed the forces and processes that resulted both in constancy and change in the characteristics of the person over the life course. But in one of the three principal domains of the ecological paradigm, the only *cited evidence* has been indirect rather than direct, more inferred than observed. I refer to the presumably ever-present influence of the person on his or her own development. The inference was mainly based on the general knowledge that the majority of early entrants into the military during the period in question were volunteers, and hence, by enlisting, had taken an action of their own free will.

In the preceding paragraph, I have italicized the words *cited evidence* for a reason. In point of fact, additional data were available in earlier assessments that could have been analyzed to provide direct evidence on the issue. These data were of two kinds. First, there were the personality scales administered at adolescence. Among the qualities assessed were the following: *goal orientation* (e.g., "high aspirations"), *self-inadequacy* (e.g., "feels victimized,"), and *social competence* (e.g., "arouses liking and acceptance"). You will recognize in these several of what I distinguished earlier as developmentally instigative characteristics. In addition, in the analyses conducted at mid-life, one of the control factors used as a covariate in assessing the effects of military schooling and adult education was "childhood IQ."

Taken together, these two types of personal characteristics meet the requirements of what I have called a "force–resource" model—one that provides not only an index of capacity but also of motivational disposition. Thus, the availability of these two types of data for the childhood period makes it possible to examine the extent to which the "recovery" from psychological disarray during adolescence was a function not only of environmental opportunities but also of the earlier cognitive assets and dynamic orientations of the individual.

The preceding "Gedanken Experiment" provides a cogent illustration of the importance and use of conventional measures of intelligence in developmental research; namely, they provide an assessment of the intellectual resources that the person has at his or her disposal for future development. The fact that such resources themselves reflect the prior interactive influence of both genetic and environmental factors underscores their theoretical significance and, hence, the desirability of including them in the research design not merely as controls, but as critical elements in the person domain of the ecological paradigm.

But even without the additional evidence that such an analysis would have provided, the scientific life story of the "Children of the Great Depression" is well worth the researcher's reading. For the particular purposes of this chapter, it provides a rich and powerful example of the uses and yield of a process–person–context model, here applied not only through the life course, but across generations. At a more concrete level, it illustrates three basic premises of an ecological paradigm of human development. The first is the principle that development occurs through organism–environment interaction through the life course, here manifested in the successive interplay between environmental stresses, personal initiatives, and environmental opportunities. Second, the study demonstrates the systems character of the human organism functioning as a whole, as reflected in the intricate interdependence of psychological resources and dispositions within the person—cognitive, emotional, motivational, and social. Finally, the research reveals the dynamic interactive relationships operating between different environmental contexts, beginning with the dramatic impact of an exosystem event—the unemployment of the father—on developmental processes taking placing in the child's family, and then radiating outward into the mesosystems of school, military service, college, and workplace, with processes and outcomes in each setting influencing their sequelae in the next.

This entire succession of environments, however, is itself embedded within the overarching context of U.S. society and its distinctive institutions, customs, belief systems, and aspirations at particular critical points in its history—economic depression, war, and economic recovery. In the words of my Cornell colleague, Rick Canfield, what Glen Elder and his coworkers have done is to deliver on Vygotsky's promissory note without ever having owed the debt. Thus, their work gives elegant support to the central Vygotskian thesis that psychological development, in all its aspects, is a function of the flow of history. In accord with that thesis, the generalization applies in the cognitive realm no less, and perhaps even more, than in any other. Across the centuries, there have been special ecologies for special qualities of mind — ancient Athens, Alexandria in its prime, Florence in the 15th century, Paris in the 19th, Vienna before World War II, and Berlin just afterward — not to mention New Orleans, and the College of the City of New York!

But once again, Hecuba, what is she to us and we to her? What do such flowery, and far-flung generalizations have to do with what we do? I feel reasonably confident that few are about to undertake a three-generational study across historical time. Nevertheless, the work of Elder and of other students on the impact of human history on human development does have relevance for what we do. That relevance lies in the fact that whatever psychological phenomena we study, they are taking place in a particular culture at a particular point in its history. And, as we have seen in Elder's work, the prevailing Zeitgeist of the period leaves a heavy imprint not only on what people think, but how they learn to think — or don't. As I have argued elsewhere (Bronfenbrenner, 1989c), the present crises we are experiencing in American education and, thereby, in the competence of the American work force, have to do not only with the way in which we teach reading, math, and science in our schools. The roots of our difficulties lie in the major changes now taking place in American society that are disruptive to basic processes of psychological development and cognitive growth.

The preceding considerations raise a question regarding the extent to which the processes, contexts, and personal characteristics analyzed by Elder and his colleagues — all of these distinctively American in provenience — are applicable to other groups with differing cultural and historical roots and experiences. The concluding section of this exposition addresses this challenging query.

Cognition in Context: Microprocesses in a Macroworld

Some provocative findings bearing on this issue appear in a series of reports from two collaborative programs of research, one directed by Sanford Dornbusch at Stanford University (Dornbusch, 1987; Dornbusch, Ritter, Leiderman, Roberts, & Fraleigh, 1987), and the other by Laurence Steinberg, now at Temple University (Mounts, Lamborn, & Steinberg, 1989; Steinberg, 1989). Taking as their point of departure the classic and frequently replicated work of Diana Baumrind (1966, 1971, 1973; Baumrind & Black, 1967) on the superiority of authoritative parental styles over either permissiveness or authoritarianism, both groups of investigators have demonstrated that these parental patterns have reliably and dramatically different, and even contradictory, cognitive effects when separately examined in the four principal ethnic groups in the United States—Whites, Blacks, Hispanics, and Asians.

Specifically, in the first study, Dornbusch and his colleagues (1987), using a sample of over 7,000 adolescents enrolled in six high schools in the San Francisco Bay area, found that, in general, effects on school performance of parental style, and of other family characteristics as well, were substantially greater for Whites than for any other ethnic group. The Whites benefited most from an authoritative style, suffered most from authoritarianism, and were the only group to show a significant negative impact of permissiveness. Next in line were the Asians, but, for them, only authoritarianism produced its expected negative impact, albeit in reduced measure; permissiveness had virtually no influence; and the effect of the presumably optimal authoritative style was not only nonsignificant, but negative in sign. By contrast, for Hispanics, authoritativeness showed some positive effects, but authoritarianism exerted an influence only on females. Finally, for Black students, none of the three parenting styles produced any significant effects whatsoever.

I should mention that the foregoing pattern of results was still in evidence after control for the following possibly confounding factors: the subject's gender and age (14 to 18), parental education (used as a measure of social class), and family structure (one-parent, two-parent, and stepparent). The control was accomplished by calculating separate regression equations within each ethnic group, with all of these factors entered as covariates. (By now, I expect at least a raised eyebrow—if not a rising gorge—when you hear that familiar formula.)

Steinberg and his colleagues obtained essentially the same pattern of varying, if not contradictory, findings. Perhaps the most striking paradox is one highlighted by Dornbusch. Taking note of "the success of Asian children in our public schools," he commented as follows:

> Compared to whites, Asian high school students of both sexes reported that their families were higher on the index of authoritarian parenting and lower on the index of authoritative parenting. Yet, counter to the general association of such parenting patterns to grades, the Asians as a group were receiving higher grades in school. In addition, while authoritarian parenting was significantly associated with lower grades among Asians, there was no significant relation between grades and the other two parenting styles. This article concludes with more questions than answers in examining Asian parenting practices and school performance (Dornbusch et al., 1987, p. 1256)

How is one to make sense of such a melange? Why should the "same" socialization processes lead to such contrasting outcomes in different ethnic groups? An ecological paradigm reminds us that the outcome of a socialization process depends not only on the behavior of the socializing agent but also on the characteristics of the person being socialized. This was indeed the line of inquiry pursued by both groups of investigators. The personal quality selected for study was what Steinberg called "work orientation" measured by the adolescent's response on a 10-item scale composed of statements like the following: "Hard work is never fun," "I finish any work I'm supposed to do." Note that this concept meets the criteria for what I have referred to as a developmentally instigative characteristic of the person.

The measure of work orientation turned out to be a stronger and more consistent predictor of academic performance than was parental style. But, as with parental behavior, the effect of this orientation was more powerful among White and, especially, Asian students, and weakest among Blacks.

Equally instructive was an analysis reported by Dornbusch (1987) in which both types of variables were combined, thus permitting an assessment of their possible synergistic effects in what I have referred to as a force-resource cognitive match. The pattern of results provides a clue to the mystery, but, I hasten to add, hardly a solution. Specifically, work orientation predicts grades more strongly among families in which the level of authoritarianism is low, with the difference being most pronounced among Blacks — especially Black males — and least evident among Whites — especially females. In fact, for sons of Black authoritarian parents, the correlation is not merely low and unreliable, but negative in sign. Black families also obtained the highest scores on authoritarianism, and Whites the lowest.

What these findings suggest is that processes of cognitive socialization, and perhaps cognitive outcomes as well, may have different meanings, and hence different effects, in different contexts. In the absence of further clues from the data, we do well, in the continuing effort to detect some order in the seeming confusion, to return once again to the formal definition of the macrosystem and its specification of the critical elements embedded in this overarching environmental context. These specified elements are: developmentally instigative belief systems, resources, hazards, lifestyles, opportunity structures, life course options, and patterns of social interchange.

One has only to see the words "resources" and "hazards" — let alone "opportunity structures" and "life course options" — to recognize that these are hardly equally distributed among the four ethnic groups as they exist in the American context.

But is not that problem met by the control variables included in the analysis — in particular, social class (as indexed by parental education) and the three forms of family structure—two-parent, one-parent, and stepparent? After all, the analytic procedure employed, that of treating such potentially confounding factors as covariates in a regression analysis, is one of the most generally accepted and widely used in contemporary social research.

By now it should be clear that the answer to the question just posed is a resounding "No!". Moreover, the rejection is based even more on theoretical than on methodological grounds. The grounds are that such an analytic procedure assumes that the processes or relationships under investigation operate in the same way and to the same degree with respect to each of the person and context characteristics being treated as control variables. It is precisely this assumption, of course, that is challenged by an ecological paradigm. It is not that the paradigm rejects the assumption as invalid a priori, but rather that the question always be left open both as a theoretical and empirical possibility.[10]

In the present instance, it is highly unlikely that the assumption is justified, primarily for the reason that both of the contexts in question possess the stipulated characteristics of macrosystems. To be more precise, the intersection of the two domains with each other defines a set of four macrosystems, each of which meets the formal definition. As I have written elsewhere:

> In the last analysis, what defines the macrosystem is sharing in common the kinds of characteristics specified in the above formal definition (i.e., similar belief systems, social and economic resources, hazards, life styles, etc.). *From this perspective, social classes, ethnic or religious groups, or persons living in particular regions, communities, neighborhoods, or other types of broader social structures constitute a subculture whenever the above conditions are met.* This also means that, over the course of history, newly evolving social structures have the potential of turning into subcultures by developing a characteristic set of values, life style, and other defining features of a subculture. A case in point is what can now justifiably be called the "institution of single parenthood" in the United States. Another example is the two-wage-earner family. From an ecological perspective, the test of whether the label of subculture is legitimately applied to both of these phenomena is the demonstration that such structures do in fact exhibit the defining characteristics specified in the above definition of a macrosystem. There is a

---

[10]The assumption also has its methodological analogue in statistical theory; in that context it is known as "the assumption of homogeneity of regression." When the assumption is not justified, the use of statistical controls can produce distorted results that have no correspondence in reality. What, then, can be done? Both on theoretical and statistical grounds there is the same simple answer: Each process must be examined separately in the context or population in which it occurs.

growing body of research evidence indicating that the criteria are indeed well met. (Bronfenbrenner, 1989a, p. 229)

From this perspective, the designs employed in both the Dornbusch and the Steinberg studies represent a confounding of macrosystems defined by ethnicity, with others distinguished both by social class and family structure. This confounding could be clarified, however, by applying a more differentiated design to data that are already available. Given the large sample size in both of these studies, it would probably be possible to stratify most ethnic groups by both of the latter factors and then examine the socialization processes in each. Especially revealing would be a comparison of ethnic differences in the effect of family styles separately for the two most contrasting groups: middle-class two-parent families and poor single-parent households.

In general, one would expect that, within each ethnic group, the effects of parental style on school performance would be higher in two-parent middle-class families than in single-parent disadvantaged households. But, at the same time, this difference should be less pronounced the greater the degree of discrimination and denigration to which each ethnic minority is subjected in American society. Specifically, the very term *denigration* points to Blacks as the group for whom parental styles may make little difference even in those families with both parents present who have achieved middle-class status. In any event, the results of such an analysis should provide a clearer — and one would hope more theoretically coherent — picture of ethnic differences in cognitive socialization as they vary, or persist, across both class and family structure.

Even before such a model is applied, however, its very conceptualization already permits a more coherent interpretation of the paradoxical findings reported by Dornbusch, Steinberg, and their colleagues. Thus, an analysis of the developmental research literature in an ecological perspective (Bronfenbrenner, 1989c) indicates that the impact of family processes and conditions decreases with age, with the decline being most rapid and most pronounced for families living under the most disadvantaged circumstances. The finding that family styles were most predictive for Whites and Asians, less so for Hispanics, and least for Blacks is consistent with trend just discussed.

Nor were parental styles the only family characteristic to exhibit the same pattern of decreasing predictiveness across ethnic groups ranked by socioeconomic status. In reporting results of the separate analyses conducted for each ethnic group, Dornbusch and his colleagues cited regression coefficients for all control variables, including both social class and family structure. These, too, showed a similar decline in parental power across the four ethnic groups (Dornbusch et al., 1987, p. 1254, Table 3).

At a broader level, the preceding findings are consistent with the general ecological hypothesis (Bronfenbrenner, 1989a, 1989b) that, by adolescence, the power of constructive family processes is effectively undermined in macrosystems characterized by high levels of stress and disorganization.

This hypothesis calls attention to another major finding in the research of Dornbusch and his colleagues. The finding emerged from the initial analysis of the entire sample, including all four ethnic groups, and is described by the authors as follows:

> But the mean grades of students in pure authoritarian or pure permissive families were not the lowest. The lowest grades were found among students whose family parenting style is inconsistent, especially with combinations that include authoritarian parenting . . . We speculate that inconsistency in the home environment creates anxiety among children, and that the anxiety reduces the relation between students' effort in school and the grade received. (Dornbusch et al., p. 1255)

Regrettably, the investigators did not include the measure of parental inconsistency in their separate analyses for each ethnic group. The results of other studies (see Bronfenbrenner, 1986, 1989a) indicate that inconsistency in parental behavior is more likely to occur both in disadvantaged and in single-parent families. Hence, a design that permits assessment of its presumed disruptive synergistic effects should further contribute to disentangling and clarifying the distinctive contribution of ethnic macrosystems in contrasting socioeconomic and structural contexts.

Moreover, there is evidence in the reported results suggesting that such a distinctive contribution in fact exists. It is seen primarily in the already mentioned paradoxical findings for the Asian sample. Thus, it is difficult to see how socioeconomic conditions and family structure could account for the academic success of Asian students despite the fact that their families were both more authoritarian and less authoritative than were White parents.[11] Nor do these structural factors explain the fact that the Asians were the only group not showing a significant gender difference in academic performance favoring females over males. (The means for the two genders for Asian students were essentially identical.) Asians were also the group most handicapped by having either a single parent or a stepparent.

---

[11]Unfortunately, because of limitations in sample size, it was not possible to conduct independent analyses for each of the ethnic subgroups within the Asian sample. Dornbusch (1987) was able, however, to carry out, within both the Asian and Hispanic samples, a separate analysis by generation, with the following result. The earlier a family had emigrated to the United States, the more that pattern of socialization effects resembled that of U.S. Whites. Regrettably, the report cites only correlations and does not include average scores by generation either for parental variables or for academic achievement.

Perhaps a key to such structural variation lies in the extent to which parents employing different styles also engage in progressively more complex activities — that is, in processes more closely related to the development of cognitive competence. The inclusion of measures of such processes as elements in a force–resource model could help to clarify these issues. But all this would require getting additional information not now available.

With respect to analyses of existing data, I do not mean to imply that the mere employment of a design that also incorporates the factors of socioeconomic status and family structure will resolve such mysteries. We need but recall that these factors are solely class-theoretical concepts to recognize that the most they can contribute to our knowledge is to indicate which persons in what contexts are most affected by the processes being assessed. To realize the full potential of an ecological paradigm, the research design must go beyond the conventional labels used to distinguish various social groups in a society. It is necessary, in addition, to gather specific information about one or more of the substantive domains specified in the definition of the macrosystem.

Even with this further substantive differentiation, however, the design would remain a process–context model that leaves unexplored, for example, any intellectual resources or developmentally instigative cognitive characteristics of the person that might also affect the differential impact of parental styles among different ethnic groups living in otherwise comparable macrosystem worlds.

Cognition and Culture. In such a process–person–context model, it is important to recognize that the person domain is also culturally rooted. A growing body of research testifies to the validity of this proposition. It begins with the ethnographic studies of the English anthropologist, W. H. R. Rivers (1926), on whose ideas Vygotsky drew in developing his theory of the sociohistorical evolution of the mind. That theory, in turn, served as the basis for the extraordinary expedition to remote regions in Soviet Asia, conceived by Vygotsky and carried out by his students — Luria and Zaporozhets, with the aim of assessing the impact on thought processes brought about by the social and technological changes associated with the Russian Revolution (Luria, 1931, 1979).

In the present generation, the same thesis has received more sophisticated and systematic support from the work of contemporary ethnologists, and psychologists. As an example of a recent, concerted effort to assess cognition in context, I can do no better than to cite the work of my colleague, Stephen Ceci (1990), an experimental psychologist briefly turned anthropologist who then returned to his root discipline by putting the laboratory itself in context. In a series of experimental studies, Ceci and his colleagues demonstrated that the same cognitive processes, in both children and adults, varied appreciably both in complexity and efficiency as a function of the context in which they were embedded. For example, processes supporting prospective memory progressively increased in efficiency as the same experiment was conducted with samples of children in a physics laboratory, a laboratory in a home economics building, and in the children's own home (Ceci & Bronfenbrenner, 1985). In a second experiment (Ceci, 1990), the ability to educe complex visual patterns showed a quantum gain when the same stimulus patterns were depicted as small pictures of familiar objects embedded in a video game instead of by abstract geometrical figures embedded within a laboratory task. In a third study, appropriately titled "A Day at the Races" (Ceci & Liker, 1986), highly successful racetrack bettors were asked to handicap 60 actual and experimentally contrived races.

> The analysis revealed that expert handicapping was a cognitively sophisticated enterprise, with experts using a mental model that contained multiple interaction effects and nonlinearity . . . involving as many as seven variables [pertaining to the characteristics of the horse, the jockey, the other horses in the field, the weather, etc.]. (Ceci & Liker, 1986, p. 255)

Measures of expertise, however, were not correlated with the subjects' IQs, and four of the top handicappers had IQ scores in the lower to mid-80s.

On the basis of their findings, Ceci, Bronfenbrenner, and Baker (1988) concluded that "the context in which cognition takes place is not simply an adjunct to the cognition, but a constituent of it" (p. 243).

Some Preposterous Proposals

Ceci's scientific aphorism has important implications for research on cognitive development in general? The reader may recall a statement I made earlier, which, at the time, may have seemed perplexing if not preposterous. I asserted, without further elaboration, that the definition of a macrosystem argued for "the representation of characteristics of the culture, or of any other macrosystem, as a critical feature of research models for investigating developmental processes and outcomes-particularly in the cognitive sphere."

I now offer two recommendations that spell out what the term *representation* implies in terms of research design. These recommendations may make the original statement less perplexing, but probably even more preposterous.

Recommendation 1

Because the psychological meaning of particular characteristics of process, person, and context depends on the particular macrosystem in which these phenomena occur, it is important to include in every research design some assessment of the meaning to the research subjects of key elements of the model to which they are exposed. Such assessment can usually be most easily carried by interviewing a subsample of the subjects or requesting their responses to an open-ended questionnaire.

For example, in the studies of parental style, it would have been instructive to ask representatives of each ethnic group what their opinion is of a parent who is authoritarian, and what the significance of grade point average is in their lives. To illustrate what can be learned from posing such questions, I quote the response of a Chinese-American student in my class. When I asked what Asians thought about authoritarian parents, he replied, with a smile: "That's how we know our parents love us."

It should be clear that what I am recommending here is an ecological analogue to Piaget's classic clinical interview.

The second recommendation goes even farther:

Recommendation 2

To the extent that is practically possible, every program of research on human development should include, at an early stage, a contrast between at least two macrosystems most relevant to the developmental phenomenon under investigation, represented not just by a label, but by psychological substance.

Why should such an outlandish provision be desirable, let alone necessary? I offer what I hope are two compelling reasons. First, the recommended procedure provides one of the most effective checks against arriving at, and publishing, a false conclusion. Second, and even more important for scientific advance, the strategy constitutes one of the most powerful tools we have for illuminating our understanding of how developmental processes function in species *Homo sapiens*. In the words of a leading British neuropsychologist, "We are a species wired for culture." Short of trying to change human beings, an effort for which the chances of success are not particularly high, our next best hope as scientists is to try to understand how human nature does that very job. And macrosystems are where we humans do it on the grandest scale, the better or the worse for our own development — cognitive and otherwise.

*   *   *

At the beginning of this chapter I promised to present research models and fugitive findings. By now it should be clear what I meant by research models; some are real, but most are imagined, waiting for someone rash enough to try to transform methodological fantasy into methodological fact.

And what about fugitive findings? Even the meaning of this expression is ambiguous. In the Oxford English Dictionary, the adjective "fugitive" has several definitions. One is "fleeting, evanescent, subject to change"; in other words, the findings I have cited may not stand up. But there is another definition, even more disconcerting: "running away, or intending flight"; in short, escaping consequences by dodging the issues.

It is true that many of the findings I have presented relate to cognition only by analogy, and for some, a connection to cognitive development may seem more imagined than real. I am unhappily reminded of Hotspur's response to old Glendower (in *Henry the Fourth, Part I*). The latter had been expanding upon the scope of his own remarkable powers, and finished with a flourish: "I can call spirits from the vasty deep." To which Hotspur retorted: "But will they come when you do call for them?"

I must acknowledge that this chapter consists more of dreams than of data. Earlier on, I invoked Lewin's classic dictum: "There is nothing so practical as a good theory." It would seem to follow that there is nothing so useless as a bad one. I close with the ardent hope that some of the ideas presented here may turn out to be useful.

ACKNOWLEDGMENTS

I am indebted to my colleagues Richard Canfield and Stephen J. Ceci for their insightful criticisms and creative suggestions, and to Avshalom Caspi and Glen H. Elder, Jr. for copies of graphs from their research reports.

REFERENCES

Allport, G. W. (1937). *Personality: A psychosocial interpretation.* New York: Holt.

Baumrind, D. (1966). Effects of authoritative parental control on child behavior. *Child Development, 37,* 887–907.

Baumrind, D. (1971). Current patterns of parental authority. *Developmental Psychology Monograph 4,* 1–103.

Baumrind, D. (1973). The development of instrumental competence through socialization. In A. D. Pick (Ed.), *Minnesota symposium on child psychology* (Vol. 7, pp. 3–46). Minneapolis: University of Minnesota Press.

Baumrind, D., & Black, A. E. (1967). Socialization practices associated with dimensions of competence in preschool boys and girls. *Child Development, 38,* 291–327.

Beckwith, L., & Cohen, S. E. (1984). Home environment and cognitive competence in preterm children during the first 5 years. In A. W. Gottfried (Ed.), *Home environments and early mental development.* New York: Academic Press.

Beckwith, L., Cohen, S. E., Kopp, C. B., Parmelee, A. H., & Marcy, T. G. (1976). *Child Development, 47,* 579–587.

Bee, H. L., Barnard, K. E., Eyeres, S. J., Gray, C. A., Hammond, M. A., Spietz, A. L., Snyder, C., & Clark, B. C. (1982). Prediction of IQ and language skill from perinatal status, childhood performance, family characteristics, and mother-infant interaction. *Child Development, 53,* 1134–1156.

Block, J. H., & Block, J. (1980). The role of ego-control and ego-resiliency in the organization of behavior. In W. A. Collins, (Ed.), *Minnesota symposia on child psychology, Vol. 13: Development of cognition, affect, and social relations* (pp. 39–101). Hillsdale, NJ: Lawrence Erlbaum Associates.

Block, J., Block, J. H., & Keyes, S. (1988). Longitudinally foretelling drug usage in adolescence: Early childhood personality and environmental precursors. *Child Development, 59,* 336–355.

Block, J., Buss, D. M., Block, J. H., & Gjerde, P. F. (1981). The cognitive style of breadth of categorization: Longitudinal consistency of personality correlates. *Journal of Personality and Social Psychology, 40,* 770–779.

Bronfenbrenner, U. (1977). Lewinian space and ecological substance. *Journal of Social Issues, 33,* 199–212.

Bronfenbrenner, U. (1979). *The ecology of human development.* Cambridge, MA: Harvard University Press.

Bronfenbrenner, U. (1986). Ecology of the family as a context for human development. *Developmental Psychology, 22,* 723–742.

Bronfenbrenner, U. (1988). Interacting systems in human development: Research paradigms: present and future. In N. Bolger, A. Caspi, G. Downey, & M. Moorehouse (Eds.), *Persons in context: Developmental processes* (pp. 25–49). New York: Cambridge University Press.

Bronfenbrenner, U. (1989a). Ecological systems theory. In R. Vasta (Ed.), *Six theories of child development* (pp. 185–246). Greenwich, CT: JAI Press.

Bronfenbrenner, U. (1989b, April). *The developing ecology of human development: Paradigm lost or paradigm regained?* Paper presented at a symposium on "Theories of Child Development: Updates and Reformulations" at the biennial meeting of the Society for Research in child Development, Kansas City, MO.

Bronfenbrenner, U. (1989c). *On making human beings human.* Unpublished manuscript.

Bronfenbrenner, U., & Crouter, A. C. (1983). The evolution of environmental models in developmental research. In P. H. Mussen (Series Ed.) & W. Kessen (Vol. Ed.), *Handbook of child psychology: Vol. 4. History, theory, and methods* (pp. 357–414). New York: Wiley.

Caspi, A., Elder, G. H., Jr., & Bem, D. J. (1987). Moving against the world: Life-course patterns of explosive children. *Developmental Psychology, 22,* 303–308.

Caspi, A., Elder, G. H., Jr., & Bem, D. J. (1988). Moving against the world: Life-course patterns of shy children. *Developmental Psychology, 24,* 824–831.

Ceci, S. H. (1990). *On intelligence: A bioecological view of intellectual development* (Century Series in Psychology). Englewood Cliffs: NJ: Prentice-Hall.

Ceci, S. J., & Bronfenbrenner, U. (1985). "Don't forget to take the cupcakes out of the oven": Prospective memory, strategic time-monitoring, and context. *Child Development, 56,* 150–165.

Ceci, S. J., Bronfenbrenner, U., & Baker, J. G. (1988). Memory in context: The case of prospective memory. In F. Weinert & M. Perlmutter (Eds.), *Universals and changes in memory development* (pp. 243–256). Hillsdale, NJ: Lawrence Erlbaum Associates.

Ceci, S. J., & Liker, J. (1986). A day at the races: IQ, expertise, and cognitive complexity. *Journal of Experimental Psychology: General, 115,* 255–266.

Cohen, S. E., & Beckwith, L. (1979). Preterm infant interaction with the caregiver in the first year of live and competence at age two. *Child Development, 50,* 767–776.

Cohen, S. E., Beckwith, L., & Parmelee, A. H. (1978). Receptive language development in preterm children as related to caregiver-child interaction. *Pediatrics, 61,* 16–20.

Cohen, S. E., & Parmelee, A. H. (1983). Prediction of five-Stanford-Binet scores in preterm infants. *Child Development, 54,* 1242-1253.

Cohen, S. E., Parmelee, A. H., Beckwith, L., & Sigman, M. (1986). Cognitive development in preterm infants: Birth to 8 years. *Developmental and Behavioral Pediatrics, 7,* 102-110.

Cole, M. J., Gay, J., Glick, J., & Sharp, D. W. (1971). *The cultural context of learning and thinking.* New York: Basic Books.

Cole, M., & Scribner, S. (1974). *Culture and thought.* New York: Wiley.

Connolly, J. A., & Doyle, A. (1984). Relation of social fantasy play to social competence in preschoolers. *Developmental Psychology, 20,* 797-806.

Dornbusch, S. M. (1987, April). *Adolescent behavior and school problems: The importance of context.* Paper presented at the meetings of the Society for Research in Child Development, Baltimore, MD.

Dornbusch, S. M., Ritter, P. L., Leiderman, P. H., Roberts, D. F., & Fraleigh, M. J. (1987). The relation of parenting style to adolescent school performance. *Child Development, 58,* 1244-1257.

Elder, G. H., Jr. (1974). *Children of the Great Depression.* Chicago: University of Chicago Press.

Elder, G. H., Jr., & Caspi, A. (1988). Human development and social change: An emerging perspective on the life course. In N. Bolger, A. Caspi, G. Downey, & M. Moorehouse (Eds.), *Persons in context: Developmental processes* (pp. 77-113). New York: Cambridge University Press.

Elder, G. H., Jr., & Caspi, A. (1990). Studying lives in a changing society: Sociological and personological explanations. In A. I. Rabin, R. A. Zucker, & S. Frank (Eds.), *Studying persons and lives* (pp. 201-247). New York: Springer.

Elder, G. H., Jr., Downey, G., & Cross, C. E. (1986). Family ties and life chances: Hard times and hard choices in women's lives since the 1930s. In N. Datan, A. L. Greene, & H. W. Reese (Eds.), *Life-span developmental psychology: Intergenerational relations* (pp. 151-183). Hillsdale, NJ: Lawrence Erlbaum Associates.

Elder, G. H., Jr., Van Nguyen, T. V., & Caspi, A. (1985). Linking family hardship to children's lives. *Child Development, 56,* 361-375.

Gjerde, P. F., Block, J., & Block, J. H. (1986). Egocentrism and ego resiliency: Personality characteristics associated with perspective-taking from early childhood to adolescence. *Journal of Personality and Social Psychology, 51,* 423-434.

Laboratory of Comparative Human Cognition. (1983). Culture and cognitive development. In P. H. Mussen (Series Ed.) & W. Kessen (Vol. Ed.), *Handbook of child psychology: Vol. 1. History, theory, and methods* (4th ed., pp. 295-356). New York: Wiley.

Leont'ev, A. N. (1932). The development of voluntary attention in the child. *Journal of Genetic Psychology, 40,* 52-83.

Leont'ev, A. N. (1982). *Problems in the development of mind.* Moscow: Progress Publishers. (Original Work published 1959)

Leont'ev, A. N. (1978). *Activity, consciousness, personality.* Englewood Cliffs, NJ: Prentice-Hall. (Original Work published 1975)

Lewin, K. (1931). The conflict between Aristotelian and Galilean modes of thought in contemporary psychology. *Journal of Genetic Psychology, 5,* 141-177.

Lewin, K. (1935). *A dynamic theory of personality.* New York: McGraw-Hill.

Lewin, K. (1943). Forces behind food habits and methods of change. *National Research Council Bulletin, 108,* 35-65.

Lewin, K. (1946). Action Research and minority problems. *Journal of Social Issues, 2,* 34-46.

Luria, A. R. (1931). Psychological expedition to Central Asia. *Science, 74,* 383-384.

Luria, A. R. (1979). *The making of mind.* Cambridge, MA: Harvard University Press.

MacDonald, K., & Parke, R. D. (1984). Bridging the gap: Parent-child play interaction and peer interactive competence. *Child development, 55,* 1265-1277.

May, M. A. (1932). The foundations of personality. In P. S. Achilles (Ed.), *Psychology at work* (pp. 81-101). New York: McGraw-Hill.

Morrison, F. J. (1988). *The "Five-to-Seven Shift Revisited: A natural experiment."* Paper presented at the meeting of the Psychonomic Association, Chicago, IL.

Mounts, N. S., Lamborn, S. D., & Steinberg, L. (1989, April). *Relations between family processes and school achievement in different ethnic contexts.* Paper presented at the biennial meeting of the Society for Research in Child Development, Kansas City, MO.

Plomin, R., & Daniels, S. (1987). Why are children in the same family so different from one another? *Brain and Behavioral Sciences, 10,* 1-16.

Plomin, R., & Nesselroade, J. R. (1990). Behavior genetics and personality change. *Journal of Personality, 58,* 191-220.

Pulkkinen, L. (1982). Self control and continuity from childhood to late adolescence. In P. Baltes & O. Brim (Eds.), *Life span development and behavior* (Vol. 4, pp. 64-102). New York: Academic Press.

Pulkkinen, L. (1983a). Finland: The search for alternatives to aggression. In A. P. Goldstein & M. Segall (Eds.) *Aggression in global perspective* (pp. 104-144). New York: Pergamon Press.

Pulkkinen, L. (1983b). Youthful smoking and drinking in longitudinal perspective. *Journal of Youth and Adolescence, 12,* 253-283.

Rivers, W. H. R. (1926). *Psychology and ethnology.* New York: Harcourt, Brace.

Rogoff, B. (1990). *Apprenticeship in thinking.* New York: Oxford University Press.

Rutter, M., & Quinton, D. (1984). Long-term follow-up of women institutionalized in childhood: Factors promoting good functioning in adulthood. *British Journal of Developmental Psychology, 2,* 191-204.

Scarr, S. (1988). How genotypes and environments combine: Development and individual differences. In N. Bolger, A. Caspi, G. Downey, & M. Moorehouse (Eds.), *Persons in context: Developmental processes* (pp. 217-244). New York: Cambridge University Press.

Scarr, S., & McCartney, K. (1983). How people make their own environments: A theory of genotype-environment effects. *Child Development, 54,* 424-435.

Steinberg, L. (1989, March). *Parenting academic achievers: When families make a difference (and when they don't).* Paper presented at the annual meetings of the American Educational Research Association, San Francisco, CA.

Steinberg, L., & Brown, B. B. (1989, March). *Beyond the classroom: Parental and peer influences on high school achievement.* Invited paper presented to the Families as Educators Special Interest Group at the annual meetings of the American Educational Research Association, San Francisco, CA.

Super, C. M. (1980). Cognitive development: Looking across at growing up. In C. Super & M. Harkness (Eds.), *New directions for child development: Anthropological perspectives on child development* (Vol. 8, pp. 59-69). San Francisco: Jossey-Bass.

Vygotsky, L. S. (1929). II. The problem of the cultural development of the child. *Journal of Genetic Psychology, 36,* 415-434.

Vygotsky, L. S. (1978). *Mind in society.* Cambridge, MA: Harvard University Press.

Vygotsky, L. S. (1979). Consciousness as a problem in the psychology of behavior. *Soviet Psychology, 17,* 3-35.

Vygotsky, L. S., & Luria, A. R. (1956). *Psikhoilogicheskie vozzreniia Vygotskogo* [Vygotsky's views on psychology]. In L. Vygotsky (Ed.), *Izbrannye psikhologicheskie issledovaniiia.* Moscow: Academy of Pedagogical Sciences.

Wachs, T. D. (1979). Proximal experience and early cognitive intellectual development: The physical environment. *Merrill-Palmer Quarterly, 25,* 3-41.

Wachs, T. D. (1987a). Specificity of environmental action as manifest in environmental correlates of infants's mastery motivation. *Developmental Psychology, 23,* 782-790.

Wachs, T. D. (1987b, April). *Comparative salience of physical and social environmental differences*. Paper presented at the biennial meeting of the Society for Research in Child Development. Baltimore, MD.

Wachs, T. D. (1989). The nature of the physical micro-environment: An expanded classification system. *Merrill-Palmer'Quarterly, 35,* 399–419.

Wachs, T. D. (1990). Must the physical environment be mediated by the social environment in order to influence development?: A further test. *Journal of Applied Developmental Psychology, 11,* 163–178.

Wachs, T. D., & Chan, A. (1986). Specificity of environmental action as seen in environmental correlates of infants' communication performance. *Child Development, 57,* 1464–1474.

Wertsch, J. V. (1985). *Vygotsky and the social formation of mind.* Cambridge, MA: Harvard University Press.

Acknowledgments

Chickering, Arthur W. and Linda Reisser. "The Seven Vectors." In *Education and Identity*, 2d ed. (San Francisco: Jossey-Bass, 1993): 34–52. Reprinted with the permission of Jossey-Bass Publishers Inc.

Weathersby, Rita Preszler. "Ego Development." In *The Modern American College*, edited by Arthur W. Chickering and Associates (San Francisco: Jossey-Bass, 1981): 51–75. Reprinted with the permission of Jossey-Bass Publishers Inc.

Perry, William G., Jr. "Cognitive and Ethical Growth: The Making of Meaning." In *The Modern American College*, edited by Arthur W. Chickering and Associates (San Francisco: Jossey-Bass, 1981): 76–116. Reprinted with the permission of Jossey-Bass Publishers Inc.

Goldberger, Nancy Rule, Blythe McVicker Clinchy, Mary Field Belenky, and Jill Mattuck Tarule. "Women's Ways of Knowing: On Gaining a Voice." In *Sex and Gender*, edited by Phillip Shaver and Clyde Henrick (Newbury Park, Calif.: Sage, 1987): 201–28. Reprinted with the permission of Sage Publications, Inc.

Baxter Magolda, Marcia B. "Students' Epistemologies and Academic Experiences: Implications for Pedagogy." *Review of Higher Education* 15 (1992): 265–87. Reprinted with the permission of the *Review of Higher Education*.

Kitchener, Karen S. and Patricia M. King. "The Reflective Judgment Model: Transforming Assumptions About Knowing." In *Fostering Critical Reflection in Adulthood: A Guide to Transformative and Emancipatory Learning*, edited by Jack Mezirow and Associates (San Francisco: Jossey-Bass, 1990): 159–76. Reprinted with the permission of Jossey-Bass Publishers Inc.

Fowler, James. "Moral Stages and the Development of Faith." In *Moral Development, Moral Education, and Kohlberg*, edited by Brenda Munsey (Birmingham, Ala.: Religious Education Press, 1980): 130–60. Reprinted by permission of the publisher, Religious Education Press, 5316 Meadow Brook Road, Birmingham, Alabama, U.S.A.

Atkinson, Donald R., George Morten, and Derald Wing Sue. "A Minority Identity Development Model." In *Counseling American Minorities: A Cross Cultural Perspective*, 2d ed. (Dubuque, Iowa: Wm. C. Brown, 1983): 35–47. Reprinted with the permission of Wm. C. Brown Communications Inc.

Helms, Janet E. "Toward a Model of White Racial Identity Development." In
    Black and White Racial Identity: Theory, Research, and Practice (New York:
    Greenwood Press, 1990): 49–66. Reprinted with the permission of
    Greenwood Press.
Cass, Vivienne C. "Homosexual Identity Formation: Testing a Theoretical Model."
    Journal of Sex Research 20 (1984): 145–67. Published by permission of the
    Journal of Sex Research, a publication of The Society for the Scientific Study
    of Sex, Inc.
Astin, Alexander W. "Student Involvement: A Developmental Theory for Higher
    Education." *Journal of College Student Personnel* 25 (1984): 297–308.
    Reprinted with the permission of the American College Personnel
    Association.
Markus, Hazel Rose and Shinobu Kitayama. "Culture and the Self: Implications for
    Cognition, Emotion, and Motivation." *Psychological Review* 98 (1991):
    224–53. Reprinted with the permission of the American Psychological
    Association. Copyright 1991.
Bronfenbrenner, Urie. "The Ecology of Cognitive Development: Research Models and
    Fugitive Findings." In *Development in Context*, edited by Robert H. Wozniak
    and Kurt W. Fischer (Hillsdale, N.J.: Lawrence Erlbaum Associates, 1993):
    3–44. Reprinted with the permission of Lawrence Erlbaum Associates, Inc.